SHAW ABROAD

The Annual of Bernard Shaw Studies
Volume Five

---

continuing

The Shaw Review

Stanley Weintraub, *General Editor*

John R. Pfeiffer
Bibliographer

Rodelle Weintraub
Assistant Editor

Editorial Board: Elsie B. Adams, California State University, San Diego; Sidney P. Albert, California State University, Los Angeles (Emeritus); Charles A. Berst, University of California at Los Angeles; Robert Chapman, Harvard University; Louis Crompton, University of Nebraska; Bernard F. Dukore, University of Hawaii; Frederick P. W. McDowell, University of Iowa; Michael J. Mendelsohn, University of Tampa; Ann Saddlemyer, Graduate Center for Study of Drama, University of Toronto; Barbara Bellow Watson, City University of New York; Jonathan L. Wisenthal, University of British Columbia.

SHAW
ABROAD

Edited by
Rodelle Weintraub

The Pennsylvania State University Press
University Park and London

Extracts from Shaw's plays and prefaces, unless otherwise noted, are based upon the Bodley Head *Collected Plays with their Prefaces* (1971–74).

Quotations from published Bernard Shaw writings are utilized in this volume with the permission of the Estate of Bernard Shaw. Shaw's hitherto unpublished writings © 1985 The Trustees of the British Museum, The Governors and Guardians of the National Library of Ireland, and the Royal Academy of Dramatic Art.

Quotations from the unpublished diaries of Sir Horace Plunkett are used with the permission of the Plunkett Foundation for Co-operative Research, London.

Library of Congress Cataloging in Publication Data

Main entry under title:

Shaw abroad.

  (Shaw ; v. 5)
  1. Shaw, Bernard, 1856–1950—Journeys—Addresses, essays, lectures. 2. Dramatists, Irish—20th century—Biography—Addresses, essays, lectures. 3. Voyages and travels—Addresses, essays, lectures. I. Weintraub, Rodelle. II. Series.
PR5366.A15 vol. 5   822'.912 s   [822'.912]   84-43058
ISBN 0-271-00384-7

CONTENTS

ACKNOWLEDGMENTS

The editor personally and on behalf of the contributors wishes to thank Dan H. Laurence, who graciously assisted those contributors who called upon him, and Stanley Weintraub, who shared with contributors the Shaw diaries he is editing and without whose support and encouragement this volume could not have been brought to fruition.

ACKNOWLEDGMENTS

Rodelle Weintraub

INTRODUCTION

Before Shaw the man had begun travelling, Shaw the dramatist had begun using far away places as the settings for his plays. *Widowers' Houses*, his first play, opens in Germany, on the Rhine. It was begun in 1884, before his first visit to the Continent. *Arms and the Man*, which could have been set in the part of Yugoslavia he would visit in 1929, was set in the Bulgaria he never saw. The Italian setting for *Man of Destiny* may have come from a picture he had seen in London, although *Candida*, which is set in London, grew out of his exposure to Italy and pre-Raphael art. As early as 1896 he "travelled" to the New England he would never see to set *The Devil's Disciple* in the American colonies at the time of the Revolution, and his only experience with the American Wild West would be an overnight trip to the Grand Canyon two decades after he had written *The Shewing-Up of Blanco Posnet*. After his first "visit" to America, he would "travel" to another continent, to the Egypt of the Roman occupation for *Caesar and Cleopatra* and to contemporary Morocco and the Atlas Mountains for *Captain Brassbound's Conversion*. *Man and Superman's* Ann Whitefield pursues John Tanner through France to Spain over roads Shaw was later to travel himself, and *John Bull's Other Island*, his first Irish play, was written before he physically returned to the island he had left in 1876. For these early plays Shaw used the materials of others' travels and was scrupulously careful about the detail for his setting.

From the time he left Ireland until he married Charlotte Payne-Townshend, Shaw seldom travelled out of England. With few funds to expend, he waited to visit the Continent until he could do so as a critic, earning his way as he studied other cultures and art. Travelling with the boys, he visited Belgium, Holland, France, Germany, and Italy, energetically and exhaustively exploring the streets of cities new to him, visiting cathedrals and museums, going to the theater, the opera, and the Passion Play at Oberammergau.

The pattern set in Shaw's first visit to the Continent was to be repeated in all of his travels. Immediately upon arriving in Antwerp on 17 April 1889, having endured a difficult night on the Channel boat, he set out to see the churches and pictures. That he was disappointed—he found Antwerp like Limerick but duller, the Cathedral a "whitened doghole" and the paintings in the leading gallery a "horrible experience"—did not dissuade him from seeking out churches and art wherever he would travel. He also looked for theater. The *Theatre de la Monnaie* in Brussels offered French tragedian Jean Mount-Sully in an *Oedipus* Shaw put in the same category as the churches and art of Antwerp. At Amsterdam he reviewed the new Dutch opera, *Brinio*, at the Park Theatre, and complained that no "stretch of international courtesy" could make the work worth the half-guilder admission price. He enjoyed the Dutch production of *A Doll's House* at the Municipal Theatre in Haarlem, describing it as "very successful," which was also his impression of the Ryksmuseum in Amsterdam; the museum at the Hague, he felt, did not make up for the disgusting smell of the canals. He was delighted with the galleries in Utrecht. A great walker, he strolled through the Jewish quarter in Amsterdam which Rembrandt had captured in his painting. He found restaurant meals "terrible," but in dairy-conscious Holland there were ample eggs, cheese, cocoa and chocolate, apples, oranges, cakes, and pastries to keep the energetic—and vegetarian—traveller going. Obtaining sufficient and satisfying food would be more of a problem in other countries. In Germany he was reduced to eating fish. His remarks about food in Russia, which were received as mean-tempered criticism, may have been veiled praise. "Black bread and cabbage agree with me—and I have had plenty of both" (p. 137), which suggest the unavailability of anything but peasant food, may have been a simple statement that in Russia he, a vegetarian, ate well. After another dreadful Channel crossing, he immediately began his usual regimen, revising an article, reviewing a play.[1]

After his marriage, Shaw accompanied his peripatetic wife on her flights from England, her household, her servants, and perhaps from herself. To humor her and to have her company, Shaw returned to Ireland and to the Continent, driving almost every road in France while quarreling with her much of the way. He claimed he went unwillingly, for he was "like a tree" (p. 252) wanting to be firmly rooted to one spot. But exhaustion and overwork—too many commitments, appointments, and demands upon his time and his person—drove him to seek rest and anonymity in their travels while restlessness and a need to work caused him to work on vacation just as hard as he worked at home.

By the time he had reached his seventies, his fame made private travel impossible. Going anywhere was like taking part in a "royal progress" in which the sovereign and the jester were the same person. Local nobility and officials called upon him; heads of state and cabinet ministers met with him; reporters and photographers flocked about him; newspaper, radio, and even film interviews were demanded; crowds on the streets shouted his name as he passed. Only by taking to the seas, despite his nausea and seasickness, could he find rest and privacy. As he wrote Molly Tompkins, "I now take my holidays on ships going as far round the world as possible, as I find that in this way alone can I work continuously and rest at the same time."[2] But ships dock, and reporters found their way on board to interview him even before the ship was safely berthed in the harbor. While he claimed that mob interviews terrified him and that he dreaded attention, he continued to hold the interviews and to do and say the provocative things that assured him of an eager crowd at the next stop. Reporters rushed to report whatever "preposterous" or "outrageous" things he might say, often grateful that he could and did say what they did not dare. What they could not or would not do was report his statements as serious commentary on the problems of society, civilization, and government.

After World War I, as his disappointment with democracy and government as it was practiced in the 1920s and 1930s became more profound, his pronouncements became more extreme. Outside of Russia he proclaimed the Soviet system superior to all others, for he recognized that any criticisms he might make of "utopia" would be snatched upon and exaggerated. He also realized that any praise he would, and did, bestow on what was at the time the only socialist experiment would be derided. In Russia he condemned the excesses of Stalinism. Russians ignored his comments, as did a young Englishwoman who, influenced by his writings, had gone to Russia and joined the revolution. After his trip to Russia she wrote him that it did not matter whether he approved of the results or not, for the experiment no longer needed him.[3] South Africans, amused and annoyed by his rejection of their sun-trap, are still trapped in the quagmire he condemned and are still political and economic slaves to the system that he recognized was enslaving them. Chinese students and bureaucrats scoffed at his telling them they should and must become communists. The Japanese War Minister brushed aside Shaw's warnings that the result of war was always what was least expected and that great empires which engaged in war were often dissolved by the wars.

Did the travels have any effect upon the traveller? The young Shaw, visiting Europe as a novice, developed his artistic and aesthetic skills as he honed his writing ones. Plays such as *Candida* owe their genesis to those early visits. The middle-aged tourist found ideas as well as settings that resulted in plays like *Saint Joan* and *The Six of Calais*. The elderly Shaw, on his progresses, collected ideas and settings which he put into such later works as the film version of *Major Barbara*, *The Simpleton of the Unexpected Isles*, *Geneva*, and *Buoyant Billions*. The time spent on board ship or at out-of-the-way resorts made possible the writing of *Saint Joan*, *The Black Girl in Search of God*, *Village Wooing*, *The Millionairess*, *On the Rocks*, and *The Apple Cart*. From his first travels to his last, Shaw worked as hard as a tourist as he did at home in England. He even wrote travel reports for the Royal Automobile Club. His itineraries, even when he was in his seventies, would have defeated most other travellers. Shaw's recreation remained always an activity as intensive as his work; as he grew older his shipboard travels became his opportunities to write un-interruptedly. His seasons abroad educated, refreshed, and renewed him, and the locales he visited and ideas to which he was exposed were incorporated into his writings.

Even before the War of 1939–45 and Charlotte's death in 1943 his travels had ended. He had long complained about travelling with her, writing to his Austrian translator Siegfried Trebitsch in 1911 that married people should never travel together, for they blame each other for whatever goes wrong and drive each other mad. But when Charlotte became too frail to leave home, he travelled no more, seldom even going into London although he kept his flat there. Without her, the "tree" went no farther than his garden.

Notes

1. *CL*, 1, 208 and *Diaries*.

2. Peter Tompkins, ed., *To a Young Actress: The Letters of Bernard Shaw to Molly Tompkins* (New York: Clarkson N. Potter, Inc., 1960), p. 164.

3. Typescript letter. Anna Louise Strong to Shaw, 24 July 1931. British Library, vol. 50520, f. 110.

John J. Weisert

A WAGNER PILGRIM: G.B.S. IN GERMANY

Shaw's interest in things German long predated his first-hand experience of the Germans. Goethe, Nietzsche, Schopenhauer, and Wagner as translated for English readers were powerful attractions for him. Although he never permitted himself to be seduced by its poets and thinkers into passively accepting the conclusions which such men propounded, they were always handily ready as chiding examples to set before his countrymen, whose philosophy rarely developed beyond a comfortable pragmatism.

The Wagner Festival performances regularly mounted at Bayreuth resulted in three Shavian visits—1889, 1894,[1] and 1908. In 1890 he visited the Passion Play at Oberammergau. He had intended to make the pilgrimage to Bayreuth in 1891 as well, but could not, having failed to heed his own warnings to his readers that tickets must be procured well in advance.

On Monday, 22 July 1889, Shaw prepared for his first pilgrimage to Bayreuth, having had a few German lessons from the Sonntag sisters in Hampstead. He called at Cook's for information about costs and railway connections, learning that the rail tickets he required came to six pounds, sixteen shillings, and tenpence. A *Baedeker* for South Germany cost him an additional five shillings, while his Festival Theatre admission added a further four pounds to his bill at Thomas Cook's travel agency. But Shaw knew that in addition to his theater admissions being borne by the *Star*, for his music column, the *English Illustrated Magazine* had promised him seven and a half pounds for an article on Bayreuth. He could even afford to add to his travel library the next day, purchasing, for four shillings sixpence, the *Baedeker* covering the Rhine portion of the journey. By mid-week he had confirmed his accommodations, and left on Thursday, 25 July, from Holborn railroad station at 1:40 p.m. for Queensborough.

The traditionally wretched Channel crossing had its traditional effect, which was still felt the next day when Shaw arrived at Cologne in the early afternoon. In Cologne Shaw inspected the venerable cathedral (regretting all modernizations), especially its stained glass windows, and the nearby Wallraf-Richartz Museum, which specialized in Roman remains from the vicinity as well as medieval artifacts. As he left the cathedral it began to rain. In his haste to don his mackintosh he split it, "like a trick coat in a farce," making the wet weather he later encountered in Germany less bearable. Unable to find a way to mend it (time and his German were both problems), he left that afternoon for the Rhine journey en route to Würzburg.

The night journey by train was unpleasant. He felt stuffy and sick. It was not easy in Germany to be a vegetarian, and it is possible that (as he would do elsewhere in Germany) he had eaten local fish. At Würzburg the next day he changed trains, leaving the city in the late afternoon for Bamberg, where he arrived in the early morning. He hurried through the town to see the cathedral, for the *Baedeker* pointed out that the figures of Adam and Eve on the south side of its eastern transept were the first life-size representations of the naked human body since antiquity. The guidebook also noted the equestrian statue at the cathedral as the image of the knightly man of the Hohenstaufen period. Because this side trip had caused him to miss breakfast, he took his morning meal just before the train left at ten.

Shaw reached Bayreuth three and one-half hours later. (He recalled that two cheerful young women in his carriage had enlivened the journey but had not prevented his falling asleep.) The room secured for him was at Leonard Lieb's, 18 Maximilian Street, up several flights of stairs. It was cheap but comfortable. Depositing his luggage, he strolled about town, looking for Wagner's house and the local churchyard which *Baedeker* identified as the last resting place of Liszt.

"What is Bayreuth like?" he would ask, rhetorically, in an article he wrote for a London paper, *The Hawk*.[2] "Well, it is a genteel little Franconian country town among the hills and the woods of Bavaria. . . . It is not old enough to be venerable, nor new enough to be quite prosaic; and the inhabitants either live in villas on independent incomes or else by taking in one another's washing and selling confectionery, scrapbooks, and photographs." There were also street fountains, monuments to local burghers, a lunatic asylum, a "very quaint XVIII century opera house," the Wagner Theatre "halfway up the hill," and the "inevitable" *Sieges Turm* commemorating the victory over France in 1870–71. The main street, he noted, was named for half its distance the Maximilianstrasse, for the other half the Richard Wagnerstrasse. And behind Wagner's undistinguished villa was the Master's grave: "buried in the back garden, sir," Shaw overheard an indignant Englishman say, "like a New-foundland dog."

There would be no life in Bayreuth beyond that of a country village, Shaw wrote, "without Wagner." He could find walks in such scented woods "in the next county to Surrey." But, he noted, there was also the author Jean Paul Richter buried and memorialized at Bayreuth. It is doubtful that he or any of his contemporaries from England then sampling the town's attractions had as much as a nodding acquaintance with even the titles of books by this author, let alone his idiosyncratic writings. Richter's countrymen had dubbed him *"Der Einzige"*—the unique man—and even today he is inaccessible to most readers of any nationality.

Shaw got to bed early, for the next day, Sunday, 28 July, he was to experience his first opera at Bayreuth, *Parsifal*, with the curtain at 4:00 P.M. After rising, he walked the pinewoods around the town, then made for the theater. There he joined his friends William Archer and Edward Dibdin (then art critic for the *Liverpool Courier*), with whom he would dine afterward on the "heavy" German food he disliked. After the third act, he wrote, "I had just enough energy to go home to my bed."

On Monday, 29 July, *Tristan and Isolde* was sung, beginning as usual in the late afternoon. Shaw used this morning to write a notice of *Parsifal* for the *Star*, mailing it to London before the performance began. The next morning he did the same for *Tristan*, observing that to enjoy the opera "it is only necessary to have had one serious love affair." He then went hiking with Archer and Dibdin as far as the Café Sommet, and from there to the Fantasie; he did not return until late in the day, for there was no operatic presentation on Tuesday.

Wednesday's performance was *Die Meistersinger*. With no review to write, Shaw planned to visit the Eremitage with Dibdin, but when Dibdin failed to meet him he went alone. The Eremitage was composed of two *Lustschlösser* (pleasure palaces) surrounded by parks, fountains and pseudo-ruins fashionable in the previous century. A later *Baedeker* assured the pilgrim that "for certain aspects of the culture of the 18th century this is an illustration of splendid immediacy." At the time of Shaw's visit the upper castle contained numerous portraits of princely families, the lower one being a Temple of the Sun lined with rock crystal. Shaw was apparently not impressed enough to mention either palace.

As Shaw was leaving his room to go to the opera, Dibdin reappeared, and the two went to the theater by way of the Roman bath, sketching it until curtain time. By now weary of Bayreuth, Shaw was wearied further by the performance, unable to reconcile the interpretation, like that of a "student and philosopher," with singing that resembled "an improved foghorn." Fortunately, before he left the next evening, he was to hear his second *Parsifal* ("a wonderful experience"). On Thursday morning he wrote his notice of the previous day's opera and then went sightseeing, this time to the old opera house, which had been completed, in the Italian Baroque style, in 1748. Shaw, Dibdin, and Archer then checked out of their rooms and left their luggage at the station, to be picked up an hour before midnight.

The next morning—only a few hours later—the sleepy travelers arrived at Nuremberg, secured rooms, and caught up on their sleep before "doing" the town. In the late afternoon they reboarded their train, this time for Frankfurt, where they arrived mid-morning the next day and checked into the Golden Eagle Hotel. Dibdin and Archer were travel-jaded, but Shaw was eager to see things. All three went to the art museum, but while Archer and Dibdin returned to the hotel to eat, Shaw (less than eager for the food) went to the cathedral, where, as in Cologne, he was trapped by a downpour. He went on anyway, visiting the town fortress, where he was horrified by the instruments of torture on display. Nevertheless they would later make real for Shaw the line he would give to the Executioner in *Saint Joan*, for when the Executioner is asked about such implements, Joan is sufficiently shaken by his response to sign a confession in which she does not believe.

The three friends traveled together as far as Aschaffenburg, Archer and Dibdin going on to Darmstadt, Shaw returning to Frankfurt, where he visited the Goethe house, cathedral, municipal museum, and Staedel Institute (now the Art Museum). He left for Mainz in the early afternoon and managed to squeeze in a sidetrip to the Mainz cathedral before boarding a Rhine steamer to Coblentz. He arrived there at eight in the evening and then proceeded to Bonn. In Bonn he walked through the town, perhaps to taste its academic flavor, before he continued to Cologne, where he permitted himself five hours of sleep.

Shaw would later characterize the Rhine journey as quickly growing stale to the traveler, but like many others he did not descend for a meal until his boat had passed the Lorelei rock. He was dismayed to learn that the railway station at Cologne was not open all night and that he would have to find a bed in the middle of the night. On his third try he succeeded.

The next day, a Sunday, he left Cologne early in the morning, reaching Vlissingen (Flushing) in Holland at noon, Queensborough eight hours later, and Holborn Viaduct shortly after nine in the evening. Monday morning he slept until half-past-ten. He was not a good traveler, he would tell his *Star* readers. After being rocked for five hours in a Dutch railway carriage, he had been ready "to look death in the face with a smile of welcome." Now that he was on solid ground again he could look back on the Rhine between Bonn and Coblentz as an experience "better than a dozen press reviews of different schools of land-scape. Cologne Cathedral, too, has affected me, I am extremely suscep-tible to stained glass, and the old glass there transports me, whilst the new glass [there] makes me long to transport it—with bricks." He also mentioned that he wished his return could be by "Channel Tunnel."

Shaw's encounter with the cult of Wagner on its home soil left him with curiosity about another semi-religious, semi-dramatic unfolding of a plot of epic ambitions also regularly presented in Germany. In August 1890, with his Fabian friend Sidney Webb, also a religious skeptic, he went to see the *Passion Play* as enacted at Oberammergau. In a letter from London dated 17 August 1890, to William Archer, who was him-self then in Bavaria, Shaw described his dissatisfaction with the per-formance and with the village, a community that seemed to be run by "two women who speak all languages, and run the Burgomaster's office and the post office alternately." Shaw and Webb had applied too late for seats under roof, and at first rejoiced, on the sunny Saturday afternoon, at the five shillings saved. "Our rejoicing was shortlived. At about eight in the evening a horrible dust storm suddenly charged into the village, turning the balmy eve into a scene of darkness and confusion. . . . By the time we were abed, the dust was succumbing to rain. In the morning it was raining as if it had no idea of leaving off; and what is more, it did not leave off."

Sodden, Shaw enjoyed the ritual play even less. In his *World* theater column, Shaw told Archer, he "denounced Meyer[3] as a stick, grumbled at his perpetual pose as the Man of Sorrows . . . and being such an in-sufferably superior person that the wonder was, not that they crucified him, but that they stood him so long." Josef Mayr was apparently over-whelmed by the significance of the role he was playing and performed it woodenly, while "secular people"—the villagers in minor roles—earned Shaw's praise.

The trip to Oberammergau was also an excuse to visit Munich and its galleries, to examine the "glorious cathedral" at Ulm, to sleep away the day in Stuttgart, and to go on to Strasbourg (then Strassburg, since 1870, and until 1918, a German city), where, Shaw wrote Archer (*CL* 1, 254–56), "I paid two marks . . . to go to the tiptop of the cathedral spire. I outfaced agonies of terror that no typewriter can describe. . . ." The "naked flight of steps" was outside the steeple, "at a height that makes me sick to remember." Still far from the "apex of the thing" Shaw told his guide "*Ist genug.*" Yet when he was "safe in the street" he wished he had not given in.

A night in Brussels preceded a calm Channel crossing, and Shaw was again in Fitzroy Square.

Shaw's second pilgrimage to Bayreuth took place in July 1894. This time he went from Darmstadt (17 July) to Würzburg, sightseeing there before going on to Nuremberg, where he arrived in early evening. Reaching Bayreuth the next day, he lodged with the Kapper family at 1 Hintere Damenallee. Again there was an initial *Parsifal*, in which Theodore Reichmann "did not sing a note of it in tune. . . . I was wrong in fearing that [the second act] might be worse than the first. A man should not fear impossibilities."

Yet he was back on the soil of Wagner's inspiration and was confident that authentic Wagnerian emanations would emerge from some performance if he were patient. On the following day, a Friday, he found the atmosphere of the Master in the first Festival production of *Lohengrin*, an improvement he attributed to the amount of action "carried by the chorus, which gives immense vivacity and interest to several of the scenes by means of quite simple business. . . ." As there was no performance on Saturday, 21 July, he went to the Fantasie Hotel to meet English friends. The next day, however, featured a performance of *Tannhauser* followed on Monday by yet another *Parsifal*, then performed only at Bayreuth. The first two acts of *Tannhauser* were dreary bows to German prudery, Venus herself "defying even the boldest admirer to see her ankles"; however the third act restored Shaw's faith in the Bayreuth magic.

Shaw left for Nuremberg by the late evening train on Tuesday, after the performance, taking the shortest route to Ostend and then home. From London he wondered about the efficacy for most people of going to Bayreuth to purchase the spirit of music with which they have no rapport "at a pound per performance at the bar where Wagner has left it on tap. . . ." He himself would not return to Bayreuth until 1908, his 1894 visit having coincided with his giving up professional music criticism. He would return to Germany, on occasion, by motor car in later years when the attraction of Bayreuth was past. The Wagner Theatre, his principal reason for crossing the Rhine, had been "the utmost perfection of the pictorial stage . . . framed by a proscenium . . . , and . . . its machinery could go no further." Nevertheless, he wrote in 1922, in a preface to a fourth edition of *The Perfect Wagnerite*, "I must also admit that my favorite way of enjoying a performance of *The Ring* is to sit at the back of a box, comfortable on two chairs, feet up, and listen without looking. The truth is, a man whose imagination cannot serve him better than the most costly devices of the imitative scenepainter, should not go to the theatre, and as a matter of fact does not." Shaw's Germany was largely that of the Wagner pilgrim, and was now left to his capacious imagination.

Notes

1. Music criticism is quoted from *Shaw's Music*, ed. Dan H. Laurence (London, 1981); other information on Shaw's travels, except where specified, is from the revised Stanley Weintraub version of the Stanley Rypins transcript of Shaw's shorthand diaries, entries for July/August 1889 and July 1894 (in press). I am grateful to Rodelle Weintraub for making these available.

2. *The Hawk* (the text is from *Shaw's Music*) was edited by George Moore's feisty brother Augustus, and Shaw's writing may reflect Augustus Moore's editorial preferences.

3. Shaw's misspelling of Mayr's name, if not a mere typographical matter, may reflect his having already written twice about Johann Mayr, an early German operatic composer.

Elsie B. Adams

IN PURSUIT OF ART: SHAW'S ITALIAN TOURS OF 1891 AND 1894

I

In his Preface to *Plays Pleasant* (1898), Bernard Shaw alluded to two visits to Italy as contributing to his concept of "a modern pre-Raphaelite play." His Italian visits, he asserted, along with his observation of English pre-Raphaelite art, inspired him with the underlying vision that governs *Candida*. Shaw called English pre-Raphaelite art "more hopeful" than the Italian art he had seen, for the English art "was the work of living men, whereas modern Italy had . . . no more connection with Giotto than Port Said has with Ptolemy." The statement implies a rejection of both "dead" Italian art and modern Italy. Did Italy offer anything, then, other than the inspiration for *Candida* to the young journalist and future playwright? Did it sharpen his aesthetic sense or enrich his spiritual values?

Shaw's first visits to Italy were with the Art Workers Guild, in tours organized in 1891 and 1894 by Thomas Okey, a basketmaker and an instructor at Toynbee Hall in Whitechapel. The tours were modelled after the cooperative Toynbee Travellers' Club, which, according to Okey, had been founded in 1887 "to extend the educational advantages of foreign travel to East End students."[1] Okey, who later held the endowed chair of Italian Studies at Cambridge, was valuable to the club because of his proficiency in languages. When in 1891 he was asked to join the Art Workers Guild, he organized similar tours for that group.

The Art Workers Guild, founded in 1884, grew out of the St. George's Art Society, which had been founded a year earlier and was composed mainly of architecture pupils of Norman Shaw. Part of the Arts and Crafts movement of the 1880s, the Art Workers Guild included "Handicraftsmen and Designers in the Arts," with "the Unity, the Interdependence, the Solidarity of all the Arts" its central idea.[2] May Morris, writing of the guild, recalled that it consisted at first mostly of painters and architects but came to include almost "every conceivable artistic craft."[3] In 1891, and again in 1894, Shaw was invited to accompany the guild on its pilgrimages to Italy;[4] in 1921, he became an honorary member.

The 1891 two-week tour included visits to Milan, Verona, Venice, Padua, Mantua, and Pavia, with a week in Venice. The Art Workers Guild travellers met at Holborn Viaduct on the morning of 16 September to depart by train for Dover (and from there to Ostend, Brussels, Basel, and Italy); they returned to London on 4 October. According to Okey, "We were a merry party of twenty-seven, with one or two exceptions, young artists and craftsmen, visiting Italy for the first time, and eagerly responsive to the peculiar emotions which a first experience of Italian art and history excites."[5] Among Shaw's companions were his friend Emery Walker, an engraver, typographical expert, and member of William Morris's Society for the Protection of Ancient Buildings; and Sidney Cockerell, a friend of Ruskin, and Morris's secretary (later director of the Fitzwilliam Museum). Shaw, Walker, and Cockerell were roommates at Mantua and Pavia. Okey's published memories of the trip include a letter from Shaw to Morris from Venice on 23 September and several anecdotes about Shaw. Okey noted that "Few of us . . . had any suspicion that we had with us the future great dramatist of the twentieth century."

The future dramatist's vegetarianism posed a practical problem for the tour's organizer. As Okey explained, "Italians cannot understand anyone, except on religious grounds, refusing to eat meat when able to include it in his diet. Mr. Shaw, in the early stages, was actually suffering from insufficient food (even *maccaroni al sugo* he refused—the gravy was repugnant to him), until at length I hit upon the expedient of seeing the head-waiter on our arrival at the hotel, and explaining to him that one member of our *comitiva* was under a vow. This was at once understood, and for the remainder of the *Italienische Reise* Mr. Shaw travelled as a devout Catholic under a vow to abstain from flesh, wine, and tobacco."[6]

Hesketh Pearson is the source of another amusing anecdote concerning Shaw at this time: "He was lunching on one of his tours with the Art Workers' Guild at a cafe in Milan when the members wanted to have their bills separately. This being too complicated for their scanty Italian they appealed to Shaw to explain. He racked his brains and suddenly remembered a line from the Italian version of Meyerbeer's *Les Huguenots: Ciascun per se; per tutti il ciel.* (Each for himself; and heaven for us all.) He said casually, '*Ciascun per se*'; the waiter said, '*Si, si, signore*': and his credit as a master of Italian was firmly founded."[7]

Another practical problem, mentioned by both Okey and Shaw, was posed by Italian insects. Shaw's letter to Morris ends with a reference to the fact that the faces and necks of Walker and Cockerell are "mosquito pastures—all red spots"; Shaw explained that he had escaped by burning noxious pastilles. His system for discouraging fleas, he added, was to perspire so much that the dampness produced rheumatism in the fleas ("which must be a hideously unpleasant complaint for an insect which has to jump for its life every few seconds") (*CL* 1, 312). The prevalence of "small beings" in the quarters at Pavia led Okey to a digression in which he described (complete with illustration) a wicker bug-trap he, as an expert basket maker, had made.

For Shaw's impressions of Italy on this trip we rely on his letter to Morris. Shaw's shorthand diary, which he kept from 1885 to 1897, yields for the dates of this and his subsequent Italian tour only departure and arrival times, destinations, names of hotels, and notes of Fabian activities back in London. It contains no reports of places visited nor impressions of them. The long letter to Morris, on the other hand, provides copious comments on Shaw's touring companions, his impressions of Italian architecture, and his estimate of what constitutes "a permanent, living art" (*CL* 1, 309–12).[8]

The letter expresses Shaw's irritation with his travelling companions, "most of whom have taken up art as the last refuge of general incompetence." He complained that they were incapable of appreciating beauty, that they admired things for the wrong reasons (e.g., citing Ruskin instead of forming their own opinions), and that they were conned into buying fake "antiques." He satirized their attempts to speak French and Italian, and feared that they left meager tips. He frankly preferred "the blank Philistines, who shew a healthy preference for the penny steamers, the sunsets & the Lido."

William Irvine, in *The Universe of G.B.S.*, concluded that on this trip Shaw himself turned into "a hopeless Philistine."[9] And it is true that Shaw's criticism of Italian architecture in the letter to Morris borders on Philistinism. The Milan cathedral "disgusted" Shaw: ". . . it struck me as representing the result of giving a carte blanche order for the biggest thing of the kind that could be done. Every sort of decoration is heaped up and elaborated and repeated. There are windows miles high & acres broad, with nothing in them but hundreds of little piffling pictures like pages out of Cassell's Illustrated Family Bible—not even a joke in them except the stealing of Adam & Eve from Coreggio's Venus & Mercury in the National Gallery. I greatly prefer St Pauls. . . ." The Frari, SS. Giovanni e Paolo, and San Rocco "are nothing but enormous barns." He had not yet looked inside St. Mark's, but was disappointed with its exterior.

Shaw's estimates of the Italian architecture he saw on his 1891 trip are remarkably similar to those in an 1855 Ruskin-influenced book by a celebrated architect of Victorian Gothic, G. E. Street (1824–1881). Street was disappointed with the churches of Venice, preferring Northern to Southern church architecture, and especially preferring English: "The churches in Venice in no respect came up to my anticipations. There is, indeed, not a tithe of the real delight experienced in visiting them which I remember having felt in visiting the churches of much smaller cities in France, Germany, and our own dear England."[10] The churches of Santa Maria Gloriosa dei Frari and of SS. Giovanni e Paolo were "not pleasing"; the Milan cathedral was "depressing" and lacking "repose." In contrast, San Ambrogio offered a transition from the world to church: "Here the atrium gives time and space to throw off all worldly thoughts, and to enter entirely into the religious feelings proper in such a place" (p. 222). Likewise, San Zeno is "one of the noblest examples of a very noble type of church"; its cloister allowed him to feel "most deeply the great and religious effect of the church." In a passage anticipating Shaw's argument in "On Going to Church," Street regretted that churches in both Italy and England were no longer filled with sincere worship. San Zeno's "exceeding grandeur appeared to deserve a better fate than the careless irreverence to which it seems now to be abandoned. To see all these painted or coloured walls, all these marble piers, and all that vast expanse of wall and roof shut up and desolate, apparently half-used and never filled with a throng of worshippers, reminded me too strongly of the sad and similar fate of our own dear English cathedrals. . . . To some men it is a comfort to find that their neighbours are no better than themselves . . . , but . . . to my mind a noble church disused is a subject only for mournful recollection, just as a noble church much used and filled with crowds of worshippers is . . . an object for our emulation and admiration" (p. 102). The only point of disagreement between Street and Shaw in reaction to the Italian churches is over St. Mark's: Street found it "religion-inspiring," seeing it as "some fairy-like vision" in which "its real charm lies . . . in its beautiful colour" (p. 124). Shaw expressed disappointment with the exterior of St. Mark's in that he "expected above all things colour, and it is *scraped clean*." My guess is that Shaw, reading Street almost like a guide-book, expected magnificent color. (Shaw was no doubt also led to expect color from Ruskin's assertion in *The Stones of Venice*, 1853, that one's respect for St. Mark's rests "on its value as a piece of perfect and unchangeable colouring.")[11]

Shaw's complaint that the building had been "*scraped clean*" is an allusion to the "anti-scrape" campaign of Morris's Society for the Preservation of Ancient Buildings (founded 1877). Shaw and others on the tour (Walker, for example, who was a member of the S.P.A.B.) were horrified by their encounters with Italian architecture which they found threatened with nineteenth-century "restoration." Ruskin had written in opposition to such restoration, which involved demolition of the original and its replacement with new work supposedly in the spirit of the original. An influential medievalist and architect characterized the restorers' attitude thus: "To restore a building is not to preserve it, to repair it, or to build it; it is to reinstate it in a condition of completeness which could never have existed at any given time."[12] Curiously, Shaw came to the conclusion that total destruction was the only way to avoid such specious "restoration." He concluded his letter to Morris with an allusion to his "old iconoclastic idea of destroying the entire show," since "Italy seems to me a humbug." The same point appears in a later letter to Emery Walker: "since my trip to Italy, I have definitely made up my mind that all ancient buildings ought to be demolished as soon as possible. I am still sound on the restoration question; but this logically involves the repudiation of preservation, which always means restoration & nothing else" (CL 1, 343–44).

In spite of his extravagant attacks on Venetian architecture, it is a mistake to dismiss Shaw's criticism as an example of hopeless Philistinism. In it were the beginnings of an aesthetic theory, a theory which calls for organic, everyday, innovative art. Like Ruskin in "The Nature of Gothic" (1853), Shaw preferred northern to Italian architecture, finding the latter "not organic" but "flagrantly architecture for the sake of ornamentality." Just as Shaw was elsewhere to reject art for its own sake, by which he meant non-organic art, mere confectionery instead of substance, he here rejected architecture which "does not grow in the great way." Like Street, he isolated the churches of San Ambrogio in Milan and San Zeno in Verona as places where "I felt happy"—an idea he was to develop at length in his 1896 essay "On Going to Church." But even in San Zeno, with its beautiful porch and tower, he found "the organic nature of the porch & arches . . . not carried far"; the porch is out of proportion with the rest.

Shaw, toward the end of his letter, looked forward to a new art which would not rely on "old bricks." Nor would it depend on the extraordinary or spectacular: "I do not believe that a permanent, living art can ever come out of the conditions of Venetian splendour, even at its greatest time. The best art of all will come when we are rid of splendour and everything in the glorious line." These lines anticipate Shaw's conviction that the artist should deal with "real life at first hand" and discover "drama in real life."[13] They show that, though Shaw was at times exasperated with his tour companions and unimpressed with Italian monuments, he nevertheless found in his first experience of Italy ideas and impressions that were to surface later as part of his aesthetic.

Shaw's second tour of Italy, also organized by Okey for the Art Workers' Guild, was made in 1894 from 5 September to 23 September. From Basel the group went to Pallanza, Milan, Florence (for a stay of nine days), Pisa, Genoa, and Como (where they left for London via Basel, Brussels, and Ostend). Okey writes that in Genoa Shaw requested entrance to the Carlo Felice theater, where he examined "the construction, arrangements, and measurements of the stage—an incident whose significance became intelligible in later years." (Presumably Okey is referring to Shaw's later work as a playwright.) Okey also remembered that in Genoa Shaw threatened (probably in jest) to destroy a realistic sculpture of Jenner vaccinating a child.[14] Otherwise, the information we have of this trip comes from Shaw, who in the Preface to *Plays Pleasant* wrote that in Florence "I occupied myself with the religious art of the Middle Ages and its destruction by the Renascence." Just beginning his career as playwright, he observed that "the time was ripe for a modern pre-Raphaelite play. Religion was alive again, coming back upon men, even upon clergymen, with such power that not the Church of England itself could keep it out." This statement, connecting his playwriting, pre-Raphaelitism, and religion (admittedly an unorthodox one, as his remark about the established church demonstrates), suggests that just as his earlier Italian tour had sharpened his aesthetic perceptions, his second visit awakened his religious sense. He began to go to church again.

II

In "On Going to Church,"[15] Shaw used his Italian experience to argue for the recreative and restorative power of church-going. The essay was published in 1896 in the first issue of Arthur Symons' short-lived avant-garde magazine, *The Savoy*. "On Going to Church" continues Shaw's attack on "splendour and everything in the glorious line" begun in his letter to Morris in 1891. Again the cathedral at Milan, a "petrified christening-cake," is contrasted unfavorably with San Ambrogio. In Florence, San Lorenzo, "built to the pride and glory of God (not to mention the Medici)," and the Santissima Annunziata, an example of church restoration which displayed "wealth and elegance as a guarantee of social importance," contrasted with Santa Maria Novella, Santa Croce, and San Miniato—churches "built as a sanctuary shielded by God's presence from pride and glory and all the other burdens of life." But the importance of "On Going to Church" is not in its criticism of church architecture: it is in the argument that Shaw makes for spiritual regeneration, which he finds in going to church.

The essay begins with an attack on fine art that is "produced by the teapot, the bottle, or the hypodermic syringe." Finding that many artists rely overmuch on unwholesome stimulants (including meat-eating), Shaw noted that his "experiment of not eating meat or drinking tea, coffee, or spirits" has not placed him at a disadvantage. He did not, however, advocate "abstinence, pure and simple." All artists need stimulation, he said; and for him such stimulation lies not in food and drink but in going to church, where he found "rest without languor and recreation without excitement."

The essay relies on a series of contrasts, beginning with the contrast between artistic stimulation produced by drugs and that produced by church-going. It also contrasts artists who work for a comfortable living with those who sacrifice everything and everyone, including themselves, to the perfection of their art. Shaw rejected fashionable, architect-designed churches exuding "respectability and talent" for "real" churches built by artisans who love their craft and have "the true votive spirit." Finally, he contrasted conventional religion, as exemplified by the joyless genteel Irish Protestant church of his boyhood or by "the innumerable daily services which disturb the truly religious visitor" in Roman Catholic Italy, with "the real religion of to-day," i.e., his unorthodox, iconoclastic faith: "I am a resolute Protestant; I believe in the Holy Catholic Church; in the Holy Trinity of Father, Son (or Mother, Daughter) and Spirit; in the Communion of Saints, the Life to Come, the Immaculate Conception, and the everyday reality of Godhead and the Kingdom of Heaven."

In arguing for church-going as a substitute for drinking gin and smoking hashish, Shaw was doing more than being witty and outrageous. Going to church is meant literally, but it is also used as a metaphor for freeing the human spirit. In a remarkable passage anticipating the Jungian notion of a house as symbolic of human consciousness, Shaw said:

> Any place where men dwell, village or city, is a reflection of the consciousness of every single man. In my consciousness there is a market, a garden, a dwelling, a workshop, a lover's walk—above all, a cathedral. My appeal to the master-builder is: Mirror this cathedral for me in enduring stone; make it with hands; let it direct its sure and clear appeal to my senses, so that when my spirit is vaguely groping after an elusive mood my eye shall be caught by the skyward tower, showing me where, within the cathedral, I may find my way to the cathedral within me.

It is a conventional enough idea—that a church should foster spiritual introspection and allow the soul to "open all its avenues of life to the holy air of the true Catholic Church." But the cathedral/spirit analogy puts a new light on Shaw's comments on Italian churches. His praise of San Ambrogio, San Zeno, Santa Maria Novella, Santa Croce, and San Miniato and his rejection of other churches reflect not only his architectural preferences but his philosophical position.

Shaw's attacks on the churches he dislikes focus on pretentiousness and a failure in faith. He deplored "the decay of religious art from the sixteenth century to the nineteenth" caused by "an eclipse of religion by science and commerce" as demonstrated by the Milan cathedral, San Lorenzo, and the Santissima Annunziata. The Milan cathedral he called a "costly ornament." In Florence, he found San Lorenzo a masterpiece architecturally but a monument to "talent, power or rank," alluding to the Medici support of Brunelleschi's fifteenth-century restoration of the church.[16] The Santissima Annunziata he condemned as "carefully and expensively brought up to date," a monument to snobbery. Shaw thus objected primarily to what he believed to be commercial rather than religious motives that went into the Renaissance and post-Renaissance art of these churches.

Influenced by Ruskin and Morris, Shaw believed that in the middle ages religious art—including church architecture—grew out of a genuinely religious impulse, out of a reverend and loving spirit subsequently lost but capable of being recaptured. With a knowledge of the cathedral within, Shaw said, a modern craftsman "might build churches as they built them in the middle ages." He believed that modern art capable of moving the religious spirit can be produced by "a craftsman who has picked up the thread of the tradition of his craft from the time when that craft was a fine art [i.e., from the middle ages]," or by someone "who had tried to learn what she could from the early Florentine masters and had done the work in the true votive spirit." It is no surprise that the Italian churches that Shaw preferred are all medieval churches, literally pre-Raphaelite churches, i.e., churches built before Raphael (1483–1520).

Both in the letter to Morris and in "On Going to Church," Shaw admired San Ambrogio in Milan, a Romanesque church built in the eleventh century over a fourth-century foundation. Shaw praised the altar, "made of gold, jewels, filigree, mosaic &c," and the "free & beautiful work in the capitals of the pillars in the courtyard, and in the carving of the panels in the choir stalls"; most important, however, is his implication in his comparison of San Ambrogio with the Milan cathedral that the former was built by more devout craftsmen. In Florence, the Gothic churches Santa Maria Novella (begun in 1279) and Santa Croce (ca. 1294–1301) and the twelfth-century Romanesque church of San Miniato are examples of truly religious sanctuaries. The twelfth-century Ro-

manesque San Zeno Maggiore in Verona and San Ambrogio are cited in
the letter to Morris as the only places where Shaw "felt happy" on the
way to Venice.[17] What these churches have in common is not architectural style but their age. "In the older churches you forget yourself, and
are the equal of the beggar at the door, standing on ground made holy
by that labour in which we have discovered the reality of Prayer." For
Shaw they represented art produced in reverence and inspiring reverence, allowing one to touch "the cathedral within."

In "On Going to Church" Shaw also glanced at English churches, noting with approval the village churches which keep their doors open for
all those who wish to enter. He lamented the tendency to keep churches
locked and "guarded in the spirit of that Westminster Abbey verger
who, not long ago, had a stranger arrested for kneeling down, and explained, when remonstrated with, that if that sort of thing were toler-
ated, they would soon have people praying all over the place." He mentioned the successful efforts of a Parson Shuttleworth, of St. Nicholas
Cole Abbey, to make the church attractive as a place of rest at mid-day:
the parson guaranteed "immunity from sermons, prayers and collections," had the organist play Bach and Wagner, and put out a shelf of
books for reading in the church. In contrast are the pious committees
and clergy who impede the construction of churches that encourage
worship and create instead "purposeless, respectable-looking interiors
. . . irreconcilable with the doctrine of Omnipresence . . . in a place that
must needs be intolerable to Omniscience."

Clearly the religious spirit—the "cathedral within"—that Shaw
sought in church is not associated with a respectable, conventional religion. A clergyman—for example, Parson Shuttleworth—may have that
spirit, but so may self-proclaimed atheists, like Shaw. Shaw spoke elo-
quently of the repressive, narrow religion which stifled his spirit as a
child: ". . . it prejudiced me so violently against church-going that
twenty years elapsed before, in foreign lands and in pursuit of works of
art, I became once more a churchgoer. . . . When I at last took to church-
going again, a kindred difficulty beset me, especially in Roman Catholic
countries." In Italy, Shaw found the services not conducive of worship,
the priests unclean, and the sacristans primarily interested in tips.

"On Going to Church" argues that the church should transcend sec-
tarianism, that it should be open to all, and that it should in its exterior
and interior design reflect the reverend spirit of those who built it and
of those who enter it. The essay, in its references to "real churches" (i.e.,
those inspiring rest and recreation) and "real religion" (i.e., the religion
"made possible only by the materialistic-physicists and atheist-critics who
performed for us the indispensable preliminary operation of purging
us thoroughly of the ignorant and vicious superstitions which were

thrust down our throats as religion in our helpless childhood"), helps to explain the passage in Shaw's Preface to *Plays Pleasant* which says that, in Italy, he realized that "Religion was alive again, coming back upon men, even upon clergymen. . . ." It was this revitalized religious sense, which Shaw associated with his 1894 trip to Florence, that called for "a modern pre-Raphaelite play," i.e., a play that would emulate the votive spirit in which medieval art was produced.[18] But it would be better than Italian art, because it would be, like the work of Morris and Burne-Jones, the work of a living man and because it would eschew "splendour and everything in the glorious line," demonstrating instead the godhead of everyday reality.

In summary, what can we say that Shaw gained in the 1891 and 1894 Italian tours? How did they affect him and his work? First we must note that there is a kind of stubborn chauvinism in Shaw's art preferences: he preferred Morris and Burne-Jones to Florentine masters, and St. Paul's to the Milan cathedral. He was also distrustful of Italian magnificence, preferring instead Shavian common sense. But his tours of northern Italy provided him with a way of focussing his nascent aesthetic theories. His 1891 letter to Morris, his 1896 essay "On Going to Church," and his 1898 Preface to *Plays Pleasant* all suggest that, in the Italian experience, he was observing a connection between art and morality (not, let me hasten to add, conventional ideas of good and evil), and he was developing the idea later expressed in "The Religious Art of the Twentieth Century" (Preface, *Back to Methuselah*, 1921): "Indeed art has never been great when it was not providing an iconography for a live religion. . . . until we have a great religious movement we cannot hope for a great artistic one." He found the last great age of faith reflected in medieval art, and saw the collapse of that faith and of great art in post-Raphaelite art. He used Italian church architecture as illustration of this theory, but explained that "You may read the same history of the human soul in any art you like to select." It would be claiming too much to say that in Italy Shaw became, in the traditional sense, a religious man; rather he "became once more a churchgoer." The churches of Italy offered him a place where he could reach "the cathedral within" and then, spiritually renewed, create an art to reflect that living religion.

Notes

1. Thomas Okey, *A Basketful of Memories: An Autobiographical Sketch* (London and Toronto: J. M. Dent, 1933), p. 66.

2. Quoted in May Morris, *William Morris: Artist, Writer, Socialist* (New York: Russell & Russell, 1966), I, 83–84.

3. Introduction, *The Collected Works of William Morris* (New York: Russell & Russell, 1966), XVI, xxiii. May Morris quotes, pp. xxii–xxiii, one of the original founders, W. R. Lethaby, on the Guild: "An Associated Art Society of Painters, Sculptors, Architects and actual workers in the minor arts, with the objects (1) of promoting association, and forwarding the cause of Art, (2) of helping Decorative Art, and especially restoring certain art handiworks now almost lost or entirely forgotten, (3) of spreading a knowledge of principles among the several trades and the public. . . . The Society should discuss current Art; permanent collections should be formed by it; each craft should lecture on its own methods and have loan exhibitions of its works; and finally, the instruction of the public should be attempted by tracts, pamphlets, letters, and articles."

4. Archibald Henderson, *George Bernard Shaw: Man of the Century* (New York: Appleton-Century-Crofts, 1956), p. 185, believes that the artist and socialist Walter Crane invited Shaw; it is equally plausible that William Morris's and Shaw's friend Emery Walker invited Shaw. A letter to Walker on 11 August, 1891, has Shaw sending Walker a check for his share of the expenses (each person paid £13–10–0) and asking Walker if Shaw's journalist friend, H. W. Massingham, could be included in the expedition. (Massingham did not go.)

5. Okey, p. 118.

6. Okey, pp. 125–26.

7. *Bernard Shaw: His Life and Personality* (London: Collins, 1942), p. 309. The same anecdote is reported in Archibald Henderson, *George Bernard Shaw: His Life and Works* (Cincinnati: Steward & Kidd, 1911), p. 500.

8. The letter, with minor variations, appears also in Okey, pp. 119–25, and Henderson, *George Bernard Shaw: Man of the Century*, pp. 185–88.

9. New York, London and Toronto: McGraw Hill (Whittlesey House), 1949, p. 122.

10. *Brick and Marble in the Middle Ages: Notes of a Tour in the North of Italy* (London: John Murray, 1855), p. 139. Street designed the American church of St. Paul's in Rome (1872–76), for which Burne-Jones designed the mosaics in consultation with Morris, and in which the floor tiles were directly after Morris and possibly by him. Shaw, through his friendship with Morris, most certainly would have known Street's work.

11. John Ruskin, "St. Mark's," *The Stones of Venice*, vol. 2, in *The Works of John Ruskin*, ed. E. T. Cook and Alexander Wedderburn (London: George Allen, 1904), vol. 10, 97.

12. Viollet-le-Duc, in *Dictionnaire raisonné de l'architecture française du XIe au XVIe siècle* (Paris, 1854–68); quoted in Carroll L. V. Meeks, *Italian Architecture 1750–1914* (New Haven and London: Yale University Press, 1966), p. 224.

13. "A Dramatic Realist to His Critics" (1894), in Dan H. Laurence, ed., *Selected Non-Dramatic Writings of Bernard Shaw* (Boston: Houghton Mifflin [Riverside Edition], 1965), pp. 323, 338.

14. Okey, p. 126.

15. In *Selected Non-Dramatic Writings of Bernard Shaw*, pp. 378–90.

16. The history of the restoration of San Lorenzo, the Medici church, supports Shaw's criticism of it. Brunelleschi's rebuilding of the older church was "financed with the methods of modern capitalism," i.e., through bank interest on bank funds, and was "exclusively a product of high-level planning, bureaucratic adroitness, a well-oiled banking administra-

tion, and an agreement between a very few money-aristocrats supported and encouraged by the political organs of the city" (Eugenio Battisti, *Filippo Brunelleschi: The Complete Work*, trans. from the Italian by Robert Erich Wolf [New York: Rizzoli, 1981], p. 174). For the complicated and interesting history of San Lorenzo, see Battisti, pp. 173–96.

17. As a matter of fact, some of the churches which Shaw praises were modernized after the Middle Ages: Santa Maria Novella after 1456, and Santa Croce in 1857–63, with an effect "more industrial than religious" (Meeks, p. 220). See also F. M. Godfrey, *Italian Architecture Up to 1750* (New York: Taplinger Publishing Co., 1971).

18. For a full discussion of this point, see my "Bernard Shaw's Pre-Raphaelite Drama," *PMLA*, 81 (October, 1966), 428–38.

Ishrat Lindblad

A GOOD HOLIDAY: SHAW VISITS SWEDEN

"On Saturday next, I start for Stockholm by sea, via Gothenburg and the Gotha Canal. As my wife has never been to Bayreuth, we shall go there at the end of July," wrote Shaw on 29 June 1908 to his German translator, Siegfried Trebitsch (*CL* 2, 794). His letter makes it clear that his main reason for taking the trip is to "break away from my work and have a good holiday, as I'm pretty nearly at the end of my tether." The Shaws set sail, according to plan, on board the *Thulebaten* on 4 July, and arrived, two days later, in Gothenburg, where they were received by Shaw's Swedish translator and host throughout the trip, Hugo Vallentin.

Considering the kind of publicity that famous authors on tour are given nowadays, even when they want peace and quiet, it is surprising to find that Shaw's visit was treated with only perfunctory interest. There are a few interviews with portraits in the daily press, a humorous sketch by Hugo Vallentin in *Puck*, the magazine he edited, an account of Shaw's visit to Strindberg's *Intima Teatern*, and a passing reference to his presence in Stockholm in a few of Strindberg's letters.[1] None of the original photographs or sketches of Shaw have been preserved in the Swedish public libraries or archives, even though the cartoon (Fig. 1) which appeared in *Puck* is by the well-known artist Edward Forström, whose work is represented in the collections at both *Kungliga Biblioteket* and *Stadsmuseet*. Forström's sketch is said to be inspired by G.B.S.'s quip: "What a crazy country. They search my luggage but not my character. It is far more dangerous!"

In addition to the material described above, there is a section on Shaw's sojourn in Stockholm in Herbert Grevenius's *Shaw rebellen*, of which an English version was published in *The Shavian*.[2]

Since, by the standards of today, Shaw had given himself plenty of time for his visit (he arrived on July 6th and left on July 18th), he seems to have been able to enjoy the kind of holiday he needed. In Gothen-

G. BERNARD SHAWS ANKOMST TILL SVERIGE.

(EFTER G. B. S:s EGEN IDÉ.)

G. B. S.: Ett sådant tokigt land. Dom undersöker mina koffertar. men inte min karaktär. Den är mycket farligare.

FIG. 1. Cartoon by Edward Forström published in *Puck*, No. 29, 18 July 1908. Text of cartoon translates as follows: G. Bernard Shaw's Arrival in Sweden (Based on GBS's Own Idea). *GBS:* What a crazy country. They search my baggage, but not my character. It is much more dangerous.

burg he went to the Art Museum and picked out the work of Anders Zorn, Bruno Liljefors, and Richard Bergh with the unerring instinct of a true connoisseur. The next day he boarded the *Motala Ström* in order to make the journey up to Stockholm through the famous Göta Canal.

Shaw could not resist commenting on the absurdity of calling one of the most beautiful routes in Sweden "the canal route," a name which he associated with an "enormous gutter full of boats being drawn by mules trudging along the embankment."[3] But then he added mischievously: "Of course, if it had been named something romantic like 'The route through the Lakes' you would have hordes of tourists trying to crowd their way past the locks. And so, I for one, will do what I can to perpetrate the notion that Sweden is a frightful place, where bears wander through the streets and the people live on cod liver oil."

Upon their arrival in Stockholm, on 9 July, the Shaws stayed at the now-defunct Hotel Rydberg in the heart of the city at Gustaf Adolf's square. Their schedule for the next few days looks very much like that of an ordinary tourist. On Friday 10 July, they explored the old town and the southern part of Stockholm, made famous by Strindberg's descriptions of its quaint charm. Then they lunched with Hugo Vallentin and his secretary, Ebba Byström, at Stockholm's most exclusive restaurant, *Operakällaren*. Byström, later known as Lady Ebba Low, would succeed Vallentin as Shaw's Swedish translator. The luncheon was followed by an afternoon at *Skansen*, the open-air folk museum, and dinner at the nearby restaurant *Hasselbacken*, where Shaw was amused by the band's standing up to play "God Save the King" in his honor.[4]

The next day was equally busy, with a tour of the Nordic Museum and a trip to the sailing resort of Saltsjöbaden, where they were invited to dine by their faithful guide, Hugo Vallentin. The Shaws spent the weekend at the Grand Hotel in Saltsjöbaden but there remains little record of their activities for the rest of the week.

Naturally, the Swedes were eager to ask Shaw for his impressions of Stockholm. A German tourist had recently visited the city and pronounced it to be excessively dull, with the result that *Dagens Nyheter* had begun a series of entertaining articles about "This tedious city." Leonard Vitt interviewed Shaw, who said he found it very dull when he discovered that the churches in Stockholm were often closed: "When a person like me is getting ready to storm the house of God and a policeman creeps up from behind a bush and threatens to arrest him and that in a foreign language, he is bound to feel a bit discouraged."[5] Apparently the free-thinker Shaw always made a point of visiting places of prayer: "temples, pagodas, cathedrals, basilicas—wherever they may be. After all, these buildings represent an expression of a people's innermost longings, their highest dreams, their worship of the invisible." With a characteristically Shavian turnabout he then went on to say that he regarded a service in a church as a "disturbance of the peace," but feared that in Sweden there seemed to have been "a Voltaire who had gained the ear of the people. Over here I feel that I am in the midst of a revolutionary era living under the benign, if somewhat godless, rule of the Goddess of Reason."[6] The conversation is noteworthy because, in spite of Shaw's bantering tone, it reveals something of the complexity of his attitude to religion.

Shaw's commitment to socialism, a topic on which Shaw could be quite serious, was a burning issue in Sweden at the time of his visit. His arrival was overshadowed by the explosion, in Malmö harbor, on 12 July, of a bomb on board the *Amalthea*, where some British strikebreakers were being housed during a strike of the Swedish stevedores. When a reporter from the leading left-wing daily *Socialdemokraten* interviewed Shaw, he was more interested in presenting the socialist than the dramatist who was already familiar to a bourgeois public. He quotes Shaw on poverty: "Perhaps you have heard Cromwell's opinion of the House of Lords—'it is useless, dangerous, and should be abolished'? Well, those are exactly the words I used in my best speech in the East End of London. To have such a large class of poor workers is both useless and dangerous. The entire class should be abolished."[7] The reporter then goes on to remind his readers that Shaw's Fabian pamphlets have been translated into Swedish by Anton Andersson and A.C. Lindblad. Copies of these were presented to Shaw by members of the Social Democratic Party "as a sign of their recognition of the international nature of this movement and of the significance of the use of literature as an instrument to further the socialist cause." The sincerity of the Social Democrats' appreciation of Shaw's efforts on behalf of socialism is called into question by the fact that Shaw's brand of it is described as "opportunism salted with witty paradoxes." It seems that the Social Democrats in Sweden dismissed Shaw as an "armchair socialist" in much the same way as Henry Straker in *Man and Superman* dismisses John Tanner.

In addition to questioning Shaw on his political opinions, reporters were eager to ask him for his views regarding censorship and freedom of speech. The subject was one of considerable current interest, owing to the Swedish government's decision to file a suit against Tolstoy for the distribution of anti-military flyers in Sweden. Shaw had an anecdote ready for the occasion. He told them how he himself had almost been imprisoned for his opinions at least three times. The nearest escape had been during a political rally in the 1880s when socialists were forbidden to meet in public and the first speaker at such a meeting ran the risk of imprisonment. Naturally, Shaw was eager to be the man, but he was not chosen for the honor because a volunteer from the rival party, which was larger, was preferred. Shaw was chosen as the second speaker and thus forfeited the coveted prison sentence.[8]

Those who were more interested in aspects of Shaw's work other than his politics found that their purposes were better served by the conservative daily *Svenska Dagbladet* which devoted more space to covering Shaw's visit than did *Socialdemokraten*.[9] Indeed, the editors of *Svenska*

Dagbladet could congratulate themselves on its being the first newspaper to publish an interview with Shaw. Their representative, "Yvette," met the Canal boat at Södertälje and made the journey up to Stockholm in Shaw's company, thus making the most of her opportunity to obtain information for her paper.

Their conversation centered on the subject of the women's suffrage movement in England and Shaw's cordial support of it. He maintained that he thought that women have great administrative ability, and that they are often better able to relieve social distress through practical measures than men, who tend to indulge in high-flown sentiments instead.[10]

Other reporters were eager to question Shaw on his ideas concerning women, and Shaw himself asked: "Do you know why my portraits of women are always so excellent? I never bother to imagine a womanly character. I always presume that women are just the same as I am and write away quite happily."[11] Still, they wondered if his plays appealed especially to women. "Yes, women like my plays" claimed Shaw, "and all that I have written are nothing but 'women's plays.' The best proof is that my latest play, *Getting Married*, has annoyed men and critics."[12] Somewhat jestingly, he proceeded to suggest that every critic should be married to a gifted woman who could write a second review of all the plays they saw together, and wondered what kind of plays Strindberg would have written if this practice had been customary in Sweden.

This comment led naturally into a discussion of Shaw's views on the kind of women Strindberg portrays:

> First, I must admit that I have not read much of Strindberg. I do not know one word of any of the Scandinavian languages, and up to just half a year ago I did not know that Lappland was in Sweden. But I have read some of his plays. Women, as portrayed by Strindberg, do exist, but the type is rare. It's a good thing that such portraits are available. The more that is done to get rid of the sentimental romantic woman in literature the better.[13]

Although this statement of Shaw's suggests only a slight acquaintance with the work of Strindberg, an earlier letter from Shaw to his biographer, Archibald Henderson, gives the impression that he is rather familiar with Strindberg's ideas:

> I have read one book and one play by Strindberg; but here again I was perfectly familiar with his peculiar hatred of women-idolization through the writings and conversation of Ernest Belfort Bax, whose essays attacking bourgeois morality were published here before Strindberg or Nietzsche had been heard of. (*CL* 2, 554)[14]

There can be little doubt that Shaw held Strindberg in high esteem. In the preface to *Three Plays for Puritans* (1900) he refers to him as "the only genuinely Shakespearian modern dramatist."[15] It is reasonable to assume that the unconventionality of Strindberg's ideas on marriage as expressed in his collection of short stories *Giftas* (1884), along with his conception of woman as the pursuer in the "duel of sex," appealed to Shaw. Admittedly, Strindberg's view of the vampire female engaged in a death struggle is much bleaker than Shaw's debunking of the Victorian ideal of womanhood. Moreover, Shaw creates several women who are capable of taking on traditionally male roles. There is, however, no denying an element of influence, nor the fact that Shaw himself tried to arrange a meeting with Strindberg.

Soon after his arrival in Stockholm, Shaw contacted Strindberg with the request that he be given permission to visit him the same afternoon.[16] Strindberg's reply that he would be sick at two o'clock has already been made famous by Shaw's various versions of it. It is interesting to see how Shaw's imagination worked on the incident, twisting the tale to suit the teller.

His first account of the meeting is contained in his letter to William Archer:

> I achieved the impossible—a meeting with Strindberg today. He said "Archer is not in sympathy with me." I said "Archer was not in sympathy with Ibsen either; but he couldn't help translating him all the same, being accessible to poetry, though otherwise totally impenetrable." After some further conversation, consisting mainly of embarrassed silence & a pale smile or two by A.S. & floods of energetic eloquence in a fearful lingo, half French, half German, by G.B.S., A.S. took out his watch & said, in German, "At two o'clock I am going to be sick." The visitors accepted this delicate intimation & withdrew. (*CL* 2, 802)

The picture postcard of a portrait of Strindberg which Shaw sent to Granville-Barker reporting the same incident, shows how Bernard Shaw had begun to embellish the story and use it to perpetrate the legend of G.B.S.:

> This great man reached the summit of his career when he met the immortal G.B.S. at the Theatre Interne at Stockholm on the 16th July 1908 at one o'clock in the afternoon. At 1.25, he said in German, "At two o'clock I am going to be sick." On this strong hint the party broke up.[17]

Subsequently, Shaw embroidered his account still further in a conversation reported by his friend Judge Henry Neil.[18] By the time he was interviewed by the Danish portrait artist, Ivan Opffer, in 1928, fiction had taken over completely:

> I wanted to exchange some ideas with him and went down to Paris where Strindberg was staying at the time. I wrote to him and eventually got a

reply. He informed me that he never met anyone before two o'clock in the morning and suggested a day, or rather, a night.

I had taken along Mrs Shaw as an interpreter since she knew French better than I did. Strindberg lived at Montparnasse in Rue de la Grande Chaumière in old Ton Tons pensionat. We drove there in an old taxi and were shown into Strindberg's room. But when he saw my wife he stared wildly at her and said: "I am always sick at two o'clock in the morning." We apologized hastily and disappeared rapidly.[19]

In spite of the circumstantial detail presented in this report, it is improbable that Shaw ever met Strindberg in Paris. Strindberg lived there between 1883 and 1889 on one occasion, and on another between August 1897 and April 1898 after his "Inferno" crisis. During those years Shaw had just begun to make his name. Moreover, the unlikelihood of Strindberg's having made exactly the same remark on two quite different occasions strongly suggests that Shaw's tale is based on his meeting with Strindberg in 1908.

A study of the Swedish sources provides a more accurate, albeit duller, version. According to August Falck, a friend and collaborator of Strindberg's during his years at *Intima Teatern*, and the leading actor in many of his plays, Strindberg contacted him while he and his leading lady, Manda Björling, were holidaying on the island of Ornö in the archipelago of Stockholm. He did this in order to request the two actors to return to the city and give an afternoon performance of *Fröken Julie* for Shaw's benefit.

The performance was given on 16 July, which was also the date of the opening night. It is possible that Strindberg would have asked for a dress rehearsal in any case, but ostensibly his purpose was to oblige Shaw. Here is Falck's account:

> Bernard Shaw was in Stockholm and had been in touch with Strindberg who did not know how to receive him. He also seemed to regret the fact that he had been terribly rude to Shaw, for as soon as he had arrived in Stockholm he had contacted Strindberg and asked if he could pay a visit the same day at two o'clock, whereupon Strindberg had only replied: "At two o'clock I will be sick."[20]

Apparently Strindberg was eager to make amends, for he accompanied Shaw and his wife to the theater and saw the play himself for the first time. Falck especially noticed the pride with which Strindberg showed Shaw around the theater which he himself had founded just the year before. Although Falck was naturally more interested in Strindberg's reaction to the play than in Shaw's, he did wonder how much Shaw would be able to get out of seeing such a naturalistic play in a language he did not understand. Evidently Strindberg was greatly

moved, and both he and Shaw came backstage afterwards to congratulate the actors:

> Shaw thanked us with a charming smile but did not say much. It was
> evident that he had not been able to gain much from such a perform-
> ance. No doubt he had expected an experimental theater with daring
> ideas in form and color and what did he see? A small naturalistic stage
> of the most genuine kind. Even if he had been able to understand that
> the precision of the dialogue and the way in which the actors played to
> each other was unusually intense judged by the conventions prevalent
> here at the time, he was nonetheless prevented, because of the language,
> from enjoying the details in the same way as Strindberg was able to.[21]

Whatever Shaw may or may not have got out of the afternoon's performance, he was gracious enough to attend the opening one the same evening.[22]

Strindberg complimented his actors immediately, but did not hesitate
to take them to task in the letters he wrote to them later. In one of his
letters to Falck he says: "Shaw was even more severe in his criticism than
I was, but I will not repeat his words."[23] Since most of Strindberg's objections relate to Falck and Björling's delivery of their lines, it is probable
that he is referring to Shaw as having confirmed his opinion.

Falck's account makes it quite clear that Strindberg spent more time
with Shaw than the alleged twenty-five minutes recorded on his card to
Granville-Barker. It is understandable that Strindberg, who knew virtually no English and was, indeed, a sick man, should have told Shaw
that he would not be fit to receive him the same afternoon if Shaw had
contacted him, without previous notice, and suggested a meeting the
same day. That Shaw should have found it more interesting to concoct
an amusing anecdote than to tell people that Strindberg personally
showed him around his theater and asked two of his leading actors to
return from the countryside in order to perform for him, facts which
would have enhanced his own importance, is more difficult to explain,
and adds yet another facet to his complicated personality.

In a letter that he wrote to Strindberg two years later, Shaw reminded
Strindberg of their meeting (although he remembers it as having taken
place in 1909 and not, as it did, in 1908). The tone of his letter suggests
that the meeting between them was a congenial one. He mentions that
Strindberg was kind to Hugo Vallentin "in connection with our visit to
you" and even indicates that if he "had time I would pay another visit to
Stockholm and tell you all this by word of mouth" (*CL* 2, 907). Shaw also
seems to know Strindberg sufficiently well to be able to anticipate that,
being dissatisfied with it himself, he would have strong reservations
about giving permission for the production, in London, of one of his

early plays, *Lycko Pers Resa*. Because of these reservations Shaw's proposal came to nothing.

The letter reveals an interesting difference of opinion regarding the stage requirements of Strindberg's work. Shaw contends that "in spite of all you [Strindberg] say, . . . your Intimes Teater is far too small even for Fröken Julie, and that nothing smaller than the Opera House is big enough for you" (*CL* 2, 903). Since Strindberg's idea of an intimate theater was extremely close to his heart, and *Intima Teatern* represented the realization of the aesthetic ideals he expounds in the preface to *Fröken Julie*, it is hardly likely that Shaw's opinion on the subject would have carried much weight. When Strindberg rejected the ideal of a naturalistic theater he turned towards symbolic, expressionistic drama, which remained more suited to an intimate theater, rather than towards a Wagnerian vision of total theater on a grand scale.

Even though these two major figures in twentieth-century drama confronted each other only briefly, it is difficult to dismiss the impact of their meeting. For Strindberg, soon to die, it was of little consequence. For Shaw, already an admirer of Strindbergian drama, it was to have consequences years later when he reconsidered his rejection of the Nobel Prize for Literature ("a lifeboat thrown to a swimmer who has already reached the shore") in 1926. Rather, he chose to accept the award if the prize money could be used for an Anglo-Swedish Literary Foundation which might fund the translation into English of such writers as Strindberg. Strindberg's works were the first to be so published.

The impact of Shaw's visit itself was to confirm an interest in Shaw's plays which was at its height when he visited Sweden. Just the year before, Harriet Bosse, Strindberg's third wife, had received much praise for her portrayal of Ann Whitefield in *Man and Superman*. Only after the award of the Nobel Prize in 1926 did interest in Shaw's work reach the same level as it had maintained between the years 1906 and 1917. Shaw, however, did not come to receive the award in person, nor did he ever revisit the country.[24]

Even before he came, Shaw had expressed an admiration for Sweden as "one of the most highly civilized countries in the world."[25] He delighted his hosts by claiming that Swedish critics were far more appreciative of his plays than British ones and he flattered them still further by arguing that Hugo Vallentin's translations must be better than the originals since they met with so much more favorable a response. In fact, he thought it would be a good idea to translate them back into English in the hope that they might fare better in England than they had done in their original form![26]

Having managed so skillfully to compliment his hosts and gibe at his

own countrymen, Shaw journeyed onward, leaving the famous columnist, Hasse Z, to lament his departure with his own brand of wit:

> Times are bad. Money is dear and Shaw has left. There was too much
> traffic on Gustaf Adolf's square and too much smoke from Blasieholmen.
> "Oh pshaw! . . . Imagine what we have to put up with all year."[27]

And Shaw himself, as he sailed away on the Baltic towards Lübeck,
summed up his reactions in his own inimitable way:

> Stockholm is a very jolly town to look at & the people very superior
> within certain limits of high mediocrity. All the art is ornamental XVII–
> XVIII century—grand ducal—Louis Quatorze &c; but there is a Codex
> Aurens [sic] in the Library (quite unknown to the inhabitants) and some
> very nice Icelandish MSS. (CL 2, 802)[28]

Well, the inhabitants have found out about the Codex Aureus, but who
can deny the "high mediocrity" of a people committed to the "middle
way"? With his gift for the telling paradox, Shaw infallibly put his finger
on an essential truth.

Notes

1. The interviews appeared in *Svenska Dagbladet*, 10 July 1908; *Socialdemokraten*, 11
July 1908; *Dagens Nyheter*, 12 July 1908; and in the weekly *Idun*, 16 July 1908, p. 345.
Vallentin's contribution appeared in *Puck*, No. 29, 18 July 1908, and was accompanied by
several illustrations. Shaw's visit to *Intima Teatern* is reported by August Falck in *Fem år med
Strindberg* (Stockholm: Wahlström & Widstrand, 1934), pp. 170–80. An extract of this account appeared in *Ögonvittnen, August Strindberg, mannaår och ålderdom*, ed. Stellan Ahl-
ström and Torsten Eklund (Stockholm: Wahlström & Widstrand, 1961), pp. 246–50.
Strindberg mentions Shaw in the following letters: To Manda Björling, dated 16 July 1908
(reprinted in Falck, *Fem år med Strindberg*, pp. 174–78); to August Falck, dated 24 July
1908, posted 27 July (original in the manuscript department, *Kungliga Biblioteket*); to Emil
Schering, dated 15 July 1908 (original in the archives of the Bonnier publishing house); to
Spånberg, dated 1 January 1912 (original in the manuscript department, *Kungliga Biblioteket*).
2. Herbert Grevenius, *Shaw rebellen* (Stockholm: Sveriges Radio, 1959), pp. 275–79;
and *The Shavian*, 2, February 1960, No. 1, pp. 7–12.
3. "Dagens Nyheters enquet om 'Denna tråkiga stad,'" *Dagens Nyheter*, 12 July 1908.
Whenever I quote from the Swedish I provide a fairly free translation in an attempt to
convey the humor in many of Shaw's remarks.
4. Grevenius, *Shaw rebellen*, p. 277.
5. *Dagens Nyheter*, 12 July 1908.
6. Ibid.
7. *Socialdemokraten*, 11 July 1908. Herbert Grevenius maintains that Shaw's visit to

Stockholm did not bring him in touch with Hjalmar Branting, the leader of the Social Democratic Party (*Shavian*, p. 10). However, the interview in *Socialdemokraten*, the newspaper of which Branting was chief editor, is signed "—r," the signature of Branting himself, and if not written by Branting was probably written by his wife, the critic, Anna Branting.

8. Ibid.

9. Grevenius maintains that the most faithful coverage of Shaw's visit was provided by the newspaper *Stockholms Dagblad* (*Shaw rebellen*, p. 277). I have only been able to find a brief report on the recent translation into German of Shaw's book on Richard Wagner (*Stockholms Dagblad*, 15 July 1908) and a mention of his presence among the first night audience of *Fröken Julie* (17 July).

10. *Svenska Dagbladet*, 10 July 1908.

11. *Idun*, p. 345.

12. Ibid.

13. *Svenska Dagbladet*, 10 July 1908.

14. The book was *The Diary of a Madman*, and the play *The Father*, in Nellie Erichsen's translation of 1899.

15. *The Complete Prefaces of Bernard Shaw* (London: Hamlyn, 1965), p. 748.

16. *Ögonvittnen*, p. 247.

17. *The Shaw-Barker Letters*, ed. C. B. Purdom (London: Phoenix House, 1956), p. 130.

18. "How My Enemies Made Me Famous and Wealthy," Broadside advertising sheet in Stanley Weintraub's collection. Published by the Centenarian Club (1930). A Swedish translation of this version was published in *Svenska Dagbladet*, 3 March 1927, and reprinted in *Ögonvittnen*, pp. 249–50.

19. *Svenska Dagbladet*, 9 April 1951. The report is based on Opffer's own version in the Danish newspaper *Politiken*.

20. *Ögonvittnen*, p. 247. In my translation I have kept closely to the text of the original. According to Grevenius, Shaw was invited to the dress rehearsal, *The Shavian*, p. 9.

21. Ibid., p. 249.

22. *Stockholms Dagblad*, 17 July 1908.

23. Letter from Strindberg to Falck dated 24 July 1908, postmarked 27 July, in the collection of the Manuscript Department of *Kungliga Biblioteket*.

24. For further details on this subject see Ishrat Lindblad, "Bernard Shaw and Scandinavia," *The Shaw Review*, 20, No. 1, January, 1977, pp. 9–15.

25. *Complete Prefaces*, p. 2. It is perhaps worth noting that he wrote this specifically on the subject of marriage in the preface to *Getting Married*, which is the play he had just been working with before leaving London for Sweden.

26. *Idun*, p. 345.

27. *Söndags-Nisse*, 9 July 1908, p. 3. I have tried to convey the pun on Shaw's name in English.

28. What Shaw refers to as "Codex Aurens" is probably the gilded manuscript of the Gospels in *Kungliga Biblioteket*. The apparent Shavian error (Aurens for Aureus) may actually be a mistranscription of the handwritten postcard.

Stanley Weintraub

A HIGH WIND TO JAMAICA

"Dis chile gwine ter Jamaica," Shaw wrote, in an invented island patois, to Sylvia Brooke, on 22 December 1910. Wife of the last white Rajah of Sarawak, she had first-hand experience of exotic tropical places, and Shaw knew his effort would amuse. Yet the joking hardly concealed his confessed need for a holiday remote from England. "Much shark, much scorpion, much mongoose, much alligator. . . . Poor chile done busted himself making chin music for election. Greatly increase other candidates' majority mostly. Him all nerves—want to cry—talk like infant—must voyage. . . ."[1] The next day Shaw wrote to an old journalist friend from the 1880s, Ernest Parke, that he and Charlotte would be sailing on the morning of the 24th from Bristol, to return 25 January 1911. "England can breathe peacefully for a whole month," he assured Parke; further, newspaper interviewers—Shaw could seldom refuse a request for an interview, and often drafted one for the would-be interviewer—would have to "join the unemployed."

Why Jamaica? The only reason he gave Parke was "Anything to avoid Christmas in England" (*CL* 2, 958). Escaping an English Christmas was hardly Shaw's real motive, although since Parke had first met Shaw in the distant 1880s, he had indeed inveighed in print against Christmas almost annually. Still, on shipboard, isolated in that miniature and ultra-conventional world, he was unlikely to be able to avoid Christmas. That the shipboard dinner menu on Christmas would offer almost nothing Shaw would eat was a further certainty.

Shaw's old friend Sydney Olivier, one of the pioneer Fabians, had moved upward from a Colonial Office clerkship to administrative posts in British Honduras and the Leeward Islands. Once returned to London he was considered ready for a minor governorship, and in April 1907 was appointed (at short notice) governor of Jamaica. It was no sinecure post. The island had just survived a massive earthquake and fire which destroyed the capital and largest city, Kingston. Olivier arrived amidst a chaos of clearing and rebuilding, and immediately wrote to London to have an architect check at the Public Works Office for a building plan for a proper King's House to replace the leveled offices of the governor.

When Shaw arrived—he had been horribly seasick as the ship rode out an Atlantic storm—the reinforced concrete King's House was already up and in use, giving Olivier's rule a certain stateliness impossible earlier. To Granville Barker in London Shaw put a good face on the voyage, but later he recalled to his secretary Blanche Patch that he had been "violently sick" for most of the fourteen days at sea.[2] Only three days of the voyage, as they neared the island, he wrote Barker, had been tropical: the earlier eleven had been "rough and rolling, especially 36 hours of rolling to 45° on New Years Day, but I got my sea legs in 48 hours and did quite a lot of reading and writing."[3]

In *Fabianism and the Empire* (1900), Shaw, with the assistance of Webb and Olivier—the two Fabians with Colonial Office experience—dealt prophetically with the future of the British lands over which the sun never set, warning that if Britain cast off the colonies, or was ousted from them, the result would be shrinkage from Great Power status to that of an impotent island nation. Further, Fabians like Webb and Olivier anticipated the sharing of natural advantages through the Imperial community, and the imposition of Western civilized values through an Imperial bureaucracy. Simplistically, believers in the Empire saw only savagery and ignorance as the other side of the Imperial coin. Thus in his "Some Impressions" prefacing a posthumous memoir of Olivier, Shaw recalled, clearly with approval, that when he visited Jamaica he had asked Olivier whether he had "tried our democratic plan" suggested in *Fabianism and the Empire*, which had gone as far as recommending that local and native councils be elected where possible to consult with "our viceroys and governors working with them as Prime Ministers rather than as despots." If so, Shaw asked, how was the idea working?

He had tried it, said Olivier, "and found that whenever he proposed a measure intelligible only to people who could see further than the ends of their noses he was invariably opposed by his democratic councils." He had learned his lesson about governance. "I now do not consult them. I do what is needed. In eighteen months or so they [will] see that I was right, and stop howling about it."

Shaw called the practice "kindly objectivity," and saw the message of *Fabianism and the Empire* apparently being carried out. This, plus some compliments to the island and its people and a few Shavianisms unaffected by place, seem to be the substance of the only interview Shaw gave while in Jamaica, in the Kingston *Gleaner* for 12 January 1911. It is possible, given the language as recorded on both sides, that the interview is self-drafted, as was Shaw's wont, or at least corrected and edited by him:

A representative of the "Gleaner" has had a very interesting interview with Mr. George Bernard Shaw, the famous Socialist author, dramatist, and lecturer, who, as an old friend of Sir Sydney Olivier, is on a visit to His Excellency in Jamaica.

"Well, Mr. Shaw, to what do we owe the pleasure of seeing you in Jamaica?" asked the newspaperman.

"Several things," he replied. "The general election in England, coming on top of a very heavy pressure of overwork, brought me to a standstill. I had to go somewhere to recover my health. Then my wife, who was in much the same predicament, wanted a respite from the cold and darkness of the English winter; and as we find, as often as not, that the south of Europe is as cold as it is at home, the only sure refuge is the tropics.

"Well, Jamaica is tropical, but not too tropical. You have no sunstroke and no snakes, and your coloured population is neither enslaved nor starved. Besides, there is a special attraction for me in Jamaica just now in the person of your Governor. The average British colonial governor is often an excellent man in his way, a gentleman and a man of affairs; but he is not always able to talk to you of his island or his province, or whatever his charge may be, in its relation to the highest European culture in philosophy, in art (I don't mean merely pictures, you understand), and in world politics. He is not always even a naturalist or ethnologist in the widest sense. For the matter of that, it is not easy to find a man anywhere, even in the European capitals, with such qualifications. But it happens that your governor possesses them. I really came here because Sir Sidney Olivier was here. He and I belonged to a small knot of men who were drawn together in London about thirty years ago by a strong common interest in—well, shall I say in the political destiny of the world? and in the great movements in literature, music, science and religion with which that destiny is connected. It happens that most of us have since become well known in one way or another.

"My personal destiny tied me to the centre of the empire, where things are always in such a complicated muddle that no individual skill can unravel them. But in the outlying parts, such as the West Indies, the problems are simple enough, and the people manageable and sensible enough, to be put right by an able man when a difficulty arises; and so Sir Sydney Olivier, being such a man, got sent everywhere there was trouble and so got detached from us and landed finally in Jamaica. If he had landed in Hong Kong I should probably have gone to Hong Kong."

"I suppose we must not tempt you into any indiscretions as regards the confidences of the King's House on the subject of the island?"

"Oh, there are no confidences with a man like your Governor," replied Mr. Shaw. "Everybody is welcome to his opinions; he is a public man in the real sense, not a diplomatic repository of disgraceful secrets. He would tell you everything he tells me: only you wouldn't believe him, though you would find out five years hence that he was exactly right."

"What are your own impressions of Jamaica?"

"I have none worth recording. You see I haven't yet got over the novelty of bananas and sugar canes and coloured villages and eighty in the shade in January. But I can tell you what is wrong with Jamaica, if you are willing to admit that there is anything wrong with it."

"We have our faults, Mr. Shaw."

"You wouldn't admit it so complacently if you really believed it. But what is wrong here is that you produce a sort of man who is only a colonial. Please don't misunderstand me. I know perfectly well that it is ten times better to be a colonial than to be a Cockney, because the average Cockney has all of the defects of the colonial and none of his advantages. But the fact remains that if a Jamaican wishes his son to be a fully civilised man of the world in the best sense—to belong to a great intellectual and artistic culture—he has to send him to Europe. Now that is not a necessary state of things. On the contrary, it ought to be far easier to build up a Jamaican culture than it is to civilise a Camberwell Cockney.

"Just consider a bit. When I speak of culture I am not using a vague general expression which seems to mean everything and really means nothing. I mean a personal equipment as definite as a Panama hat, a pair of deck shoes, and a buggy.

"You want three things in Jamaica. You want a first-rate orchestra giving performances at least once a week of the works of the great masters of modern music, from Sebastian Bach to Wagner and Richard Strauss. When a Jamaican knows Beethoven's Ninth Symphony as well as he knows the ten commandments, and feels hungry if he does not hear it well played fairly often, then he is to that extent no longer a colonial.

"And, remember, it can be done. You can import your band parts as easily as you can import *The Illustrated London News*. You can learn the fiddle or the trombone, and play B flat as written by Beethoven just as you can play it in the Gin and Scissors cake-walk. All that is necessary is to believe that Beethoven's music, though you can't pick it up as easily as Gin and Scissors, is enormously more enjoyable and lasts you all your life.

"The next thing you want is a theatre, with all the ordinary travelling companies from England and America sternly kept out of it, for unless you do your own acting and write your own plays, your theatre will be of no use. It will, in fact, vulgarise and degrade you. Don't smile incredulously. I tell you the thing can be done fairly easily.

"Over the water, when Dublin, Manchester and Glasgow got finally sickened by the trash of the touring companies, they started theatres of their own under great difficulties, and with less money, than you would have to face here. They began by producing Ibsen's plays, Granville Barker's plays, Galsworthy's plays, Hankin's plays, and the plays of Euripides and Shakespeare, not to mention my own plays. And now they are producing new plays by their own townsmen, plays of Dublin life by Dublin men, plays of Glasgow life by Glasgow men, plays of Manchester life by Manchester men—all novices at the game, and all playing it better than the conventional celebrities of Paris, London and New York.

"All you want is a band of convinced enthusiasts and an endowment of a few thousand pounds to do that here. And when you have done it and provided your Beethoven orchestra as well, your Kingston man need be no longer a colonial. People will begin to send their sons from England to old Jamaica to get culture.

"But a theatre and an orchestra are not enough. You must have good architecture and well planned towns. In Kingston you have had the advantage of an earthquake. It sounds inhuman, but if you knew how possible it is to stand in some districts of our great English towns, and simply long for an earthquake in utter despair of anything short of that making an end of our slums, you would catch my meaning. An earthquake is a very dreadful thing—hardly to be spoken about when the recollection of its horror is still sore. But, believe me, the yearly death toll and the disease rate of a badly planned, insanitary, ugly town, which we endure thoughtlessly as a routine that we are used to, is a far more terrible thing than the list of casualties in any momentary calamity, however dreadfully it may harrow our imaginations.

"If you rebuild Kingston healthily and handsomely and honestly, you will save more lives and create more happiness than the earthquake destroyed. You have already made a good start, not only as to the planning of the reconstructed town, but as to its good looks. The new King's House and Government buildings in ferro-concrete no doubt looked strange to Jamaicans who admire photographs of Buckingham Palace (which enlightened Londoners want to pull down); but I assure you that if these buildings could have been exhibited at the great Darmstadt Exhibition of architecture a few years ago, they would have been praised enthusiastically by the Germans. Your architect, Sir Charles Nicholson,[4] has done splendidly, with the Governor to back him. There, again, you see the value of Sir Sydney Olivier's culture coming in. If you work that vein for all it is worth, and see that your Building Acts are really enforced, you will produce the first condition of a high civilisation, a handsome town. And these three things will cure you of colonialism."

"You know, of course, that we have at the Jamaica Institute a library and a picture gallery to complete our education."

"To begin it, you mean. Yes; and you will find it worth your while to develop it handsomely, because your writers—you must produce Jamaican writers—must have the machinery of their profession: books of reference and so on that are too expensive for private men to buy and own for themselves; and everybody should have access to a good public library; it is a vital necessity of civilised life. But do not encourage your dreamy people to acquire a habit of killing time with books and pictures, mistaking that kind of loafing for culture. It isn't.

"Of course, you should have a gallery with good reproductions of all the great pictures of the world and photographs of the great buildings. But until you have Jamaican painters able to paint your ferro-concrete walls as Giotto painted the Arena Chapel at Padua, you will not have a real school of painting."

"You have certainly given us a long programme, Mr. Shaw."

"Well, I can only give you the lessons of my own trade. If I offered you hints on banana growing, they would be more novel than useful, though

by the look of the Prison Farm I conclude that the Governor's philosophical genius has proved applicable to agriculture. By the way, you need a
technical school of handicraft very badly. At present as far as I can make
out, it is easier to find a competent alligator in Jamaica than a competent
cabinet maker. You must realize that the old apprenticeship system is
dead; and that its place must be supplied by public enterprise. Also, I
would like to say, as an old municipal councillor, that if an English local
authority left big stones and other obstructions lying about on the sidewalks as they lie in the streets of Kingston, the police would interfere.
You ought to form a Vigilance Committee and execute somebody."

"It shall be attended to, Mr. Shaw. With that exception, can you, on
the whole, recommend Jamaica as a place to be visited?"

"I can, but I won't. Why encourage globe-trotters? Jamaica for the
Jamaicans, say I. At any rate it is the Jamaicans who must make Jamaica
and not the tourists. Still, it is well to see yourselves as others see you
from time to time. At present you don't allow a man to land unless he
has some capital. Why not refuse to allow him to land unless he has some
brains and character? That would be more sensible. However, Captain
Selfe brought you a good cargo this time—two Bishops, myself, and
some very pleasant fellow-passengers. I hope I shall be equally lucky
going back. Good morning."

One judges from the interview that Shaw had observed Jamaica and
the Jamaicans carefully and unsentimentally. Privately, he could indulge
himself in a more touristy perspective. In a letter from Kingston, written
the day before the interview was published, Shaw wrote Granville
Barker[5] that Olivier's "new post-earthquake palace is a masterpiece of
nouveau art. The trees and mountains look pleasantly theatrical through
the mosquito curtains when one wakes in the morning." Whether *art
nouveau* architecture was right for Jamaica was never questioned. All was
right with the world. It was a lovely morning. In the shade it was barely
above 70°, and Charlotte padded about in a quilted dressing gown while
Shaw, in his "Superman suit, Act III," he told Barker, took photographs
or watched the lizards and dragonflies.

The suit recalling the *Don Juan in Hell* scene from *Man and Superman*
may have been a white linen one, suggesting the Statue of the Commander. It was a reference with explicit reverberations, for Shaw's last
voyage to a warmer climate, to North Africa in April 1909, had brought
him memories of Tanner's and Straker's proposed automobile flight to
Biskra, in the Algerian interior, to flee from women. Then, from the
desert at Bou Saada, Shaw had written Barker[6] that after Biskra the
roads were almost racecourses, and that the mirages had surpassed anything he had seen before. "One lake with a particularly fresh meadow
on its banks was as near as 6 telegraph posts off: it was not until we
reached that sixth post and found the desert still scorched and barren

that Straker believed—or rather disbelieved—at last." "Straker" was Shaw's driver, but to Barker the references to *Man and Superman* were a private code as to how much the play had meant to the man who had played John Tanner and the playwright who had conceived him.

For Shaw the voyage to Jamaica—a mere footnote in his life—was so brief an excursion that he would arrive back in London at the same time as his letter to Barker—possibly on the same ship that carried his letter. He would never write a play in which he would utilize the island, but the experience would survive into his drama nonetheless. The days as guest in the King's House would be the closest that he would come to observing a benevolent despot in action, on a very small scale a Platonic philosopher-king. Almost all Shaw's postwar plays—and the 1914–18 war would soon be at hand—deal with the problem of how we might best be governed. A little of Olivier's methods and style seems to turn up in King Magnus of *The Apple Cart* (1929) and his unruly, somewhat infantile, Cabinet, which Magnus—if he is to survive as ruler—must co-opt or evade.

As Shaw remembered what happened after he left Jamaica, Olivier consulted the intrusive Americans ("who had a way of behaving as if the island belonged to the United States")[7] "as little as he consulted his infantile councils. . . . He understood thoroughly the conflict of economic interests between the planters and the black proletariat, sympathising with the oppressed negroes; but these easy-going and likeable darkies understood nothing but their immediate grievances." When tram fares were raised, they rioted, and Olivier had to put the demonstrations down. But later one aggrieved Jamaican "managed to launch a heavy stone which struck their high-handed Governor flush on his occiput." The failure to follow up Shaw's strictures in his interview about stones on the sidewalks had exacted its price.

Olivier hanged no one, but became "more indifferent to the effect of what he said on his hearers." He was replaced and returned to London. "I reminded him," Shaw remembered, "that it was hard for any British government to select for an imperial job a man who had just been reported as saying, in effect, that the British Empire might break up for all he cared." Preferring to re-define Olivier's attitude in a Shavian way, G.B.S. saw Olivier's "Fabian grasp of the appalling social danger of the imperial instincts that were keeping Downing Street under the thumb of a handful of planters in the face of millions of black proletarians." The Empire had to be run for its larger interest, if indeed there were to be an Empire.

Typically, all that is remembered of Shaw's encounter with Jamaica is that he asked the leading Jamaican writer why he had not become a boxer.[8] An indefensible racial slur to some, it was for Shaw, once a pugilist himself, a paradox he thought would be understood. Like most of his ironies, it was accepted only at its outrageous face value. What he was dramatizing, however, was the refusal of a rare indigenous intellectual to behave according to racial stereotype. As outspoken traveler he would continue to weave his misunderstood paradoxes.

Notes

1. Shaw to Sylvia Brooke, 22 December 1910, as quoted in sale catalogue #4, The Scriptorium, Beverley Hills, California, 1984, item 26851.
2. Blanche Patch, *Thirty Years with G.B.S.* (London, 1951), p. 156.
3. 11 January 1911, in C. B. Purdom, ed., *Bernard Shaw's Letters to Granville Barker* (London, 1957).
4. Sir Charles Nicholson (1867–1949), son of an architect, set up his own practice in 1893, becoming best known for his modern English Gothic church designs.
5. 11 January 1911.
6. 24 April 1909, in Purdom.
7. An echo of that thought may appear in *The Apple Cart* in the American decision to take over the British Empire indirectly by opting to join it. Quotations from Shaw's recollections here are from "Some Impressions," a preface to Margaret Olivier's *Sydney Olivier: Letters and Selected Writings* (London, 1948), pp. 9–20.
8. Quoted by Peter Fryer in *Staying Power: The History of Black People in Britain* (London, 1984).

Nicholas Grene

SHAW IN IRELAND: VISITOR OR RETURNING EXILE?

"I have an instinct against going back to Ireland," says Larry Doyle to Tom Broadbent in *John Bull's Other Island*, "an instinct so strong that I'd rather go with you to the South Pole than to Rosscullen." There can be little doubt that Larry here speaks for his creator. The character in the play has been away from Ireland for 18 years—any longer period would have strained the credibility of the waiting Nora Reilly as an eligible heroine. Shaw himself, when he wrote *John Bull* in 1904, had been out of Ireland for 28 years, just ten years longer than Larry, and had never set foot in it again, not even to attend his father's funeral. Yet the following year he returned for the first of what was to become a series of all-but-annual visits which continued until 1923. This peculiar pattern raises intriguing questions about Shaw's relationship with his native country. Why did he have such a strong "instinct" against going back to Ireland? How did he feel about it when he did return? Were his visits to Ireland merely holidays abroad, or did he think of himself as an Irishman coming home?

Certainly, as Larry Doyle would not have gone back without the urging of his partner Broadbent, Shaw might never have returned without the persuasion of his wife. Charlotte Shaw had strong feelings for Ireland, particularly for the area of West Cork where she grew up, and she very much wanted to take her husband back to see it. It was she who arranged that they should spend the summer of 1905 at Derry, the large late-Georgian house near Rosscarbery built by her grandfather, where she had spent most of her childhood. It was to be a family holiday shared with her sister and brother-in-law, the Cholmondeleys. Shaw stipulated only that a sufficiently quiet room should be provided in which he could work (writing *Major Barbara* as it turned out) and reluctantly agreed to the plan.[1] It is perhaps always difficult for one spouse to enter into a social environment which is wholly the other's, but in

Shaw's case there were added complications. Charlotte, as a Townshend, was related to a whole clan of Townshends and Somervilles that made up the backbone of county society in West Cork. (The little Protestant church in Castle Townshend, not far from Derry, has to this day a whole wall devoted to the genealogy of the Townshend/Somerville families.) Slightly further afield within the county, Charlotte was on familiar visiting terms with the Kingstons of Mitchelstown Castle, the Bandons of Castle Bernard. Into this world Shaw the "downstart" from Dublin did not easily fit.

He would have fitted in much more easily if he had not been Irish, but Protestant Anglo-Ireland was a small community and Shaw's origins, and his lowly position within the social hierarchy of that community, would have been instantly identified. Edith Somerville—of the writing partnership Somerville and Ross—had reacted sharply and significantly to the news of her cousin Charlotte's marriage in 1898:

> Charlotte is now Mrs Bernard Shaw and I hope she likes it. He is an advanced socialist (all the same he has kept his weather eye open). They were married at a registrar's office. . . . Of course he is an awfully clever man. He began as office boy in Townshend French's agency office in Dublin, and now he is distinctly somebody in a literary way, but he can't be a gentleman and he is too clever to be really in love with Lottie, who is nearly clever, but not quite.[2]

We see here the sort of hostility and prejudice that Shaw was likely to encounter in Anglo-Irish society: fear of his socialism, cynical suspicion that he had married Charlotte for her money, envy of his literary success, but above all the sense that the downstart had become an upstart. It is summed up even more pungently in a later letter of Miss Somerville: "Charlotte seems perfectly happy and delighted with her cad, for cad he is in spite of his talent."[3]

Of course Shaw was quite capable of overcoming such prejudices. Even the vitriolic Edith Somerville was impressed when the "cad" made his appearance, as she noted in her diary: "Charlotte, Sissy and G.B.S. drove over from Derry for lunch. He was very agreeable and quite affable."[4] When the Shaws stayed at Mitchelstown Castle, then the largest private house in Ireland, they were honored with the immense King's bedroom, and Lady Kingston was reported as saying that "Mr Shaw is always most pleasant to me."[5] In 1906 they stayed at Lismore Castle, the Irish home of the Dukes of Devonshire.[6] Nora Robertson, who met the Shaws as a young woman when staying at Bantry House, suggests that Shaw may not have found "the visits to country houses as uncongenial as his admirers might wish to imagine. . . . He was not himself reared in the Big House but he was only a generation removed from it."[7] Indeed, but that one generation made all the difference. Shaw could make himself agreeable to Charlotte's friends and relations, but that is not the same thing as being accepted as one of them. In England Shaw's position was all but classless; he was regarded only as a well-known writer, famous or notorious depending on the point of view. In Ireland by contrast he was quite specifically *déclassé*, the Dublin office-boy who had married above himself and had achieved a somewhat suspect fame and fortune by his writing. There is nothing to indicate that Shaw did not enjoy his summer in Derry, nor yet the visit the following year to Castle Haven Rectory, a beautiful small Georgian house close to Castle Townshend with a garden running down to the Atlantic. But he struck at the continued round of visits to the county families—the "Bandons and Castletowns and Kingstons & other Irish peers in their castles"[8]—he did not join Charlotte in Castle Haven in 1907, and thereafter they spent their holidays in Ireland in hotels or with friends outside Charlotte's home area of West Cork.

Yet if Shaw felt somewhat uncomfortable in his wife's social milieu, he had a much fiercer reaction to his own native city. In the Preface to *Immaturity*, written in 1921, he put the matter coldly and bluntly:

> When I left Dublin I left (a few private friendships apart) no society that did not disgust me. To this day my sentimental regard for Ireland does not include the capital. I am not enamored of failure, of poverty, of obscurity, and of the ostracism and contempt which these imply; and these were all Dublin offered to the enormity of my unconscious ambition.[9]

It was this sort of feeling which kept him away from Dublin until 1908, and even then, as he said, "a curious reluctance to retrace my steps made me . . . enter Dublin through the backdoor from Meath rather than return as I came, through the front door on the sea."[10] The squalor of Dublin remained as he remembered it, as he told Lady Gregory: "It looked to him just as before, the houses had never been painted since, and the little shops had eggs in the windows, with mice and rats running over them, and rubbish that looked as if on its way to the dust heap."[11] However famous and prosperous he himself had become, arriving back in Dublin in a motor-car—still driven only by the very wealthy—having visited the seaside-town of Skerries where he had helped an impoverished cousin to set up a boarding-house,[12] the sense of belonging to this slum city remained a real horror. In 1913, on a later visit, he wrote to Mrs. Patrick Campbell: "I drove into Dublin today and cursed every separate house as I passed."[13]

But it was not only memories of shabby-genteel poverty in Synge Street which made Dublin repugnant to Shaw. The depth and ambiguity of his feelings about his native place emerge in his reaction to two of its

best-known characteristics, Dublin talk and Dublin laughter. Lady Glenavy once asked Shaw why he never came to Dublin:

> He replied, "What has Dublin got that I should go there?" I could not
> think of anything but said, "Good talk." Shaw said, "Who talks in Dub-
> lin?" Hesitatingly I said, "Oliver Gogarty." He snorted, "Silly Dublin per-
> siflage!"[14]

Yet Shaw himself was a talker, goodness knows—Nora Robertson meeting him for the first time thought she "had never heard anyone talk so
much and so uncritically."[15] Oliver Gogarty, of the "silly Dublin persiflage," confessed that he had not cared for Shaw because he hogged the
conversation![16] The talking habits which were built into the persona of
G.B.S. sounded different in their place of origin. Father Leonard, whom
Shaw was to meet later and who became a friend and adviser when he
was writing Saint Joan, recalled his first public lecture in Dublin in 1910,
on the Irish Poor Laws:

> Shaw began by making very exaggerated statements. I thought that he
> was using the technique that he used in England to startle and upset
> people; when he made these outrageous statements in Dublin, where
> they were used to them, they all began to laugh. He got quite annoyed
> and he said, "This is no laughing matter, I'm perfectly serious." They all
> laughed twice as much. I think he recognised his mistake, for from then
> on he spoke very seriously, and he was listened to very attentively.[17]

In a land of hyperbole only understatement is effective.

It was the laughter of Dublin which Shaw most hated. His reaction to
Ulysses is well-known: "I should like to put a cordon round Dublin;
round up every male person in it between the ages of 15 and 30; force
them to read it; and ask them whether on reflection they could see anything amusing in all that foul mouthed, foul minded derision and ob-
scenity."[18] One suspects that in this there is the Puritanical Shaw's memory of his own sexually frustrated Dublin adolescence, voiced also by
Larry Doyle in his great "dreaming" speech in John Bull:

> And all the while there goes on a horrible, senseless, mischievous laugh-
> ter. When youre young, you exchange vile stories with them; and as
> youre too futile to be able to help to cheer them, you chaff and sneer and
> taunt them for not doing the things you darent do yourself. And all the
> time you laugh! laugh! laugh! eternal derision, eternal envy, eternal folly,
> eternal fouling and staining and degrading.

Yet the tendency to mocking laughter was not merely an adolescent
phase but something endemic in Dublin which Shaw himself shared, as
he confessed to the audience of his last Dublin lecture in 1918: "From
his childhood he had imbibed the habit of derision. He had tried to get

out of it, but he could not, quite. In spite of living in England, he found that curiously cackling derision breaking out in him, and he wished he had been born somewhere else than in Dublin."[19] Here as with so much to do with Dublin, there is in Shaw's reaction a pronounced element of self-disgust. *His* talk was not mere persiflage, *his* iconoclastic laughter was not aimless and derisive mockery like that of most Dubliners. The family resemblance was not flattering.

The social and spiritual constrictions represented by the cramped terrace house where Shaw's family lived in Synge Street were set against the imaginative impression made by the land and seascape to be seen from Torca Cottage, Dalkey. "It is the beauty of Ireland that has made us what we are," he declared in his ninetieth year. "I am a product of Dalkey's outlook."[20] On motoring tours in 1908 and 1910, the Shaws explored many of the beautiful parts of Ireland which they had not visited before. In 1908 they travelled up from the south to Connemara and stayed for two weeks at Mallaranny (*alias* Mulranny), the Great Southern Hotel far out on the west coast of Mayo. Their 1910 tour of the north of Ireland started badly, as Shaw explained to Harley Granville Barker in a letter written on his 54th birthday, 26 July 1910:

> From our landing at Belfast on Sunday morning it rained hard for 36 hours, causing a steady rise in Charlotte's temper. In that downpour we drove round the Antrim coast to the Giants Causeway. In that downpour I sat under my umbrella in my aquascutum, like a putrid mushroom, whilst a drenched mariner rowed me round the cliffs and told me lies about them. In that downpour we drove back next day to Lough Bay, only to find the hotel too revolting to pass the night in. In that downpour we pushed on to Antrim, only to find two hotels there so loathsome that we simply turned tail and returned to Belfast where the hotel we didnt go to (Charlotte at the last moment consented to stay at the Grand Central after heaping insults on the manager and ordering the instant repacking of all the luggage) was burnt to the ground with some slaughter and much concussion of the brain through the people who jumped out casting themselves from the third floor head foremost. [*CL* 2, 940]

The Northern Irish themselves hardly made a more favorable first impression than their hotels or their weather: "The ugliness of these towns, and the slightness of the provocation on which the inhabitants raise up their voices and call one another sanguinary liars is quite astonishing."[21] Yet in spite of the continuing bad weather—"Carrick to Bundoran—rain, rain, rain," Shaw wrote glumly in his diary for 8 August[22]—he saw a great deal of the countryside of Donegal, staying at Rosapenna in the north for a week, and then travelling gradually south through Counties Sligo and Roscommon. A visit on 12 August to the Shannon Pot, source of the longest river in Ireland, made enough of an impression to be remembered in an article on "Touring in Ireland" six years later:

> In the north there are no stone fields, but you come to a common green one with a little stagnant pool in the corner, and from that magic pool you are amazed to see a rush of waters through a narrow, deep, sinuous ditch, which ditch is the mighty Shannon emerging from the underworld.[23]

But by far the most memorable sight of Shaw's 1910 tour was the Skelligs, the tiny islands off the coast of Kerry which he visited from Parknasilla on 17 September. Though today one can go to the islands by motor-boat and a helicopter lands supplies for the lighthouse keepers, Shaw's dramatic description still represents vividly the extraordinary experience of travelling to the Skelligs:

> Yesterday I left the Kerry coast in an open boat 33 feet long, propelled by ten men at 5 oars. These men started at 49 strokes a minute, a rate which I did not believe they could keep up for five minutes. They kept it without slackening half a second for two hours, at the end of which they landed me on the most fantastic and impossible rock in the world: Skellig Michael, or the Great Skellig, where, in south west gales, the spray knocks stones out of the lighthouse keeper's house, 160 feet above calm sea level. There is a little Skellig covered with gannets—white with them (and their guano)—covered with screaming crowds of them. The Bass rock is a mere lump in comparison: both the Skelligs are pinnacled, crocketed, spired, arched, caverned, minaretted; and these Gothic extravagances are not curiosities of the islands: they *are* the islands: there is nothing else. The rest of the cathedral may be under the sea for all I know: there are 90 fathoms by the chart, out of which the Great Skellig rushes up 700 feet so suddenly that you have to go straight upstairs to the top—over 600 steps. And at the top amazing beehives of flat rubble stones, each overlapping the one below until the circles meet in a dome—cells, oratories, churches, and outside them cemeteries, wells, crosses, all clustering like shells on a prodigious rock pinnacle, with precipices sheer down on every hand, and, lodged on the projecting stones overhanging the deep, huge stone coffins made apparently by giants, and dropped there, God knows how. An incredible, impossible, mad place, which still tempts devotees to make "stations" of every stair landing, and to creep through "needle's eyes" at impossible altitudes, and kiss "stones of pain" jutting out 700 feet above the Atlantic. [CL 2, 941–42]

Shaw never forgot this experience, and to the end of his life he maintained that "whoever has not stood in the graveyards at the summit of that cliff, among those beehive dwellings and their beehive oratory, does not know Ireland through and through."[24] The Skelligs remained a highpoint in his assertion that Irish scenery was like nothing else on earth.

Shaw enjoyed travelling in Ireland, but from 1910 on it was often to stay with friends that he returned—two friends in particular, Lady Gregory and Sir Horace Plunkett. It is not quite clear when Shaw and Lady Gregory actually met, but their first extended exchange of letters came with the controversial production of *The Shewing-up of Blanco Posnet* by the Abbey in 1909. Shaw had known Yeats for many years, even before the Avenue Theatre's first production of *The Land of Heart's Desire* and *Arms and the Man* in 1894. It was with Yeats that he corresponded over *John Bull* in 1924.[25] It is often implied that *John Bull* was deliberately, humiliatingly rejected by the Abbey, but there were genuine practical problems of casting which would have made it impossible for the then partly amateur company to produce it, and Shaw did not take offence at the rejection. In 1909 he accepted enthusiastically the Abbey's offer to put on *Blanco Posnet* in defiance of the Lord Chamberlain's ban on its production in England—by a legal quirk the Lord Chamberlain's writ did not run in Ireland. It seems to have been Lady Gregory who took the initiative for bringing *Blanco Posnet* to the Abbey. Through the summer of 1909 there were constant letters to and fro between her and Shaw discussing the public controversy over the play. Although Shaw was in Ireland at the time, he refused to come up from Kerry to Dublin to assist at rehearsals or even to attend the first night, claiming that he wanted all the credit to go to the Abbey.

In 1909 there was talk of Shaw visiting Coole Park, Lady Gregory's home in County Galway, but it was in 1910 that he went there for the first time. Yeats must have been staying there also, for there is a photograph of him taken by Shaw in the garden at Coole from this date.[26] On this visit or a later one, Shaw was asked to carve his initials on the famous "autograph tree," a much coveted honor when staying at Coole, and the bold G.B.S. is still visible. Over the years Lady Gregory came to consult Shaw quite often on business matters, but they seem to have become close friends after the Shaws' second visit to Coole in 1915. From then on, he is addressed in letters as "G.B.S." rather than "Mr Shaw" and "Mrs Shaw" becomes "dear Charlotte."[27] Lady Gregory's enjoyment of their visit was expressed at the time in a letter to Yeats of 16 April 1915: "The Shaws are here. They are very easy to entertain, he is so extraordinarily light in hand, a sort of kindly joyousness about him, and they have their motor so are independent."[28] There is a splendid photograph (Fig. 1) of Lady Gregory, Shaw, and the "motor" in which if one looks closely one can see a small child at the steering-wheel. The child is Richard Gregory, Lady Gregory's grandson, and the two children with an adult in an upstairs window looking on are her two granddaughters, Anne and Catherine. Anne Gregory, in her amusing memoirs of her childhood at Coole, remembers Shaw's visits with great pleasure, though

FIG. 1 Shaw and Lady Gregory in front of Coole Park, April 1915.

she was horrified to learn from his example that adults were prepared to cheat at games![29] Here, as in so many reminiscences of Shaw, it is apparent that, although he was childless himself and seemed to show relatively little interest in children in his writing, he took great delight in playing with them and had enormous gifts for amusing them.

The visit to Coole in 1915 was a productive one in many ways. It was on this occasion that Augustus John painted his portraits of Shaw, and there are varying accounts as to how this came about. According to Lady Gregory, she suggested inviting John because Charlotte expressed regret that Shaw had never been painted by a really good artist. John's painting of Lady Gregory's grandson Richard was a bonus which she was overjoyed to be given but which she could not have afforded to have commissioned.[30] John himself suspected that the painting of Shaw was only a bait to lure him into doing the portrait of Richard.[31] And Anne Gregory reports that John really wanted to paint her and her beautiful golden hair (celebrated in Yeats's poem to her) but that Lady Gregory had forced him to paint Richard, the heir to the estate, instead![32] Though later he was to express great admiration for Shaw, at the time John took a jaundiced view of his subject—"a ridiculous vain object in knickerbockers."[33] Shaw, apparently unaware of such disparaging thoughts going through the head of the artist, described the results to Mrs. Patrick Campbell:

Augustus John painted six magnificent portraits of me in 8 days. Unfortunately, as he kept painting them on top of one another until our protests became overwhelming, only three portraits have survived: and one of these got turned into a subject picture entitled Shaw Listening to Somebody Else Talking, because I went to sleep while I was sitting, and John, fascinated by the network of wrinkles made by my shut eyes, painted them before I woke, and turned a most heroic portrait into a very splendid painted sarcasm.[34]

The reference to the six versions painted on top of one another can be explained in terms of John's layered technique of portraiture; of the three extant portraits, one is in Shaw's Corner at Ayot St. Lawrence, one in the Fitzwilliam Museum, Cambridge, and one (more poetically described as "The Sleeping Philosopher") in the collection of Her Majesty the Queen Mother.[35]

The visit to Coole also supplied Shaw with a setting for his only two dramatic pieces with an Irish background apart from *John Bull. O'Flaherty V.C.*, written in 1915 partly to revive the flagging fortunes of the Abbey, partly to assist the British recruiting campaign in Ireland (by the characteristically Shavian argument that joining the army afforded an ideal opportunity for Irishmen to get out of Ireland), was set "at the door of an Irish country house in a park." The country house is identified specifically as Coole in a letter to Lady Gregory of 14 September 1915,[36] and the details of the scene—"under the window is a garden seat with an iron chair at each end of it"—correspond exactly to a photograph of Shaw himself with notebook in hand sitting on the garden seat outside the house. Another photograph in the same collection (Fig. 2),[37] may have been used as an *aide-memoire* by Shaw when he came to write the section of *Back to Methusaleh* entitled "Tragedy of an Elderly Gentleman." It shows Shaw, holding a camera, sitting on a bollard on a small pier with a distant prospect of hills. It is very tempting to identify this as Burren (or Burrin), the little quay on the coast of Galway near Mount Vernon, the house belonging to Robert Gregory, not far from Coole. Certainly there is a striking resemblance to the scene set in *Back to Methusaleh*:

> Burrin pier on the south shore of Galway Bay in Ireland, a region of stone-capped hills and granite fields. It is a fine summer day in the year 3000 A.D. On an ancient stone stump, about three feet thick and three feet high, used for securing ships by ropes to the shore, and called a bollard or holdfast, an elderly gentleman sits facing the land. [*BH* 5, 491]

Although in the play the Irish have been supplanted as the inhabitants of Ireland by the long-livers, the landscape remains the same. Shaw visited Coole only once more—in 1918—but he and Lady Gregory remained good friends. After the Dublin authorities had made it clear that

FIG. 2 An Elderly Gentleman (Burgunder Collection)

they would not allow *O'Flaherty V.C.* to be produced in 1915 (they failed
to see it in the Shavian light of "A Recruiting Pamphlet"), Shaw helped
Lady Gregory to pick a season of his plays to be performed at the Abbey
in the winter of 1916 (including the first Abbey production of *John Bull*).
Significantly he saw this as the introduction of "foreign work," in default
of new plays by young Irishmen, and he urged that some plays of Ibsen
should also be included.[38] When Lady Gregory's son was killed in 1918,
Shaw wrote in praise of him in terms which strikingly foreshadow Yeats's
two great poems, "An Irish Airman Foresees His Death" and "In Memory of Major Robert Gregory": "To a man with his power of standing up
to danger—which must mean enjoying it—war must have intensified his
life as nothing else could; he got a grip of it that he could not through
art or love. I suppose that is what makes the soldier."[39] Shaw, so often
regarded publicly as fierce and choleric, was to Lady Gregory "the gen-
tlest of my friends."[40]

Sir Horace Plunkett met Shaw on his 1908 visit to the west of Ireland,
as Plunkett's diary for 18 September 1908 records: "At Mallaranny met
the Bernard Shaws after dinner. He was delightful. I never knew a more
brilliant conversationalist. He is hopeless about Ireland of course, but I
think I could make him a little hopeful if I saw more of him."[41] It was
Sir Horace Plunkett's mission in life to make people more hopeful about

Ireland. He worked very hard to promote agricultural reform and founded the Irish co-operative movement, using the poet AE (George Russell) as one of his agents. Kilteragh, the large and elaborate house which he built for himself in Foxrock, County Dublin, was planned as a social center to which he invited a wide variety of writers, artists, and politicians whom he believed could help the cause of progress in Ireland. Among such was Shaw, who came to Kilteragh for the first of a series of visits in 1913. Although Shaw had little or no interest in agriculture—like Larry Doyle he thought that "we Irishmen were never made to be farmers"—he was prepared to believe in Plunkett's co-operative movement and to support his work for progress in Ireland generally. Shaw, like Plunkett, did not favor separatist Irish nationalism. Though Shaw allowed that Sinn Féin (We Ourselves) was "an inspired title," he maintained that "until we get rid of the Irish idea and get hold of the human idea—the true Catholic idea—we shall never be real Irishmen."[42] This was not to stop him from defending the 1916 Rising and protesting vehemently against the execution of its leaders, but by and large Shaw shared with Plunkett that most uncomfortable and unrewarding position, the middle ground of Irish politics.

When Plunkett was appointed to chair the Irish Convention in 1917, Shaw at last saw an opportunity to take an active part in his country's political life, and he tried hard to have himself nominated as a member of the Convention. The Irish Convention was among the first of what has now become a dismally long series of attempts to get together all shades of political opinion in Ireland to work out a solution of the country's intractable problems. (As I write in 1983, another such assembly rumbles on unproductively in Dublin.) Shaw believed that his own position, as an Irishman but an outsider, without commitments of party or creed, would make his contribution to the Convention a specially helpful one. In spite of Plunkett's best efforts, Shaw was not appointed to the Convention, but he continued to offer his advice in long letters to Plunkett, who kept Shaw informed of the progress of the discussions. Shaw's hope for the future of Ireland was based on the supposition that in an independent Irish parliament there would be a strong socialist presence and that the Ulster workers would be won away from their unionist position by the prospect of advancing their labor interests. He had as little time for Sinn Féin as for Ulster unionism, and in a series of articles for the *Daily Express*, entitled "How to Settle the Irish Question," he ridiculed the intransigence of both of them, particularly the Sinn Féin suggestion that the Irish question should be settled at the Peace Conference at the end of the war.[43] In suggesting a federation of all four of the countries in the British Isles, each with its separate parliament as well as a federal parliament, Shaw differed from Plunkett, who looked to Dominion status for Ireland. For Shaw this federation would have represented just the right degree of recognition of the separate national identities, while maintaining the basic principle of internationalism which for him was so crucial.

The Irish Convention came to nothing, but Shaw continued to support Plunkett's political schemes, such as the Irish Dominion League, and his paper *The Irish Statesman*. He took part in a debate with G.K. Chesterton (another of Plunkett's invitees to Kilteragh) in Dublin in October 1918 on the question of whether private property was necessary to human happiness, Chesterton speaking one week and Shaw replying the following week. An incident recalled by Lady Glenavy at Shaw's lecture, though not recorded in the press reports of the time, is indicative of his mood of the period:

> Shaw was talking about bread, how it should be as much public property as the streets one walked in. A man in the pit got up and asked why Mr Shaw didn't speak of something that really mattered, like the seven hundred years of English oppression of the Irish people. Shaw paused for a second, then arms folded, stepped forward to the edge of the stage; a long arm shot out, one finger extended admonishingly. He said, "Mark my words, *God is not mocked*. As surely as the ichthyosaurus disappeared from the face of the earth, so will man cease to exist if he is unable or unwilling to adapt himself to his surroundings."[44]

The words, recalling those of Hector Hushabye in *Heartbreak House*—"I tell you, one of two things must happen. Either out of that darkness some new creation will come to supplant us as we have supplanted the animals, or the heavens will fall in thunder and destroy us"—suggest Shaw's bitter revulsion at the short-sighted nationalism of his own country and the no less short-sighted nationalism which had brought about the catastrophe of the war. His last visit to Dublin was a brief stay at Kilteragh in 1922, where he met Michael Collins, the I.R.A. guerilla leader, who was by then one of the founders of the newly established Free State. Three days after this meeting, Collins was dead, shot in an ambush. Years later Shaw recalled the toll which the Troubles had taken on the man known in nationalist hagiography as "the Laughing Boy": "His nerves were in rags: his hand kept slapping his revolver all the time he was talking pleasantly enough."[45] In the following year, 1923, Kilteragh also was to fall a victim to the Civil war between the Free Staters and the Republicans. Its burning was a terrible blow to Plunkett, who had worked so long and with such disinterested intentions for the Irish people. With Kilteragh burned and Plunkett living in England, there was one less reason for Shaw to go back to Ireland.

Although through his friendship with Lady Gregory Shaw was to some extent involved with the Abbey, and his relations with Plunkett gave him a specific link with Irish politics, most of Shaw's trips to Ireland were holiday visits spent in first-class hotels in the south and west of Ireland. It was still the heyday of the railway hotel, of the sort planned for Rosscullen by Broadbent and Doyle. Mallaranny, where Shaw stayed in 1908, was a characteristic example: one arrived at the little station and had only to walk 50 yards to reach the hotel with its spectacular and unexpected view over the Atlantic. The favorite of the Shaws, however, was the Great Southern Hotel at Parknasilla where they first stayed in 1909, and to which they returned very often in later years. Parknasilla, a large Victorian building set in some three hundred and fifty acres of its own grounds beside the Kenmare river estuary, had a great deal to offer to someone of Shaw's temperament: long walks in the almost endless rhododendron woods, swimming in the tidal pools, the mild weather characteristic of the Southwestern Atlantic Coast, the mountains not far away. Charlotte and her sister Mrs. Cholmondeley also became very attached to it and sometimes went to stay there without Shaw, as, for example, in 1916 when the memory of the Rising made him unwilling to go to Ireland.[46] Although Parknasilla is included in Shaw's rather blasé generalisation that in Ireland "the first-class hotels are like first-class hotels anywhere else: in fact, that is the only complaint one makes of them,"[47] he seems to have thoroughly enjoyed staying there.

Of course for Shaw a holiday was not time off work but a period in which there were no interruptions from work, no lectures, committee meetings, or rehearsals to stop him from getting on with his writing or dealing with his correspondence. The periods in Ireland were extremely productive, like most of Shaw's summers: the bulk of *Major Barbara* was written at Derry in 1905,[48] and *Saint Joan* was completed at Glengariff and Parknasilla in 1923. Although he was proud of his ability to write anywhere, even on trains or buses, Shaw seems to have preferred writing out of doors. A story is told of a little green tent which was set up in the grounds of Parknasilla to be used as a sanctum for Shaw to write in—anticipating his garden summer house in Ayot St. Lawrence—and of the children teasing him by throwing stones at it, a game Shaw responded to with amiable ferocity.[49] Yet Shaw found plenty of time for amusement and social activities at Parknasilla as well. He made friends with other guests at the hotel. It was here that he met Father Leonard and another Vincentian priest, Father Joseph Sheehy, who was holidaying with him; it was here also that he made the acquaintance of Lord and Lady Glenavy, important figures in the establishment of the Irish Free State and friends of D.H. Lawrence and Katherine Mansfield. He visited local beauty spots, such as Garnish Island off Glengariff with its exotic gardens of sub-tropical shrubs and flowers—"like a scene in one of Gluck's operas," he recalled.[50] We hear of him boating on the Kenmare river, or going for long car-rides with the Glenavys when he used to startle the Kerry villagers with songs trolled out at the top of his voice from the high back seat of the car. Lord Glenavy remembered him "silent and depressed on only one drive, when we took him to Puck Fair in Killorglin. The tethering of a he-goat, for the days of the fair, on a platform on the top of the high wooden tower struck him as barbaric. He could see no inspiration from it, for the crowd on the street and in the pubs."[51] Quite apart from the cruelty to the Puck ("puckan" is the Irish for a billy-goat), Shaw was unlikely to have been enthusiastic about a festivity which derived as much of its enjoyment from alcohol as Puck Fair did.

The long holidays at Parknasilla were a success, apparently none more so than the *Saint Joan* summer of 1923. And yet after that summer, the Shaws never returned to Ireland. It is difficult to understand exactly why not. Some few days before he left Parknasilla, Shaw had a bad fall when walking on the rocks and was in considerable pain before help could be summoned from the hotel. This might have left an unhappy impression, but would surely not have been sufficient to stop him coming back another year. The Irish Civil War of 1922–23 brought much that was painful, not only the shooting of Collins and the burning of Kilteragh, but the destruction also of Derry, Charlotte's old home. Yet the Shaws had continued to come to Ireland particularly faithfully through the years of the Troubles, with visits in 1919, 1920 (twice), 1922, and 1923. Shaw even went so far as to write a letter to the *Times* in July 1923, arguing that Ireland was perfectly safe for holiday-makers.[52] It is hard to see that the Shaws would have set their faces against Ireland in less troubled times. It seems likely that a number of more or less accidental circumstances may have contributed to their not returning to Ireland. It was always Charlotte rather than Shaw who took the initiative in arranging holidays (one suspects that without Charlotte he might never have left England to the end of his days). In 1924 and 1925 they went to Scotland and for the rest of the twenties they holidayed on the Continent, in Italy, France, and Switzerland. In the 1930s the Malvern Festival came to occupy much of the time which had been spent on summer visits to Parknasilla. By the time Shaw was given the Honorary Freedom of Dublin in 1946, he quite understandably pleaded old age and infirmity as reasons for not returning to receive the honor in person. Yet whatever the accidental and arbitrary circumstances which led him never to revisit Ireland, the very fact that such circumstances were sufficient to outweigh any desire to go back tells us a good deal about the ambivalent feeling Shaw had for his native country.

In many ways Shaw remained a loyal Irishman all his life. *The Matter with Ireland*, with its collection of material from 1886 when Home Rule was a live political issue, to 1948 when Ireland finally severed all links with England and declared itself a Republic, shows that he never lost interest in Irish public affairs. He continued to give time and money to Irish causes even after he no longer came back for visits. In 1932 he accepted Yeats's invitation to become the first president of an Irish academy of letters. In 1899 Shaw had inherited from his uncle, Walter Gurly, some few pieces of property in Carlow. In 1918 he donated one of these, the more or less derelict eighteenth-century Assembly Rooms, to the town of Carlow for conversion into a Technical School. In 1944 he handed over the rest of his Carlow property to the municipality, a transfer which made necessary a special act of the Irish parliament. If Shaw the socialist found it embarrassing to have been an owner of Irish property who lived in England, he knew how to make the most of the embarrassment: "I am an absentee landlord," he declared in his letter to the Carlow County Council, "having spent of the 88 years of my life only one day in Carlow."[53] Shaw hoped that *Saint Joan*, which was partly written in Ireland, might be filmed in Ireland; there is a contract dated 8 September 1947 with a group of Irish businessmen for this purpose. Its preamble reads, "the Author is desirous that his plays shall employ and develop the dramatic genius of his fellow-countrymen and make Ireland's scenic beauties known in all lands."[54] Among Shaw's other benefactions to Irish institutions one can include the gift of the manuscripts of his novels to the National Library of Ireland. The National Gallery of Ireland, as one of the principal legatees of his will, still draws a substantial income from the Shaw Estate.

No one was ever likely to take Shaw for an Englishman: His voice was always identifiably Irish; his educated Dublin accent, with its clearly pronounced "r's," was easily distinguished from Received Standard English. Yet his attitude towards his nationality remained ambiguous. "I am by birth a British subject," he said in 1948:

> I have always so described myself when applying for passports, though I never stood up nor took my hat off while the English national anthem was played until Ireland became a so-called Irish Free State. I am also a registered citizen of my native Ireland.[55]

St. John Ervine, with an Ulsterman's scorn for Irish nationalism, casts an ironic light on this statement: "To please his wife, who had the extraordinary sentimentality about Eire that is felt by many English people, he became a registered citizen of the Irish Republic in his old age, only to feel appalled by the fear that he might lose his British nationality as a result of this act."[56] Although it is absurd to call Charlotte English, it is true that she felt much more attached to Ireland than Shaw and "always seemed hurt when G.B.S. mocked at it and derided it."[57]

There was a part of Shaw that did feel deeply about Ireland, especially about its landscape, and he had more than a little sympathy with Peter Keegan's claim for Ireland as "holy ground." "Religious genius," he claimed in the Preface to *John Bull*, "is one of our national products; and Ireland is no bad rock to build a Church on." Yet there is quite as much, if not more, of him in Larry Doyle, the Irish exile whose bitterness about his own country contains elements of self-hatred and self-disgust. There is a curious tone almost of triumph in Shaw's projection in *Back to Methusaleh* of a time when "the Irish race [has] vanished from human knowledge." Having been born in Ireland, by his own account, had made him "a foreigner in every other country,"[58] but he certainly did not feel at home in Ireland itself, and as far as one can tell he never for a moment considered going back to live there permanently. If it served his turn to be an Irishman abroad in England, making possible the claim to a detached perspective on the English, at some level he contrived to avoid the emotional strains and uncertainties of his Irishness by making himself a holiday visitor, a tourist, in his native country.

Notes

1. See Janet Dunbar, *Mrs G.B.S.* (London, 1963), pp. 208–9. The first draft of *Major Barbara*, started in London but largely written in Cork, is known as the "Derry manuscript." See *Bernard Shaw, Early Texts: Play Manuscripts in Facsimile. Major Barbara*. Introduction by Bernard F. Dukore (New York & London: Garland Publishing, 1981).
2. Letter from Edith Somerville to her brother Cameron, quoted by Maurice Collis in *Somerville and Ross* (London, 1968), p. 127.
3. Ibid., pp. 127–28.
4. Ibid., p. 128.
5. Nora Robertson, *Crowned Harp: Memories of the Last Years of the Crown in Ireland* (Dublin, 1960), p. 90.
6. 4–6 October 1906, noted in Shaw's catalog of "Travels and Movings," British Library Add. Ms. 50711A.
7. *Crowned Harp*, p. 87.
8. Letter to Beatrice Webb, dated 5 October 1905, quoted in Janet Dunbar, *Mrs G.B.S.*, p. 210.
9. *Immaturity* (London, 1931), p. xxxiii.
10. Ibid.
11. Reported in *Seventy Years: Being the Autobiography of Lady Gregory*, ed. Colin Smythe (Gerrards Cross, Bucks., 1974), p. 447.
12. See the correspondence with J.C. Shaw in the British Library, Add Ms. 50514.
13. *Bernard Shaw and Mrs. Patrick Campbell: Their Correspondence*, ed. Alan Dent (London, 1952), p. 106.

14. Beatrice Lady Glenavy, *"Today we will only Gossip"* (London, 1964), p. 128.
15. *Crowned Harp*, p. 94.
16. See W.R. Rodgers, *Irish Literary Portraits* (London, 1972), p. 140.
17. Ibid., p. 132.
18. Quoted in James Joyce, *Letters*, vol. 3, ed. Richard Ellmann (London, 1966), p. 50.
19. Lecture on "Literature in Ireland" given to the Dublin Literary Society on 26 October 1918, reported in *The Irish Times*, 28 October 1918.
20. See "Shaw Speaks to his Native City" in *The Matter with Ireland*, ed. Dan H. Laurence and David H. Greene (New York, 1962), p. 291.
21. *CL* 2, 941.
22. Engagement diary for 1910, British Library of Political and Economic Science, London.
23. *The Matter with Ireland*, p. 93.
24. Ibid., p. 291.
25. Their correspondence has been published by M.J. Sidnell in "Hic and Ille: Shaw and Yeats," in *Theatre and Nationalism in Twentieth-Century Ireland*, ed. Robert O'Driscoll (Toronto, 1971), pp. 156–78.
26. The photograph, from the collection of Colin Smythe, is reproduced in Edward Malins and Patrick Bowe, *Irish Gardens and Demesnes from 1830* (London, 1980), p. 144.
27. The bulk of the correspondence between Shaw and Lady Gregory is in the Bernard F. Burgunder collection in Cornell University Library and in the British Library.
28. *Seventy Years*, p. 474.
29. Anne Gregory, *Me and Nu: Childhood at Coole*, ill. Joyce Dennys (Gerrards Cross, Bucks., 1978), pp. 26–29.
30. Lady Gregory, *Coole* (Dublin, 1971), p. 32.
31. See Michael Holroyd, *Augustus John*, vol. 2, *The Years of Experience* (London, 1975), p. 46.
32. *Me and Nu*, p. 47.
33. *Augustus John*, II, p. 47.
34. *Bernard Shaw and Mrs. Patrick Campbell*, p. 175.
35. See Malcolm Easton and Michael Holroyd, *The Art of Augustus John* (London, 1974), p. 156.
36. Burgunder collection, Cornell.
37. The negatives of this whole group of photographs, most of them excellent, are in the Burgunder collection. I am very grateful to the staff of the Cornell University Library for making available to me extremely clear prints of them.
38. Unpublished letter to Lady Gregory, dated 3 September 1916, Burgunder collection, Cornell.
39. Quoted in *Seventy Years*, p. 558.
40. The phrase Lady Gregory used in dedicating *The Golden Apple*, one of her later plays, to Shaw. See Lady Gregory, *Collected Plays*, vol. 3, ed. Ann Saddlemyer (Gerrards Cross, Bucks., 1970), p. 100.
41. The Plunkett diaries are in the Plunkett Foundation for Co-operative Research in London; there is a microfilm copy in the National Library of Ireland. I am grateful to my colleague Dr. Trevor West of Trinity College Dublin for information about Plunkett and for drawing my attention to the diaries.
42. "Mr Bernard Shaw: Special Interview," *Freeman's Journal*, 3 October 1910.
43. See *The Matter with Ireland*, pp. 140–63.
44. *"Today we will only Gossip,"* p. 29.
45. *Bernard Shaw and Alfred Douglas. A Correspondence*, ed. Mary Hyde (London, 1982), p. 134. At the time Shaw wrote a heartening letter of sympathy to Collins's sister: see *The Matter with Ireland*, p. 258.

46. As he makes clear in an unpublished letter to Lady Gregory of 22 August 1916 in the Burgunder collection, Cornell.

47. *The Matter with Ireland*, pp. 95–96.

48. The evidence suggests that it was only a part of the trial scene and the Epilogue which were actually written in Ireland, but most of the play was revised at Parknasilla. See Brian Tyson, *The Story of Shaw's* Saint Joan (Kingston, Ontario 1982), pp. 6–9.

49. This story was passed on to me by Dan Laurence, whose informant had heard it from General Sir Richard Goodbody, who had been one of the stone-throwing children.

50. See letter to James A. Whelan dated 9 November 1939, reproduced in facsimile in the *Evening Echo* (Cork) 19 January 1977.

51. W. R. Rodgers, *Irish Literary Portraits*, p. 133.

52. *The Matter with Ireland*, pp. 264–66.

53. See "Shaw's Ties with Carlow," *Carloviana*, 1, No. 4, N.S., December 1956. I am grateful to the Carlow County Council Librarian for making this and other articles about Shaw available to me. The one day Shaw spent in Carlow was 30 September–1 October 1910.

54. A carbon copy of this contract is in the Burgunder Collection, Cornell; on it Shaw pasted a handwritten note that the Irish scheme failed because it could not attract sufficient funding.

55. *The Matter with Ireland*, p. 296.

56. St. John Ervine, *Bernard Shaw: His Life, Work and Friends* (London, 1956), p. 110.

57. *"Today we will only Gossip,"* p. 128.

58. *The Matter with Ireland*, p. ix.

Bernard Shaw

CROSSING SWITZERLAND: THUN TO ZÜRICH. THE TRUTH ABOUT THE BRÜNIG PASS AND THE SPEED LIMITS.

From a distinguished literary Member of the R.A.C. we have received the following comments on the subject of touring in Switzerland.

The difficulties of the passage from the Lake of Geneva to Feldkirch (as to police hostility, etc.) are exaggerated; and the published particulars are mostly wrong. The Brünig Pass need not be avoided. What happens is this. On entering Switzerland from Savoy, you can come from Aigle over the Col de Pillon and the Saanen-Moser Pass to Thun without interference. But from Thun you must start at nine in the morning, as the road to Interlaken (north bank of the lake) is closed to automobiles at ten. This, or earlier, is the pleasantest hour for the drive: so there is no hardship.* The speed limits through the villages are practically the same as in England or France, as they are not taken literally, though the people are nervous about automobiles, and are determined to be considerately treated by drivers, and not scattered and scared. In the refreshment room of the Brünig railway station, at the top of the pass, you get for two francs a permit marked to be delivered up at Hergiswil, 25 miles off, in two hours' time. (This is correct as calculated: your speed limit is the average of 18 miles in the country and 6 through the villages). *After* your permit is handed to you it is suggested that you should lunch at the refreshment rooms or, if you prefer it, at the hotel. As it is about noon, this also is highly convenient, for you are hungry and want to dispose of as much of your time allowance as possible without moving. When you

---

*The closing is now, we learn, at 8 A.M.—ED. [of the *R.A.C. Journal*]

start, you have only one hour of your permit to fill up during your drive to Hergiswil, and, as a good deal of it is down the pass and through scenery that nobody wants to scorch through, or through villages that nobody *ought* to scorch through, you are not delayed or hardshipped by the permit; and you get through to Lucerne in good time. In fact, except for the two francs, the net result to a really considerate driver is very much what it would be in France. In these circumstances the advice sometimes given to avoid this very pleasant road by the lakes, and to make a detour by Langnau, and even by Bern, is really an explosion of temper at the regulations. If the Swiss would only steam-roll their roads instead of leaving the stones loose, there would be no reason to complain; for the speed limits are the same as the French, and are enforced by fines instead of by summary imprisonment as in France. The real grievance is the total prohibition over large areas, including the Engadine. On the open roads one drives without molestation exactly as in England. There may be Swiss Kingstons or Godalmings; but the hotel keepers do not regard a journey from Thun to Zürich as anything unusual for one day. Total prohibition apart, the regulations are just what they are in France; that is, quite impossible either to observe or to enforce, but leaving the motorist hopelessly "in contravention," if he provokes interference by inconsiderate driving or displays of sportsmanship, which latter are especially obnoxious to the Swiss temperament.

It has to be borne in mind that the agitation against automobiles in Switzerland has created something of a scare there. Even young and sturdy pedestrians rush to the wall and squeeze their backs to it—sometimes even their faces—to let an automobile pass them six feet away. There is more obvious dislike, and less curiosity and interest, than in the adjacent countries; consequently the driver who thinks he can drive as close to people's nerves as to their skins without annoying them will soon find himself in the clutches of the local democracy.

The correct thing to do if trapped is to refuse to pay the fine summarily to the policeman (who gets a percentage!), and to deposit at the police office a covering sum as guarantee, taking care that the receipt is for a guarantee, not for a fine. The deposit leaves you free to continue your journey. But first put your case in the hands of a local solicitor, who will defend you when the case comes for trial. You are quite likely to save money by this procedure, as it eliminates the percentaged policeman, and puts you in the hands of a properly qualified judge. If all motorists acted in this way, mere brigandage on the part of the police would cease.

On the whole, the worst objection to crossing Switzerland is the cost, which, after France, is appalling to the frugal. In the season, hotel charges at the best houses are stiff in Thun, monstrous at Lucerne, outrageous in Zürich. Swiss hotel keepers welcome automobilists, but they have not yet realised that in the case of motorists a hotel has to compete with all other hotels within a radius of ten miles, instead of within a radius of a mile, as in the case of customers with less command of loco-motion. On the contrary, they are still in the stage of assuming that an automobilist must be rich beyond all concern for hotel bills, instead of recognising that in most cases a motor car costs so much that its owner can hardly afford to be extravagant in anything else. Possibly when pe-destrians and railway tourists realize this, they will welcome automobil-ists as the most powerful agents in the reduction of travelling expenses.

There is, by the way, a pleasant new hotel (Sport Hotel) at the Saanen-Moser railway station which may serve to rescue some of our motorists from the huge crowd of trippers at Les Diablerets.

July-August, 1911.

[Bernard Shaw, unsigned, in the *Royal Automobile Club Journal*, 1 September 1911, p. 165]

Jean-Claude Amalric

A PLAYWRIGHT'S SUPERTRIPS: SHAW'S VISITS TO FRANCE

For almost half-a-century, Shaw was a frequent visitor to France, generally coming on holiday, travelling not to meet people nor to give extensive interviews, but to rest, to recuperate from overwork, and to sightsee. He and Charlotte motor-toured, usually with a chauffeur, all of the major and many of the minor roads in France, visiting churches and museums, and taking thousands of photographs. He almost always travelled incognito, because, as he wrote to J. N. Pesara, he did not want to be recognized as a public figure but preferred travelling in France as a private and unknown person.[1]

Shaw had a reading mastery of French but felt ill at ease speaking French and understanding spoken language. He had written to Augustin Hamon, his French translator, "Say that as I read French quite easily, [Brieux] need have no hesitation in writing to me direct; but that I hesitate to inflict letters of my own on him, as my French is extremely Britannic and must be positively painful to a man of his literary sensibility" (*CL* 2, 893). Shaw prudently observed that "No man fully capable of his own language ever masters another."[2] It is true that Shaw could read French. He boasted that he had read Marx's *Das Kapital* in Deville's French translation before any English translation was available. The letters he wrote in French to Jules Magny, to Lugné-Poe, and to Rodin, show that his assessment of his ability to write French was correct. They are fluent but not always correct. As for spoken language, he confessed his inadequacies, as when he attended plays in French. "I am very sorry but I cannot learn languages . . . unless I have read the play beforehand or asked somebody during the interval what it is about, I must either struggle with a sixpenny 'synopsis' . . . which invariably misses the real point of the drama, or else sit with a guilty conscience and a blank countenance, drawing the most extravagantly wrong inferences from the dumb show of the play."[3] His natural shyness made it difficult for him to speak to foreigners. When he had to get his car across the German and French frontiers (he wrote Mrs. Patrick Campbell), he spoke "German fluently to the Frenchmen and French fluently to the Germans and understanding neither of them (I am the most deplorable of linguists); all this is simply tragic for me, who am so shy that I would rather write three plays than ask my way anywhere."[4] Asked if Shaw spoke French well, Rodin replied, with his characteristic grave and exact veracity: "Monsieur Shaw ne parle pas bien; mais il s'exprime avec une telle violence qu'il s'impose."[5] As a result his direct contact with French people was more limited than the relationships he established with Frenchmen by correspondence.

Shaw's first visit to Paris took place in April 1890. Although the year before he had gone to Belgium and the Netherlands, he had not entered France. Accompanied by his friend Sidney Webb, Shaw remained in Paris a week and reported his activities in *The Star* as "Corno di Bassetto." Shaw had gone to Paris primarily to attend the "Soirée Musicale et Littéraire du Vendredi Saint" in which Sarah Bernhardt performed the dual role of the Virgin Mary and Mary Magdalen in Edmond Haraucourt's mystery, *La Passion*. Shaw reported that "Sarah sung—sung as usual, holding the book in her right hand and waving her left in the air with a rhythmic persuasiveness."[6] But when another actor delivered a sort of Sermon on the Mount some forty minutes long, he was interrupted by the audience in spite of the intervention of the author! Shaw also went to Saint-Saëns's new opera *Ascanio* at the Opéra, but, in spite of the quality of the singers, did not appreciate the music. "The tragic scenes are secondhand Verdi; the love scenes are secondhand Gounod; the 'historic' scenes are secondhand Meyerbeer."[7] He was even more bored by a *Joan of Arc* by Barbier and Gounod, with Bernhardt in the title role. He enjoyed a performance of Molière's *Le Bourgeois Gentilhomme* at the Comédie Française, though he found the traditions of the House of Molière "to consist of equal parts of gag and horseplay."[8] This opinion was confirmed five years later when he wrote, "In the Comédie Française, there is nothing but costly and highly organized routine, deliberately used, like the ceremonial of a court, to make second-rate human material presentable."[9] Shaw's initial opinion of Paris is very severe. "Paris is what it has always been: a pedant-ridden failure in everything that it pretends to lead."[10] Shaw and Webb also went to the Père Lachaise Cemetery to see the burial place of the "Communards," the victims of the Paris Commune. An official, insisting on the less disparaging term *Federal*, told them that they should speak of "Les Fédérés." A few months later, in August, the two friends passed through Strasbourg on their way back from Oberammergau, where they had attended the *Passion Play*.

Though Shaw travelled through France to go to the International Socialist Congress that was held in Zürich in August 1893, he did not return to Paris until November 1896, when he stayed for three days. Shaw resided somewhat awkwardly in the same lodging house as the artist Bertha Newcombe, who a few years earlier had painted the portrait of him known as "The Platform Spellbinder" and had fallen in love with him. To Shaw, who had already met Charlotte Payne-Townshend, whom he would marry, Newcombe was merely a friend. While in Paris he wanted to see two important plays: Ibsen's *Peer Gynt*, produced by Lugné-Poe, the great French director, and Eugène Brieux's *Les Bienfaiteurs*, produced by Coquelin, which Shaw was unable to attend. Shaw's review of *Peer Gynt* appeared in the 21 November 1896 *Saturday Review*. After declaring that Paris had humiliated the English stage by producing this important play before London did, Shaw praised the excellent performance in spite of some cuts made by the director and some arguable interpretations. Shaw had met Lugné-Poe during his London visit in March 1895, when he produced Ibsen and Maeterlinck. "Artistically first rate. Man of genius, by the Lord," Shaw had written to Richard Mansfield (*CL* 1, 508).

In 1905–6, Lugné-Poe wanted to produce *Mrs Warren's Profession*, but he would not accept Shaw's terms and the negotiations broke down. Shaw answered Lugné-Poe's indignant letter with a biting rejoinder. "I am a shark eager to devour French artists and French theatres as I am devouring English, American, German, Austrian and Scandinavian artists and theatres. . . . I have conquered London, Berlin, Vienna, New York, Budapest and Stockholm; and I shall conquer Paris in due time. Would it not amuse you to take part in the campaign?" (*CL* 2, 729–30).

After Shaw's marriage, he and Charlotte began their long tours of France. Charlotte, although she was not a good traveller, was fond of travelling. For Shaw the writer, the committee man, and the public speaker, the trips were a means of escaping the hectic pressure of activity and the involvement of his daily life in London. On the eve of their departure in April 1901, Shaw wrote to his friend Pakenham Beatty, promising that he would read a recommended book "when I come back from Provence, whither I fly, more dead beat than words can express, tomorrow morning. I haven't had a day off for seventeen months" (*CL* 2, 225). To find such escape, the Shaws set off on long cruises, such as the six weeks' Mediterranean Cruise in September 1899, or on exhausting motor tours, usually driven by a chauffeur. Shaw's motor trips took two forms: either a large circular tour with many stops at interesting places, or the exploration of a particular region, sometimes directly reached by train, with a few more stops on the way back. In the first tour, which began on 7 April 1901, the Shaws went from Marseilles to Paris by way of Bordeaux.[11] Considering the state of the roads and the discomfort of the cars in the early decades of the twentieth century, one is astounded by the length of Shaw's itineraries, both in terms of mileage and of motoring days.

Shaw returned to Paris in 1906 for three weeks to sit for his bust by Rodin.[12] Shaw and Charlotte went to Meudon every day except when Rodin fell ill, which delayed the sittings. Shaw considered Auguste Rodin the greatest sculptor of his epoch, and the greatest artist France or the world had produced for several centuries. He thus describes Rodin's mastery:

> The busts [Rodin's] are of real men, not of the reputations of celebrated persons. Look at my bust, and you will not find it a bit like that brilliant fiction known as G.B.S. or Bernard Shaw. But it is most frightfully like me. It is what is really there, not what you think is there. . . . A succession of miracles took place as he worked. In the first fifteen minutes, in merely giving a suggestion of human shape to the lump of clay, he produced so spirited a thumbnail bust of me that I wanted to take it away and relieve him from further labor. . . . But that phase vanished like a summer cloud as the bust evolved, I say evolved advisedly; for it passed through every stage in the evolution of art before my eyes in the course of a month. . . . Rodin's hand worked, not as a sculptor's hand works, but as the Life Force works.[13]

Rainer Maria Rilke, who was Rodin's secretary at the time, was struck by the mysterious collaboration which existed between sculptor and model:

> Hardly ever has a portrait been so much aided in its making by the subject it represents as this bust of Bernard Shaw. Not only that he stands excellently (with an energy in his keeping still and with such an absolute giving of himself to the hands of the sculptor), but he knows how to collect and concentrate himself to such a degree in the part of his body which, within the bust, will after all have to represent so to speak the whole Shaw, that the nature of the man springs over from it unbelievably heightened intensity, feature by feature, into the bust.[14]

On 21 April, the Shaws, Alfred Langdon Coburn, and Sidney Cockerell were present at the unveiling of Rodin's sculpture "Le Penseur" (The Thinker) outside the Panthéon. Shaw was so impressed by this statue that the next day he asked Coburn to photograph him nude in the pose of "The Thinker," his true role in life. Coburn did. The photograph was exhibited at the London Salon of Photography. Shaw naturally took advantage of his stay in Paris to attend plays and concerts and to visit museums: he saw *The Wild Duck* at the Théâtre Antoine, and he attended a performance of Beethoven's Ninth Symphony.

As the Shaws happened to be in Paris on 1 May, they went to the Place de la République to see a demonstration of workers for a limitation of working hours. There was a clash with the police and the soldiers, who soon put down the riot and arrested a number of demonstrators. The Shaws were shocked by this brutal repression. "In the afternoon we went to the Place de la République, where Charlotte clung to lamp posts to see over people's heads, and got so furious when she saw a real crowd charged by real soldiers that she wanted to throw stones. By dignified strategy, which did not at any time go to the length of absolutely running away, we left the field without wounds" (CL 2, 621). The *Illustration* of 5 May spoke of "revolutionary violence" and contrasted that violent day with the English May Day, a festival of flowers and may-poles.[15] Shaw contested this view of the demonstration in the *Labour Leader*:

> The only message that occurs to me is that it will presently be well to organise some means of protecting the public against the police and the military. The Government here wishes to win the general election by suppressing a revolution. Unluckily there is no revolution to suppress. The Government therefore sends the police and the dragoons to shove and charge the lazy and law-abiding Parisians until they are goaded into revolt.[16]

Shaw's next tour took place in April 1907. The Shaws traveled across northern France, from Le Havre to Rheims and Amiens.[17] Shaw was glad, once more, to stop writing and working for a while. He found the old Norman abbeys of Jumièges and St.-Wandrille very fine, and Rouen very interesting because of the Joan of Arc associations. The cathedral of Rheims is probably the French monument Shaw admired most. He was to come back to Rheims in 1912 "for the sake of its dateless unique French sculpture, especially a Virgin whom I intended some day to put into a play."[18] In the Preface to *Heartbreak House*, he noted again: "In point of appeal to the senses, no theatre ever built could touch the fane at Rheims: no actress could rival its Virgin in beauty. . . . Its picture glass was glorious even to those who had seen the glass of Chartres" (*BH* 5, 53).

In 1910, the Shaws and Mary Cholmondeley started on another long tour, visiting Rouen, Le Mans, Poitiers, Périgueux, the whole range of the Pyrénées from Atlantic Coast to Mediterranean coast, Toulouse, the Languedoc and the Limousin, Blois, and Chartres, returning through Beauvais and Amiens.[19] Shaw was still not fond of Paris, perhaps for literary reasons: he had more difficulty having his plays produced there than in the other European capitals, and their critical reception was far from enthusiastic till the triumph of *Saint Joan* in 1925. He wrote to Hamon in 1910: "I shall carefully avoid passing through Paris on my way south" (CL 2, 915). He also said in 1924 that he was now too old to educate Paris, that it was too far behind and he was too far ahead. The Shaws suffered two snowstorms, a very cold temperature, east wind, and rain. Charlotte fell ill in Bayonne, but a few days later, Shaw "put her into the car and rattled her off to Saint Jean de Luz and Biarritz to see how she could stand it. The result was quite satisfactory" (CL 2, 920). They were also stopped by the snow on the Col du Puymorems; April is not quite the most favorable season to drive through high mountain passes. Shaw was unabashed and delighted, although it took four attempts before they could break through to Ax-les-Thermes. He wrote to Granville Barker: "The scenery here is magnificent, stupendous valleys and gorges, with snowy summits on the back cloth, but we are quite light-headed with the perpetual journeying. . . . I drive half the day, lie deliriously awake half the night; and am visibly waning towards my grave" (CL 2, 921). The tempers of the two ladies were sometimes affected by the weather conditions and Shaw's determination to go on. "Charlotte abandoned all semblance of good humor; tried to make herself ill (unfortunately in vain), . . . snubbed the landlady . . . refused the food . . . declared that all her life she had hated and loathed being shut in by mountains; made it clear that she also hated and loathed me" (CL 2, 922).

A few days after the Shaws' return to London, Eugène Brieux, the French playwright, was received at the Académie Française. Three of his plays, Le Trois Filles de M. Dupont, Les Avariés, and Maternité, translated by St. John Hankin, John Pollock, and Charlotte Shaw respectively, had just been published in England by the Stage Society. Shaw, who admired him very much, had written the preface, "Three Plays by Brieux." L'Illustration announced this London edition and published a part of Shaw's preface in a translation by A. Hamon, together with a portrait of Shaw. The latter was presented as "a sociologist, a dramatist, and a drama critic," but the introductory notice concluded: "Yet he still remains a somewhat upsetting, heterodox man in the eyes of his countrymen, and those who belong to the school of common sense consider him as an extravagant, paradoxical mind."[20]

In 1911, the Shaws were abroad for more than three months, one of their longest motor trips in Europe.[21] They went through Picardie, Champagne, Lorraine, and Alsace, then visited the Savoie and the Alps, stopping at Annecy, Grenoble, Chamonix. Then they went to Switzerland, Germany, Austria, and Italy. In September they were in France again, touring in Touraine and Brittany, going back to Boulogne through Normandy. The Shaws spent ten days at Port-Blanc in Brittany with Augustin Hamon, Shaw's French translator. A socialist author and editor of the journal L'Humanité Nouvelle, Hamon had become Shaw's translator in 1903. He had accepted reluctantly, as his familiarity with English was slight, but Shaw insisted on being translated by a man who knew and shared his ideas and, as Henderson says, "Shaw's Britannic obstinacy was greater than Hamon's Bretonic stubbornness."[22] In 1907, Hamon lectured on "Bernard Shaw et son théâtre" at the New University, Brussels, and published one of the first studies of Shaw in French, *Le Molière du XXe Siecle: Bernard Shaw*, in 1913. Shaw constantly encouraged him and, in spite of friends' entreaties, would never hear of finding an abler translator. Vicomte Robert d'Humières, a dramatist and the stage-director of the Théâtre des Arts, where *Candida* was presented in 1908, had criticized Hamon's translation. Shaw wrote to Hamon: "In making the translation, you were working from an English original; and you produced a version under the direct influence of that original. The Marquis [Vicomte d'Humières], unobsessed by this original, starts perfectly fresh on your French version and instantly sees how it can be made more French and more clear. You have occasionally made an obscure translation because, as the meaning was not quite clearly into your head by the original, you could not become conscious of the obscurity in the translation" (*CL* 2, 776–77). Shaw was always convinced that if Hamon's translations were attacked, it was because they were faithful renderings of his subversive ideas. Shaw had planned to visit the Hamons in 1906, but the sittings for the bust by Rodin were delayed and Shaw had to postpone the trip until 1911.

In 1912, the Shaws motored again through France and Germany from 27 July to 8 September.[23] The car broke down in Germany and it had to be carried back to Lunéville by train to the Lorraine-Dietrich factory of its makers. Leaving Charlotte at Bad-Kissingen for a cure, Shaw spent twelve days in Nancy at the Hôtel Excelsior, waiting for his car to be repaired. As he explained to Mrs. Campbell, Shaw had great difficulty in "getting horses to drag her [the car] to the nearest railway station, negotiating for transport with a country station master, persuading her into a truck after baffling the plans of the shunters for smashing her by impossible methods, following her to the frontier, getting her across it through a French station and a German station."[24] During this period, Shaw saw a performance of *The Merchant of Venice* at Bussang on August 25, by the Théâtre du Peuple. Moved by its Shylock's loss of his daughter, Jessica, Shaw wrote to Harley Granville Barker, "The version was an 'adaptation musicale de Paul Vidal,' which meant that an American organ played freely at all the sentimental passages, and Bassanio burst into song most unexpectedly again and again. . . . Shylock was very good indeed. . . . His calling of Ola! J. C. Kah! Ola! J. C. Kah! was thrilling. His exit in the trial scene was perfect."[25] Then the Shaws drove to Gérardmer and Rheims. They stopped at Domrémy "for the sake of St Joan of Arc."[26] They also visited Artois and Picardie, Soissons, Lille, and Arras. "I found Arras a Spanish town, dating from the days of Alva. . . . Its facades, made up of rows of ornamental gable-ends, were unlike anything else in France that I had seen; and though its cathedral was pseudo-classical in the late Renaissance manner . . . , there was a medieval town-hall."[27] While going through Calais, Shaw recalled the story of its six burgesses as illustrated by Rodin's famous group and toyed with the idea of writing a play about them. "Whiling the last evening stretch of the journey by inventing a play on the Rodin theme of the Burgesses of Calais, which, like the play about the Rheims Virgin, I have never written down, and perhaps never will."[28] But Shaw was mistaken. He did eventually write *The Six of Calais* in 1934, "A Medieval War Story by Jean Froissart, Auguste Rodin and Bernard Shaw."

In 1913, the Shaws made their last long tour in France.[29] Their subsequent visits were either short trips or longer stays in one region only. From 6 September to 17 October, they went south through Orléans to the Massif Central, spending ten days in Valence, then west to the Atlantic coast, where they took another ten-day stop in Biarritz before heading back north. Orléans could not but interest Shaw because of the historic associations with "The Maid." He wrote to Mrs. Campbell:

> Strangely enough, I have never been in Orléans before, though I have been all over the Joan of Arc country. . . . I shall do a Joan play some day, beginning with the sweeping up of the cinders and orange peel *after* her martyrdom, and going on with Joan's arrival in heaven. . . . I should have . . . Joan producing an end of burnt stick in arrest of Judgment. . . . "It's what is left of the two sticks a common English soldier tied together and gave me as I went to the stake; for they wouldnt even give me a crucifix; and you cannot damn the common people of England, represented by that soldier because a poor cowardly riffraff of barons and bishops were too futile to resist the devil." . . . One of my scenes will be Voltaire and Shakespeare running down bye streets in Heaven to avoid meeting Joan.[30]

Later on in his Preface to *Saint Joan*, Shaw also mentioned Anatole France's *Life of Joan*, but explained why France's attitude to Joan was unfavorable. Shaw had met Anatole France not in France, but in Italy, where they happened to visit the Sistine Chapel in Rome on the same day. France made an official visit to London in 1913. There were a meeting with the Fabian Society and the Socialist Party and an immense banquet at the Savoy, attended by the literary elite including Kipling, Bennett, Masefield, and Galsworthy. Shaw said a few words of welcome and France delivered a speech entitled: "Let us work together for the peace of the world." Shaw admired France's works. He wrote in 1921: "On his comic side, Anatole France is Dickens's French double, disguised by culture. In one of his earliest stories, Jocaste, the heroine's father, is a more perfect Dickens comic personage than Dickens himself ever succeeded in putting on paper."[31]

Shaw also sent several reports of his travels to the Royal Automobile Club, one of which was published in the *R.A.C. Journal*. These reports are careful, accurate descriptions of the routes to follow, of the difficulties of the road, or of available accommodation.

> This route cuts straight through the middle of the district on the right (west) bank of the Rhône. It is easy to miss the road to St Julien en Chapteuil, as the Faubourg St Jean and the Route d'Yssingeaux, by which one leaves Le Puy, has two important looking turns to the right a few miles out, and the second is the one to take (Le Puy to Valence). . . . This is a much tougher job for the driver than the previous days (from Mende to Millau). . . . As the picturesque Chateau de la Caze is now a hotel and is only 4 miles or so further on, it might be worth trying it for lunch. . . . Mende is inevitable though the hotel accommodation is not luxurious (From Vals to Mende). . . . In Privas, the landlord of the Croix d'Or, who is also the cook, has lived in Liverpool and welcomes English visitors (From Valence to the Gorges du Tarn).[32]

Charlotte, who had had a severe cold in Valence and was already suffering emotional distress because of Shaw's infatuation with Mrs. Campbell, often quarrelled with her husband during these prolonged tours. Shaw told Mrs. Pat, "After two perfectly frightful scenes with me, in which [Charlotte] produced such a case against my career and character as made Bluebeard seem an angel in comparison, she quite suddenly and miraculously—at a moment when murder and suicide seemed the only thing left to her—recovered her intellectual balance, her serenity, and her amiability completely, and became once more (after about two years) the happy consort of an easygoing man."[33]

In 1917, Shaw was invited by Sir Douglas Haig to visit the front and write about it. After some hesitation, Shaw decided to go.[34] "Joy Riding at the Front" appeared in the *Daily Chronicle* and was reprinted in *What I Really Wrote About the War*. He was received as a distinguished visitor at the Headquarters at Boulogne and insisted on going to see Ypres. Though struck by the horror, Shaw still retained his humor. It was a way of remaining self-possessed. "A man lying by the roadside was not a tramp taking a siesta, but a gentlemen who had lost his head. There was no Belgian carillon, but plenty of German music: an imposing orchestration in which all the instruments were instruments of percussion."[35] Shaw also revisited Arras, which he had seen in 1912: "The cathedral, a copy of a copy, looked better as a ruin than when it was intact. The Town Hall . . . is now a subject of gentle regret."[36] The Somme front struck him by the complete destruction of every village and landscape. "The Somme front in the snow and brilliant sunshine was magnificent. The irony of the signposts was immense. 'To Maurepas'; and there was no Maurepas. 'To Contalmaison'; and there was no Contalmaison. . . . I went to the windmill of Pozières, and saw a little mound on which the windmill may have stood."[37] The same desolation had been noted by G. Babin in *L'Illustration* in March: "The places we went by are hardly any more than geographical names, a few letters printed on a now inaccurate map."[38] Nevertheless, Shaw, the incorrigible jester, said he had enjoyed himself enormously during the week, in spite of the biting cold! The censorship imposed on war correspondents prevented him from expressing his ideas on that war and on the places he visited, at least at that time. On 1 February he was invited to lunch with the Commander-in-Chief, Sir Douglas Haig, who showed him some experimental weapons that were being tried out. Haig entered in his diary: "Mr. Bernard Shaw came to lunch. An interesting man of original views. A great talker!"[39] At Trezennes, where Major Robert Loraine commanded the 40th Squadron, Shaw attended the dress rehearsals of *The Inca of Perusalem* and *O'Flaherty V.C.* done by the men and the officers. On his way back, Shaw stopped at Boulogne to see his friend Sir Almroth Wright, the bacteriologist, who superintended military hospitals. Wright had been the prototype for Sir Colenso Ridgeon in *The Doctor's Dilemma*. Shaw had thus had the opportunity to have a firsthand look at the war, at the soldiers, and at what he called "a diabolical phenomenon."[40] He said as a conclusion to his final *Daily Chronicle* article that the war was largely in the hands of the politicians who were responsible for it.

The Shaws did not come back to France until 1928, when they spent six weeks on the French Riviera in July and August, suffering from the heat wave at the beginning.[41] Shaw enjoyed sea-bathing and lounging, but reproached himself with doing so instead of working. Staying first at Agay, then at Cap d'Antibes, at the Hotel Beau-Site, Shaw went on excursions to Monte-Carlo, Menton, Nice, and the beautiful hinterland of Haute Provence. He had lunch with Frank Harris in Nice, because Charlotte would not hear of entertaining "Frank Casanova" at the hotel in Cap d'Antibes.[42] The *Nouvelle Revue Française* had published Frank Harris's "George Bernard Shaw" in 1925,[43] in a translation of August Bréal. It was the text published in *Contemporary Portraits* with some cuts; and it was followed by Shaw's corrective essay, "How Frank ought to have done it." On 3 September, Shaw proceeded to Geneva in order to attend the League of Nations meeting.

In 1931, the Shaws travelled from London to Marseilles to join the Hellenic Travellers' Club tour. On the return journey, they passed through Paris, from 23 April to 6 May. He hoped to remain incognito at a performance of George Pitoëff's production of *The Apple Cart*, but was recognized. The *Nouvelles Littéraires* told the story: "Shaw attended a performance of *La Charrette de Pommes*, paying for his seat and his wife's. . . . Recognized by one of the actors, he consented to come and salute the audience and congratulate the cast. . . . [He said to G. Pitoëff] You played my King Magnus as democratically as I hoped. I am grateful to you for doing so, for it was not the case in England, in Poland and in Germany."[44] The Pitoëffs and the Hamons had had lunch with the Shaws on 10 April and Shaw also met H. Granville Barker in Paris. Charlotte was ill during this period and was still in bed on 2 May.

In 1932, they travelled through France once more, on 15 and 16 December, from Calais to Paris and Monte-Carlo to join the *Empress of Britain* at Monaco, to embark for a world tour. On 28 March 1935, they docked at Marseilles on their tour round Africa aboard *S.S. Llangibby Castle*. These were Shaw's last visits to the French soil.

After so many years of wanderings through France, Shaw could say he knew France and its landscapes very well. Could he have said that he knew the French and their everyday life? This is not so obvious, if we turn to Shaw's works to find images of French people. If we except the historical figures around Joan of Arc and the Napoleon of *The Man of Destiny*, there are few French characters in the plays. One of the brigands in Act III of *Man and Superman*, Duval, is an "unmistakeable Frenchman" and a Social-Democrat; some of his cues are in French. Duvallet, in *Fanny's First Play*, is more developed. He is a well-mannered, engaging young marine officer, and his speech on the differences between the French and the English is well-known. Shaw uses him to criticize English traits and manners, and Duvallet's professed admiration for all the aspects of the English character is in fact an amusing satire of English society: "If you were a Frenchman, stifled in prudery, hypocrisy, and the tyranny of the family and the home, you would understand how an enlightened Frenchman admires and envies your freedom, your broadmindedness, and the fact that homelife can hardly be said to exist in England" (*BH* 4, 427–29). In the novels and plays, a certain number of French phrases and of complete sentences are to be found, but they are generally introduced for the sake of comedy.

Many of Shaw's remarks on the French in general often mirror traditional British prejudices rather than original, personal judgments. Hilaire Belloc is, according to Shaw, a Frenchman, "a French peasant, greedy, narrow, individualistic, ready to fight like a rat in a corner for his scrap of land, and, above all, intensely and superstitiously Roman Catholic."[45] France is self-centered, "a country ten times more insular in its preoccupation with its own language, its own history, its own character, than we, who have always been explorers and colonizers and grumblers." (*BH* 4,573) The Frenchman is nevertheless a very formidable fighter at war; and O'Flaherty wants a French wife because she would be a good cook. France is often considered as materialistic, but the Frenchman is superior to the Englishman because of his intellectual virtuosity. Such hasty or commonplace judgments, whether favorable or unfavorable, are in fact used by Shaw as foils, to stress an aspect of English manners or to criticize a facet of the English character.

But Shaw's real contact with French thought, French art, French literature, and French science comes from his readings, his correspondence, and his activities as music or art critic, rather than from his stays in France. It would take volumes to explore Shaw's knowledge in that field, to study possible influences, to mention his likes and dislikes, and to trace all the references to French culture in his works. From Ingres to the Impressionists, from Bizet to Gounod, from medieval sculpture to Rodin, from Molière to Voltaire, from Dumas fils to Brieux, from Pasteur to Lamarck, from Joan to Napoleon, there is a long list of Frenchmen and Frenchwomen whom Shaw criticizes, or admires, in whom he recognizes kindred spirits in the realm of ideas and of art. The land and the people of France may be said to have exerted a significant influence not so much on the traveller—aside from *Saint Joan* and *The Six of Calais*—as on the artist and the thinker.

Notes

I am indebted to Michael Holroyd and Rodelle Weintraub for interesting documents and information on Shaw's routes and travels through France.

1. Letter to J. N. Pesara, 24 April 1929, Cornell University. (Communicated by M. Holroyd.)

2. "La Princesse Lointaine," 17 June 1895, B. Shaw. *Dramatic Opinions and Essays* (New York: Brentano's, 1906), vol. 1, p. 144.

3. *BH* 2, 784.

4. *B. Shaw and Mrs. P. Campbell. Their Correspondence*, ed. A. Dent (New York: A. Knopf, 1952), letter of 19 August 1912, p. 34.

5. "Mr. Shaw does not speak well, but he expresses himself with such violence that he commands attention." Reported by A. Henderson in *George Bernard Shaw: Man of the Century* (New York: Appleton-Century-Crofts, 1956), p. 791.

6. "Paris: A Pedant-ridden Failure," *The Star*, 11 April 1890, *Shaw's Music*, ed. D. H. Laurence (New York: Dodd, Mead & Constable, 1981), vol. 2, p. 24

7. Ibid., p. 20

8. Ibid., p. 23

9. 30 March 1895. *Our Theatres in the Nineties, Ayot St. Lawrence Edition of the Works of Bernard Shaw* (New York: Wise and Co., 1931), vol. 23, p. 80.

10. *Shaw's Music*, p. 25.

11. Their complete itinerary included Marseilles, Arles, Saint Rémy, Avignon, Nîmes, Toulouse, Bordeaux, Tours, Chartres, and Paris.

12. 15 April to 8 May, at the Hotel Palais d'Orsay.

13. "Rodin," *The Nation*, 1912, reprinted 24 November 1917 in *Pen Portraits and Reviews* and in *Shaw: An Autobiography*, ed. S. Weintraub (London: Max Reinhardt, 1970), vol. 2, pp. 64–66.

14. Letter to S. Fischer, 19 April 1906, quoted by S. Weintraub in *Shaw: An Autobiography*, vol. 2, p. 271.

15. *L'Illustration*, 5 May 1906, pp. 281–83, 291.

16. *The Labour Leader*, 11 May 1906, quoted by D. H. Laurence, *Collected Letters*, vol. 2, p. 620.

17. 30 March to 11 April: Le Havre, Yvetot, Caudebec, Rouen, Beauvais, Laon, Rheims, and Amiens.

18. "Bombardment," *Daily Chronicle*, 5 March 1917, *What I Really Wrote About the War* (London: Constable, 1931), p. 247.

19. 30 March to 2 May: Boulogne, Neufchâtel, Rouen, Le Mans, Poitiers, Périgueux, Bayonne, Biarritz, St.-Jean-de-Luz, Tarbes, St.-Girons, Perpignan, Bourg-Madame, Quillan, Tarascon, Toulouse, Carcassonne, Albi, Cahors, Tulle, Limoges, Blois, Chartres, Evreux, Beauvais, Amiens, and Boulogne.

20. *L'Illustration*, 7 May 1910, p. 412.

21. 19 June to 4 October: Boulogne, Amiens, Doullens, Coucy, Soissons, Rheims (3 days), Châlon, Nancy, Gérardmer, Ballon d'Alsace, Belfort, Pontarlier, Annecy, top of Mont Cenis, Grenoble (5 days), La Grande Chartreuse, Chambéry, Albertville, Beaufort, Haute Combe, Chamonix, Thonon, Evian, les Diablerets. (Switzerland, Germany, Austria, Italy) Courmayeur, Albertville, Chambéry, Belley, Bourg, Bourges, Aignan, Tours, Saumur, Angers, Rennes, St.-Briac, Port-Blanc (10 days with Hamon), St.-Brieuc, St.-Lunaire, Granville, Caen, Bayeux, Rouen, and Boulogne.

22. *Bernard Shaw: Man of the Century*, p. 495.

23. 27 July to 8 September: Boulogne, Hesdin, Doullens, St.-Quentin, Hirson, Sedan. (Germany. Car broke down; continued via railroad.) Nancy (12 days awaiting repair of the car), Freiburg, Gérardmer, Neufchâteau, Bar-le-Duc, Rheims, Soissons, Ham, Péronne, Bapaume, Arras, Lille, Dunkerque, Calais, and Boulogne.

24. *B. Shaw and Mrs. P. Campbell, Their Correspondence*, p. 34.

25. MS postcard, 26 August 1912. Shaw Collection, Humanities Research Center, Austin, Texas (communicated by D. H. Laurence).

26. *What I Really Wrote About the War*, p. 247.

27. Ibid., p. 248.

28. Ibid., p. 249

29. 6 September to 17 October: Rouen, Orléans, Moulins, Mont-Dore, Le Puy, Valence (10 days) Vals les Bains, Mende, Albi, Toulouse, Lourdes, Pau, Biarritz (10 days), Bordeaux, La Rochelle, Nantes, Le Mans, Rouen, and Boulogne.

30. *B. Shaw and Mrs. P. Campbell, Their Correspondence*, p. 163.

31. "Tolstoy, Tragedian or Comedian?" *International Magazine*, 1921, *Pen Portraits and Reviews* (London: Constable, 1931), p. 262.

32. MS notes, Shaw Collection, Humanities Research Center, Austin, Texas.

33. *B. Shaw and Mrs. P. Campbell, Their Correspondence*, p. 166.

34. 28 January to 5 February: Boulogne, Trancourt, Rollencourt, Arras, St.-Eloi, Ypres, Bailleul, Etaples, Montreuil, St.-Omer, Amiens, the Somme front, Aire, and Boulogne.

35. *What I Really Wrote About the War*, p. 249.

36. Ibid., p. 251.

37. Ibid., p. 252.

38. *L'Illustration*, 3 March 1917, p. 183.

39. R. Blake, ed., *Private Papers of Douglas Haig* (London, 1952), p. 194–95. Quoted by

S. Weintraub, *Journey to Heartbreak, The Crucible Years of Bernard Shaw* (New York: Weybright and Talley, 1971), p. 220. One will find many details of this visit to France and Belgium in this book.

40. *What I Really Wrote About the War*, p. 253.

41. 15 July to 3 September: boat train to Agay (5 days), then Cap d'Antibes. Excursions to Vence, Cannes, Thorens, Monte-Carlo, Menton, Sospel, Var, Goyes de Coron, Fréjus, Beauvallon, St.-Raphaël, Monaco, and Nice.

42. *The Playwright and the Pirate: Bernard Shaw and Frank Harris, A Correspondence*, ed. S. Weintraub (University Park: Pennsylvania State University Press, 1982), p. 214.

43. *Nouvelle Revue Française*, No. 142, 1 July 1925, pp. 36–52, 53–73.

44. *Les Nouvelles Litteraires*, 2 May 1931, p. 10.

45. "The Chesterbelloc," *The New Age*, 15 February 1908, *Pen Portraits and Reviews*, p. 73.

Charles A. Berst

PASSION AT LAKE MAGGIORE: SHAW, MOLLY TOMPKINS, AND ITALY, 1921–1950

In "Sailing to Byzantium," Yeats expresses the despair of a man whose body is old while his instincts remain young. He finds himself a frustrated scarecrow, aching for sensuality, seeking a soul-song:

> An aged man is but a paltry thing,
> A tattered coat upon a stick, unless
> Soul clap its hands and sing . . .

These lines, written in 1927, might well have been venting Bernard Shaw's similar dilemma. Yeats's imaginative answer to the frustrations of age was to seek a mystic transmutation, to become an "artifice of eternity." But this hardly served earthly realities and later, far less poetically, he sought youthful virility via glandular operations. Meanwhile Shaw—some nine years older—was pursuing a more appealing answer. On an island in Lake Maggiore in northern Italy dwelt a seductive Calypso whose song tempted him from his worldly occupations to her youth, beauty, and passion. In 1913 he had written Stella Campbell: "Oh the two beauties I was born to love! Ireland's and Italy's, how they scorch my veins."[1] Although the reference was to Charlotte and Stella (whose mother was Italian), now it applied to a much younger woman who offered his old age a rejuvenating throb of romance.

The enchantress of Lake Maggiore was Molly Tompkins, a young American admirer who, in 1921, had captured his attention and, rapidly, his affection. Molly's presence at the lake led in no small measure to the remarkable fact that from 1926 to 1931 Shaw returned to Italy after an absence of more than twenty years, sojourning in the north of that country and its immediate environs for a total of nearly eight months. Just after his seventieth birthday in the summer of 1926 he traveled to Stresa, booked rooms in a waterfront hotel near Molly's island, and stayed for two months. In 1927 he returned for another two months. In 1928 he spent seven weeks at Cap d'Antibes, a Riviera resort within a day's drive of Lake Maggiore, then he skirted Italy to spend two weeks equally close in Geneva; in 1929 he vacationed for a month on the then-Italian island of Brioni in the Adriatic, followed by an excursion to Dubrovnik and a return via Venice and Molly's demesne; and, after a trip to South Africa in the winter of 1931, he took a Mediterranean tour, stopping for three weeks in Venice on the way back.

Molly and Italy thus amount to a significant chapter in Shaw's life, one casting a tantalizing light on his old age. Intriguing as the romance of this chapter is, his biographers up through the 1950s appear to have been unaware of it. Henderson, Harris, Pearson, Irvine, and Ervine mention not a word about Molly. Between them they record a few details of Shaw's two Italian tours in the 1890s, the reception of his plays in Italy, and his favorable comments on Mussolini, but except for a few paragraphs about his holiday with the Gene Tunneys on Brioni they overlook his eight months in the region. Most notorious and widely observed elsewhere are his views on Italian fascism, but these relate only peripherally to his travels.[2] The prevailing accounts of these years of Shaw's old age include plays, politics, even pugilism, but certainly not passion. The general conception of him after his affair with Stella, the First World War, and *Back to Methuselah*, is one of a famous, contentious sage, witty and resilient but drying up (as oldsters ought to do), with a tough old heart devoted to nonromantic worldly activities. His famous affairs now echoes, his major source of recreation seemed to lie in traveling abroad with Charlotte in a wedlock which, as he admitted—and regretted—remained unconsummated. Against this context the idea of G.B.S. pursuing a siren jars like a satyr play.

It is only fair to observe that Shaw kept his biographers in the dark about his relationship with Molly, much as Dickens concealed his affair with Ellen Ternan who, like Molly, was shapely, intelligent, a mediocre actress, and many years the great author's junior. Not until 1960 did it come to light with the publication of *To a Young Actress: The Letters of Bernard Shaw to Molly Tompkins*, which was followed in 1961 by *Shaw and Molly Tompkins: In Their Own Words*, both edited by Molly's son, Peter.[3] The existence of these books hangs on a thread of luck. If a bomb had destroyed a certain Roman palazzo during World War II, if its occupants had been careless of others' property, if the fascists had discovered an OSS radio in its cellar and dispatched the owners, the details of Shaw's Italian romance would have been lost, and Molly would be only a footnote. In a chest in that cellar, not far from some hand grenades, lay a bundle of Shaw's correspondence to her, over a hundred letters dating from 1921 to 1940. Molly had left them behind in 1941 when, after seventeen years in Italy, she barely escaped the war by sailing on the last American Export liner from Lisbon. These letters, plus eight written up to 1949, comprise *To a Young Actress*. Apparently just one of Molly's letters to Shaw survives, although her son estimates that she must have written nearly a thousand. *Shaw and Molly Tompkins* is a compilation of her reminiscences (tied down by Shaw's letters) which her son recorded in the 1950s and edited shortly thereafter. Since these books appeared they have been dealt with only briefly, first by C. G. L. Du Cann in *The Loves of George Bernard Shaw* (New York: Funk & Wagnalls, 1963), and recently by Margot Peters in *Bernard Shaw and the Actresses* (Garden City, N.Y.: Doubleday, 1980). Peters includes a valuable extract from Molly's one surviving letter.

Fortunate as it is that source materials exist, they have limitations which call for a weighing of evidence and attentive probing between the lines. Shaw's letters to Molly display his usual frankness and spontaneity, combined with the rhetorical delight he nearly always took in expressing himself. He had good reasons, however, to temper utter candor about touchy personal matters: at exactly the time he started this correspondence, Stella Campbell was bothering him for permission to publish his early love letters to her, and later she repeatedly pressed the request. Not only was he abashed at the thought of being thus bared, but he refused most strongly for his wife's sake. He knew that they would be published eventually because all of his letters had a commercial value, especially amorous ones. Consequently when he wrote to Molly he was freshly aware that he should watch his step lest once again he appear too fallible or foolishly infatuated. On the other side of the relationship, Molly's reminiscences must also be taken with caution since they deal with events long after they occurred, through the memory and censorship of a woman, now a grandmother, who was reporting them to her son and posterity.

It is surprising that the correspondence and reminiscences are as candid as they are. They complement each other tellingly, Shaw's letters anchoring Molly's account to the immediate scene, her account filling gaps between the letters, presenting her side of the story, and providing firsthand glimpses of the lively personality that attracted G.B.S. Still, on both sides personal discretion and the knowledge of eventual publicity urged restraint about the most intimate details, and these must be surmised in light of the restraint and the evidence. What follows, therefore, combines synthesizing, cross-referencing, and interpretation aimed both at bringing together two sources and at penetrating two filters. What, then, were the essential ingredients of Shaw's last love affair, especially as it climaxed in the romantic environs of Lake Maggiore?

In December 1921 Molly Tompkins and her husband Laurence, with their two-year-old son in tow, made a pilgrimage from Atlanta, Georgia, to London, specifically to seek out G.B.S. She had hopes of becoming a Shavian actress; Laurence was a sculptor. They planned to establish a theater for the production of Shaw's works, she to perform in its plays, Laurence to design and manage it. Attracted by their charm, energy, and spirit, Shaw quickly sparked to a warm relationship: he introduced them to his literary friends, swam with Laurence at the Automobile Club, and took them on trips to the countryside, to a Fabian summer school, and to the Shakespeare Theatre at Stratford-on-Avon.

Molly soon became the focus of Shaw's attention: twenty-four years old, audacious, vivacious, and attractive yet tripped up by her American-isms and naïveté, she was a type of Eliza—an unsculpted Galatea. Pyg-malion Shaw, now sixty-five, was not only captivated by her charm and adoration but invigorated by the challenge she posed. Molly clearly had more ambition than ability. She needed basic training. Accordingly, he sent her off to the Royal Academy of Dramatic Art, closely followed her progress there, saw that she took phonetics lessons, and coached her on stage speech himself. Again and again his letters of the first year have a Higgins-like ring: he advises her on discreet ladylike makeup; he ad-monishes her to get rid of her Americanisms "And keep your figure and dont live on chocolate creams"; he composes a long epistle on stage ar-ticulation; and at last he brings *Pygmalion* to the surface: "I exhort you (in the manner of Higgins) to remember that you are a human being with a soul and the divine gift of articulate speech, and not a confection-ers shop" (*Letters*, pp. 12–32).

In a very notable respect, however, the letters move beyond Higgins: they display an open, bantering affection. In the first, Shaw drops the phrase, "if you love me"; in the third he declares "And yet you have the face to pretend that you love me"; in the fourth he admonishes, "Dont say years for ears in my plays or I will never love you any more"; in the fifth he sets up a date; and soon afterwards he observes, "You will grow out of your Shavian infatuation (alas! for I hope it is a great pleasure to you)."

Molly promoted her acting talents for all they were worth, and per-haps a bit more. Headstrong with ambition, she irritated Claude Rains, her instructor at The Royal Academy. No matter. She left the Academy, sought roles wherever she could find them, charmed theater managers, and achieved some initial successes. An early description of her which provides third-party evidence of why she made such a mark with G.B.S. and the managers (and later with Italian genteel society) appears in a letter Sir Johnston Forbes-Robertson wrote Shaw about her perform-ance in a poor play: "I saw the exquisite young thing play her utterly worthless part and was much impressed. She made bricks without straw bravely. It seems to me she has a powerful personality which gets over the flats. She moves beautifully, and makes all the others look commonplace by her high distinction" (*Tompkins*, p. 94). Although Shaw's presence as a friend no doubt forwarded Molly's acting career, he had too much professional integrity to intercede with theater managers on her behalf. Rather, he prodded her personally and critically, enjoying her crush on him and the flair of her letters which, he tactfully suggested, might point to a future more in literature than on the stage. But Forbes-Robertson, also smitten by Molly, favored her ambition. Still handsome and famous in retirement from acting, he courted and escorted her to London theaters many a night—while his wife was away in Australia.

Forbes-Robertson's observation of Molly's powerful personality, beautiful body movement, and high distinction conveys her forcefulness, elegance, and sensuality. To isolate her sensuality would be to misrepresent the appealing combination; nonetheless it was a quality in which the other two apparently peaked, making her especially enticing. Shaw wrote to Forbes-Robertson about a theater manager "who had been led away by her good looks into offering her the leading part in a production of Androcles & The Lion," and when the famous actor had been carried away by those same looks, Shaw advised Molly that "A clever young woman has to choose between stupid and vigorous young men and clever and—shall I say goatish old ones? See Misalliance passim. But do not be too hard on the poor old things" (*Letters*, pp. 55, 59). As a drama critic years earlier he had found himself bound to London theater and had likened himself to a tethered goat.[4] Now, wryly, he found that like Forbes-Robertson and John Tarleton of *Misalliance*, he was a bit of an old one, tethered by fancy to a young creature who aroused the libido of many a male.

Arresting visual evidence of Molly's fleshly attraction is a drawing of a voluptuous reclining nude (Fig. 1). With her arms stretched behind her head, the nude's body arches backward, her pelvis turns forward, and one leg is raised. Laurence drew this figure as Lilith, intending a Shavian connotation. Molly recalls, "When Shaw saw the sketch he chuckled, thinking, as did everyone else, that I had posed for it: actually, though Laurence always seemed to put a little of me in everything he did, the model was an unsuccessful actress" (*Tompkins*, pp. 36–37; drawing, p. 97). That "little" of Molly was later to attract aristocratic Latin lovers, including a crown prince. The likelihood that it also attracted Shaw is suggested by a picture postcard he sent her in March 1922 when she asked him about her costume for a student production of *You Never Can Tell*. The card (Fig. 2) reproduces Rubens's "Judgment of Paris," in which three nudes—Hera, Athena, and Aphrodite—stand seductively in a ro-

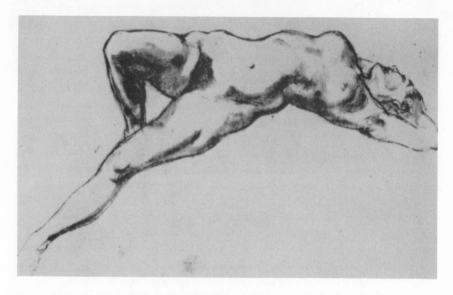

FIG. 1. "Lilith," by Laurence Tompkins: "Laurence always seemed to put a little of me in everything he did." From *Shaw and Molly Tompkins*, p. 97.

mantic copse. Shaw has labeled these "Dolly," "Mrs. C.," and "Gloria," after characters in the play. Closely, longingly observing the goddesses is a handsome, half-draped, seated male—Paris—whom Shaw has dubbed "G.B.S. [slightly idealized]." Rubens includes a sly detail which Shaw's sharp eye was not likely to have missed: a shepherd's staff rests on Paris's thigh where it is covered by a drapery; its lower portion protrudes outward from between his slightly parted legs, at which spot his left hand rests on it. In a corner crouches Cupid—a hint, regarding the legend, that Aphrodite will win the contest as to which is the fairest goddess, and give Paris the love of the most beautiful woman in the world as a reward. Shaw adds a fertile Valentine touch to the allusion by identifying Cupid as "The B.S. Baby." Molly was to play Gloria; G.B.S., like Paris, was to observe. In a wide margin on the card he notes: "This is how it really ought to be dressed" (*Letters*, p. 20).

What Shaw wrote Molly late the next year must remain conjectural, but evidently some of his letters motivated her housekeeper-secretary to attempt blackmail. Molly recalls Shaw telephoning her about it and laughing, "I'm too tough for that sort of thing." The housekeeper left and, unfortunately, the letters went with her.[5]

Molly's small stage successes apparently resulted more from the striking figure she cut than from natural aptitude. In her reminiscences she

FIG. 2. "The Judgment of Paris": GBS (un)costuming Molly for *You Never Can Tell*. ("K.B." is Kenneth Barnes, principal of The Royal Academy of Dramatic Art). From the original postcard, reproduced in *To a Young Actress*, p. 20.

claims that she would do her best in rehearsals and then stiffen in performance. Whatever the case, the ups and downs of provincial theater life discouraged her. After the failure of her last play in July 1924, she declared that she did not really care for acting, that she had undertaken it only because Laurence wanted her to; instead, she decided, what she wanted was "to live." Laurence, ever indulgent, mentioned Italy. Carrara would offer him marble; nearby was a seaside hotel. Where better to "live"?

The abruptness with which Molly dropped her stage career and left England was consistent with her impulsive temperament. Nonetheless there appears to have been another motive which she suppresses in her account of the situation: the strong attraction she felt towards Shaw had come up against a dead end. For all her sprightly openness in her reminiscences, Molly consistently soft-pedals her own romantic passions. Yet abundant evidence suggests that passion was a counterpart of her sensuality and that by this time her affection for Shaw had moved beyond nominal infatuation. A notable sign of this appears in a letter he wrote her on 10 June 1924 in which he recognizes her love but then dodges, counters, and plays with it in a manner that might well have prompted any amorous woman to think of sunnier climes. He moves into the subject of their relationship by declining her invitation to attend a performance of her latest play:

> Wimbledon is out of the question: I am stuck down here working; and my mate does not like to be left alone in the domestic cage in the evenings. Besides, I want to see you at work at longer intervals now that you are learning. I am too professionalized to be able to see you in a human way when you are on the stage. It is for the young to sit in ecstasy and wait for you at the stage door at the end, bouquet in hand.
>
> Is it not delightful to be in love? I will pose for you to your heart's content. You will find it described in Heartbreak House as far as it can be described. It has happened to me twice. It does not last, because it does not belong to this earth; and when you clasp the idol it turns out to be a rag doll like yourself; for the immortal part *must* elude you if you grab at it. . . .
>
> Why a poor old domesticated drudge, slaving to keep pace with his work and (worse) his wretched business, should be suspected of being Don Juan, heaven knows! . . .
>
> When I tell you of my movements I am not warning you off. Little liar: how dare you? . . . [*Letters*, pp. 71–72]

Of the letters which survive, this is Shaw's most romantically intimate up to that time—well over half of its 800 words are concerned with love. He addresses her as "My dear Mollytomps," speaks of the voluptuous "Song of Solomon," and introduces a teasing censorship in the middle with a fragmented "But really, Mrs Tompkins, this is hardly a subject — ." What it reveals, however, is an affection stronger on the woman's part than on the man's, and a shift in Shaw from the role of an infatuated Higgins toward the heartbreak terms of a prudent Shotover. Shaw's claim that he is not warning her off clearly responds to her suspicion that he was doing exactly that. This suspicion could well have been reinforced one month later when she either expressed doubts about going abroad, or asked his advice about it. He supported the idea strongly:

> I see no reason on earth why you should not go to Italy. Everybody should go to Italy. Goethe's visit to Italy produced an extraordinary effect on him. My first visit to Italy produced Candida. But remember that the spring and the end of autumn are the best times to go. The hot season, with no rain and clouds of mosquitos, is very trying on the plains. And Carrara has no reputation as a pleasure, health, or culture resort. You must stay in Venice for at least a week, and go out to Torcello in a gondola (if there is one left); for Venice is a quite peculiar place: Then there is Verona, with a lovely church (San Zeno) and a charm of its own. Mantua is a stinking place, with pictures of extraordinary cleverness and beastliness by Giulio Romano, atoned for by the frescoes of Mantegna in

the Archives. Besides, you can walk along the marshes and see the green frogs taking headers off the dock leaves as you approach. I was never in Ravenna; but I still want to go there to see the mosaics. In Milan, which is unavoidable, and about as romantic as Manchester, do not fuss about the cathedral (a sort of fortified wedding cake) but do not miss San Ambrogio: it will give rest to your soul, which the cathedral will only worry. [*Letters*, p. 73]

Molly's restless spirit was thus spurred toward Italy not only by her flagging acting career but by the frustrating coolness of a hero who seemed quite content to have her go, and even provided cues for an itinerary. Ironically, however, her departure in the summer of 1924 was the beginning of the most important stage of their relationship. For the next two years Shaw's letters followed Molly and Laurence on their peregrinations, from which they alighted for short stays in a villa at Forte dei Marmi (near Carrara) and in Paris. These letters are distinctive for their colorful overviews and vignettes of Italian places, culture, and people—and for a repeated motif of marital infidelity, coquetry, and philandering. Molly's absence appears to have sparked a glimmer of Don Juan in Shaw, despite his recent laughter at the notion. Soon after her departure he had second thoughts. In two letters that fall he extols the virtues of Russia over Italy, then lightly hints that he would like to go there with her: "You ought to go to Russia: Italy is *vieux jeu*. . . . It seems so ridiculously old fashioned and prim to be touring Italy in the footsteps of the Victorians when this land of terror, romance, hope, and dawning is open to you with no worse discomforts than the road from Pisa to Carrara. . . . Living in Italy is like living on Bath buns and strawberry ices: delicious, but you cannot keep it up. Perhaps going to Russia with you would be the same. Anyhow I shant go: my wife wouldn't let me" (*Letters*, pp. 78–80).

By the next February Molly was already caught up in an affair with an attractive Italian man—the first of many throughout the years. Shaw responded by rebuking her as a coquette who steals other women's husbands. He paralleled her to himself as a philanderer, and sympathized with the innocent parties: "I dont suppose [his wife] will shoot you; but if she does, no Latin jury will convict her, any more than they would convict Lawrence if he gave you the thrashing you deserve." He observes that, like himself, "You go about the world writing prefaces without the least intention of writing the books; and the sooner you realize that what is fun to you is heartbreak and homebreak to your victims, the better." The parallel is not precise, since there is evidence that Molly was sometimes quite prepared to write the books; but it suggests a poignant subtext. As Shaw's sentiments come so soon after she left England, they apply to her potential threat to his own home, one which, he implies, could have been reciprocal: as a coquette and a philanderer, each could have raised havoc with the other's marriage. Two days later the thought was still on his mind: "I will not come to Italy to share the fate of Achilles. Besides, I am very nearly as bad as you" (*Letters*, pp. 82–83). In having written him about her affair, Molly reveals not only their intimacy but, perhaps, some desire on her part to tantalize him; his response nibbles at the bait but deflects the hook.

Despite his censure of Molly's coquetry, Shaw's letters during these months reveal that her lively correspondence and his memories of Italy stimulated him to a fresh awareness of an instinctive, sensual mode of existence. Beneath his Nordic prudence was a delight in the open emotions and free spirit of the Italians. In two letters of the following June and one in early August, he juggles Nordic prudence with thoughts of marital infidelity and fleshly temptation:

> You must really get a profession. Playtime will not last forever. And Lawrence may bolt anyday with some irresistible signorina who will spend every rap he possesses. . . .
> Lawrence will certainly be vamped, and elope. You have trained him to be imposed on.
> . . . I like the Scots (though the Shetlanders, by the way, are Norse) because they combine the noblest sentiments and the loftiest imagination with an utter inability to resist the slightest temptation, whether of the world, the flesh, or the devil. Like the Italians, by the way. [*Letters*, pp. 84–87]

This last concludes with a reference to another of her affairs and an affirmation of his most recent role with her: "I hope Ettore (or is it Akeelay?) will fall in love with someone else—his wife, for instance—before there is any serious trouble. As for you, better remain faithful to me, your ancient Shotover."

Ancient or not, this Shotover was beginning to feel stirrings. Moments came when he found himself beset by an Italian temptation toward the world, the flesh, or the devil. In the winter of 1926 he dallies with the thought of youthful love:

> I snatch this moment late in the evening, when I should not write at all. I am alone here, my wife having gone up to town. It is the anniversary of Mozart's birth in 1756 (I followed in 1856); and his Little Night Music is coming through on the wireless. It is a mild night; and I am sitting at the fire with my typewriter on my knees, like a sailor with his lass.

He describes being kissed on the street by an American lady and struggling, whereupon he plunges to the heart of his relationship with Molly:

> . . . [You] do not understand that dotards of seventy must not assume that beautiful females who admire their works would like to be pawed by

them. There is a shyness of age as there is a shyness of youth. And that is only the cheapest out of a dozen reasons why a man, especially an old man, does not always devour his natural prey.

And then, your romance has lasted a long time without spoiling. There are moments, of course, when you want to consummate it. But they pass; and the romance remains. You get tired of waiting; but suppose there were no longer anything to wait for!

But these things do not fit into words and arguments. They belong to the Elysian fields (not those through which you rush the Renault, but those that Gluck set to music in Orfeo) into which we both want to escape to meet each other, and in which we never shall meet except in imagination. But we shall do as well on this solid earth as we need; for next time you will not be so tongue tied, to say the least. [*Letters*, pp. 90–91]

These passages have a quality of wistful reverie. In the context of a late and mild night, an absent wife, music, the image of a sailor and his lass, kissing, with an impulse to paw and devour thwarted by the shyness of age, comes the thought of Molly's long-lasting romance with him, her desire to consummate it, her impatience at waiting. This he answers with an acknowledgement of his own desire—"we both want to escape to meet each other"—but he elevates the fulfillment of this desire to myth, music, and imagination. As a worldly compromise he chooses the excitement of the desire itself, but adds a titillating "next time." Within the bounds of reverie, this could hardly lay forth the elements of their attraction towards one another more explicitly. Revealing himself and the sensual magnetism between them, Shaw's emotions and thoughts intertwine in a genuine confession and expression of romantic longing, reflecting little less than—(with G.B.S. at sixty-nine, the obvious word somersaults)—love.

Early the next summer "next time" came closer with a jolt. It appeared that the Tompkinses might be settling down at last. Laurence had begun to establish a studio in Paris, but Molly was enchanted by a small island off the shore from Pallanza on Lake Maggiore and employed her famous charm to persuade its owner, Prince Vitaliano Borromeo, to rent it to them for half price. Consequently they found themselves closing up Laurence's studio while the house on the island was being renovated. A postcard from Shaw on 12 July expresses his palpable delight, and his giving in to temptation: "At last an address! You mean the Borromean island in Lago Maggiore, dont you? I must go and have a look at it if I survive my 70th birthday the Monday after next. . . . I am forced to go on working instead of taking a leaf out of your book (which is what I need)" (*Letters*, p. 92).

Shaw's mention of his birthday has more trauma behind it than one might suspect. Although he frequently complained of his age, the idea

FIG. 3. San Giovanni Island, Lake Maggiore: "I cannot tear myself away from the Isola Molli." From a postcard purchased by Charlotte, reproduced in *To a Young Actress*, p. 97.

of passing into his seventies was unusually painful to him. A few months before, Charlotte had written Siegfried Trebitsch about his chagrin at the prospect of having the occasion celebrated in Austria and Germany: "Can anything be more unkind than to call the attention of all Europe to the fact that a man is 70? If he was 17 or 170—not 70! . . . G.B.S. is really *very vexed about this*. I have seldom seen him more so."[6] Time's wingéd chariot was haunting Shaw with unusual oppressiveness. What better way to thwart it for a moment than to sport, while he could, at Lake Maggiore?

By the first week in August, Shaw and Charlotte checked into the Hotel Regina at Stresa, a short boatride away from the Borromean Islands. Molly was still in Paris, so he immediately sent her two picture postcards of the islands, drawing pointers on them and querying, "Is it this one? All the others look too big for the price"; "I thought at first it might be this—the Madre. But the house looks too large for three." Forthwith he began circling her vicariously. On the seventh he took a boat around the islands; by the tenth he had located the right one (Fig. 3): "I cannot tear myself away from the Isola Molli. I sailed round it again today" (*Letters*, pp. 93–95).

Meanwhile, fame's curse attended him. His plays had gained a foothold in Italy with a production of *Arms and the Man* in 1909, and from

1915 onward many had been produced there with great success. They had been well translated by Antonio Agresti, promoted by the famous actress Emma Grammatica, applauded by Pirandello, and had achieved widespread sales in book form.[7] Hence he found little of the anonymity he had enjoyed on his former trips. Foreign travel now, even on holiday, involved recognition, and sometimes this could be disconcerting. He reports to Molly that "a most appalling thing happened at noon. The hotel porter dashed in and announced the Princess Borromeo, the governor of the provinzia of Novara, half a dozen mayors and ex-mayors, and countless marchesane, principesse, contesse, baronesse d'ogni grado nobile. Charlotte and I stood aghast; but there was no time to fly. The princess fortunately talked English, and unbent before my blarney. With perfect tact she took her crowd away after a short visit; but they all invited us to call" (*Letters*, p. 96).

More congenial to him were frequent swims in the lake, tours in the surrounding hills, and friendships. Across the lake at Cerro lived Cecil Lewis, an Englishman whose playwriting ambitions he had mildly encouraged the year before.[8] He befriended the British conductor Albert Coates, a neighbor of the Lewises; and in a suburb of Pallanza lived Prince Paul Troubetskoy, the sculptor who had done a bust of him in 1912, and who promptly had him posing for two new likenesses. These men and their wives made for good company. Besides swimming or touring with one or the other, Shaw had ready talk of playwriting, music, and art. He had left London "stupid with fatigue" from work on *The Intelligent Woman's Guide to Socialism and Capitalism*. By 22 August, Charlotte observed that "G.B.S. gets better & better. I think I shall have to bring him to live here!" (*Letters*, pp. 96, 97). The holiday, it would seem, was ideal—except that Molly was proving to be temperamental.

For the first six weeks she was aflutter. Against a backdrop of seemingly placid visits, picnics, and excursions, Molly played out a personal drama of moodiness, irritability, sulkiness, even fury. She had hastened to the lake shortly after she heard from Shaw, taking a room in her favorite hotel at Baveno, about two miles from Stresa. Her subsequent movements reflect the extremity of her moods. In her reminiscences she recalls two trips back to Paris—the first in a pet over Charlotte, the second in a fury over Shaw—followed in each case by speedy returns to the lake. Dates of the *Letters* suggest that on the first occasion her stay in Paris was much longer than she reports or, more likely, that she made at least one more trip. In any event, personal turmoil spurred her back and forth. So slight an occasion as a picnic with the Shaws, Lewises, and Coateses on Molly's island reveals how out of sorts she was: "It was a lovely day, but by evening the sky was clouded over, blighting the beauty of the trees and flowers on the island, setting my nerves on edge" (*Tomp-*

kins, p. 137). For her the excursion was a failure. In contrast Shaw seemed to enjoy himself thoroughly, although he professed to hate picnics, and Charlotte wrote her later: "The Island looks very sweet. I often look up to the place where we had that most wonderful dinner!" (*Letters*, p. 100). Shaw was puzzled by Molly's behavior: "Your life seems to be one of considerable quite unnecessary friction. But I will not preach" (*Letters*, p. 101). This last is on the back of a postcard picturing him seated outside his hotel, very much at ease.

For Molly, Shaw's presence at Lake Maggiore amounted to a stunning turn of events: the idol for whom she and Laurence had crossed an ocean, the world-renowned genius who had generously played Higgins to her aspiring Eliza, had now reversed roles—he had crossed a continent to seek out *her*. The circumstance dazzled. It was one to live up to moment by moment. And increasing the tension, disorienting and flustering her, was her passion for him. She waited until she was in Paris to communicate some of this to Shaw. Her letter brought an impatient response: "Yes, yes: I got your bothersomely honest letter. I sent you a card this morning to say so. If you have started being afraid of me, all is over. . Lots of people are: that is why they hate me. The fear of God may be the beginning of wisdom; but the fear of Man is the beginning of murder" (*Letters*, p. 99).

More obviously frustrating for Molly was the presence of Charlotte, whose Victorian propriety and domestic possession of G.B.S. she felt as a constant rebuff. Molly craved a free, happy, fulfilling time with her hero; Charlotte sat in the way like a heap of domestic baggage. And worse, Molly perceived the old woman as an insidious rival stanching the pulse of romance. On her first pouty trip back to Paris, Laurence exposed her feelings:

> "You can't be jealous of Charlotte!"
> "I'm not. But she's so smug!"
> "You *must* be jealous. Were you impossible to B.?"
> "No. Just sulky. I didn't want to be sulky and silent and hard inside but I just got all tied up and was."
> "So you walked out on them when they had gone all the way to Italy to see you and your island."
> "I didn't exactly want to leave." [*Tompkins*, p. 139]

Molly's jealousy survives in her reminiscences. With claws scarcely concealed, she details Charlotte's black dresses, black swimsuit, priggishness, stiffness on informal occasions, stifling veneration of "G.B.S.," and slights (perhaps more imagined than real) toward herself. At one point her feline eye fastens on a stuffed canary which adorned Charlotte's swimsuit; at another she suspects that high-powered binoculars on the balcony of the Shaws' room were used by the old woman to spy on the activities of "B." and herself across the lake.

Considering Molly's youth, beauty, and amorous instincts, and the susceptibility to romance which Shaw had displayed with Stella Campbell, Charlotte had good cause to be wary. Nonetheless, her few letters to Molly appear to be friendly, supportive, even chatty. They convey a sense of security. After all, Molly was little more than a girl and had a kind husband and young child. G.B.S. might be somewhat infatuated, but he was well ensconced in the connubial nest. He read her Molly's correspondence (at least most of it), and could be perceived more as a fond, admonishing father figure than anything else. Still, Charlotte must have known that a visit to Molly's new environs was at least one motive for the holiday, and there are signs that the enticing young beauty was a test of her composure. Molly recalls a scene in which Shaw alluded to the women's covert conflict:

> The next day Charlotte said she had "letters," so Shaw and I went to Coates without her.
> "I like it best without Charlotte," I said.
> Shaw's eyes twinkled as they did when he was amused or very happy.
> "You and Charlotte have got to come to some arrangement," said Shaw. "Stop being so polite to each other. The strain is terrible. Can't you tell her to go to hell, once. You'd both feel better afterwards."
> "But I couldn't," I answered. "She is much too old."
> As Shaw winced I realized they were just the same age; only to me he was so full of gaiety and vitality he had no age. He seemed to be Peter's when he talked and played with Peter, my age when he talked to me. [*Tompkins*, p. 132]

Molly's report reflects her bias, but it is supported by an increasing chill in Charlotte's correspondence to her over the years. In two letters of the summer of 1926 Charlotte calls Molly "my dear," sends "Our love to you both," and signs herself "C.F.S." (*Letters*, pp. 97, 100). By November 1931 this changes perceptibly into a desire to see Molly and Laurence *together*, "Yours Sincerely," and "C.F. Shaw."[9]

As the key figure of a bizarre triangle, attached to a sixty-nine-year-old matron and adored by a twenty-nine-year-old charmer, Shaw found himself the focal point of competing temperaments, ages, and value systems. He must have experienced a small thrill of the familiar, since such competitions had long since characterized his plays. On the one side was his wife, strong in her Victorian propriety; on the other side was his youthful adorer, ready to trample on propriety and follow her impulses. Regarding marriage, sensuality, and sex, Charlotte had the instincts of Mrs. Grundy while Molly had those of D. H. Lawrence, whose works she devoured. For Charlotte, marriage meant fidelity, sensuality was suspect, sex was dirty. Her success at holding Shaw in a sexually unconsummated marriage was a testament to her devotion and great domestic convenience to him, to his appreciation of this, and to a deep strain of personal puritanism which lay beneath his worldliness. For Molly, marriage meant a home base open to the sport of touching other bases, sensuality was the pulse of existence, and sexual involvement was a natural culmination of sensuality. These attitudes appealed to another side of Shaw. Years before he had challenged Victorian value systems, stressed personal freedom, and extolled instinct over reason. Now he had sought out an amorous woman in a hedonistic locale.

Molly's reminiscences depict details of the free-flowing sensuality of the holiday environment, providing an inkling of its appeal to G.B.S. and revealing her own relish in such matters. Amidst this sensuality Shaw was not so entirely out of place as it might seem. In matters of the flesh he could not compete with younger bodies, but after his sittings for Rodin in 1906 he had posed in the nude for Alvin Langdon Coburn, mimicking Rodin's "Thinker" surprisingly well for a man of fifty. At other times he had been the exuberant subject of nude photographs taken out of doors.[10] Although sensuousness was scarcely his overt style, Molly responds to a distinctive magnetism when she finds that "he was so full of gaiety and vitality he had no age." The gaiety rose in part from Shaw's inbred disposition towards Irish blarney and gallantry which, he observes, had given him the reputation of a philanderer (*Letters*, p. 82). Vitality was among his most famous qualities, one which apparently connoted virility to Molly and many another woman. He was a wiry dynamo who could out-work, out-walk, out-bicycle, out-swim, and out-tour many a younger mortal. Molly recalls him running her ragged on a long walk and, like a young man, nonchalantly showing off at diving. Combined with the psychic force of his fame, these qualities translated uniquely into a version of that "life" she was seeking. For all his seventy years, this phenomenon exuded energies which gave an extra vibrancy to the sensuous environment.

Nonetheless Molly was beset by her nerves and frustrations, and near the end of the sixth week her moodiness nearly blew everything apart. Once again arriving in Baveno from Paris, she received a note from Shaw outlining his activities and concluding, "You can join us as you please." Smoldering at the impression of being taken for granted, she responded, "So sorry to miss you this trip. Returning to Paris immediately"—which she did (*Tompkins*, p. 140). That night the Shavian equipoise exploded: "This time I really am cross. What do you mean by it, you young devil? . . . 'Am returning immediately to Paris'!!! Return immediately to hell, you little beast, and never dare write to me or approach me or mention your poisonous island to me again as long as you live." His "G.B.S." at the end was immoderately large and fearsome. Eliza-like, Molly drank in the nectar of Shaw's tantrum; Higgins-like, his outburst revealed how much he really cared. She returned forthwith to a pacified doter: "You must behave exactly as you did before, when you were very nice. But you will spoil everything if you tomfool as you are doing now. So be good, and look in on Tuesday, clothed & in your right mind" (Letters, pp. 105–6, 107).

The breaking of the storm brought the romantic atmosphere Molly desired. She is both idyllic and circumspect about their remaining time together: "After that there were sun-filled days and quiet evenings, and every night Shaw would walk me to Baveno and then I would walk back with him halfway to Stresa and then he would return again to leave me at Baveno on the steps of the Bellevue, striding off into the night" (Tompkins, p. 142). Once again the rhythm is back and forth, back and forth; but now the compass points were not, tumultously, Paris and Italy, but, tenderly, Baveno and Stresa, "Mollissima" and "B.," pulling at one another in the night near the shores of the dark lake. One final afternoon Molly and the Shaws, attended by a host of the nobility of northern Italy, were guests of honor at a tea in the palace of the Borromeos on the Isola Bella. Afterwards Shaw dropped Charlotte at the hotel and saw Molly off on a train to Paris. That winter he wrote her, "I came back to England quite extraordinarily well and vigorous—better than I had been for some years. Partly you, I think. . . . When do you go to the Isle of The Ever Blessed Many Times Kissed?" (Letters, p. 109).

If there is any doubt that Molly was Shaw's primary motive for going to Italy in 1926, there can be none for his holiday there in 1927. In January he writes about an unpleasant trip she had taken home to Georgia, and how such experiences enter one's dreams. He observes that, in compensation, "you will have the Baveno road at night, and the Cerro passage at noon, and even the shelter at Ayot to steal into your sleep from the past." He says that were Laurence to ask, he would advise him that the day for artistic American expatriates is over, that America is beginning to offer fertile cultural ground—to which he would add: "By the way, you might leave Molly behind if you are tired of her" (Letters, p. 110). In February, hearing of Molly's arrival at her idyllic island, including, apparently, an exuberant description of her stripping off her clothes to wade ashore (Tompkins, p. 147), he responds, "That, Mollimia, very nearly sent us spinning across the channel . . . the attraction of the island is very strong" (Letters, p. 112). In March he writes, "I have just had to stop for dinner, which was accompanied on the wireless by a jazz band with a negro, or an American pseudo-negro, singing 'Let's all go to Mary's house, Mary's house, Mary's house, Let's all go to Mary's house

and have a jolly time.' Which is just what I would like to do for the rest
of the evening if it were not so far off" (*Letters*, p. 114). Mary was Molly's
given name. Accordingly, he went to her house the next summer.

The course of their relationship during that season was the reverse of
the first: it began with a long peaceful spell and ended with a short
period of turmoil. As Molly reports it, the Shaws came to the island
every morning and informality prevailed: he would read, write, swim,
or wander in the garden. Typically during the first days the foursome
would go to the mainland after lunch for a drive in search of new sights.
Shaw was particularly attracted to the many Sacro Montes in the hills.
At each he would make the long pilgrimage to the calvary at the top,
scrutinizing the lifelike statuary in each station of the Cross along the
way. In the heat of midsummer Charlotte and Laurence would sometimes remain on the island, leaving the ever-energetic Shaw and ever-
ready Molly to tour the countryside by themselves; and, as the season
went on, the two were alone together more and more. Molly focuses on
one hot day when they retreated to an isolated copse of trees by a river
and reclined in idyllic silence:

> For a long time we lay on the river bank looking down at the water, or
> up at the tree limbs and sky, content and with no need to talk. All the
> million things I had to say to Shaw were forgotten. With my hands I
> pretended to touch the leaves that patterned the sky overhead.

Eventually Shaw voiced his oft-repeated remonstrance about her laziness and suggested that she write his biography.

> "There have been many lives of me written, Molly, but you know more
> about me than anyone else. I'd like you to do it."
> "I don't know anything about you," I said slowly, "except how you are
> to me." Then after a long silence: "Tell me all sorts of things about you,
> please, from the very beginning."
> For a long time he talked in his curiously enchanting voice, and prob-
> ably because it was uppermost in both our minds talked and talked about
> his relations with women, and his reactions to them.
> At the end I stretched and said: "I'm so full of you, and the river, and
> trees, and sweetness, but still I couldn't write your life. I would make a
> fool of you and of myself." [*Tompkins*, pp. 156–57]

In its setting of heat, isolation, and languor, this scene is both circumspect and suggestive. Demurely, it coalesces strains of "The Judgment of
Paris" and D. H. Lawrence. Perhaps, as far as Molly's memory would
allow, she reports everything. Among all of her descriptions regarding
her love affairs, however, this one stands out: it is as intimately detailed
as she becomes. While the scene could be platonic, Molly's description
could also be a discreet indication that something intimate had oc-

curred, something familiar to her and adventuresome for Shaw at the age of seventy-one. Their languor, his subsequent talk of his loves, a subject which "was uppermost in both our minds," his "you know more about me than anyone else," and her stretching, with the words "I'm so full of you" would follow as a natural sequel to the consummation she desired. Being recalled after thirty years, these words could only vaguely approximate the actual ones, but if true they communicate a remarkable occasion, platonic or not. It was followed by other long, private times together. They drove through the country, ate dinners at small restaurants, watched movies—sometimes twice through—and returned so late at night that even the ever-tolerant Laurence frowned.

Despite this long period of peace and romancing, the holiday turned from tranquility to tension. And much as Molly had found it difficult to explain her edginess of the previous summer, she is imprecise about what went wrong this time. What may be inferred is that her time with Shaw was running out, and the closer they had become the more intolerable was the thought that he was destined to return to Charlotte's Victorian nest. Intervals with the Coateses and Lewises were no doubt more of a pleasure to him than to her. He could enjoy swimming and talking with them or robustly singing snatches of Wagner with Coates, in accompaniment to records, but for her such occasions were soured by the prudish old woman in black. Consequently she found herself making minor details into unpleasant scenes which usually related to Charlotte but inevitably involved Shaw. Molly recalls an exchange with Laurence after one of these scenes: *224236*

> "Do you love B.?" Laurence asked.
> "Of course," I answered, looking up in surprise. "You know I do."
> "I suppose so. But why do you have to act like such a bitch. Is it love? Or is it jealousy?" [*Tompkins*, p. 160]

To set things right on this occasion, the two took a canoe to visit the Shaws at Stresa. On the way a storm soaked them, and after dinner Shaw lifted Molly in his arms and put her into his bed for warmth. There she informed him that she was going to Milan to have an abortion. We have his response only as she recalls it, but it rings true as the gist of one who was poised between the roles of lover and Shotover, and who continued to prize the Life Force: "Please don't go to Milano, Molly. It will be my spiritual child, at least" (*Tompkins*, p. 161). Molly was determined, however, and when she returned after the abortion she sensed in Shaw's eyes and face an older man. She reports a gentle "Molly, Molly," from him, and a feeling of guilt as though she had committed murder. Although she sentimentalizes the incident, it appears to have coalesced with the abortion of their romance. Shaw continued to come daily to her island, where he held her hand in the garden, but Eden had lost its luster. Neither found much to say.

Since Molly had no incentive to retreat to Paris that summer, there is no current correspondence from Shaw to reflect his views against hers. But his letters of the next November through May tell a somewhat different story. They indicate that he found Molly's infatuation toward him and her peevishness about Charlotte far more aggressive and difficult to handle than she realized, and that, as a consequence, he felt compelled to tear himself away from her. In November he writes an account of the holiday which wryly diagnoses the situation:

> I had really a dreadful time in Stresa. I had to preserve the dignity of Mrs Shaw and Mr Tompkins (to say nothing of my own before all the world) as well as the character of Mrs Tompkins, who was determined to throw it away and lead me captive. Mrs Shaw, though resolutely kind, was naturally uneasy; Mr Tompkins was angelic but a helpless prisoner on an island; Mrs Tompkins was possessed by seventy and seven devils in addition to being the very devil herself. But for Troubetskoy and Coates I should have bolted after the first week of storms.
>
> I wonder does she ever feel any remorse. [*Letters*, p. 122]

In her rendition, Molly introduces this passage with "Of our summer, he laughed"; and comments immediately afterwards, "I felt no remorse" (*Tompkins*, pp. 163–64). She seems determined to gloss over Shaw's discomfort. Although laughter and play were an implicit element behind much Shavian correspondence and were especially strong in his love letters, the "dreadful time" he alludes to here is supported by his résumé of strained relationships.

The following January, Shaw gave evidence both of his continuing affection and of Molly's disconcerting anger at being thwarted in hers. From Cliveden, Lady Astor's country house, he wrote, "I would have you know that the Isolino and its chatelaine are not the only pebbles on the beach." But Molly was a very special pebble. He describes her as an "American lady who loved me, and then gave me a shock by looking at me with hatred in her eyes and speaking with it in her voice. . . ."

> That wicked woman is giving me absent treatments of hatred. Perhaps she has made a wax figure of me and is sticking pins into it, like Sister Helen. Only by casting her out utterly can I escape the spell; and I find that somehow I cannot do that. The old tenderness gives the witch her grip; and I languish and must presently die of her hatred. Unless she relents and sends a message of love I am a lost man, though a most innocent one. Innocent or not, her adoration was an indispensable Vitamin in my bread of life; and if I perish my blood will be upon her head. . . . you must relieve my uneasy soul by a sign of life. [*Letters*, p. 123]

This whimsical call for continued correspondence indicates that Molly's scenes had been more acrid than she reports and that Shaw, still pained and longing for the infusion of life her love had given him, sought a patching up.

Molly's immediate response was not a letter but a scenario for a play, hastily scribbled on the back of Shaw's thin sheet. Alone on the island in winter, she had once again become "a bundle of nerves." Not only had Shaw's visit ended with stress, but later that fall Laurence had taken a fancy to a young, shapely American guest, and in a fit of jealousy Molly had sent the girl packing. Now the tedium, this incident, and the past summer boiled into her first and only sustained literary effort besides her later reminiscences: she purged her tension and anger in a drama, including Laurence, the girl, and the Shaws as characters and indulging herself spectacularly as the heroine-wife who, Tosca-like, leaps from a parapet to drown in the lake. Hence she found an answer both to her own frustrations and to Shaw's repeated urgings that she immerse herself in work. This was literally her longest response to "B." Ever the unsentimental critic, Shaw praised her dialogue and characterization but promptly revised the last act, providing a comic ending: "You may write Italian opera and romantic tragedy or you may write studies of modern life; but you must not attempt to combine the two. A mixture of Tosca and Trovatore with Tchekoff is ridiculous: false beauty and bitter truth flourish apart but not together" (*Letters*, p. 125).

This critique epitomizes the disparity between Shaw and Molly, and it boded his forthcoming detachment from her. In pouring her emotions into her play, she took to an idiom which expressed her temperament: the impulsiveness, fire, and passion of Italian opera befitted her. Such qualities were thrills at the heart of the "life" she sought in Italy. By contrast, Shaw's temperament led him to face bitter truths, which, like Chekhov, he accommodated with a smile or a laugh. His revision of her play was an assertion of this temperament: it was a laugh at her Tosca— at her values, her passionate ideals—on behalf of realities as he saw them. Predictably, Molly was furious at his alteration of the play but then, having purged her emotions, she rapidly forgot it, hardly turning a hair when Laurence "lost" the manuscript.[11]

That spring their temperamental disparity came into even sharper focus. Shaw sent her a copy of his recently published *Intelligent Woman's Guide*, a work which had cost him years of labor. Molly found it boring, and told him so. Her indifference sparked an eloquent response at the end of May. Shaw starts his letter with deceptive off-handedness, briefly advising her that she can trade in her inscribed copy of the *Guide* to a bookseller and come away with a clean copy, plus thirty guineas. Then he takes off from irritation to a despairing, theatrical appraisal of her.

The Shavian Higgins is in a dressing room; the Shavian lover holds his heart in the wings. Front and center is Shaw as Shotover, surrounded by lurid mythical shades, bewailing the spiritual corruption of one of his last dreams:

> Henry [Molly's brother-in-law] is right as to the island. It is a place to spend six weeks a year in, but not a place to live in. You have no business there—no roots in it. The life you are leading is horribly wicked. . . . you are a predestinate damned soul, a Vamp fiend, neither doing justice, loving mercy, nor walking humbly with your God. You will prowl round that lake, making men's wives miserable, tormenting yourself whenever their glances wander from you for a moment, until the lake water changes to fire and brimstone and rises up and scorches you into nothingness.
>
> Lawrence works and fences; Troubetskoy sculpts; Albert and Cecil work like negroes . . . but *you*—what do you do? what will become of you? how will you face old age: With a "lifted" face, with grease paints and an iceball and rouge, with peroxided hair, an old hag desperately pretending to be a young witch. Oh Molly, Molly, Molly, Molly. I must not think about you; for I cannot save you; I have done my best and only made matters worse.
>
> Can you not learn how to live in the world: You are not a thing evil in itself; and it is impossible to believe that you *must* go to the devil by natural necessity, though my experience tells me that you will. For Mephistopheles whispers to me as he did to Faust "She is not the first." Before you were born I have had to do with sirens as seductive as you. . . . And yet you thought that when you had secured your Ogygia and lured me to its shores you could play Calypso to my Odysseus and make a hog of me. Aren't you glad you didn't succeed: After all, you have some brains in your upper half. This erotic-romantic attitude to life doesn't make you happy.
>
> If only you had a sense of humor! You could write plays if you had.
> I have no use for a woman who can't laugh at herself.
> Your spiritual values are all wrong. [*Letters*, pp. 127–28]

For sheer drama, emotion, and its withering characterization of a fallen woman, this is one of Shaw's most striking letters. His joining of the Calypso and Circe myths near the end drives home an apt personal point: like Odysseus with Calypso he had remained faithful to his Penelope; like Odysseus with Circe he had foiled the siren's attempt to turn him into a hog. Not surprisingly, he did not show up at Lake Maggiore the next summer, and Molly innocently wrote in late August to ask if he were angry with her. His curt reply came from Cap d'Antibes, a fashionable resort near Nice:

> For seven weeks, I have been hiding within a day's ride of your Renaud [sic]. I shall have left when this reaches you.
> I enclose a press cutting to make you jealous.

I am not in the least angry: why should I be? But you should not drive me away to horrible hell-paradises like the Riviera by refusing to behave yourself tactfully.

In this place when you are not bathing or driving over the mountains you are stark mad with irritable despair. . . .

All your fault. [*Letters*, pp. 129–30]

Two weeks later he sent one of his small "compliments" cards from Geneva, stating merely, "Starting for home tonight after a fortnight of the League of Nations" (*Tompkins*, p. 171).

Despite the brevity of these notes, their plaintiveness and pettishness reveal how much Shaw was still enthralled. When he claims that Molly drove him to the Riviera because of her tactlessness, he indicates clearly where he would rather be and throws the blame for their separation onto her. In confessing to hiding within a day's ride of her, he admits to playing a game of so-near-and-yet-so-far. But he finds himself the game's greatest victim, driven mad with irritable despair at being so temptingly nearby. Key words, emotions, and subjects—*hiding, jealous, angry, hell-paradise, stark, mad, despair, your fault*—indicate that he is going through acute withdrawal symptoms. Against these is a subtext expressing a compulsion: *within a day's ride, drive, driving over the mountains.* Molly was so close, so accessible: Shaw appears to have had an almost visceral urge to drive, drive, drive to her, but prudence told him he must not; so, mad and despairing, he did not. Rather, he put a lid on his compulsion and avoided the chance of a meeting by sending each note only when he was leaving the vicinity. In contrast to his vehement Shotover-like excoriation of Molly the previous May, these notes reflect a depleted humor: their brevity, their hide-and-seek twist, the desire to make the woman jealous, to tantalize, to complain, to blame—"All your fault"— and the superfluity of the card from Geneva, except to tease, all express the childlike impulses of a discountenanced lover.

What distinguished this lover was the extent to which his discomfort was of his own making. His cursing of Cap d'Antibes as a hell-paradise points less to the environment than to his own conflicting emotions and state of mind. After all, much like Lake Maggiore the Riviera offered him a luxury resort, ample sunshine, swimming, drives in the hills, and even old acquaintances: Troubetskoy came to have Shaw model further, and Shaw visited Frank Harris, who had a villa nearby in Nice. Whence, then, his petulance? The most singular missing ingredient in this paradise was Molly. Ironically, in Harris he had an uncomfortable reminder of his role with her, without the compensation of her presence. Charlotte refused to see the infamous author of *My Life and Loves*. She had been scandalized by the book, and had burned a copy page by page. In response to a luncheon invitation from him, Shaw wrote that he would come but that Harris was off Charlotte's visiting list: "Il faut souffrir pour etre Casanova. For a Victorian lady she has given her proofs of Liberalism and even of intransigence by marrying ME. . . . But Frank Casanova she will not entertain on any terms."[12] The personal barb in this association was the lingering touch of Bernard Casanova in himself, the awkwardness it had caused with Charlotte, and the quantum of suffering the present chapter of his own life and loves was bringing him. His amorous urges had at least in part moved him to this paradise, then had helped make a hell of it by conflicting with his conscience. And it could well be that these urges influenced the subsequent direction of his holiday. The trip from Nice to Geneva skirts Italy; Geneva, like Cap d'Antibes, is less than a day's drive from Lake Maggiore. Apparently magnetized and resisting at the same time, torn between his id and his superego, Odysseus traveled in an arc around Calypso's island.

Within two months of his unhappy holiday Shaw started to write *The Apple Cart*, his first play after a five-year hiatus. He composed it rapidly between 5 November and 29 December, and on 2 February he explained his ostensible motive to Molly:

> When that endless book was finished (the one you took as a personal insult) I thought I was finished; but when Barry Jackson announced a festival of my plays at Malvern in August next, with nothing newer than Joan and Methuselah and Heartbreak House, I erupted like a volcano and simply hurled out a new play, inspiringly entitled The Apple Cart. [*Letters*, p. 131]

Further inspiring Shaw was the play's subject matter: "it is all about politics except for twenty minutes in the middle between a He Man and a She Woman of my patent brand." Having been so recently immersed in the politics of *The Intelligent Woman's Guide*, he now had an opportunity to vent some of its ideas in a genre congenial to him; and for dramatic relief, personal fun, and notoriety he exploited his famous affair with Stella Campbell, providing the Interlude in which King Magnus diverts himself with his mistress Orinthia.

Shaw quickly acknowledged the Stella parallel. No one has noticed, however, that beneath his obvious motives his current affair with Molly gave him several more. For years his relations with Stella had been tepid at best. At exactly the time Molly entered his life, his letters to his former love dropped off radically: their *Correspondence* shows just one in 1923, another in 1924, then none for three-and-a-half years. Only after he had complained to Molly about his "dreadful time" at Lake Maggiore in the summer of 1927 did he briefly reopen correspondence with his old flame, writing her four letters in two months. But these are emotionally low-keyed, dealing largely with professional matters, the most notable being one in which he literally advises her to act her age: "get into the routine of the theatre as leading Old Woman, and break with your starry past."[13] In contrast was his continuing emotional involvement with his youthful, fresher flame during 1928—his longing for her, trying to patch things up, revising her play, reviling her, despairing of her and of the recent holiday on which he had found himself "stark mad" without her. On 5 November he began his new play. Three days later he sent her a card along with an enclosure: reflecting his own discomfort, it refers to her driving an Italian out of his mind.[14] On 27 November he wrote Cecil Lewis that he had just received a letter from her, and repeated the image he had thrown at her six months before: apparently Calypso was becoming tired of Ogygia.[15]

Thus when Shaw turned to his play and its Interlude, he was still wrestling with his feelings for Molly, while Stella was not only old hat but an Old Woman. This raises the distinct possibility that his current affair not only contributed to his taking up his dramatist's pen once again, but also led to his including something of Molly in his play's single romantic scene. He had tried to exorcise the enchantress of Lake Maggiore in May by dismissing her as a vamp fiend, but his discomfort at Cap d'Antibes had proven that he was still under her spell. Now the need for another play offered him a new opportunity.

The strongest evidence that Shaw's current romance was a lively factor in his creation of the Interlude lies in the scene itself. Stella was enraged by it. She declared vehemently that its portrayal of their relationship was not only libellous but vulgar and untruthful.[16] She was largely correct. The scene presents the male (presumably Shaw/Magnus) as wise and restrained, a clever and busy monarch for whom the female (presumably Stella/Orinthia) is merely a fascinating diversion from politics and marriage. The idle, self-indulgent female is the aggressor, vainly and ambitiously desiring that the king divorce his wife and make her queen. Larkish as this may be, it inverts Shaw's affair with Stella. Despite his better judgment, Shaw had fallen head over heels for her. Madly and foolishly infatuated, dubbed "Joey" the clown by his loved one, he was largely the aggressor and had to swallow his thwarted romance when she fled him and married. Although Stella was affectionate and responsive, she had been relatively discreet. Little wonder, then, that she fumed at the Interlude's apparent misrepresentation.

What Stella could not know was that the scene most strongly echoes a Shavian affair other than hers. Like Orinthia, Molly was more the idle, self-indulgent aggressor; like Orinthia, she chafed against the great man's marriage and had to swallow her thwarted impulses when he prudently asserted his connubial bond. Many details of the scene apply more to Molly than to Stella. Closer to her case are Orinthia's scorn of politics, which elicits Magnus's comment that her interests are limited to "always thinking of some man or other," and Orinthia's blunt contempt for Magnus's wife, whose dignity and importance he defends: "she is a part of my workaday self. You belong to fairyland." The name of Orinthia's son, Basil, can be taken as a mutation of Beo, the nickname of Stella's son, but it is far closer to that of one of Molly's Italian admirers, Basile; and Magnus's comment, "If I am a pig, a pigsty is the proper place for me," echoes Shaw's recent reference to Molly as Calypso/Circe. To Orinthia's complaint that she is only a diversion for him, Magnus responds much as Shaw had responded to Molly: "Keeping our distance is the whole secret of good manners; and without good manners human society is intolerable and impossible." In short, the wise, restrained Magnus is less Stella's passionate, often foolish "Joey" than Molly's discreet "B.," and the aggressive, thwarted Orinthia is less Stella than Molly. Both affairs and their personalities are played off against each other, but the Interlude tilts decisively towards the later one.

Whether or not Shaw consciously wrote the scene as an exorcism, it worked that way. Responding to Molly a month after completing the play, he casts a telling light on the heat of their former relationship and its current attenuation:

> You desire to know whether I am Thru with you. At my age one is thru with everybody, and can only beg for a little charitable tolerance from young persons. I hoarded my bodily possessions so penuriously that even at seventy I had some left; but that remnant was stolen from me on the road to Baveno and on other roads to paradise through the same district. Now they are all dusty highways on which I am safe because nobody can rob a beggar. Nothing is left except my eternal genius. [*Letters*, p. 131]

Shaw's hyperbole about age estranging him from life and youth was contradicted by his current plans. He and Charlotte were contemplating a holiday with the Gene Tunneys on Brioni, an island in the Adriatic. And once again the direction of his thoughts stretched coincidence. At that time the island was Italian territory.[17] It lies due south of Trieste, just off the Istrian Peninsula, east southeast of Lake Maggiore. To travel there, he would pass directly by the lake.

Shaw had met the Tunneys in December when, in response to Gene's declared admiration for him, he and Charlotte invited them for luncheon at Adelphi Terrace. During the conversation the prizefighter and his wife extolled Brioni's sunshine, with the result that when they returned to the island the following April they were surprised to find the Shaws staying at the same hotel. During a month on Brioni the two couples developed an enduring friendship. Tunney began the holiday by gently pulling Shaw's leg, sending him a case of cordials under the guise of a gift of fine wine from an Italian admirer; Shaw returned the joke by sampling local wine which Tunney had praised, asserting that he always did so with the wine he and his wife served guests. Charlotte basked in the congenial atmosphere, and the Tunneys felt a special affection for her. In contrast to Molly's description of a stiff, priggish, stand-offish figure in black, Tunney observed her frequent laughter and their good times together. His lively conversations with Shaw ranged from ancient Egyptian wrestling to Madame Blavatsky's Theosophy.[18] Charlotte had ample reason to laugh: she could retire by herself with an easy spirit, knowing that G.B.S. was in attentive hands, other than Molly's. To Blanche Patch she wrote: "We are both very well and getting a real rest. The Island is dull, but that is good for us! . . . Mr. Tunney is a most wonderful help. He takes Mr. Shaw off to the polo ground, or the golf course, or sailing, or something, and so keeps him from writing, which is splendid."[19]

The dullness which was Charlotte's pleasure proved to be poison for Shaw. Once again, as at Cap d'Antibes, the most singular ingredient missing was Molly, and he was similarly frustrated: "There is nobody here that we know except Gene Tunney. A settled melancholy, peculiar to the place perhaps, devours us."[20] Richard Strauss arrived and provided him with additional companionship, but he found himself escaping into miscellaneous writing, and he complained repeatedly about the weather: Brioni's icy wind reflected his mood. Finally he fled the dullness and the wind, traveling down the Yugoslav coast to Dubrovnik and its environs. There he wrote an appreciative letter about the area for the sake of reporters and a statement on world peace and international copyright,[21] but his private discontent went with him: "I have just returned from a stupendous climb (in a car) over the mountains to Cettinje, and am tired and ill humoured. I am treated here like a King: nothing can be more exhausting."[22]

Ironically, Shaw attained a fair control of conversational Italian only when his need for it was ending. Following his first trips to Italy in the 1890s, he had apologized to readers of his theater reviews about his inability to learn languages, with one professional exception: as a music critic he could command operatic Italian, but its subject matter—making love, dueling, swallowing poison, and praying—was too specialized for modern conversation.[23] By the time he sailed from Istria on his way home via Venice, however, he had spent five of his last thirty-four months on Italian soil, and at the captain's table he was sufficiently at ease with the language to inform an Italian colonel that the secret of Tunney's success was his fear of being hit on the head.[24]

In Venice the Shaws stayed at the Hotel Royal Danieli, a luxurious establishment next to the Doges' Palace, then raced right by Molly's abode on the Paris Express. From a safe distance—where he could be hit on neither head nor heart—he wrote her the next August: "I was in Italy & Jugo Slavia from the middle of April to the middle of June, and saw the isola from the train window both going and coming. . . . I was 73 last month. An awful old man" (*Letters*, p. 134).

In speeding by Lake Maggiore, traveling elsewhere and declaring himself awfully old, Shaw concluded a series of withdrawals from Molly which had taken almost two years. Although he returned to Venice for three weeks in April 1931, the visit was little more than a concluding leg of his trip to the Holy Land and he found that the city, like Molly, had lost its magnetism. He wrote her later:

> I have visited Venice three times. The third time it *bored* me!!! Get into a motor boat and go to Torcello and Chioggia. Dont attempt to look at the historical ceiling pictures in the Ducal Palace: there are so many that there had better be none at all. In the Scuola di S. Lucca there are just enough; but the lighting is bad. [*Letters*, p. 174]

His advice to seek out nearby islands echoes his impulse, five years before, to sail to Molly's isola; but now Italy itself had become an echo, and this was to be his last stay there.

Meanwhile, Molly plunged into the Italian scene. Her life traversed glamor and trauma, affluence and poverty, decadent leisure and hard work at a new profession, all spiced by affairs with aristocratic admirers. In the fall of 1928 she took an apartment in the Palazzo Orsini in Rome. Party followed party in a frantic profusion of elegance and aristocratic friendships, so much so that by early the next spring La Dolce Vita was almost too much for her. Fatigued and bored (and in retrospect recalling Shaw's warning about her "horribly wicked" life), she swallowed an overdose of veronal pills. Shaw's response to her survival was a postcard: "You really *are* a duffer—couldnt even poison yourself properly!" What she needed, he advised, was a job in a factory; what Laurence needed was a divorce and an efficient cook-housekeeper-wife (*Letters*, p. 133).

For the present Laurence took only a version of the advice about a job, setting up a painting studio for her on their island. This therapy became a form of salvation. Consistent with Shaw's repeated admonitions that she find an occupation, Molly realized more happiness in her painting than in her past five years of nebulous living. It was well that she did, because she and Laurence lost the source of their luxurious existence in the stock market crash of 1929, leaving them no choice but to close up the isola in 1930 and leave it at last early in 1931. While the fruits of luxury had led to her suicide attempt, the trials of poverty brought forth Molly's strengths. To earn a living she turned from art as a hobby to art as a profession, with Shaw rigorously criticizing her efforts

FIG. 4 Molly's superego (center) and id (in the painting, right): the artist at her London exhibition; the enchantress on her island. From *Shaw and Molly Tompkins*, p.176.

along the way. In July 1931 she asked if she might accompany him on his trip to Russia. Orinthia on a political jaunt? Molly and *Stalin*? He quickly refused. That November she gave him no warning before she visited London for an exhibition of her works (Fig. 4). He blanched: "How terrifying! What on earth am I to do with you? . . . I must know all about it before I can break the devastating news to Charlotte and arrange something." Nonetheless, Molly observed, "I found him his old self, if anything more dear and charming than ever"; and he not only approved of her paintings but bought one—notably, of the "Road to Baveno" along which they had romanced many a night five years before (*Tompkins*, pp. 213–21).

Molly's awakening to Shavian values of work and art had its counterpart in his continuing responsiveness to the sensual life she represented. Each had moved the other, if ever so slightly, toward fuller self-awareness. The afterglow of romance which prompted Shaw to buy her painting of the Baveno Road may partly account for his increased attention to sexual matters in a number of his writings following *The Apple Cart*. In the spring of 1930 Frank Harris queried him about his sex life.

One wonders whether at the age of seventy-three Shaw would have approached the subject with such relish and detail had he not so recently experienced an affair which had recapitulated much of his sexual biography. Especially intriguing is his declaration, "I was not impotent; I was not sterile . . . I never associated sexual intercourse with delinquency. I associated it always with delight . . . I preferred women who knew what they were doing."[25] Molly's pregnancy towards the end of their summer together in 1927 would be one of the very few possible corroborations of his assertion that he was not sterile. Whatever that case, he had experienced warm delight with her, and she thoroughly knew what she was doing.

Shaw's frankness with Harris and a flicker of his relationship with Molly carried over into his next play. For him, *Too True to be Good* (1931) is unusually graphic about sexual matters. When he despaired over Molly's "erotic-romantic attitude to life" in 1928 he had observed, "After all, you have some brains in your upper half," intimating the very different disposition of her lower half. *Too True* highlights this strain. In almost D. H. Lawrence fashion, its leading man analyzes an erotic-romantic woman with whom he was once "madly in love." Although she was not his intellectual equal,

> there was an extraordinary sympathy between our lower centres . . . Our lower centres act: they act with terrible power that sometimes destroys us; but they dont talk. Speech belongs to the higher centres. . . . But the lower centres are there all the time: a sort of guilty secret with every one of us. . . . That is what makes Sweetie almost superhuman. Her lower centres speak. [*B.H.* 6, 474–78.]

Two years later another Shavian protagonist answers the speaking lower centers of a woman in *Village Wooing*: "You are the dupe of thoughtless words like sensuality, sensuousness, and all the rest of the twaddle of the Materialists. I am not a Materialist: I am a poet . . ." This Shavian poet seeks love as a "magic moment . . . and when the moment comes, the world of the senses will vanish" (*B.H.* 6, 568).

During this time Shaw still wrote Molly of his affection for her—"angels will always love you, including . . . G.B.S."—but increasingly his letters stressed his age and urged that she detach her affection from him: "Turn from the setting to the rising sun / Love bettering men, and let the worsening die / For I, dear Mary, am no longer I"; "It is impossible for anyone to love me. And you?"; "You must not decentralize yourself, fixation or no fixation" (*Letters*, pp. 140, 141, 166, 167).

Molly continued to live in Italy, now combining work with romantic liaisons, but she found its old ambiance fading. In 1935 Shaw told her that he was licensing no more of his plays there until after the war. The next year Laurence divorced her. When clouds of war loomed in 1941 she deposited Shaw's letters in a chest, took leave of old friends, and departed for America.

The embers between Shaw and Molly burned low until October 1945. Then, suddenly, there was a flare, one arresting not only in itself but also for the light it throws on their past relationship. Shaw provided a spark the year before in noting his wife's death and then observing significantly, "We can write more freely now that Charlotte can never read our letters," to which he added in the margin, as if for emphasis: "I could never bring myself to write a line that could hurt her; but now I can write *anything*." The old barrier aside, Molly took him at his word. She made a proposition which nearly blew out the windows at Ayot. The ancient widower leaped to a response: "I have just received your letter, with its proposal to come across the ocean to live with me. The same idea has occurred to other women. Put it out of your very inconsiderate head at once and forever, as they have had to. No woman shall ever live with me again in that sense." His reputation, his retainers, the village, and Charlotte's memory would all be put out by the scandal: "Why have you not known all this without my having to tell you? You are no longer a young savage: you are a mature woman. . . . no more atomic bombs, please" (*Letters*, pp. 181, 184). Two days later, apparently fearing that the impulsive vamp might not wait for the mail, he dashed off a telegram bluntly forbidding her to come.[26]

Molly's rejoinder may be her only surviving letter to G.B.S. It reveals not only her verve but more than a little of her youthful passion towards him: "What a monstrous way to misconstrue my letter. Come and live with you indeed! Do you think I would give up the serenity of my independence to live with anybody on earth—and be responsible to them for my time and thoughts—even you? Hell no!" She claims that she had thought of little more than a month's visit:

> It would have given you pleasure and satisfaction to have me with you as I am now. It would have been an infinite pleasure to see you and talk to you now that I could talk without being dazed by the violence of my desire for you. . . . One thing you have never understood is that you are two B Shaws to me. It is exciting to know the Great Man, and bray about it a little. . . . Anyway I have far less interest in him than I have in the B. Shaw that gave my body and my mind and my heart peace when I lay by the side of a river or a lake, with him in Italy, or walked the Baveno Road with him. I don't want either now. The Great Man or my beloved of the Baveno Road. I wanted a short visit with somebody I could be as free as air with. . . . Somebody that you loved and who in spite of themselves loved you. And with the solid background of that love behind you (and

me) there would be no awkward snags because one or the other of us wanted (or thought they did) something the other didn't have to give. I don't want the Baveno Road in fact again. I will have it always deep and sweet in my heart.[27]

Whether Shaw misconstrued her or not, this letter zestfully underscores the possibility that his romance with Molly had climaxed more than platonically at Lake Maggiore. Her admission to having been dazed by the violence of her desire for him illuminates a plethora of amorous details in his correspondence, including his early references to her love for him, her jealousy in suspecting him to be a Don Juan, her departure for Italy when he seemed cool, his observation of her desire to consummate their romance, her skittishness at the start of the first summer at the lake and his admonition that she come clothed and in her right mind, his complaint after the second summer that she had been determined to throw away her character and lead him captive, his likening her to Calypso, and his advice—as late as 1935—that she rid herself of her Shaw fixation. The fact that he had satisfied her violent desire for a blissful spell emerges in "the B. Shaw that gave my body and my mind and my heart peace when I lay by the side of a river or a lake, with him in Italy, or walked the Baveno Road with him." This parallels and forwards the sexual implications of the languid scene in her reminiscences. Coming from a woman for whom love involved a strong sexual component, her separate clause, "with him in Italy" (introduced by "lay," followed by "my beloved"), and her reference to "the solid background of that love," imply more than platonic dallying. Her supposition regarding "something the other didn't have to give" is in a subjunctive mood between "the solid background" and "I don't want the Baveno Road in fact again." As such, it indicates that she would not expect the venerable Shaw to be the sort of lover that he had been in the past.

Molly's proposal and Shaw's vehement negative reflect their old disparity. In his emotional condemnation of her after his summers at the lake he had seemingly contradicted himself, declaring on the one hand that she had not made a hog of him, yet admitting on the other that she had stolen his "bodily possessions" when they were alone and romancing. From his point of view, however, there was no contradiction: one might well dally with a siren so long as such delights were recreation and not an occupation. Alone with Molly beneath the Italian sun and stars he could philander as far as his instincts and the holiday carried him, but he would not throw over everything else to become passion's swinish slave. Once again, Molly's amorous values reflected her deplorable lack of perspective. Although their paths had crossed delightfully, the goals of his life and hers were far apart. Yet he continued to write, to admonish, to advise.

Echoes of Shaw's Italian connection reverberated into his last days. In 1948 he wrote to Molly in Rome, where she was staying with Peter's family, and in January 1949 he sent her a photograph of himself, cane in hand, peering through the gate at "Shaw's Corner." On the back is one of his last pieces of doggerel:

> The Old Man at his gate
> As he was in fortyeight
> And still is at ninety three
> Awaiting news of thee
> Molly Bawn
>
> [*Letters*, pp. 190–91]

Thus even in his ninety-third year Shaw found himself thinking of Molly and seeking to hear from her much as he had time and again in the past twenty-seven years. His persistence over so long a period attests to a need and care for her far exceeding transitory infatuation: she offered his old age a romantic spark, an infusion of youth and love. To the extent that this spark brought him for two long holidays to Lake Maggiore, drew him to the vicinity in the two succeeding years, gave sexual zest to several of his late plays, and attracted him for the rest of his life, it punctuated his travels in a unique way.

Notes

1. *Bernard Shaw and Mrs. Patrick Campbell: Their Correspondence*, ed. Alan Dent (London: Gollancz, 1952), p. 105.

2. The most recent and substantial treatments of Shaw and fascism are those of Allan Chappelow, *Shaw—"The Chucker-Out": A Biographical Exposition and Critique* (New York: AMS Press, 1969), pp. 162–204; and Warren S. Smith, *Bishop of Everywhere: Bernard Shaw and the Life Force* (University Park: Pennsylvania State Univ. Press, 1982), pp. 138–49.

3. Both published in New York by Clarkson N. Potter. Hereafter these volumes will be cited as *Letters* and *Tompkins*.

4. 21 May 1898. *Our Theatres in the Nineties* (London: Constable, 1931), III, 405.

5. *Tompkins*, p. 99. In the *Letters*, Shaw's account of this event is different in time and circumstance. On 25 June 1925 he enquires about "one Mollie Little, who alleges that she kept house for you, and on that score asks me with extraordinary persistence for sums of money in three figures, undaunted by the dead silence into which her letters fall" (p. 85).

6. Quoted in Janet Dunbar, *Mrs. G.B.S.: A Portrait* (New York: Harper & Row, 1963), p. 276.

7. See Archibald Henderson, *Bernard Shaw: Playboy and Prophet* (New York: Appleton, 1932), pp. 829–31; *Shaw: The Critical Heritage*, ed. T. F. Evans (London: Routledge & Kegan Paul, 1976), pp. 279–84.

8. MS. letter to Lewis, 20 March 1925; Humanities Research Center, University of Texas at Austin.

9. 4 and 9 November 1931; in the author's collection.

10. See *The Genius of Shaw: A Symposium*, ed. Michael Holroyd (New York: Holt, Rinehart, 1979), pp. 59, 200; *Bernard Shaw: Collected Letters 1898–1910*, ed. Dan H. Laurence (New York: Dodd, Mead, 1972), p. 227.

11. Hence Molly's first-draft scenario is all that survives. It runs as follows: In the prologue a father and mother with a young child are at war because he is neglecting both his family and his occupation as a writer to pursue a young woman who drains all of his energies. His wife walks out with a lover of her own, and the father, though maimed by his own actions, is greatly relieved. In Act I the mother is remarried. Her daughter, now grown, learns that her stepfather is not her natural parent. Enraged and tearful, she causes such a disruption between her mother and stepfather that they separate, and she goes off, determined to locate her father. In Act II she finds him in Florence, where he is living with a mistress and is successfully engaged in his career as a writer, under a pseudonym. She takes him away, causing misery for everyone. In Act III the father and daughter are living together unhappily. There is an unsuccessful attempt to reconcile him with his former wife, whereupon the daughter leaves and marries. Finally the father returns to his work, the mother returns to her second husband, and the girl is blissful with the impression that she has taken care of everything (!). (MS. in the author's collection.)

Molly names the wife's lover, and second husband, Achilles (not "B."). Quite possibly this reflects back to her affair with an Italian of the same name in 1925 (*Letters*, pp. 82–83). Obviously the wife's melodramatic leap off a parapet into Lake Maggiore was a later thought.

12. *The Playwright and the Pirate: Bernard Shaw and Frank Harris: A Correspondence*, ed. Stanley Weintraub (University Park: Pennsylvania State Univ. Press, 1982), pp. 213–14.

13. *Shaw-Campbell Correspondence*, p. 264.

14. In the author's collection.

15. MS. letter; Humanities Research Center, University of Texas at Austin.

16. *Shaw-Campbell Correspondence*, pp. 289–90.

17. Until 1920 Istria belonged to Austria, at which time the Treaty of Rapallo assigned it to Italy. After World War II all of the area except that immediately around Trieste was acquired by Yugoslavia.

18. See Gene Tunney, "G.B. Shaw's Letters to Gene Tunney," *Colliers*, 23 June 1951, p. 17; Dunbar, pp. 277–78; Archibald Henderson, *George Bernard Shaw: Man of the Century* (New York: Appleton, 1956), p. 101.

19. Quoted in Blanche Patch, *Thirty Years with G.B.S.* (New York: Dodd, Mead, 1951), p. 186.

20. Ibid., p. 186.

21. See J. F. Lupis-Vukic, "Shaw's 1929 Program for Easing World Tensions—and How It Originated," *ShawB*, 2, No. 4 (January 1958), 1–4.

22. *Shaw-Campbell Correspondence*, p. 283.

23. 22 June 1895. *Our Theatres in the Nineties*, I, 165.

24. Tunney, p. 17.

25. *Shaw-Harris Correspondence*, p. 234. Shaw slightly bowdlerized this famous letter for publication in Harris's *Bernard Shaw* (New York: Simon and Schuster, 1931), pp. 241–45, and in *Sixteen Self Sketches* (London: Constable, 1949), pp. 113–15.

26. In the author's collection. *Shaw and Molly Tompkins* skips over this incident entirely.

27. Quoted in Margot Peters, *Bernard Shaw and the Actresses*, pp. 408–9.

Damir Kalogjera

A POLITICAL GAME: SHAW IN YUGOSLAVIA

In May 1929 the Shaws made a holiday visit to Yugoslavia, arriving in Dubrovnik by boat from the island of Brioni off Istria (at that time under Italian rule). They travelled to Montenegro and its capital, Cetinje, via Boka Kotorska, returned to Dubrovnik, and then went to Split, where they spent three days, and left by boat for Venice on 26 May 1929. This brief visit was made by the press into a considerable cultural event with political overtones.

The most comprehensive report of the Shaws' stay in Yugoslavia has come to us from Ivan [John] F. Lupis-Vukić, one of the rare Yugoslav journalists who at that time spoke English.[1] He was present at the two-hour long press conference that Shaw held at the Imperial Hotel in Dubrovnik and later spent the three days in Split in the company of the Shaws. The entire Yugoslav press, from the national dailies to the provincial rags, reported Shaw's stay. Therefore Lupis-Vukić's report can be easily verified. Shaw's visit, besides being treated as an advertisement for the burgeoning tourist industry, was felt to be politically important. It was considered so important that, according to Lupis-Vukić, "the authorities were discreetly suggesting to journalists and to me in Split to 'press' Shaw into making statements favourable to the regime and to the present state of the Yugoslav frontiers" (1950, p. 819). Shaw, however, refused to meet the press in Split after his statements concerning the Trianon Peace Treaty—a sensitive topic for the Kingdom of Yugoslavia and its borders—were misquoted by a Zagreb journalist. Instead Shaw wrote his "Program for Easing World Tensions" in longhand and left it with Lupis-Vukić, adding jokingly that the journalist might sell it one day for good money. Lupis-Vukić translated the text but was asked by provincial authorities to submit it to them prior to publication. "Three of Shaw's points were stricken out by the censor. I did not want to publish Shaw's statement mutilated and kept the present text unpublished until after his death." Thus, for purely political reasons, Shaw's statement, which had been so eagerly sought, was not published in Serbo-Croatian until twenty-one years after it had been written and left with Lupis-Vukić. A present-day reader may wonder why the Royal Yugoslav Government was so sensitive to just another of Shaw's well-known excursions into making complex matters appear simple.

The Kingdom of the Serbs, Croats, and Slovenes was formed only eleven years before the Shaws' visit. It was confirmed in 1919 by the Treaty of Versailles, to which was later added (in 1920) the Treaty of Trianon regulating the country's western borders.[2] These and some other border lines were considered controversial both by Yugoslavia and her neighbors. In addition, a recent change in the system of government increased the authorities' sensitivity. On 6 January 1929, King Alexander, who until then had ruled as a constitutional monarch but who was disturbed by the centrifugal forces operating in this multinational state, assumed dictatorial powers to protect his threatened concept of centralized government. It was on this occasion that the state adopted its name, Yugoslavia. King Alexander's coup was a blow to democratic public opinion at home and abroad. To improve the new regime's image, a supportive statement from such a popular world figure appeared to the authorities as most necessary and welcome. They did not have to wait long to be given one.

At the press conference in Dubrovnik on 21 May 1929, after giving a summary overview of the history of the British Labour Party, claiming for himself a considerable role in its foundation, Shaw, in response to journalists' questions, offered some pronouncements on certain European regimes. According to Lupis-Vukić's notes, translated from the Serbo-Croation, Shaw said:

> The most important problem of the present time is that of freedom and democracy. The way this problem was envisaged by old-fashioned English liberals had neither a healthy nor a realistic basis. And this is why: life's necessities appear to be different from what the theoreticians of freedom imagine them to be. Thus the statesmanlike decisions taken by King Alexander in Yugoslavia and Mussolini in Italy, serving a definite and good aim, become comprehensible. The old-fashioned democrats consider the events in Italy and Yugoslavia to mark the end of all liberties. On the contrary, I can tell you, as an old socialist, that before freedom is achieved, good laws need to be created and it must be ensured that these laws are respected. As concerning the concept of autocracy, I must admit that it is a good one, but still there remains the question of what happens when the autocrat himself goes.

When asked to put forward some of his general political views, Shaw said, among other things:

The world slowly realizes that there cant be real freedom without a strong and large state. There are good reasons for me to be careful about my political statements. But I can tell you that the very moment freedom is achieved, people forget that a country must be ruled. If it had not been for the wisdom of King Alexander, you might have been forced to invite Austria back. Small states are easy to overcome. If you were to be divided into Serbia, Montenegro and Croatia there would easily be someone somewhere who would swallow you. I dont say who that would be.

The authorites could not have hoped for a better gift. Shaw seemed to have been talking their own language. Still, the gift was not without a fault. Putting King Alexander together with Mussolini was a left-handed compliment in the political climate of the country. Mussolini claimed Yugoslav lands and was far from being the toast of Yugoslav public opinion, except to some extremists. Thus it may have been only the then-underground opposition who enjoyed the episode.

In the meantime, English language newspapers reported Shaw's pronouncements under the headlines: "Shaw Upholds Dictatorship," "Shaw Again Praises 'Strong Man' Rule," "G.B.S. Review of Candidates."[3] Were his kind words for dictators and the strong state another expression of the disillusion with democratically elected government that had afflicted him since the Great War or was it merely that after the princely treatment that he obtained in Yugoslavia, he wanted to be nice to the government that was behind it?[4]

Whether the authorities got what they wanted with the statements supporting the king's coup remains doubtful, but concerning the borders they definitely obtained nothing. Regarding the Trianon Treaty, he seems to have remained adamant. In the "Program" he wrote, "The Treaty of Trianon should be kept in continual remembrance as a classic example of the Great British art of How Not to Do It." And when a Zagreb journalist from the *Novosti* newspaper apparently made up a story according to which Shaw said that he never stated anything concerning political borders, Shaw became angry and cancelled his press conference in Split (1950, p. 819).

Shaw did not refrain from asking sensitive political questions on his visit to the old principality, later kingdom, of Montenegro. In 1918 it had become a province of the Kingdom of Serbs, Croats, and Slovenes, its last king, Nicholas, having been exiled. On a visit to Cetinje, the capital, Shaw asked the mayor—who, incidentally, had been mayor during the reign of King Nicholas—what the attitude of the people towards the new state was, since in Britain, Montenegrins had always been considered as members of a separate nation. The journalist of the *Politika* newspaper who reported this episode noted, significantly, that Mayor Milošević had a prepared answer. He claimed that all Montenegrins had always stood for the integration of the Serbian peoples and they did not want any other state. When Shaw asked about the mood of the people after the events of 6 January, the mayor answered that everyone was delighted, with the reporter adding the word *allegedly* before "delighted."[5]

All Yugoslavs are aware of the beauty of their coast and have been accustomed to the idea that it is there for tourists to enjoy and for the national economy to profit. Journalists expected and reported the compliments that Shaw made about it, which he facetiously overdid a little (1958, p. 1). But the following from Shaw came most unexpectedly:

> You seem to be of the opinion that everything should be sacrificed to the catering industry for foreigners since other kinds of industry can hardly be created in these bare mountain regions. The same opinion was held in Italy until Mussolini started pushing foreigners away which may be the best thing to do. You have the case in France where old olive groves are cut down to raise chrysanthemums for the benefit of American and English ladies.

To hear this in an area that saw its future in tourist trade must have produced a shock. I don't remember seeing this reported in the newspapers, and the quotation comes from Lupis-Vukić's unpublished manuscript.

During his short stay in Split, Shaw managed to get involved in a raging local dispute. Ivan Meštrović, the most outstanding Yugoslav sculptor, about whose works Shaw expressed admiration,[6] had made a huge statue of Gregory, Bishop of Nin (10th century A.D.), that was placed in the middle of the Emperor Diocletian Palace built around A.D. 300. The statue had a certain symbolic value in that spot as, according to at least some historians, Bishop Gregory had defended the traditional liturgy held in the Old Church Slavonic language against the pressure for the Latin coming from Rome. In the course of time, Bishop Gregory became the symbol of the Slav's resistance to Romanization in this area. On aesthetic grounds, a group of local intellectuals and conservationists opposed the placing of the statue in the palace. Among these was Msgr. Frane Bulić, an important archaeologist who acted as Shaw's guide. Before meeting Bulić, Shaw had expressed his fear that he would be bored in the company of an antiquarian, but he developed a liking for this eighty-year-old scholar. They conversed in French and had a good time together. Msgr. Bulić won Shaw over to his side in the dispute concerning the location of the statue, and Shaw stated publicly that if there were no way of moving Gregory's statue from the palace, one should ask the Emperor Diocletian for help to move his entire palace to a different place and leave Gregory there. The conservationists were delighted, but Gregory remained in the palace for another twelve years (1950, p. 820).

The question of language and orthography was also touched upon in the conversations with the Yugoslavs. After repeating his well-worn opinion about the English not being sure what is correct in their language and about foreigners sometimes speaking more correct English than native speakers do, he turned to Serbo-Croatian. He grasped the simplicity of the Serbo-Croatian phonemic orthography, where roughly one letter stands for one sound, and commented that Serbo-Croatian–speaking children learn how to spell in a matter of nine days while English children need nine years for that and even then they can't spell. He added, however, that the language sounded like Esperanto to him and the letters (having presumably in mind the Cyrillic script used in the eastern parts of the country) appear like hieroglyphics.

Other topics discussed with the Yugoslav journalists reported in the press included International Copyright Convention; British politics, the coming parliamentary elections, the role of the House of Lords and the House of Commons; a critical comment on the university education and educators; freedom of speech, Speaker's Corner in Hyde Park and the tolerance of London policemen; his own pragmatic attitudes to philosophical questions; his reasons for travelling and for his coming to Yugoslavia; the riches of the Yugoslav soil; social drama and the role of playwrights and audiences; and, finally, a warning to watch carefully American visitors as they, allegedly, were ready to pocket an occasional valuable antique object or tear away a page of an old illuminated missal. After going through the press reports about this visit one occasionally feels something like a cultural gap appearing between the newspapermen and their interviewee. This gap results from an inability of the reporters to establish when Shaw was serious and when he was being facetious. But, after all, this seems not always easy to establish in some of his other pronouncements and writings as well.

The short visit that the Shaws paid to Yugoslavia in May 1929 had shown the Yugoslav press to be no different from that in other countries. In giving great importance to what G.B.S. had to say, it monitored and reported every serious, casual, and obviously flippant remark he made, paying each equal attention. Shaw, on the other hand, seems to have been ready to oblige. What makes his stay in Yugoslavia somewhat special is the keen interest in his visit that was shown by the authorities, who hoped to gain some international respectability through his statements at a delicate moment when their image was rather tarnished.

The memory of this visit has been kept alive for decades by occasional articles in the press recording its various details, especially Shaw's generous pronouncements on the beauty of the Adriatic coast and the Montenegrin mountains and about the people, with the facetious note left out. While the tourist industry still tries to get some international adver-

tising out of Shaw's visit more than a half-century ago,[7] the political
game around the visit seems to have been forgotten.

Notes

1. Lupis-Vukić published a short report about Shaw's visit together with the "Program
for Easing World Tensions," which Shaw wrote for the Split journalists, in *The Shaw Bulletin*, 4, January 1958. An article, "Povodom smrti G. B. Shawa," *Republika* (Zagreb: 1950),
XI–XII, 819–23, on the occasion of Shaw's death, and a manuscript report, probably
meant for a Zagreb newspaper, which I found among Lupis-Vukić's personal papers in the
National and University Library in Zagreb, both in Serbo-Croatian, contain further details
on the visit. Other sources for this article are Yugoslav newspapers *Novosti, Jutarnji list*, and
Obzor, published in Zagreb, and *Narodna svijest*, published in Dubrovnik. Some press reports about the visit, with Shaw's statements and comments, were retranslated and printed
in British and American newspapers (Dan H. Laurence, *Bernard Shaw: A Bibliography*, Oxford: Clarendon Press, 1983). References to Lupis-Vukić's quotations and to the "Program" are from *The Shaw Bulletin* unless otherwise noted.

2. The Treaty of Trianon supplements the Treaty of Versailles and was signed in 1920.
It concerned the lands previously belonging to the Hungarian Crown of St. Stephen
which, by this treaty, were divided among Czechoslovakia, Austria, Yugoslavia, and Rumania.

3. *New York American, New York Times*, and *Daily Chronicle*, 24 May 1929 (*A Bibliography*,
p. 725).

4. "I am treated here like a King: nothing can be more exhausting." Shaw to Mrs.
Campbell, Dubrovnik 20 May 1929. *Bernard Shaw and Mrs. Patrick Campbell, Their Correspondence*, ed. A. Dent (New York: Alfred A. Knopf, 1952), p. 325.

5. *Politika*, 21 May 1929, p. 2.

6. *Narodna svijest*, 6 June 1929, p.1.

7. A 1985 Yugoslav Air brochure advertising the Yugoslav "Riviera" continues the
practice of quoting Shaw: "Those who seek earthly paradise should come and see Dubrovnik."

G.B.S. IN THE HOLY LAND: TWO 1931 INTERVIEWS

Shaw's voyage to what was then Palestine, for which Britain was the League of Nations mandatory power, also included Egypt and Syria. Two brief but characteristic interviews with Shaw on the scene appeared on the front pages of the Jerusalem-published Palestine Bulletin. *The first, on 15 March 1931, was set, or proof-read, by an employee innocent of any knowledge of Shaw's most famous play, for a reference to it, here corrected, retitled it "Sir John." The next day, "Quidnunc," the paper's columnist, observed (p. 4), "Proof reading is never fool-proof and I noticed . . . yesterday that St. Joan had been rechristened Sir John. It may be that it was the masculine character of the Maid that allowed the error to creep in. Be that as it may, the play—I have seen it performed thirteen times—is the finest work that Shaw has written and it would be difficult to find any play written in English between Hamlet and St. Joan which can come anywhere near it. It has a peculiar interest for Palestine because it is in this country that the theory of Nationalism is being tried out and it is in St. Joan that the birth of Nationalism is brilliantly discussed. . . ."*

After Jerusalem, the Shaws went north to Galilee, and thence to Syria, whence a correspondent for La Syrie *(Syria was a French mandate) reported an interview with Shaw that was picked up, in translation, by the* Palestine Bulletin *on 25 March. It was from Damascus on St. Patrick's Day (as Shaw headed his letter to Sister Laurentia McLachlan) that he wrote what may be the best travel account of his life, largely about Jerusalem and Nazareth. By the time he finished it he was in Athens, his Mediteranean cruise taking him to Venice as well while en route home. The Shaw itinerary for 1931 was far from over, however. He would soon be packing for a trip to Russia with Lady Astor.*

Bernard Shaw in Palestine

Idol-breaker Visits the Holy City

Shaw is in Jerusalem.

There was a flutter of excitement last night when Mr. Bernard Shaw was seen dining at [the] King David [Hotel].

He dined with Mr. [Gene] Tunney the boxer and although this may on the face of it seem strange, it is really all in keeping with the Shaw tradition. One of his earliest "Novels of his nonage" was the life story of a boxer and more recently he wrote a remarkable article in the then Daily News on the subject of boxing which showed that in his seventieth year he had not lost his interest in pugilism.

Shaw has been spending some days in Egypt where the Wafdist press made much of his coming. It was not, however, known to many that Shaw the iconoclast would visit the Holy City.

Mr. Shaw, apart from the fact that every Jew in Palestine has read much of what he has written, also made his appearance in the Holy Land less than a year ago, when as a licensed jester, he wrote a delightful introduction to the Hebrew edition of "The Intelligent Woman's Guide to Socialism." This introduction was published in full in the Palestine Bulletin.

When [the] Habimah [Theatre] was in London, Shaw paid a visit to one of their performances. Speaking afterwards to a member of the Habimah, Shaw said that he would write a play for the Moscow-Tel Aviv Company. He also advised it to try and produce his "Back to Methuselah."

Shaw's "Saint Joan" is being revived in London this week when Sybil Thorndike will act the Maid. Shaw's latest play "The Apple Cart" was shown at Malvern in 1929. It has many times been rumoured that G.B.S. was writing or would write a play on the Prophet Muhammed, and who knows whether his visit to Palestine may not be for the purpose of collecting local colour for his next play. St. John Philby, when he was converted to Islam, declared that Shaw's praise of the prophet had done much to help in his conversion. In "Saint Joan" there is a satirical remark about the crusader who comes to Palestine to convert the infidel and is often himself converted in the Holy Land.

Bernard Shaw on the Promised Land

A Characteristic Interview

The correspondent of La Syrie reports that he had an interview with Mr. George Bernard Shaw prior to his sailing for Europe from Syria:

I handed my card to the cabin-boy and asked: "Will you be kind enough to give this to Mr. Shaw?"

"Mr. Shaw is not at all fond of receiving visitors," replied the boy.

"Give him my card at once," I urged.

A minute later I heard the key turn twice in the lock. Mr. Shaw had locked the door.

I didn't know what to do. Happily I met the guide and told him my troubles, begging him to intercede for me. Miraculously, G.B.S. listened to his prayer and I was given the much sought after interview. A few minutes later I saw the white-bearded patriarch come toward me.

"Do you speak English?" he asked.

"Yes."

"Then let's speak French."

We sat down in one of the corners and I asked him whether he had enjoyed his trip in the East.

"Yes," he replied. "I've been to Egypt, the Promised Land and your country."

"Do you mean the Holy Land?"

"No! the Promised Land. I reiterate: The country promised to the Jews and Arabs. I sincerely regret that I have waited so long to make this journey. Too bad I didn't do it when I was 20 or 30. I'm seventy-five now—an old man."

"Is there any way of knowing your views on politics?"

"What have we to do with politics?"

I agreed with him, but continued to push my point. He said that the ghost of nationalism is beginning to make its appearance in every corner of the East: India, Egypt, Palestine, Syria, and even among the ruins of Baalbek. "When I am assured that everything is in order, it is a sure sign that nothing is in order."

Feeling it difficult to express his views on politics in French he said in English: "In every country two parliaments should be established: one to deal with economic matters and the other to deal with political affairs."

Then he bade me Good-bye.

It is said that only one journalist succeeded in interviewing Shaw in Palestine and that the interview consisted of two words: "Get out."

T. F. Evans

MYOPIA OR UTOPIA?
SHAW IN RUSSIA

Bernard Shaw enthusiastically welcomed the Russian Revolution of 1917. When he heard the first news of an uprising, he wrote in a letter to Frank Harris, "Good news from Russia, eh!"[1] He had little sympathy with the arguments of the pure Marxists, such as H. M. Hyndman, who considered the revolution premature because, since capitalism in Russia had not reached the stage that Marx had forecast as that from which a successful transformation into a Marxist system would take place, it could only fail. For Shaw, what was happening satisfied in essential principles the requirements that he had in mind when, in a contribution on "Socialism: principles and outlook" for the *Encyclopaedia Britannica*, he said

> Socialism, reduced to its simplest legal and practical expression, means the complete discarding of the institution of private property, by transforming it into public property and the division of the resultant public income equally and indiscriminately among the entire population.[2]

He did not delude himself that the tsarist system had been eliminated overnight and that a new world was arising with the dawn of the new day, but he was convinced that steps were being taken in the right direction. The Revolution was, for him, as he wrote in the preface to the 1931 reprint of *Fabian Essays*, "a most beneficient event in spite of the incidental horrors which attend all too long delayed revolutions."[3]

Before the Revolution, Shaw's own work had become known in Russia through performances of some of the plays and publication of his works: there was a "complete edition" in Moscow of nine volumes in 1910 and a second in ten volumes appeared in Moscow and Saint Petersburg in 1911. He did not have close contacts with Russian writers, although he greatly admired Tolstoy as novelist, playwright, and social reformer. These regards were not reciprocated entirely without reservation, for Tolstoy, while admiring Shaw's "very great gifts," had difficulty in appreciating Shaw's humor. Tolstoy wrote to Shaw in an undated letter, after receiving a copy of *Man and Superman*:

> ... you are not sufficiently serious. One should not speak jestingly of such a subject as the purpose of human life, the causes of its perversion, and the evil that fills the life of humanity today. ... the questions you deal with are of such enormous importance that, for men with such profound comprehension of the evils of our life and such brilliant capacity for exposition as yourself, to make them the subject of satire may easily do harm rather than help the solution of these grave questions.
>
> In your book I detect a desire to surprise and astonish the readers by your great erudition, talent and cleverness. Yet all this is not merely unnecessary for the solution of the questions you deal with, but often distracts the readers' attention from the essence of the matter by attracting it to the brilliance of the exposition.[4]

After the Revolution and the end of the war, Shaw lost no opportunity for expressing his admiration for the newly founded Soviet state and for making comparisons to the discredit of the capitalist West. It was this period in his political development that the American critic, Edmund Wilson, decried: "In his political utterances since the war, it is hardly too much to say that Bernard Shaw has behaved like a jackass."[5] Shaw referred in immoderate words of praise to the statesmanship of Lenin in leading the revolution and establishing the new state and in tones of not much less warmth to the military genius of Leon Trotsky. His appreciation of Lenin was expressed in tangible form in 1921, when he sent him a copy of his "metabiological pentateuch," *Back to Methuselah*. The well-known opinion of Lenin that Shaw was a "good man fallen among Fabians"[6] was presumably not in the mind of the author when he inscribed the book

> to Nicolas Lenin
> the only European ruler who is displaying the ability
> character and knowledge proper to his responsible
> position
> from Bernard Shaw
> 16 June 1921.[7]

That Shaw always called himself a socialist and tended, as did the Russians themselves, to use the word as synonymous with communist contributed to the growth of his fame in Russia. He became known as a sympathizer with the regime, and publications of his works and productions of his plays increased in consequence. It may, however, be something of an exaggeration to suggest, as does Christopher Sykes, that Shaw "was the only contemporary British writer whose name was known to the man in the street."[8] Still, Sykes does say that the Russians had "a taste for sages" and "GBS was a sage too." Certainly, Shaw's fame in literary and especially dramatic circles did grow towards the end of the twenties with the appearance of his play *The Apple Cart*. This had its first performance in Poland, and Shaw's giving his new play to a theater so far from England may have quickened the interest that the play would almost certainly have evoked in any event. The reasons given for the interest shown in *The Apple Cart* vary and, indeed, sometimes contradict one another. From one point of view, the play shows capitalist democracy as both a sham and a failure. With the special love that sometimes shows itself between the contending sects on the left, some Russian observers may well have taken particular satisfaction that the government of Joseph Proteus in the play, which is defeated with such ignominy by King Magnus, is ostensibly, at least, a Labour government. Other interpretations of the play, however, have seen it as a plea for absolute monarchy, which presumably would not appeal to Soviet tastes, even if the King might be thought to be capable, in the eyes of Shaw, if of no one else, of behaving with the skill and sagacity of Lenin or Stalin. For whatever reason, or combination of reasons, it cannot be doubted that *The Apple Cart* did contribute to the broadening of knowledge of Shaw in the Soviet Union. It was at about this time that he conceived the idea of paying a visit to this land in which his own political theories were becoming a reality.

It is surprising that he never seems to have thought seriously of visiting Russia earlier. In the absence of firm evidence, there is little that can be done other than to accept the statement which he made in 1937 in *The Intelligent Woman's Guide* that "I was myself offered a very handsome commission by Mr. Randolph Hearst to go out to Russia and describe what there was to see there; but I refused because I knew only too well that what I should see was Capitalism in ruins and not Communism *in excelsis*."[9] There may well have been a reluctance of Shaw's part, quite understandable, to go to Russia as the hireling of a wealthy newspaper proprietor of well-known reactionary views, who would have been only too pleased to be able to print, even in the midst of much praise, the slightest word of criticism of Russia from the pen of the eminent socialist.

It is not clear from whom the invitation derived when Shaw was asked to visit Russia in the early summer of 1931. Christopher Sykes says that the proposal "probably" originated with Madame Litvinoff (Ivy Low), the English wife of the Soviet Commissar for Foreign Affairs. The invitation was put to him more formally by Sokolnikov, the Russian ambassador in London. There are suggestions, however, that the project was the idea of Philip Kerr, whom Shaw knew through the friendship of

Lord and Lady Astor. Kerr, who was to become British ambassador to the United States during the war of 1939–45, was a liberal politician who was sufficiently broadminded not to wish to condemn the Soviet experiment without some firm evidence. Shaw does not seem to have been in any hurry to explain where, in his view, the first idea came from, but he had at one time expressed the wish to celebrate his seventy-fifth birthday in the Soviet capital. Whether this had occurred to him or was put into his head by someone else, he was greatly taken with the notion of passing this milestone in his own life in the land of new enterprise and new hope. Unfortunately, Mrs. Shaw, who was recovering from an illness, was not fit enough to accompany him (which did not stop some newspapers from reporting her as one of the party).

Shaw looked around for other friends to make the journey with him. According to Shaw's biographer, Archibald Henderson, Kerr had suggested the idea of the Russian visit because he thought that it would be very welcome to Lady Astor, who he thought needed a holiday. Lady Astor felt it an honor to be asked to look after Shaw, as it were, in the place of his wife, and Charlotte herself felt relieved that GBS would be in good hands if Nancy Astor were with him. The friendship between the Shaws and the Astors has never been fully explained. John Grigg, whose "portrait" of Nancy Astor is one of the shortest, but also one of the more penetrating, of the considerable number of essays in biography of this remarkable woman to have appeared in recent years, has said that

> when he first met Nancy, GBS must have felt that Nature was imitating Art, or that some of his own female creations had been unconscious portraits of the real woman now before him. He and his wife, Charlotte, were both charmed by Nancy and the friendship that developed was warmly understanding on both sides. GBS also had a sincere regard for Waldorf, whose interest in social engineering appealed to the old Fabian and vestryman of St. Pancras.[10]

Had it not been for the personal friendship between them, the Astors would have been the least likely companions for Shaw on his visit to the Utopia of his dreams. Two "extremely wealthy" Americans, as he was to describe them to a Russian audience during the visit, could hardly be expected to look at the Promised Land through his own enchanted eyes. Nancy said on many occasions that she would believe in socialism if only there were any possibility of its working. Both she and her husband, she with her customary brash assertiveness and he with great reticence, let it be known that they were convinced Tories and never likely to be led into any illusions about the creation that Lenin had built on the foundation of Karl Marx. Nevertheless, they were prepared to accompany a friend on an enterprise which, whatever else it might be, could not be dull. To their credit, they took the view that, even if they had no sympathy with the aims and purposes of the Soviet state, it was a fact and it could not and should not be ignored. Kerr, who became Marquess of Lothian shortly before the departure, also went with them. The party was completed by the Astors' young son, David, then only eighteen, and two other friends of the Astors, Charles Tennant and Gertrude Ely.

It is impossible to avoid some speculation on what must have been in Shaw's mind when this unlikely caravanserai was planned. He can hardly have hoped to convert the Astors to Soviet Communism. Even if he had done this, there would not have been much point in it. Nancy Astor was a well-known member of the House of Commons. The interest that attached to her through her American origin and her being the first woman to take her seat in the House of Commons was added to by the racy, impetuous, and at times irresponsible and idiosyncratic way in which she behaved as a member of that assembly. She was always an eccentric. She did not hold government office and there was little prospect of her ever doing so. A radical change of political outlook on her part, or, indeed, on that of her husband (a much less active politician), would have been a nine days' wonder but little more. There is just the possibility that Shaw may have thought that, while an enthusiastic report by himself at the end of the visit would have been greeted with skepticism because it would have been exactly what was to be expected, such a report might be more credible if supported by the more or less independent-minded Astors. It is the personal opinion of David Astor, who retains a clear and detailed memory of much of the tour and who can still recapture some of the boyish excitement of making such a journey in such company, that it was merely Shavian "impishness" that persuaded him to ask the Astors to travel to Russia with him. His sense of fun, nothing more, suggested that it would be well worthwhile to see what the Astors made of the Soviet Union, or what the Soviet Union made of the Astors—or both.

The visit has been written about a great deal, yet there is no account that gives an entirely satisfactory picture and it is now unlikely that one will ever be written. The chief reason is that none of the principal actors in the strange comedy set down anything like a carefully considered, or even imaginatively impressionistic, picture of the events of the pilgrimage. Shaw did embark on something which seemed to start as a systematic account of his impressions and reactions, but gave up. Nancy Astor, who was not given to serious writing, or even, it may be thought, to serious reading, never tried to do anything of the kind. Lothian was a student of Russian politics and had a special interest in the recent developments but he may have thought that the visit was too short, too much of a tourist trip or otherwise not a fitting foundation for anything more than a few brief "traveller's tales." Waldorf Astor did keep a diary of the trip and it is from this informative but by no means highly colored document that any main outline of the journey must derive a substantial part of its material. The best account, largely based on the Waldorf diary, is to be found in the chapter devoted to the events of the* year 1931 in Christopher Sykes's *Nancy: The Life of Lady Astor*. Understandably, Waldorf Astor in his diaries concentrates on his own impressions and those of his wife. On the other hand, Shaw was undoubtedly the star of the whole enterprise and Astor mentions the occasions, of which there were many, when Shaw was in the center of the stage. Much in Astor's diary, however, while of the greatest interest to students of the Soviet Union in the 1930s, fails to add greatly either to an idea of the impression made upon Shaw or to his reactions during the visit. Details from other sources include notes of comments made by Shaw at intervals throughout the trip as reported in the press. The accuracy of some of these, in Russian or other newspapers, has to be questioned. It is not surprising to find that, even while Shaw was on a pilgrimage, part of the object of which was to convince the rest of the world of the great example being set by the Soviet Union, his characteristic sense of humor did not desert him. Delightful as this is, it nevertheless does not always lead to a clear understanding of some of the details. Thus, when Shaw made a speech to a Russian audience on his seventy-fifth birthday he said:

> You have no idea of the courage which we showed when we risked visiting Communist Russia. Our sobbing relatives kissed us and implored us not to risk our lives on account of so dangerous an undertaking.[11]

The party, which had begun with a motor journey to Dover, and which had been joined by David Astor in Berlin, boarded the night train and reached Warsaw on 20 July. Large crowds had been on the stations at Berlin and Warsaw. There were passport difficulties which obliged Gertrude Ely to return to Berlin, but the party was joined by the American author, Maurice Hindus, and Maxim Litvinoff himself, returning for a holiday in Russia, after a League of Nations meeting in Geneva. Waldorf Astor writes of the crossing of the frontier between Poland and Russia which consisted, in fact, of two frontiers with a no-man's land between, an arrangement not unknown in the Europe of half-a-century later. There was conversation with some working girls, who Nancy Astor was assured were "volunteers" but who it seemed were part of a forced labor program. In the middle of this account appears the following (the words are by Sykes):

> Knowing that living conditions in Russia were hard, they had brought a great many provisions, none of which they needed as the authorities pro-

vided sumptuous meals everywhere. They gave their provisions away before leaving Russia, and could hardly have guessed how heaven-sent these gifts must have seemed to those who got them.

In other accounts, there are references to food having been casually thrown from the windows of the Moscow bound train. The truth about this bizarre incident, if such an event occurred, may never be discovered.[12]

Waldorf Astor records their arrival in Moscow: "If one had told the late George Edwardes or the present [C. B.] Cochran to stage GBS's arrival in 'Red' Moscow and his reception by the Proletariat they would have staged exactly what happened."[13] The London *Daily Herald*, a paper owned by the Trade Union Congress and, while not an uncritical friend of the Soviet Union, less likely to be swayed by anti-Communist feeling than the capitalist press, wrote an account including the following:

> A brass band and a guard of honour of Soviet soldiers supplemented a crowd of several thousands of people who greeted Mr Bernard Shaw when he arrived at the Alexandrovsky station, Moscow, today. Among the people on the platform were M. Lunacharsky, former Commissar for Education, M. Khalatov, head of the State Publishing Trust, and M. Karl Radek, a leading journalist.
>
> When Mr Shaw appeared in the doorway of the special car in which he had travelled, the crowd broke into wild applause. Mr Shaw smiled and waved his hat.
>
> Then two lines of soldiers were formed to enable him to pass through the crowds.
>
> Lady Astor, who had travelled by the same train, received less attention. She patted a Russian baby on the head while Mr Shaw acknowledged cheer after cheer.
>
> Outside the station the streets were packed with thousands of people, above whom dozens of Red banners waved.
>
> "Hail Shaw!" roared the crowd.[14]

If credulity is strained by this account of a welcome, which could occur today only if the leading figures were "pop stars" or possibly world champion sportsmen, the further comment of Waldorf Astor endorses the report with the words that "I hear that the only two other people who had anything like a similar reception were Gorky and Fairbanks (with Mary Pickford)." This is a comparatively restrained picture. Some journalists could not resist the temptation to add more highly colored embellishments. Thus, Walter Duranty in a "special cable" to the *New York Times* was not content with the fairly high temperature suggested by the *Daily Herald* account. According to his view of the event, "Mr Shaw posed at the station for photographs and made a big impression with his white beard and lofty stature, a whisper of 'What a noble old man!' passing through the crowd."[15]

In an age dominated by nationwide, and indeed worldwide, radio and television, it is not easy to imagine how large crowds could have been assembled at the railway station for the arrival of visitors from what must have appeared to the Russian man in the street as outer space. Admittedly, once it is seen that something special is about to happen, a crowd will gather, and banners and soldiers presumably attracted crowds. Even so, the statement about a few thousands in the station and thousands in the streets outside does give the impression that the event must have been stage-managed. It is hard to say how. *Izvestia*, the official Soviet newspaper, included an article on 21 July, the day of Shaw's arrival in Moscow, with the title, *"Bernard Shaw: Our Guest!"* It is closely printed, and the paper did not go in for banner headlines. There is nothing about this piece which, at first sight, would encourage thousands of ordinary Muscovites to subordinate normal claims on their daily time to an irresistible desire to join in a welcome to a visiting celebrity. Nevertheless, what was written in the article reflects an official, if not a popular, attitude. The article was by that same Lunacharsky who was at the head of the delegation that welcomed the travellers on their arrival in Moscow. According to the unrestrained pen of Walter Duranty, Lunacharsky "speaks six languages, looks like a university professor, and was one."[16] The underlying note of this piece of information is commendatory rather than apologetic. In his article, Lunacharsky wrote in warm terms of "the freedom of Bernard Shaw, and the brilliance and strength of his intellect." These qualities, he contended, had enabled Shaw to "disengage himself from the webs of bourgeois socialism, bourgeois liberalism and bourgeois prejudices." Lunacharsky paid warm tribute to Shaw's artistry and irony, through which he had been able to penetrate conventional attitudes, but Lunacharsky had serious reservations also. He could not think that Shaw was a socialist "through and through." Shaw, "a brilliant representative of the intelligentsia," was too free to be able to work within the kind of systematic organisation and discipline by which alone the battle against capitalism could be fought and won. In short, Shaw and people like him had been of great value to the new world that was coming into being but, "if the new world were to be fought for only by people such as Shaw, it would never be born."[17]

The visit, which was a short one, consisted largely of excursions of a more or less conventional tourist type, designed to show the achievements of the Soviet state to best advantage. His hosts found that Shaw could usually be relied upon to make roughly the kind of comment that they wished to hear. At times, his remarks were somewhat two-edged. Thus, he made a celebrated comment to the effect that he "was a Marxist

almost before Lenin was born" which contained, or could easily be interpreted to contain, the implication that, if he approved of Lenin in
general, there might well be ways in which Shaw had something to teach
Lenin and his followers. He was always ready to cast doubts on "Western
democracy," and according to a brief comment in one newspaper, he
said that "it would take England 500 years to understand Stalin's philosophy."[18] When introduced to a young Englishman who had settled permanently in Russia, Shaw is reported to have said that, if he were the
same age, he would like to stay there too. When taken to look at the
Museum of the Revolution, however, Shaw teased his hosts by saying:

> I think your Government are mad to have a Museum of the Revolution.
> It is most dangerous from their point of view. All governments hate rev-
> olutions and will do everything they can to prevent them or crush them.
> The courage of the Russian Government seems to me foolhardy.[19]

Waldorf Astor noted this in his diary and added the dry comment that
"the remark did not pass the censor." Shaw was in a similarly flippant
mood when the party visited a factory, whereas Astor found the "combined political and industrial control incomprehensible" and he was not
ignorant of the subject of factory organization. Occasionally, Waldorf
Astor, although a quiet and sympathetic character, could be provoked
into disapproval of Shaw in his less-responsible mood. Thus, Sykes records that at the end of the factory visit, Shaw

> was angrily asked why the English and capitalist press told such disgrace-
> ful lies about forced labour in the USSR, to which he is reported to have
> replied, and in this case, the report rings true: "I wish we had forced
> labour in England, in which case we would not have 2,000,000 unem-
> ployed."[20]

Sykes appears to be echoing the thoughts of Astor in calling this "a truly
detestable witticism," but there may have been, as not unusually with
Shaw, a respectable truth under the apparent uncaring comment. He
could well have been suggesting not that the Russian system of "forced
labour" should be introduced in Britain, but that, in a socialist Britain,
it should be possible to organize the economy so that there would not be
a vast number of unemployed.

More damaging and disturbing to Shaw's reputation may have been
the strange story of Madame Krynin. According to Waldorf Astor, a telegram from the United States was handed to Nancy Astor at a formal
banquet. It came from a professor at Yale University, a Russian named
Krynin, who sought assistance from the eminent visitors to the Soviet
Union in his attempts to secure the release of his wife from Russia so
that she could join him in the United States. The Astors made what
efforts they could to secure the required permission. They interviewed

officials and Waldorf went with an American journalist to visit the lady
herself. She made no complaints against the Russian authorities but
merely wished to be allowed to join her husband. The efforts of the
Astors on her behalf came to nothing, but they did try. At the same time
as the original message was delivered to Nancy Astor, a similar appeal
was made to Shaw. Accounts of this episode suggest strongly that Shaw
showed far less concern for the fate of this unfortunate individual even
while he was making speeches about the superiority of the Russian interpretation of "freedom" to that of the West.

David Astor has said that one of the things that struck him most force-
fully about Shaw was his apparent lack of interest in the surroundings
through which the visitors passed, whether these were the beauties of
the countryside or man-made creations.[21] The young man felt somewhat overawed at being in the presence of the great writer, but he found
Shaw most charming and friendly and not in the least condescending or
presuming in any way on his fame or reputation. Perhaps because Shaw
seemed in these respects so human and normal (whereas a celebrity
might have been expected not to show these qualities), David Astor
found it difficult to understand how Shaw could apparently show so
little signs of being aware of what was all around him that was different
from his home background. Neither a visit to Leningrad, generally admitted to be the most beautiful of Russian cities, nor the beautiful and
varied landscapes through which they were taken on the long railway
journey from Moscow to Leningrad and back seemed to have any appeal
to Shaw.

Not in the same category is another example of his failure to appreciate something that appealed to other people, if not to everybody. The
fact that Shaw had chosen to spend his birthday in the Soviet Union was
not lost on his hosts, and they put themselves out to think of some special way in which to celebrate this event. It is not known on what advice
they acted, or from what source came the inspiration to do what they
did, but the special birthday treat that was arranged for the writer—
rather as a special excursion might be arranged for the birthday of a
child—was a visit to the races. Shaw, without excessive discourtesy, acknowledged the thoughtfulness of his hosts by pointing out that he was
the only Irishman in existence who had not the slightest interest in
horseracing and that there was thus something of the bizarre in this
particular entertainment being made specially available for his benefit.
Not even the inclusion in the program of the "Bernard Shaw Handicap"
succeeded in evoking any interest in the proceeding on the part of the
one in whose honor it had all been devised. He celebrated his birthday
or contributed to this part of the celebrations by paying no attention
whatever to what was going on and, indeed, falling asleep. The Waldorf

Astor diary records that the day was brought to an end by a special dinner in honor of Shaw, with long speeches. Astor described Shaw's speech as "a bad effort" and Sykes says that his jokes about Britain and his fellow travelers were incomprehensible to the Russians, who, in the opinion of Sykes, had very strict notions of good manners. As to Shaw's remarks on the Astors and his other companions, it is very possible that not everyone recognized that they were not wholly serious. The main thing that Shaw insisted upon in his speech (from the scanty reports that are directly available in the Russian press) was that when he returned to Britian and spoke of what he had seen, he would be told that he had only been shown what it was deemed expedient for him to see and that the terrors would be kept from him. He would be able to say, however, "Yes, I saw all the terrors and they are getting terribly better."[22]

Consistent with the lack of interest shown by Shaw in matters of general artistic merit or importance is the fact that he made hardly any mention of the art form in which he would have been expected to show a special curiosity, the theater. When the trip was arranged, he noted that the time of year was one in which the theaters would be closed. After his return, he said that he had visited some cinemas, without, however, going into details. One special visit was arranged for the party by their hosts. In several brief mentions of the event, not consistent with each other, this is said to have been to a performance of the English play, The Beggar's Opera. (There is some ground for thinking that this may have been a performance of Die Dreigroschenoper, the version by the German dramatist, Bertolt Brecht.)

Nevertheless, there was one event, theatrical in its essential nature and almost certainly stage-managed, if paradoxically and tantalizingly, in a secretive, even furtive manner. This was an interview with Stalin. Not all the pilgrims were admitted to the presence. The Russian leader was graciously pleased to see Shaw, the Astors, and Lothian. It was agreed that no press conference or similar report should be given. David Astor can recall vividly the way in which Shaw, as chief spokesman for the group, appeared after the interview at the head of a flight of steps, looking very serious, and, after waiting for silence, announced to the reporters that Stalin had splendid black moustaches. (There are several versions of this story in print and elsewhere, but unfortunately there is no unanimity on the actual words used. Shaw's sense of fun and anticlimax nevertheless achieved a modest triumph.)

In the course of time, as was inevitable, several accounts of what was said at the interview began to appear, and it is possible to construct a picture that is fairly clear. The interview lasted nearly two-and-a-half hours. Apart from Stalin and the visitors, the only other people there were Maxim Litvinoff and an interpreter. It seems beyond dispute that, irrespective of the views expressed, Stalin made a favorable impression on his visitors. Waldorf Astor remarked that Stalin struck him as "shrewd rather than big mentally" and added that he had "quite a sense of humour and knew how to parry questions he did not wish to deal with." On the whole, the interview seems to have consisted of discussion on more or less general questions conducted by people who, although speaking different languages (metaphorically and well as literally), were determined to be civil to each other. There was one incident which has attracted much attention and may still represent the greatest moment of excitement in the entire visit to Russia. St. John Ervine in his biography of Shaw is thought to base his version of the event on the recollections of Shaw himself, and this may therefore be as reliable as any other account:

> The honours of the occasion were won by Lady Astor who, having no veneration for dictators nor any awe of eminent persons, frightened the wits out of the interpreters [it has been said that there was only one] during an interview with Stalin by asking that cunning Caucasian why he had slaughtered so many Russians. The interpreters were loth to translate it, nor did they do so, until Stalin, observing their fearful embarrassment, demanded to be told what Lady Astor has said.[23]

David Astor recalls clearly from the accounts that he received soon after the meeting that, even if Stalin may have insisted that the question be put, Shaw, too, took the same line and suggested to Lady Astor that, if the question were not put or were left unanswered, there would be no point in continuing the discussion. Stalin was told what had been said and, from all accounts except one, took the challenge blandly, explaining that some things are inevitable in a revolutionary situation and that he hoped, in Waldorf Astor's words, "the need for dealing with political prisoners drastically would soon cease." (H. G. Wells, who considered himself as great an authority on Russian matters as did Shaw, wrote of Lady Astor having annoyed Stalin to the extent of making him lose his temper. There is no evidence to support this.)[24] David Astor recalls that Stalin not only did not get angry but did not even show signs of being ruffled.

Stalin was worried about the possible part that Winston Churchill might play in British politics, obviously bearing in mind Churchill's strong anti-Soviet stance in the past. He accepted assurances that Churchill was something of a spent force on the British political scene and that he would be unlikely to prove a serious obstacle to the improvement of Anglo-Soviet relations in the future. Lady Astor asked about the treatment of children in the Soviet Union, and Shaw was greatly taken by Stalin's explanation of the legal rights which children possessed, even to the extent of being allowed to sue their parents in the courts, should this be considered justified. There was some discussion, in which Lothian took the most prominent part, of matters concerning peace proposals put forward by Lenin in 1919, which, if implemented, it was apparently suggested by Stalin, could have been the basis of a constructive and lasting settlement between Britain and her allies on the one side and the Soviet Union on the other.

David Astor remembers that they heard no rumors about the famine that was already occurring in the Ukraine. Nor did they hear anything that presaged the purges and political show-trials that were to begin within a year or two after the visit. Some of the celebrities whom they met, such as Radek, were among those who would be purged.

The visit to Russia ended on the following day. Lady Astor and Shaw had both expressed a wish to meet Lenin's widow, Krupskaya. It had not seemed possible to arrange a meeting, but, almost at the last minute, one did take place. It is not recorded that anything of significance occurred.

To David Astor, who remembers Shaw as a nice and kind man who liked to shock and had a theatrical genius for doing so and who was as gentle as he seemed virulent, the only time on the visit that Shaw had seemed natural was when he met with Stanislavky at the latter's dacha near Moscow. There was no posturing nor publicity parables. The two men greeted each other with real warmth and talked shop to each other.

The remark of Shaw's that was given greatest prominence in press reports of the homeward journey is, to say the very least, somewhat questionable. It concerned Russian food. Thus, the opening lines of the news item in the *Observer* for 2 August 1931 were as follows:

> "Black bread and cabbage agree with me—and I have had plenty of both" was Mr Bernard Shaw's first remark when he stepped out of the Northern Express at the Schlesische Bahnhof today on his return from Russia.
>
> "Yes, there is plenty of food in Russia," he said, "But I must look after my luggage."

There is no evidence that the visitors saw people going short of food and it is probable that, if there were evidence of starvation or near-starvation, it would have been effectively concealed. Shaw's insistence on "black bread and cabbage"? Nobody can say that he did not consume some of these estimable commodities when he was in Russia, but all the evidence suggests that the visiting party were fed very well indeed with such delicacies as caviar—which Shaw could not eat—and were not obliged, as this comment would suggest, to eat as the peasants did. The trouble with this superficiality of Shaw's is that it makes it so difficult for other remarks, not on the surface quite so ridiculous, to be taken as they should. Thus, he is reported in the same paper to have said "emphatically": "It is torture to get back again after being in Soviet land. After you have seen Bolshevism on the spot there can be no doubt but that capitalism is doomed." The contention that "capitalism is doomed" has the ring of a clear judgment based on experience, but Shaw held that view before he went to Russia. The proverbial aphorism to the effect that "travel broadens the mind" may only too often be matched by the opinion that it frequently serves to confirm the traveller in his prejudices.

Perhaps the nearest Shaw came to a considered statement of his reactions to his visit came, not in a more sustained piece which he later began to write but abandoned before it showed any signs of fruitful development, but in the speech which he gave to the summer school of the Independent Labour Party at Didswell Park on 5 August 1931. Even here, he covered himself by saying that his speech was only "a rough and chatty description" and that "if the Soviet leaders were present here, they would regard me as one of the most monstrous paradoxes, to say nothing of liars, that ever existed." [25] In the speech he said—sometimes in almost the same words, sometimes in slightly different forms— much of what he had already said on and after the journey. He varied between more or less serious comment, such as his emphasis on what he considered the abolition of class distinctions in Russia, to more personal matters, such as his statement that "I personally can't sleep if there are other people in the room but they [that is, Russians in general] can't sleep unless there are other people in the room." If one main line of thought emerges, it is that the Russians had seriously decided as a matter of fundamental policy to put up with hardships for a period in order that benefits would accrue later. Such a policy—the Five-Year Plan— would not be accepted in England, whether by capitalists or workers. He declared that "the Socialism which has established itself is Fabian Socialism." There was laughter at this, but he responded by saying that he was "perfectly serious" and, later in the speech, he added "I say it is Fabian Socialism and its inspiration is a religious one all through. And here I am speaking the exact and careful truth."

It could not have been any surprise to so experienced a controversialist as Shaw to find that his comments during and after the Russian visit drew forth much fire from different directions, some of it from very big guns indeed. Two of these were G. K. Chesterton and Winston Churchill. Writing in G K 's Weekly on 1 August 1931, the former, mastering paradox as ever, declared that Shaw should not only have been accompanied by the wealthy American, Lady Astor, but also by an even more wealthy American, Mr. Rockefeller. This was because, as Chesterton put it, "the great Socialist entered the world of Socialism, at the exact moment when it had ceased to be Socialistic." Chesterton based this view on the idea that Russian economic policy had changed. He did not say, with Shaw, that it had become Fabian; on the contrary, he maintained that it had become capitalist.

> There is no Czarism to fight, but also there is no Leninism to fight for; and the vacuum of commercial compromise in which the whole epoch has ended really leaves the Socialist army confronted, like the old Napoleonic army, with a single inevitable word; which is Retreat. . . .
>
> I only look on at a tragedy, in which a great man who has missed the true conception of liberty touched a great revolution, which missed the true conception of right; and they never met, until one was old and the other dead.

Winston Churchill, unlike Chesterton never a friend of Shaw, made a sharper attack. His view of Shaw as a jester, of no great intellectual weight or political consequence, was always tempered by a recognition of Shaw's mastery of prose style. In the article, which appeared in the *Sunday Pictorial* on 16 August 1931, however, Churchill was not in the mood to make concessions. Presented with a pair of targets, in the form of two of his favorite antipathies, Shaw and Lady Astor (his own American antecedents never seemed to have softened his hostility towards his fellow Conservative eccentric), Churchill let fly. He enjoyed himself at Shaw's expense: "His spiritual home is in Russia; but he lives comfortably in England, which he derides and abuses on every occasion." He found equal pleasure in pointing out the shortcomings and contradictions of Lady Astor: "She applauds the policies of the Government from the benches of the Opposition. She denounces the vice of gambling in measured terms, and keeps an almost unrivalled racing stable. She accepts Communist hospitality and flattery, and remains the Conservative member for Plymouth." These courtesies out of the way, Churchill made his more serious attacks on a country "ruled by terror, fanaticism and the Secret Police" and on the "moral and intellectual myopia" of observers who could ignore such things.

In the same paper, the following week, Shaw wrote a reply. It is short and does not deal in any detail with more serious parts of Churchill's piece. He gives back personalities for personalities when he refers to Churchill's "Russophobia" and says that, in the interview with Stalin, "we suggested that Stalin should invite Mr Churchill to Russia and let him blow off steam on the spot. Stalin laughed heartily and intimated that he would be delighted to have Mr Churchill in Moscow."[26] In a series of exchanges with other correspondents in the columns of *The Times* during these later weeks of August, Shaw concentrated on defending what he considered the superiority of "Russia's solution of the democratic problem so far." Thus, in a letter on 20 August, he said that "liberty does not mean liberty to idle and sponge. The political machinery is built for immediate positive use; and it is powerful enough to break people who stick ramrods into it. In short, it is much more democratic than Parliament and party."

In the middle of all this sparring about ideas of democracy and the failures of different political systems to create any acceptable model of democracy in practice, it is all too easy to forget that Shaw was a dramatist. At the time he went to Russia, he was the greatest living writer in the English-speaking theater and most probably in the theater of the entire world. *The Apple Cart*, his last play before the visit, is never placed among his best, but most judges would say that, with all its faults, it still shows clear signs of his greatest virtues. Some may have hoped that, whatever the effect of the Russian experience on the politician and the economist, there might have been some profitable consequences for the dramatist. It was not to be. There are references to Russia, of course, in the new plays that were produced after his return. In *Too True to be Good* (1931), several of the characters wish to go to a place called Beotia, the Union of Federated Sensible Societies to which "everybody wants to go" but for which it is almost impossible to obtain visas, as so many English have already gone there that "their lunatic asylums are too full already." In *On the Rocks* (1933), a conservative Prime Minister goes into retreat in the middle of an economic crisis and returns, having read Marx, to declare that therein lie the remedies for the ills of capitalism but "I'm not the man for the job. . . . And I shall hate the man who will carry it through for his cruelty and the desolation he will bring on us and our like" (*BH* 6, 734). There are routine defences of the Soviet system of democracy in the prefaces to *The Simpleton of the Unexpected Isles* and *The Millionairess*, both of which were written in 1934, but there is nothing in either play to suggest that Shaw has been able to incorporate in the essential fabric of his imagination as a dramatist any substantial image of a new society. In *Geneva* (1938), he makes great sport, as war approaches, by conducting a conversation piece, at the center of which are thinly disguised representations of the dictators, Hitler, Mussolini, and Franco, and a British Foreign Secretary who combines in himself all the more amiable, but not necessarily any of the most competent, characteristics of everyone who has ever held that demanding post. For reasons best known to himself, Shaw did not accept the challenge of putting Stalin on the stage alongside his fellow dictators, but he did include in the cast a Russian Commissar. The most dramatically effective element contributed by this character to the play is that he causes, albeit inadvertently, the death of an English bishop. This distressing event takes place as the result of heart failure when the reverend gentleman suddenly discovers that the cultured and civilized foreigner with whom he has been enjoying a conversation is, in fact, a Russian communist.

As the war approached and finally broke out, Shaw tended to concentrate his dialectic resources on proclaiming, in season and out, the immense superiority, in every way, of the Soviet Union to the Western democracies on the one hand and the dictatorships on the other. He indulged in spirited controversies, not least with the editor of the *New Statesman*, Kingsley Martin, and the text of his letters and the editorial replies was issued by the Russia Today Society as a pamphlet in 1941. The title of the body, under whose auspices these observations were given to the world, is an indication that the stronger sympathizers with the Russian cause felt that there was valuable publicity to be gained from the name of Shaw.

Nimble-footed as ever, Shaw, whatever the counter-arguments, clung to his simple contention that Stalin was always far more likely to be right on any given subject than was anyone else. The Russians were therefore right to seek some kind of common front against the dictators, right to enter the Nazi-Soviet pact, and, in the fullness of time, of course, right to resist the German invasion of Russia and to combine with the allies of the West, including the United States, to destroy the Axis powers. Thus, all that happened proved Shaw right, for the simple and obvious reason that his dialectical skill left no way in which he could be shown to be wrong. It is not too much to say that his reputation as a political thinker failed to keep pace with his esteem as a dramatist at this time. While productions of his plays, with their mixture of intellectual clarity and entertainment value in the widest sense, continued to astonish those who did not know them already, it was increasingly difficult for audiences at such war-time productions in London as those of *Heartbreak House*, *The Doctor's Dilemma*, and *Arms and the Man* to realize that their author was the same person as the indefatigable but erratic letter-writer who regularly fired salvoes of advice to world statesmen from his point of vantage at Ayot St. Lawrence in the Hertfordshire countryside.

As repercussions of the 1931 visit to Russia began to grow faint, there came, some years after Shaw's death, an opportunity or an inducement to consider it in a new light. Late though this was in chronology, it would be wrong not to comment on this posthumous assessment of the 1931 event. In 1964, a Shavian scholar, Dr. Harry Geduld of Indiana University, discovered in the British Museum a lengthy Shaw fragment with the title, *The Rationalization of Russia*.[27] This was what Shaw had decided to write, or all that he cared to preserve, as an account of the Russian visit. Some scholars have doubted whether he ever wrote any more—certainly, no additions have come to light—and many have doubted whether what he did write was really worth the trouble. The fragment, which is no more than eighty pages long, does not add to the knowledge of the visit that had emerged during the third of a century that had elapsed between the return from Moscow and the publication. The critic of *The Times Literary Supplement* probably voiced the majority view when he declared that the piece shows no development in Shaw's ideas, though the critic may have lost some of his support by going on to say that "during the latter part of his life, Shaw never *developed* any ideas; he merely played a series of increasingly boring variations on a few dogmatic themes."[28] There are many who would say that Shaw could hardly have been boring even if he had tried. There was too much life in his writing, even in the repetitive observations on the downfall and futility of capitalism, the excellence of Soviet solutions and—what tended to displease most readers—his apparent enthusiasm for the liquidation of opponents of the regime or other deviants. It must be admitted, however, that there are still outstanding flashes, as, for example, the following general-purpose condemnation of the educated classes, in which Shaw is clearly not limiting himself to the Soviet Union:

> I have often said myself that if I were a revolutionary dictator my first care would be to see that persons with a university education, or with the acquired mentality which universities inculcate and stereotype, should be ruthlessly excluded from all direction of affairs, all connection with education especially with their own children, and if not violently exterminated, at least encouraged to die out as soon as possible. Lenin shared my views and attempted to carry them into action.

In the opening pages of *Everybody's Political What's What?*, published in 1944 and described, almost certainly by the author himself, as "the final fruit of his political experience," Shaw makes an admission that is present in *The Rationalization of Russia* but not so clearly or succinctly expressed. This is the recognition that all had not always been perfect in Russia since the revolution. In one of his earlier writings, he referred with glee to the young revolutionary socialist who "is apt to be catastrophic in his views—to plan the revolutionary program as an affair of twenty-four lively hours, with Individualism in full swing on Monday morning, a tidal wave of insurgent proletariat on Monday afternoon, and Socialism in complete working order on Tuesday."[29] With the Soviets, he was now prepared to state, it had been different, although, under wise counselling, they had managed to improve:

> During the ten years after the Bolshevik Revolution of 1917 in Russia, the Communist government, though up-to-date and even ahead of it in social theory and knowledge of the facts, made so many legislative and administrative mistakes that the survival of the Communist State and

even of the Russian people still seems miraculous and providential. The Bolsheviks knew what they wanted but did not know how to get it. And if the heads of our Old School Ties could be emptied of everything political they learnt at school or at home and refitted with Lenin's mental furniture and faculty, they would make all his mistakes over again, and bring the country even nearer to starvation and ruin, without any guarantee that the circumstances would allow us to pull through as Lenin did.[30]

As a one-line summary of the strange comic episode of Shaw's relations with the Soviet Union, of which the visit in 1931 was the central item, there is probably none better than Shaw's own remark, recorded by the prominent civil servant and diarist Thomas Jones, who noted that, in a conversation about Russia in March 1920, Shaw "said Russia had made the mistake of following Marx instead of Shaw!"[31] The remark sounds conceited, of course, and might be thought a typical piece of Shavian hyperbole. It enshrines, however, Shaw's continuing belief in the Fabian approach to socialism as superior to the direct revolutionary path.

As recently as January 1984, it was reported by the Soviet newsagency Tass that some photographs of Shaw had been discovered during repair work to an old building in Minsk, the capital of Byelorussia. The source of the collection had not been ascertained, but it was noted that Shaw had been welcomed at a border station near Minsk in 1931 by the Soviet writer Fyodor Gladkov. The director of the Byelorussian Museum of Literature and Art, receiving the newly found collection, is quoted as saying that "they show interesting moments in the life of the writer, whose books and plays evoke much interest among Soviet readers and theatergoers."[32]

After the visit to Russia, Waldorf Astor received a letter from a friend of both Shaw and himself, J. J. Mallon, Warder of Toynbee Hall in East London, very much of the left but by no means incapable of detached criticism. There had been some talk of his accompanying the party to Russia (and one report did include his name as among those who went) and he was naturally eager to hear the impressions of his friends when they returned. He wrote to Astor on 6 August 1931: "GBS is too ecstatic. I await your considered and candid pronouncement on the visit before I believe his dithyrambs. How I wish I had been with you!" Waldorf Astor replied the next day:

It is no good my trying to put on paper what my impressions of Russia are. When I talked to the Bolsheviks, I was never quite certain whether they were lunatics or whether I was the lunatic. It was often so impossible to find any common grouond on which to discuss any philosophy of life. But Russia is going ahead and is not going to fail. Read Philip's talk to the Liberal Summer School, much more balanced than GBS. Incidentally, GBS amused himself pulling the legs of the Reds quite frequently. Whenever we visited any place, the inevitable book was brought and the distinguished visitor was expected to write his views in the book. Most visitors appeared to have gone out of their way to plaster the Russians with praise whether their efforts deserved it or not. Not so GBS! Let me illustrate this. After visiting a factory he wrote in their book. "My father drank too much. I have worked too much. I hope your Five Year Plan will succeed but when it does, for heaven's sake stop and take a rest."[33]

Notes

I wish to express my thanks to David Astor for his invaluable assistance and to Dr. J. A. Edwards, the Keeper of Archives and Manuscripts, the Library, The University of Reading.

1. 30 March 1917 in S. Weintraub, ed., *The Playwright and the Pirate* (University Park: The Pennsylvania State University Press, 1982), p. 69.
2. *Encyclopedia Britannica*, 1926, 13th edition, vol. 31.
3. *Fabian Essays* (London: George Allen and Unwin, 1962), p. 264.
4. Aylmer Maude, *The Life of Tolstoy* (Oxford University Press, 1953), vol. 2, p. 461.
5. Edmund Wilson, *The Triple Thinkers* (London: John Lehmann, 1952), p. 167.
6. The source of this widely quoted aphorism has not been traced.
7. The inscription is reproduced in facsimile in *The Shavian*, 2, no. 7 (1963), p. 11 in an article "Shaw in the Soviet Union" by Boris Gileson. The inscribed copy of *Back to Methuselah* is in the Lenin Library, Moscow.
8. Christopher Sykes, *Nancy: The Life of Lady Astor* (London: Collins, 1972). All the quotations from Sykes are from chapter 16, pp. 377–410.
9. *The Intelligent Woman's Guide to Socialism, Capitalism, Sovietism and Fascism* (London: Penguin Books, 1937), p. 431.
10. John Grigg, *Nancy Astor: A Lady Unashamed* (Boston: Little, Brown and Company, 1980), p. 117.
11. *Pravda*, Moscow, 29 July 1931. (The translations of this item and those in notes 17 and 23 are by A. T. B. Evans.)
12. The explanation could be that the visitors kept the food that they had brought with them until they felt that they had no need for it and then distributed it.
13. Diary entry by Waldorf Astor, quoted by Sykes. All the quotations from this diary are as quoted by Sykes.
14. *The* (London) *Daily Herald*, 21 July 1931.
15. Walter Duranty, *New York Times*, 22 July 1931.
16. Ibid.
17. *Izvestia*, Moscow, 21 July 1931.
18. *New York Herald Tribune*, 19 July 1931.
19. Quoted by Sykes.
20. Quoted by Sykes.
21. David Astor gave his impressions to the author in conversation.
22. *Pravda*, Moscow, 29 July 1931.

23. St. John Ervine, *Bernard Shaw: His Life, Work and Friends* (London: Constable, 1956), p. 518.

24. When Wells himself visited Russia in 1934, the *New Statesman* issued a supplement giving a verbatim record of the conversation between Stalin and Wells (27 October 1934). Shaw contributed a comment on 3 November and a further contribution on 17 November.

25. The speech is reported in full in the *New Leader*, 7 August 1931, pp. 6–7.

26. *Sunday Pictorial*, 23 August 1931.

27. Harry M. Geduld, ed., *The Rationalization of Russia* (Bloomington: Indiana University Press, 1964).

28. "G.B.S.S.R.," *Times Literary Supplment*, 7 May 1964.

29. *Essays in Fabian Socialism* (London: Constable, 1932), p. 42.

30. *Everybody's Political What's What?* (London: Constable, 1944), p. 6.

31. Thomas Jones, *A Diary with Letters, 1931–1950* (London: Oxford University Press, 1954), p. 456.

32. *Daily Telegraph*, 21 January 1984.

33. The letters from J. J. Mallon and Waldorf Astor are in the Astor family papers, University of Reading.

Leon Hugo

UPSET IN A "SUNTRAP": SHAW IN SOUTH AFRICA

Shaw visited South Africa twice. The first visit began in Cape Town on 11 January 1932 and ended in the same city on 18 March 1932. The second visit began in Durban on 28 April 1935 and ended in Cape Town on 24 May 1935. Charlotte accompanied him on both occasions.

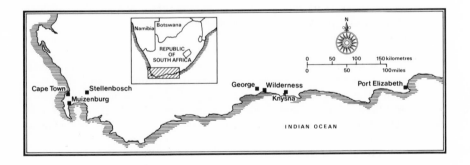

I

Shaw's arrival for his first visit was awaited with excitement in Cape Town. Local Fabians and other socialist bodies declared a truce and asked that Shaw be accorded a civic welcome. The mayor refused, saying he had been given to understand that Shaw was in need of rest: his was a private visit and a civic reception would not be welcome. One wonders

whether Shaw would have agreed. A headline in the morning newspaper, *The Cape Times*, asked: "What Will G.B.S. Say to South Africa?";
a chatty article answered the question by foreseeing a delectable clash if
he behaved in his customary way.[1] The evening paper, *The Cape Argus*,
welcomed him on the day of his arrival in a sonorous leader, the first of
several editorial commentaries the local English press devoted to him
during his visit. The *Argus* leader illustrates both the importance Cape
Town attached to Shaw's visit and the "neo-colonial" perspectives of the
time.

G. B. S.

Mr. Bernard Shaw's arrival in Cape Town this morning has been hailed
as an event of national importance. It is probable, in fact, that only the
advent of Don Bradman or Mahatma Gandhi would have aroused
greater general interest. This juxtaposition of names shows Mr. Shaw's
essential greatness. Man is a ball-hitting animal and, therefore, Bradman,
as the greatest living hitter of balls, rightly is the English-speaking world's
No. 1 in the publicity list. Gandhi similarly is a combination of saint,
rebel, prisoner and humorist, which the world regards as irresistible. Mr.
Shaw shares their high distinction solely by reason of intellect—not usually a claim to the consideration of a public which prefers its brilliant men
to be dead. Nowadays Mr. Shaw's opinion about every new idea, every
new country, every new political move, is earnestly sought. By reason of
their official positions, Mr. Ramsay MacDonald and Mr. Baldwin may
open the conversational innings, playing nice orthodox cricket with the
idea. But when Mr. Shaw appears the play changes in character. The idea
may prove to be not an idea at all. Often it is hit, with bitter blows, to all
parts of the field. Mr. Shaw assures the unthinking world of entertainment. It is too often forgotten, or overlooked, that behind his brilliance
and his unexpectedness, there is a sound method and a complete ideol-
ogy. For the substance of Mr. Shaw's contribution to modern controversy
is probably greater than that of any other living man. . . .
   Probably the greatest difference between this generation and its
predecessors is the refusal of the individual to bow down and worship
the idols of the past. People are learning to make up their own minds, to
form their own ideas. They accept or reject institutions and habits more
and more after an intellectual process of their own and less and less because such an institution or habit has been "the done thing." For this
change Mr. Shaw must bear the major burden of responsibility. He has
made the world laugh, he has made it angry, he has even driven it finally
to think. How will South Africa react to Mr. Shaw and he to us? No doubt
our politics and our native policy will strike him as atonishingly funny.
But, if our weather behaves nicely, our sun, and our respectful interest
in Mr. Shaw, may lead him to deal lightly with our very obvious shortcomings.

The comparison with Bradman must have occasioned a chuckle in
Shaw's hotel suite that evening.[2]

CAPE TIMES, TUESDAY, JANUARY 12, 1932.

Mrs Bernard Shaw, who arrived yesterday in the Carnarvon Castle, accompanied by her husband.

FIG. 1. This cartoon by Wyndham Robinson evidently delighted Shaw. (*Courtesy of the Cape Times*)

When the Shaws arrived on the *Carnarvon Castle* on Monday, 11 January 1932 (Fig. 1), press photographers swarmed round him, a movie camera team persuaded him to give an impromptu "talkie" on board ship, reporters hung on his every word, welcoming committees (the Cape Town Fabian Society, the Cape Town Publicity Association) hovered. One of his first questions to the Fabians was whether natives were admitted to trade unions in South Africa.[3] More and more people came on board. Charlotte fled to the privacy of her cabin, but Shaw was in his element. An audience of nearly a hundred crowded into the first-class reception hall to look at him and hear him speak. The press interview turned into a semipublic lecture. "There is no crisis in Europe," he said.

"There is only an appalling muddle. I think it is the beginning of the Marxian break-up of capitalism. . . . But capitalism will take a long time to break up; it will see me out, and that's all I'm worrying about. . . . The trouble is that English writers are not revolutionaries. I, on the other hand, am."

A reporter told him that Frank Harris's biography of him was being hotly criticized in South Africa. Shaw replied: "I don't care at all about Frank Harris's fantastic opinions about me. The trouble is that public men are blackmailed by their biographers. The only thing to do is to threaten to sue their publishers, or finally to get hold of their books and put the facts right. Otherwise all sorts of fantastic inventions about one's private life get about, which may be quite serious for one's relations. That was what I did with Frank Harris's book. In this the only parts that are accurate are the parts I wrote myself."[4] He mentioned his latest play, *Too True to be Good*, which was "all bundled up and ready for the stage," and tantalizingly, since this was all he said about it then and later, a new book he had been working on during the voyage from Southampton. He did not yet know, he said, what it was going to turn out, except that it was to be about Russia, "which nobody knows anything about."[5] He spoke about money and the burning issue of that time of economic depression, the gold standard: "I know to my cost that every £ sterling I have is worth only 14s. here, and I've been hoping all the time that South Africa would go off the gold standard. Foolishly, you are making a party question of it. Party politics are all wrong. . . . You put one party into Parliament to govern and then put in another party to keep them from governing. . . ."[6]

A large crowd followed him as he disembarked and walked along the quayside. One man kept shouting "Bernard Shaw!" as though the name in itself was as good a welcoming slogan as one could want. The Shaws were driven to the Queen's Hotel, where they remained during their stay in Cape Town. Here a *Cape Times* reporter got the scoop of the day—an exclusive interview in which Shaw spoke at length on a typically Shavian diversity of subjects.[7]

He began by commenting on the question of the "black proletariat":

> It seems to me to create an appalling problem. The white man with a trade or profession or owning property is in a strong position, but when you have "poor whites" up against black men with a lower standard of living, what can you do with them? Simply drop them in the water?

Later in the interview, after a few remarks about the "breakdown of morality" since the war, he returned to the question of race and color, giving it a religious bias. His comments are particularly interesting in the light of the fable he wrote a few weeks later, *The Adventures of the*

Black Girl in Her Search for God. The germ of this book may well be discerned here:

> The average modern Christian does not realize he is not a Christian, and does not know what it is to be a Christian. Yet he is making a Christian of the negroes.
>   One does not know what is going to happen. Civilization is like a tree. It grows to a point and then perishes. We do not know that the next civilization may not be a black civilization. There is a danger in natives taking their Christianity with intense seriousness, because they will find out their teachers only profess to be Christians. The best thing would be to develop their intelligence and make them sceptics.

The absence in England of a religion concerned with human conduct and the presence of "true religion" only in Russia came next.

> Where will you get genuine religious fanaticism? You get it in Russia. They have a religion and they believe in it. The man who is religious is working for something outside himself. . . . He carries out the Christian doctrine that "all are equal"—he may say "before Marx." No one believes here that the black man is the equal of the white, that the professional man is the equal of the retail shopkeeper, equal in the sight of God—but the Russians do believe it. The child there is taught to work for the State and the community.

Next came a digression on trade, which was "a drawback to human existence. . . . If you asked a business man what was his idea of a derelict place, he would say the Garden of Eden, because Eve gave Adam the apple instead of trading it. . . ." The interviewer brought Shaw back to the subject of religion and elicited a lengthy response on the "tremendous moral force" that science was beginning to exert:

> . . . Today science is becoming a formidable force. As long as it remained materialistic it made men cowards and scoundrels. They would not admit anything outside their own bodies. They had a horrible determinism and a dreadful fatalism. They could not do anything.
>   But now science is becoming really scientific. Now it is getting hold of men's souls, and men are discovering there is something outside themselves. . . .
>   The moment science becomes religious, as it is becoming, men will find in it what they are seeking. If they go to ordinary religion they find it is mixed up with things that no educated man can possibly believe. When they turn to science, religion will become scientific and politics will become scientific, as has happened to some extent in Russia. . . .

Shaw then expounded his belief in a Life Force—"some urge in men towards development"—and "nearly jumped out of his chair in horror" when asked about personal immortality: "Think of me living for ever—

that the world could never get rid of me. No one could stand it. Think
of your General Hertzog living for ever as an angel."[8] There was a little
more on the Life Force and the interview came to an end. The report is
unusually long and thorough. It induced a violent but fortunately isolated reaction.

In the afternoon Commander Newton of the Cape Town Publicity
Association[9] took the Shaws for a drive round the city. This included a
visit to the Rhodes Memorial on the western flank of Table Mountain,
where G. F. Watts's equestrian statue, "Physical Energy,"[10] appears to
have captured Shaw's special interest. He was reported as saying it was
one of the finest things of its kind he had ever seen.

He was undoubtedly worth more than one day's publicity. What, for
example, about the famous man's famous vegetarian diet? For breakfast
on Tuesday 12th he had porridge, a grapefruit, bread and marmalade,
and a cereal drink. The *Argus* reminded its readers that Shaw did not
drink tea or coffee. For lunch, breaking off a sight-seeing tour of the
Cape Peninsula at the Lord Nelson's Hotel, Simon's Town, he had lettuce
and tomato salad and "all the different varieties of nuts that could be
found in Simon's Town." Thereafter Cape Town left his diet to its right-
ful privacy, although it seems that those responsible for arranging his
visit had an anxious time ensuring that menus were right.

What were his plans? "Seeing South Africa and saying nothing," Shaw
told the *Argus*. The irony of this remark does not seem to have struck
anyone. Shaw loathed sight-seeing and loved talking; he was constitu-
tionally incapable of reversing these tendencies. Soon, despite earlier
denials, he had agreed to address the University of Cape Town Lunch
Club, the Cape Town Breakfast Club,[11] a public gathering at the City
Hall, the University of Stellenbosch, and finally the nation—the last to
be accomplished by a link-up of radio stations across the country.

Tuesday was quiet, Wednesday busy. It began with an appointment
with a newspaper photographer in the hotel grounds. Shaw reminisced
at length on his experiences before the camera. During his visit to Russia
the year before (in 1931), ". . . they were making a film about Lenin.
They asked me to appear in it, and I did so. I even told them how to do
it." There had to be a re-take of a short piece because something had
gone wrong. At the re-take Shaw had a necktie on, whereas in the original he had been without one. "So there is a movie film of George Bernard Shaw in which half-way through a tie miraculously appears on his
shirt front and then a moment or two later vanishes just as miraculously."[12]

He addressed the University Lunch Club at midday. The venue was
the old Opera House restaurant. An all-male audience (women gradu-
ates of the University were excluded, to their considerable chagrin)

crowded into both the main and adjoining rooms. The address was broadcast locally, evidently with great success. As the radio columnist of *The Cape Times* said, ". . . Mr. Shaw brought to the microphone qualities of diction, dynamic forcefulness and personal distinction which made yesterday's relay one of the most notable ever broadcast in the history of the station."[13]

Shaw began[14] by remarking that the university question was perhaps one of the most important in modern society. Were he to become an absolute dictator, one of his first actions would be to do to the universities what Henry VIII had done to the monasteries. He would abolish them. "I should probably sell Eton, Harrow, Oxford and Cambridge to American visitors. . . . You see, universities are not fulfilling their proper social functions. Of course, I don't know anything about your universities here. All I know is that your university building in Cape Town appears to me to belong to a rather crude state of architecture."

He discussed university elections. Anyone with any reputation for intellectuality was never elected, either for the university seat in Parliament or for the rectorship. "The person who is elected is usually the very crudest description of politician, a politician who has never been under the slightest suspicion of having been educated, so far as one can judge from his utterances."

What, he asked, was the business of a university? It was not to create a professional class. "The university is there to produce mental civilization. No matter what a man is, whether he is a professional man, a soldier, a parson, or even a politician—the object of sending him to a university is that he shall have a civilized mind and not a savage mind."

The universities of England and Germany were turning out men who were highly qualified technically, but were mental savages. Shaw explained the global implications of this kind of mis-education. Science and technology were placing the most extraordinary powers of destruction in the hands of men who for the most part were incapable of dealing with them and using them in a civilized way. War, he said, was an extraordinarily effective way of changing things, but it almost always did the opposite to what was aimed at by the men who made war. Those who had made the Great War of 1914–18 had certainly not expected it to establish Communism in Russia or destroy the three empires which were the backbone of the old European regime.

In further illustration of the way a war waged by "savage minds" could backfire on the makers, he said:

> I hardly like to come nearer home, but I remember the South African War. I remember the university-savage-schoolboy kind of popular feeling at the beginning of that war, when nothing too contemptible could be said about, or attributed to the Boer.[15] The word Boer lent itself to

alliteration. Whenever a Boer saw a white flag he immediately, we were told, fired on the bearer of that flag, and whenever he saw a Red Cross he immediately fired on the stretcher-bearer. He even did what no Englishman would ever have dreamt of doing, he fired flat-nosed bullets at the enemy.

Well, you know what happened in that war. You know that we were determined that the Orange Free State and the Transvaal were not going to be independent and the Empire was going to be the Empire. We fought the Boers and, after being licked an extraordinary number of times to our great surprise, still in the end Providence is on the side of the big battalions and we were victorious in a sense. With what result? We won the war and at the present time the Orange Free State and the Transvaal are bullying the British Empire.

They can show more independence—more real independence—than ever President Kruger dreamt about.

He had, he told his audience, been prophesying the day when England would enter on its last fight for independence—a fight waged by the Dominions, led perhaps by South Africa, "and with a very large share from the Irish Free State."

He would, he said, tell his audience a "secret." He recalled an incident of the Great War. The Germans had accused the British of using flat-nosed bullets. "We had to apologise and confess that it was an unfortunate mistake which would not recur. The ammunition had been supplied owing to an unfortunate oversight from some which had been left over from the South African War!"

After the luncheon, Shaw, Charlotte, and a small party of friends, with the inevitable newspapermen in attendance, went up Table Mountain by cableway. He admired the view from the tea-room at the summit (Fig. 2) and impressed the *Cape Times* reporter with his agility. "How are you enjoying our sunshine, Mr. Shaw?" "At my time of life, young man, you are beyond the youthful delusion of enjoying things. You are only too pleased if nothing unpleasant happens." An autograph hunter asked him to add a message to his signature. "At my time of life, you have exhausted all your impromptus." He had attended an exhibition of indigenous art that morning; he told the *Cape Times* reporter he had been greatly impressed by the quality of the paintings (Fig. 3).

This ended Shaw's public appearances for the week, although the newspapers continued to carry snippets of gossipy news and anecdotes. At the weekend the *Argus* remarked: "On the whole Cape Town has been extremely polite to Mr. Shaw and has respected his wish for a restful holiday. Mr. Shaw, for his part, has been quite exceptionally polite to Cape Town—so far."

On Monday of the second week (18 January) he visited Stellenbosch and was the guest of the University at a luncheon in Dagbreek, the men's

FIG. 2. At the tea-room on Table Mountain. (Photo: courtesy of the *Cape Times*)

residence.[16] His address was characteristic. As *Die Burger* reported part of it:

> Students should not have lectures from one Professor only. Suppose both Professor Jones and Professor Robinson lecture in history. Jones has a low opinion of Robinson. Both should appear before a class and, while Robinson delivers his lecture, Jones should be allowed to criticize him and show that he too knows nothing about the subject.[17]

The remainder of the week was quiet. One assumes that he took advantage of the hot dry weather to enjoy the surf at Muizenberg.[18] A special room had been set aside for him at the pavilion on the beach front. He also swam at nearby St James. It was here that one naughty schoolboy bet another naughty schoolboy sixpence he wouldn't "duck" Shaw. The second schoolboy, whose desire for wealth obviously exceeded his respect for greatness, did the dreadful deed—after asking Shaw's permission.[19]

On Friday evening, 22 January, his eye caught the following headline in the *Argus*: "Who then is this G.B.S.?"[20] The report that followed, a summary of an article in the current issue of *The Southern Cross*, the Roman Catholic weekly newspaper, contained more than a hint of controversy: as reported by the *Argus*, the article in question verged on defamation, if not libel. The writer, Father O.R. Vassall-Phillips, granted Shaw his "gift for writing good and nervous English, and above all plays

FIG. 3. Admiring a Dutch "Old Master" in one of Cape Town's art galleries, Shaw praised contemporary South African art. (Photo: courtesy of the *Cape Times*)

that strike the imagination." For the rest, Shaw was marked out by "almost incredible intellectual arrogance . . . egolomania . . . passionate determination to get himself always into the limelight . . . conceit." Vassall-Phillips's attack gathered in fury as it proceeded: ". . . the more extravagant his statements the better he seems pleased . . . he will hesitate or stop at nothing, and seems to rejoice in making statements which he knows will be deeply offensive . . . he is as arrogant and insolent as he is pretentious and crafty. . . . Withdraw your imposture and general offensiveness from men in Cape Town who still believe in Christ and Christianity . . . you are not wanted."[21]

Shaw's reply appeared in the *Argus* the next day, on January 23.[22]

> You have given the currency of your large and unsectarian circulation to certain statements connected with my name by Father Vassall-Phillips in a Roman Catholic journal.
>
> The first statement is that a large number of persons attach some importance to my words. I hope this is true; but I fear that Father Vassall-Phillips would be hard put to it to produce any practical evidence of it.
>
> But, as he believes it to be true, he must also believe that, in claiming

my authority for any sort of doctrine, he is giving importance to that doctrine.

He then claims my authority for the doctrine that no educated men believe in Christianity, because I do not believe in it myself.

Yet I gather from the rest of his article as quoted, that he does not wish to discredit Christianity, though he clearly does wish—very unchristianly—to discredit me.

In short, he uses the cross as a stick to beat me with, without stopping to consider what the effect of his assault will be on the large number of people who, he believes, will vote against Christianity if they are led to believe that I am opposed to it.

Now it is the way of priests to lose their heads when Christ is in question. They are unable to forget that they crucified him. And they seem equally unable to remember it.

If I venture, as I have done, to say a word on Christ's behalf, as against Barabbas, they rend their garments and shriek "Blasphemy!" as of old.

But if I point out that Christ is still, as of old, despised and rejected of men, especially educated men, they warn people not to listen to me, as they have adopted Him and made Him respectable.

There is no pleasing them.

Anyone who is interested in my view of Christ and Christianity will find it set forth at length with all the lucidity I can command in the preface to my play, "Androcles and the Lion."

Of Father Vassall-Phillips's view I know nothing except what I gather from your quotations from his article.

I therefore have no right to criticise it at large. But all my cards are on the table; and I should rather like him, for the good of his soul, to study them before he next calls me to judgment.

Father Vassall-Phillips's reply appeared on the front page of the *Southern Cross* the following week.[23] Like his first article, it is notable mainly for its distracted quality. He admitted that he had not read *Androcles and the Lion*; his attack on Shaw had been induced solely by the interview in *The Cape Times* of 12 January.

A more rewarding experience during the second week of the visit was a flight over the Peninsula. Newspapers carried pictures of Shaw and Charlotte getting into the aircraft, sitting in it, getting out of it. It was not Shaw's first venture into the air but the flight over Table Mountain and other scenic splendours provided, he said, one of the biggest thrills he had had in years.[24]

He attended a symphony concert at the City Hall and was asked what he thought of the Municipal Orchestra and local music generally. The conductor, William Pickerill, was doing a fine job with very limited resources. Shaw was certain Pickerill could arrange to play Wagner's *Ring* for a concertina, two Jew's harps, and a saxophone, but it was scarcely fair to expect him to do this. Jazz, he added, was played abominably in Cape Town.[25]

There is no record of public engagements during the third week, although it was probably at this time that the Prime Minister, Hertzog, entertained him and Charlotte at his official Cape Town residence, Groote Schuur ("Big Granary"). The entire Cabinet was present for what was evidently an afternoon reception. According to a *Cape Times* columnist writing after Shaw had left the country (there was of course no newspaper coverage of the occasion), Shaw and Hertzog got on extraordinarily well and were observed in the garden in animated conversation.

Shaw's meeting with General Smuts went rather differently. Fortunately it has been recorded—by the rueful hostess herself. Sarah Gertrude Millin, who knew Shaw, invited him to meet Smuts at a private luncheon party. "Here," she said to herself, "will be historic talk":[26]

> Each tried conscientiously to produce it. Smuts told a story about his guerrilla work in the Boer War . . . and mentioned Shaw's friend, T. E. Lawrence. Shaw, hearing only part of Smuts's comment, thought he was referring to D. H. Lawrence and responded, "Every schoolgirl of sixteen should read *Lady Chatterley's Lover*." As Smuts seldom read novels and had never read Lawrence or heard of *Lady Chatterley's Lover*, he saw no reason why every schoolgirl of sixteen should not read *Lady Chatterley's Lover*, and, in his eager, polite way, he said: "Of course, of course." So nothing was provoked there.
>
> Then Shaw tried another subject. He said that for a country to go off the gold standard was simple robbery. South Africa, committed too long to the gold standard, was at the time pining away, and Smuts (though I don't know whether Shaw had been in the country long enough to notice it) was going from platform to platform passionately preaching "Off gold." Here was no nonsense about novels, lovers and schoolgirls; Smuts gripped his lips thinly and tightly together and made no response. After that the lunch soon ended.[27]

Shaw delivered his promised address on the rationalization of Russia on Monday, 1 February, the beginning of his fourth week in Cape Town. When first asked by local Fabians to give the talk, he had demurred, saying he did not want to strain his "nice Irish voice." He had changed his mind on learning that microphones would be installed. "Let them all come," he said. They did. The City Hall was packed. The audience overflowed onto the stage. His listeners ranged from Cabinet Ministers to what the *Argus* described as "various species of Socialist." It was a record audience and it paid record prices to get in.

It could have been a major occasion. For many in the audience no doubt it was; but, judging from the report in the *Argus*,[28] Shaw let himself down. He spoke for over two hours. The first hour he gave a witty generalised preamble on such matters as politics *vis-à-vis* natural history, the rarity of political intelligence, the political intelligence of the Fabian Society, and hence the desirability of being governed in South Africa, not by retired businessmen and farmers, but by active Fabians. The eventual focus of his address was Russia and the triumph of Bolshevism, the leaders of which he described fulsomely. He was reported as saying:

> Trotsky and Lenin, like all true Fabians, first joined the Provisional Government Party in Russia, got into the enemy's camp, spread their opinions and made an opposition. They then formed the Soviets. . . . One of the first things Lenin had to do was to shoot the syndicalists. It was no longer a question of shooting the enemies of the revolution. He had to purge his own ranks. . . . During the counter-revolutionary wars Trotsky performed the most amazing feats of organisation. . . . Probably he will go down with Napoleon, Caesar and Alexander as one of the great military figures in history. . . . Stalin was an opportunist who survived because he was successful. Stalin did not look at the Marxist bible. He took whatever steps were necessary and organised on the system of trial and error. People who opposed the Government were liquidated.

Shaw concluded by praising the Russian system of collective farming and advising South Africa to follow suit: "If you want to make South Africa or any part of Africa a land flowing with milk and honey you must do it on the largest scale and get your fertiliser from the air."

An *Argus* leader of 2 February tactfully pointed to the dichotomy between Shaw's Socialism and Bolshevik Communism and asked how it was possible for a Fabian to sympathise with a tyranny.[29] The Fabian Socialist in question would certainly have retorted that a Bolshevik tyranny was preferable to a Capitalist tyranny, but this would have been an evasion. As the leader said: "We want to know much more about moral values," and Shaw failed to say anything about these.

A week later, on the eve of his departure from Cape Town, on Saturday 6 February, Shaw gave his broadcast talk.[30] This was one of the first times, if not the first time, that a national link-up of radio stations was attempted. Fifteen hundred miles of telephone wire carried his voice to Johannesburg, Durban, Pretoria, and Bloemfontein. "Hullo, South Africa. Bernard Shaw speaking from Cape Town." He had, he said, been asked to say nice things on his departure from Cape Town, but he asked to be excused. Saying nice things was not his business. It was the job of the Prince of Wales (who had visited South Africa in 1925) to say nice things.

> Mine is to say all the things that he could not have said without shaking your loyal attachment to the Imperial Throne.
>
> For instance, His Royal Highness pointed out very truly that the most important source of Cape Town's income is its sunshine. He said nothing about its moonshine as he is not allowed to meddle in party politics.

He praised the climate. Cape Town was not easy to leave. It was a "sun-trap."

He directed his talk away from "nice things" to more thought-provoking things. The finest sun-trap in the world was all very well, but it depended on what one caught in it. Sun-traps tended to catch people with plenty of money and nothing to do. One could easily, if one were short-sighted enough, become dependent on the money they spent. This was all very well as long as their money lasted. "But suppose it should suddenly dry up!"

He pointed to what had happened in Russia, where the money that had maintained "sun-traps" or similar indulgences had dried up suddenly and decisively. It was, he said in effect, sheer foolishness for a city or a country to build its economy on such weak foundations.

> Now what has happened in Russia may happen elsewhere. These are times in which everybody should be brought up to earn his or her own living.
>
> What is more, he should be brought up to earn it by working for workers and not for unproductive Plutocrats whose riches may vanish in a single night of revolution.

He did not want to frighten Capetonians out of building beautiful hotels and houses. They would not be wasted. On the contrary, they would be wanted as much as ever when the rich of all lands had gone the way of the Russian grand dukes. "What you have to do is to abolish your slums, for which, let me tell you, Cape Town deserves to be destroyed by fire from Heaven."

Shaw now widened the context of his remarks to consider South Africa as a whole. Could the country ever be self-supporting? During his address at the City Hall the previous Monday he had touched on South Africa's agricultural poverty and recommended what amounted to the Russianization of farming. He now repeated this advice: nationalize agriculture, which he did not think would be beyond the capability of South Africans, even though it would cost millions in mental as well as metal currency.

He spoke at some length in this vein and then, as though in reply to the *Argus* query about "moral values," he turned away from material considerations to focus on "a very serious part of the business."

> One of the first things I noticed when I landed was that I immediately became dependent on the services of men and women who are not of my own colour. I felt that I was in a Slave State, and that, too, the very worst sort of Slave State.
>
> I mean the sort in which the slaves are not owned by masters who are responsible for their welfare, nor protected by stringent laws from ill

treatment, but one in which they are nominally free, like white people, and can be thrown into the streets to starve, without pensions or public relief, when nobody happens to need their services or when they are old and are displaced by the young.

This state of things makes wise people uneasy. Foolish people think that the danger is that the slaves will rebel and refuse to do any more work. But that is not the real danger at all; and even if it were it would not matter, because white men can still easily suppress rebellions even if they have to employ black men to help them.

No, the real snag in the business is that if you let other people do everything for you you soon become incapable of doing anything for yourself.

You become an idler and a parasite, a weakling and an imbecile; and though you may also become a very pretty lady or gentleman you will be helpless in the hands of your slaves, who will have all the strength and knowledge and character that come from working and from nothing else. . . . Even the things that you still can do for yourself he can make you ashamed to do.

He actually dictates your ideas of right and wrong, respectable and disreputable, until you are his mental as well as his bodily slave, while all the time you flatter yourself that you are his lord and master. . . .

There is only one way of escaping this fate where slavery exists, whether the slavery be black or poor white.

Take my own case. The slave who fetches and carries for me, who cooks and sweeps and dusts for me, who does rough, muscular or mechanical work for me, sets me free to do work of a higher kind just as surely as to idle and loaf.

If I do the higher work, the slave will look up to me and never grudge me his service if I acknowledge its value to me and treat him decently. In fact his industry will no longer be slavery, for we shall both be doing our bit, I for him and he for me.

But if I make the downward choice and idle and loaf, woe betide me; for there is no future now in the world for idlers and loafers.

If white civilisation breaks down through idleness and loafing based on slavery—and remember that modern historical research has discovered that half a dozen civilisations like ours have already broken down through just that canker in them—then, as likely as not, the next great civilisation will be a negro civilisation.

Anyhow, black or white, it will be built up by workers, not by parasite ladies and gentlemen.

Shaw concluded his talk with words of appreciation to South Africa for her hospitality. "I broadcast my thanks to you from a heart full of gratitude and a stomach full of peaches. Good night and good luck."

His popularity fell after this broadcast. People had wondered what he would say if he said anything. He had now said something and a lot of people did not like it. Shaw had, perhaps knowingly, stood on quite a number of sensitive toes. There were letters to the papers, the general predictable drift of which was that Shaw should clean up the English back yard before criticizing anyone else's. *The Cape Times* reported the talk in full but offered no comment. The *Argus* took pains in rebutting Shaw's advice about South African agriculture, but said nothing about the other issues he had raised. *Die Burger* contented itself with a brief sentence: "Mr Shaw gave a farewell broadcast to Cape Town on Saturday evening and said what he thought of the city in his own idiosyncratic way." There were ripples in even the London press. *The Times* said nothing, but one or two of the more popular dailies heatedly reported Shaw's "rudeness to his hosts." No one appears to have tried to answer Shaw's charge about the "slave state" in which he found himself or argued against his perception of moral degeneracy among the white "masters."

Shaw and Charlotte left Cape Town the next day (on Sunday, 7 February) but they did not leave South Africa. Shaw had taken a driving test in Cape Town and been given a license. He and Charlotte, accompanied by Commander C. P. Newton, now motored along the Garden Route to Knysna, where they intended staying a few weeks before continuing to Port Elizabeth, thence by boat to Durban, and home via the East coast of Africa.

Shaw fancied himself behind the wheel, but he did not drive well. He had an accident between George and Knysna, driving the car off the road. Shaw and Commander Newton, who was in the passenger seat next to him, were unhurt. Charlotte, in the back seat, was flung violently forward while suitcases and other luggage fell over her, leaving her bruised and shaken. Shaw, fearing a deluge of reporters and other unwanted enquirers, tried to minimize both her injuries and the accident itself. He told Blanche Patch something of the truth: ". . . the injuries are only bruises and sprains and a troublesome hole in the shin plus two black eyes. . . ." As Blanche Patch remarks: ". . . quite enough one would say, for a venerable lady of seventy-six."[31]

The accident induced them to change their plans. They would not go on to Durban but remain at Knysna[32] and return to Cape Town when Charlotte had recovered. They would go home via the West coast aboard the *Warwick Castle*.

Newspapers got wind of the accident, of course. Both *The Times* of London and the *New York Times* carried reports. Shaw felt that the correspondent for *The Cape Times* had his facts wrong, and sent a telegram:

> I most indignantly deny that I drove into a ditch.
> I have never done such a thing. I cleared
> a ditch;
> a hedge;

a fence;

a formidable bunker;

and several minor cross-country obstacles when the ingenious construction of an apparently straight and safe stretch of South African road
deflected me into the veld.

I challenge your Mossel Bay correspondent to emulate that feat. . . .[33]

It was during this enforced stay at Knysna that Shaw wrote *The Adventures of the Black Girl in Her Search for God,* instead of, as he says, writing
a play in the ordinary course of his business as a playwright.[34] He had
been in South Africa for nearly eight weeks and it was inevitable that his
impressions of the country and its people should find their way into the
book, universal fable though it is. The setting, Africa, and the black girl
herself are obvious derivations; similarly, the forest she enters in her
search could be, and in Shaw's mind probably was, the dense coastal
forest of that part of the Eastern Cape where Knysna is situated. Some
details—the "mamba snake" and the "sort of cobra called a ringhals,"
for example—also place the story in southern Africa. A few words of
Dutch-Afrikaans origin occur in the text: the "knobkerry," the black
girl's cudgel, is one; the "ringhals," a spitting cobra, is another; "baas,"
meaning "master," is another. For a South African the most amusing
borrowing is "tickey," meaning a three-penny bit—banished from the
national English vocabulary with the introduction of a decimal currency
in the 1960s. The passage in which "tickey" is used suggests that Shaw
was rather taken with the word.[35]

The Black Girl in Search of God is an oddity in Shaw's literary and public
career at that time, when the problem of good and effective government—politics—was his main concern. Almost everything he said and
wrote from *The Apple Cart* onwards testifies to this. Why, then, this re-
version to religious themes? Could his South African experience have
had something to do with it? One can only speculate, but it is possible
that Father Vassall-Phillips's attack on Shaw, and his reply, prompted
him to go back some twenty years (to *Androcles and the Lion*) and decide
that some embellishment of an old theme would be worth his while. And
it is just possible that his encounter with South African society, mixed
and divided as it was and still is, could have prompted him to take his
black girl on her quest, and in particular to her confrontation with the
Caravan of the Curious.[36]

On the day of his arrival in Cape Town, Shaw had spoken about the
"appalling problem" of the "black proletariat" and gone on to remark,
"We do not know that the next civilization may not be a black civilization."[37] The lady ethnologist in the Caravan is more forthright, "I keep
telling you . . . that the next great civilization will be a black civilization.

The white man is played out. He knows it, too, and is committing suicide as fast as he can." The black girl's rejoinder, which is both an endorsement of the lady ethnologist's opinion and a denunciation of "the man-beating slave-driver and the trampling baas," echoes what Shaw had said in his radio broadcast about the moral corruption that can overtake a lazy, self-seeking people. She is far more outspoken than Shaw had been, possibly because in travelling from the Western to the Eastern Cape, Shaw had come face to face with a situation that Cape Town had only hinted at. A black person in the Western Cape in the 1930s was a comparative rarity. The "slaves" Shaw would have observed were the Cape Coloureds—people of mixed descent—who enjoyed full political rights at the time, although their economic and social status reduced them to the servitude that Shaw deplored. During his stay at Knysna Shaw would have found himself in a racially very mixed society with relatively few whites, many Coloureds, and perhaps as many blacks, whose position was and still is at the bottom of the political, economic, and social ladder. The discrimination against the Coloureds of Cape Town was marked enough to disturb Shaw, but it was—and remains—mild compared with the discrimination against the blacks of the Eastern Cape and elsewhere in the country. Hence the black girl's fierce attack on white exploitation and dominance and her disturbing vision of the future. Her wish for a true God who will destroy the false gods of the white man and not destroy her own people in turn is, of course, a central Shavianism, but in the context of Shaw's sojourn at Knysna it has marked local implications.[38]

One exchange during the black girl's confrontation with the Caravan of the Curious is worth quoting in full because it echoes what Shaw had already said and anticipates what he was still to say:

> "It would throw them back on the doctrine of the survival of the fittest" said the first gentleman dubiously; "and it is not clear that we are the fittest to survive in competition with them. That girl is a fine specimen. We have had to give up employing poor whites for the work of our expedition: the natives are stronger, cleaner, and more intelligent."
> "Besides having much better manners" said one of the ladies.

The "poor whites" (a South African coinage) were a product of socio-economic pressures of the 1920s and 1930s: thousands of Afrikaners were forced off the land and migrated to the cities where, usually unskilled in everything except farming, they were forced to seek jobs in competition with equally unskilled blacks. This was a problem Shaw knew about before arriving in South Africa; it may be recalled that he asked a rhetorical question about simply dropping the "poor whites" in the water, which, in a sense, the Caravan of the Curious does by employing blacks as bearers. The "poor whites" of the Knysna region, of whom Shaw spoke in his final interview, were a distinctive species: forest-dwellers, wood-choppers for the most part, they were as backward and degenerate as only in-breeding and the isolation of nearly a hundred years can make a community. The conflicts in South Africa disturbed Shaw far more than his public statements suggest. In a letter to Emery Walker, from Cape Town, Shaw lamented what he saw as insoluble problems caused by the competition for unskilled employment between poor whites and the blacks, who were paid next to nothing and provided with neither pensions nor unemployment insurance, and by the conflicts between the antagonistic white populations, the Dutch and the English.[39]

He and Charlotte left South Africa on Friday 18 March, a month after the motor accident. He chartered all the seats on the Union Airway Junker and returned to Cape Town with Charlotte, now recovered from her injuries. They went straight to the *Warwick Castle*. An *Argus* reporter followed them on board and secured a final interview with Shaw.

> In many ways South Africa is dull though beautiful. If I told you the whole truth about it you would never publish it.
>
> When I spoke over the wireless in Cape Town when I was here before, I said more or less what I thought about the South African people.
>
> Since I have been out into the country I have seen more of them and particularly the Dutch.[40]
>
> I think they are a fine, upstanding race, particularly well built and interesting because they have been so long isolated from the world. Outside events have not touched them. The French Revolution and other great developments in Europe have passed them by.
>
> All they need is education. Make them take an interest in things and be intelligent. And, above all, ban the Bible; take the Bible away from them. They depend too much on it.
>
> I do not think your natives are psychologically more interesting than the white races. But they are more intelligent—they are the only people who can do your work—and they have far better manners.
>
> You ask me whether South Africa will ever "go native." I think the question should be: "Will the native ever go South African?" He seems to get little opportunity of doing so.
>
> You ask me whether South Africa needs a five-year plan. . . . This country does not need a five-year plan. You have too much self-denial already. There are thousands of people in the country starving—thousands of natives with scarcely enough food to keep them alive. . . .
>
> What you want to do is to shoot your poor whites—every one of them. You should also shoot many of your rich whites.
>
> At Knysna—a very beautiful stretch of country—I came on large numbers of absolutely degenerate people—people with no intelligence, absolutely hopeless as stock for South Africa. You ought to shoot them all.[41]

He went on to speak briefly about his new work: "It is not a book at all—it is merely a large pamphlet which an enterprising publisher would make into a book. It deals with a native girl's search for God. Whatever I think about South Africa," he concluded, "it has made me well."

II

Shaw and Charlotte arrived in Durban on Sunday, 28 April 1935, for their second visit to South Africa, having travelled down the east coast of Africa in the *Llangibby Castle*. Blanche Patch, quoting letters from Shaw and Charlotte, reports that the voyage had been less than restful. Storms round the Iberian peninsula, Shaw working furiously on the final draft of *The Millionairess*, notwithstanding a persisting head-cold, stops at several ports-o'-call on the east coast, where shipboard and dockside bustle and noise disturbed them greatly—these familiars of sea-travel (and Shaw's compulsion to work "thirty-six hours a day") did not augur well for the peaceful holiday they were both seeking.[42] And, of course, the ship had scarcely docked before the reporters came on board. They found Shaw finishing his breakfast, recovered from his cold and in a genial mood.[43]

He was first asked to talk about drama. "Excellent! That's just the one subject about which I know absolutely nothing!" Asked whether he would name any successor to John Galsworthy or himself, he refused, then added: "There are a great number of very clever people about, but I don't know. I don't go to the theatre now as I am too old for that. But, you know, there are just as good fish in the sea as came out of it." He spoke about *The Millionairess*, the text of which had been posted back home from Mombasa. He told the reporters that the heroine was a "sort of female Cecil Rhodes." There was no politics in it except the politics of money. "Hitherto my plays have been for the most part fables, plays written for children. Now I have amused myself writing a play something in the manner of Ben Jonson. You are to regard me, if you please, as the modern Ben Jonson." He was asked if there were "any long pieces of dialogue" in the new play. "Of course there are some long speeches, but on the whole it is an exceptional play in comparison with my others in that the dialogue is rather crisp and short. It is a study of character, an exhibition of certain modern contemporary types we see around us."

Shaw then spoke about the situation in Europe. He had not heard about Ramsay MacDonald's critical article in "The News Letter" on Germany; when told something about it he "smiled grimly" and said it was just like his old friend Ramsay: "He's not to be beaten stringing fine words together." When asked if he saw any hope in Lloyd George's "New Deal," he replied, "Not a hope. Lloyd George missed his chance years and years ago. He ought to drop politics and concentrate on literature, for which he has a tremendous flair. I have personally strongly advised him to do so." Shaw then discussed Hitler at some length:

> Hitler was a nobody, but he was the one person who knew, and realised first, that if he re-armed, the other Powers would talk about it and do nothing else. That is what put him at the top of the tree. When he got there, I said that every German—no matter whether he was a German-Jew or German-Communist—must vote for Hitler. I said that as Germans they could not refuse to vote for Hitler.
>
> When our bluff was called it was our business to have admitted the situation. We could see what was happening and what he was going to do with Germany. But instead of that our stupid people went on nagging at him and Hitler said outright: "If you go on like that Germany will leave the League of Nations." We could not prevent him. If Germany did not have a sense of grievance under the Treaty of Versailles the people would divide on political issues and Hitler would lose his power. Our stupidity lay in not recognising what put Hitler where he is and where he wanted to be. As H.G. Wells said, we were like a lot of governesses.

These sentiments were, of course, in line with what Shaw was saying about Hitler and Germany in the mid-thirties. Similarly, his denunciation of armaments conferences as an institution for the gratification of the weak-minded is a typical Shavianism of the period: "All they come to is the question: 'Could we not say we will kill each other with 10-inch shells rather than with 16-inch shells as the former don't cost so much?'" As was to be expected, he spoke about Russia—as the one great bulwark of the world's peace.

Africa came next. Shaw criticized people for saying that the problem in Africa was between white and black. It was much more difficult than that because the black races were so numerous and complicated. It was an extraordinary problem. As for Abyssinia, he did not know what was going to happen. Mussolini was like Hitler and if he made up his mind that Abyssinia was worth going for he would go for it and the situation would become "extremely difficult."

This ended the interview. It was the first and last of its kind that Shaw gave during his three-week stay in Durban. He made it clear on arrival that he was not prepared to address any public or private gatherings; he had, he said, retired from the public platform for good (he was nearly seventy-nine years old) and was in need of a holiday. Although he made several public or semipublic appearances during his visit—two or three times in person, several times in print—the people and press of Durban respected his request for at least a modicum of privacy. Shaw reciprocated by being a model guest who left behind him an impression of "an elderly Irish gentleman of great personal charm, with a keen sense of fun, of unfailing courtesy and positive kindness"—an impression as unlike the "churlish egotistic Shaw" of the Cape Town visit as it was possible to conceive.[44]

Shaw was not to be allowed to escape scot-free. The Durban branch of Rotary apparently asked him, even before he disembarked, to attend their lunch on Tuesday 30 April. Shaw first refused, then hesitated, and then, some time later, agreed. He was not to be the official guest speaker—this was Norman Tiptaft, a Fabian acquaintance and a prominent British Rotarian—but of course Shaw spoke. More than the usual interest attended his talk because of his notorious remark in Hong Kong that the Rotary had degenerated into a "luncheon club." He wasted no time in reasserting this view, giving it an ironic twist that anyone who knows *Socialism for Millionaires* will appreciate:[45]

> What I said was that Rotary was very speedily becoming a mere luncheon club, the members of which had no idea of what the original intentions were. And, after all, a luncheon club is a very harmless thing.
> But now I find that it is not only a luncheon club, but also a charitable organisation.

The original ideas behind the formation of Rotary were for the improvement of business. In the past it had been accepted that an employer of labor was the master of a nation; this was not the case today.

> You must be aware of the truth of what I have said—that your grip has slipped and that you are getting more into the hands of the financier and more and more into the hands of the international financier who, as long as he can get his profit all over the world, cares nothing for you locally. . . .
> You really want to organise your profession, to establish scholarships at the University for the study of business as a science. You have got to realise that commerce is not a thing you just pick up. There is such a thing as commercial science and the employer has the right to say I am a man of science. . . .
> Next time I go to a Rotary Club I shall be still more disparaging. I want to wake you up and draw your attention to your own affairs. You have a great power.

The talk was evidently not long—the official guest speaker had to be given his chance—and perhaps of less moment than other Shavian utterances during the South African visits. Other speakers at the luncheon tried good-humoredly to rebut Shaw's remarks. All the same, and in spite of the rebuttals, what Shaw said to Rotary is probably still relevant.

That evening (Tuesday 30 April) Shaw gave a short radio broadcast from his suite at the Marine Hotel.[46] Maurice Webb was his host at the microphone. Shaw spoke about landmarks in English literature. Judging from the short report in the *Natal Mercury*,[47] it was a slight, informal discussion in which Shaw drew attention to the attitudes of Walter Scott, Thackeray, and Dickens to the institutions of their day. In *Little Dorrit* Dickens had forecast the decay of the Parliamentary system. "Starting life as a Parliamentary reporter, he had seen the utter futility of the system. . . . Within the past few years we have seen this wonderful Parliamentary sytem go absolutely smash—kicked into the gutter by men like Hitler, Mustapha Kemal Pasha and Mussolini, and any leader who had a really strong realistic sense. . . ."

After the radio broadcast Shaw was allowed to enjoy a more-or-less private holiday. He was still to be cornered by reporters, still to give the newspapers two[48] self-drafted interviews and still to be the guest of honor at several functions, but he and Charlotte were, by and large, spared the public harassment that seemed an invariable component of his fame. He was very active socially, the arrangement being that Durban Shavians, Fabians, and other interested people would take turns entertaining him and Charlotte.

Maurice Webb wrote an appreciation of the Shaws' visit after they had left Durban, summarizing what were obviously a full three weeks:

> But for that one stipulation ["No speeches"] the famous playwright has been indulgent and amenable in the extreme. He has dined here and lunched there, and "tea-ed"—though he does not drink tea—everywhere. His range has been catholic. Not only has he called formally on the mayor, visited the homes of the wealthy on the Berea, seen our library, museum and art gallery, lunched with Rotary, called at the Jewish Club, listened to symphony concerts and a lecture at the Library Group; he has also explored the less vaunted parts of our town that lurk behind Grey Street, called on Mr Champion at the African Workers' Club—an act of courtesy as Mr Champion could not call on him—has listened to Mr Roux preaching Communism, and has discussed the Grey Shirt movement with its Natal leader.[49]

One of Shaw's public appearances was not without a touch of the bizarre. King George V's Silver Jubilee was celebrated in the second week of May and in Durban festivities got under way on Sunday 5 May with the Indian Silver Jubilee Sports. Shaw was guest of honor with two all-in wrestlers, the Masked Marvel and Ali Bey, the "Terrible Turk," and seems to have foregone most of the limelight to these two celebrities.[50] No doubt the creator of Cashel Byron (and the friend of Gene Tunney) took this in good part. On another occasion Shaw and Charlotte were taken to watch a Zulu war dance near Durban. Shaw enjoyed himself thoroughly. He attempted a few steps of the dance and said in a short speech that the singing of the Zulus had given him great pleasure. He was sure Wagner had found his inspiration for *The Flying Dutchman* in Zulu music. The Zulus had impressed him as a fine race.[51]

A reporter buttonholed him after a symphony concert at the City Hall. How was one to make the orchestra popular? Shaw said, "It is quite simple, you must never allow the hall to be half-empty. Avoid that and you will encourage the players and convince the people it is popular. Once you give them that idea you won't be able to keep them away. . . ." But how was one to get people to attend in the first place? "Quite simple. You have a lot of convicts here. Well, they must have wives and sweethearts; go out and get them, put the men in dinner suits and the women in evening dress and fill the hall with them. . . ." It would take courage to do that, said the reporter. "Oh, no. You don't need courage to make a success of things. All you need is audacity."[52]

He and Charlotte visited Pietermaritzburg[53] at the beginning of their second week, on Tuesday 7 May. They spent the night at the Imperial Hotel and motored further inland the next day to gain a distant view of the Drakensberg ("the mountains of the dragons") and a close-up view of the waterfall at Howick. They returned to Durban on Wednesday evening. The visit to Pietermaritzburg was important in that the local newspaper, *The Natal Witness*, secured, not only a routine interview, but also, a week later, an article by Shaw on the Silver Jubilee. *The Natal Witness*, once Shaw had visited Pietermaritzburg, responded by being more enthusiastically Shavian than the two Durban newspapers combined. In addition to the reports and articles already referred to, there were two leaders and—surely a newspaper "first"—a charming entry on the children's page.[54]

The interview[55] seems to have amounted to an open invitation to Shaw to talk about what he wished. He spoke a good deal about Russia in the familiar Shavian terms of the 1930s—although he allowed himself some mild criticism of one or two aspects of the Soviet system. He spoke at length, and generously, about eminent contemporaries. He was reading the proofs of Sidney Webb's book on Russia. "His [Webb's] is probably the most highly developed investigatory brain for social and political problems in Great Britain or anywhere else," said Shaw. He thought that the book would prove to be the standard contemporary work of its kind.[56] He spoke of his personal liking for both General Hertzog and General Smuts, but did not discuss South African politics beyond remarking that a system that organized the "natives" within a specific legislative framework savored of impertinence. Asked to comment on a large advertisement hoarding next to the main road from Durban, he pronounced it "Fine."

His article on the Royal Jubilee appeared a week later.[57] Like all the Dominions, South Africa—or at any rate the English-speaking section of the population—had been putting on a loyal display. In Natal, the most English of the four provinces of the Union, this built up to an orgy of flag-waving and patriotic gush. Shaw's article was a perfectly pitched and witty riposte, and it is perhaps churlish to suggest that it is not as rounded-off as one might wish.

> "Would it be indiscreet, Mr Shaw, to allude to the fact that though you have talked on many things since your arrival in Durban, you have said not one word about the Jubilee?"
>
> "Does it matter?"
>
> "Well, it is a bit remarkable, isn't it? You are one of the glories of King George's reign just as Shakespeare was one of the glories of Queen Elizabeth's."
>
> "Elizabeth would have been greatly surprised to hear you say so. There is not a scrap of serious evidence that she ever heard of Shakespeare or ever amused herself with plays. I suspect that if you told the King that I am one of the glories of his reign—though no doubt I am—he would conclude that you must be mad."

The "interview" continues in this serio-jocular vein while Shaw points to what in his opinion are two of the undoubted "glories" of the time, Augustus John and Edward Elgar, and says that King George has never had his portrait painted by John and never listened to a symphony or an oratorio by Elgar. "And he has never heard an entire play of mine, though I believe the late Earl of Oxford once planted on him at a private party an act of *John Bull's Other Island* many years ago."

> "And when, as one of the greatest events of his reign, the new Shakespeare Memorial theatre was inaugurated at Stratford-on-Avon, and even the Chinese Ambassador felt bound to grace the occasion and listen to Mr Baldwin's best oratory in praise of our great national poet, marking the occasion as a supreme one from the high artistic point of view, the King said he preferred to go to a football match. And he did—to the cup ties."
>
> "Were you dreadfully shocked, Mr Shaw?"
>
> "Shocked! Nonsense: I was delighted. It was not only a perfectly honest personal gesture; it was symbolic and representative. It was all England. I am old enough to remember the aged Emperor William of Germany, the Kaiser's grandfather, being driven like a sheep to Bayreuth to hear the first performance of Wagner's Ring in the new festival playhouse there, though he must have hated Wagner's music and was not devoted to any sort of music. It set me thinking of the need for a Society for the Prevention of Cruelty to Monarchs. Why should the King have

let himself be dragged to witness a not too distinguished performance of
Henry IV, in which he takes no interest, when there was a presumably
superb game of football available and when he had the heart of the nation behind him in his choice? The King does not like the theatre, never
goes to it, and very possibly believes that the nation would be healthier
and holier without it. . . ."

The expected Shavian paradox soon begins to emerge. Taking as his cue
the suggestion that the King "ignored" the theater, Shaw rejected the
idea, pointing out that theater managers, actors, actresses, and even
playwrights, have been knighted. What, however, about the very eminent names in literature without a handle to them?

"Be reasonable, my friend. A King cannot chuck titles about at the risk
of having them thrown back in his face; nor, since a title is a conventional
honour, can they be fittingly bestowed on unconventional persons, however gifted. Take, for instance, three of the most eminent names in Georgian literature: Colonel Lawrence of Arabia, H.G. Wells and Gilbert
Chesterton. Add myself if you like, since by your smiling I perceive you
are about to do so. Lawrence could have had any rank he liked, but he
insists on being a hermit. H.G. Wells' fame is international and would
bear any official dignity worthily; but Wells is a professed Republican and
. . . not a loyal subject to the Crown. In Chesterton's case the Pope has
been beforehand with the King and made him a Knight of the Order of
Gregory the Great, thereby getting the King out of a difficulty; for Chesterton, though the most imposing figure in literature since Dr Johnson,
and much more gifted, is the head of a Distributist League of the most
extensive subversiveness and is, like Mr Belloc, by implication a Jaco-
bite. . . .

"As for myself, I am a Red Marxist Communist of 50 years' standing,
a persistent friend of the Russian Revolution and the Soviet State and
the prophet of a modern religion which would make short work of the
Thirty-nine Articles. Ask the King to confer on me the Order of the
Garter—and I should consider anything less an insult—and he will reply: 'Am I the defender of the faith or am I not?' Besides, a title would
compromise me horribly: look at the trouble I got into with the Left
Wing because I wrote a play in which a King is the hero instead of the
villain! Where none of these difficulties and objections occur the King
comes up to the mark splendidly as in the case of Elgar. Elgar was in the
best sense a courtier: he loved the pomp and circumstances of royalty
and carried himself as he so often directed his music to be played, *nobil-
imente*. Well, the King, on his own initiative, delighted to honour Elgar:
he did everything for him short of listening to his symphonies. When he
had a royal chance he rose to it. Then what have we to complain of?
Absolutely nothing. And that is my contribution to the Jubilee."

There is a tailpiece about conferring titles on the inconspicious who
deserve recognition of their work and not conferring titles on the con-

spicious who do not need and may not deserve them. If, Shaw concludes, the King were obliged, in addition to his usual public duties, to listen to the political speeches of those two "great platform artists," Ramsay MacDonald and Lloyd George, to sit out Elgar concerts, and to witness performances of *Back to Methuselah*, he would instantly abdicate. "And he has no heartier supporter in that attitude than myself. I tell you again that he has done all for us that can reasonably be expected, and more. And so, Long Live the King!"

T.E. Lawrence died on Sunday, 19 May. Blanche Patch cabled the news to Shaw and Charlotte, but it is doubtful whether her message reached them before the Monday newspapers and *The Natal Advertiser*'s opportunistic request to him to write an article on Lawrence. Blanche Patch says: "His death was Greek tragedy to them. They met it like Stoics."[58] Despite his feelings, and the imminence of his and Charlotte's departure from Durban, Shaw complied. The article, which is in the usual Shavian form of an interview, betrays Shaw's haste and, for all its flashes of insight, his complete unawareness of the mystical strain in Lawrence's make-up.[59]

> "With the single doubtful exception of myself . . . no man of our time has had such a power of setting journalists and even diplomatists to tell lies about him as Lawrence. Look at the obituary notices! They are all headed 'Mystery Man.' Yet there has never been any mystery about Lawrence since the end of the war. He changed his name twice; but everybody knew it as well as when the King changed his name from Guelph to Windsor.
>
> "All the Powers of Europe would have it that he was spying in India, when a word of enquiry would have ascertained that he was routining prosaically in the ranks in Dorset, in Plymouth, in Lincolnshire, taking not the smallest interest in politics, dropping in on his friends whenever he was on leave at incredible distances on the famous bicycle that killed him in the end, and busy with books and boats and the Schneider Cup trials, and all sorts of immediate and homely jobs about which he talked freely to everybody.
>
> "The mysterious missions to Asia were really visits to Bumpus' bookshop in Oxford Street. . . ."

Lawrence's essential non-mysteriousness is given further illustration in ensuing paragraphs. He would be in the middle of the stage with ten limelights blazing on him and everybody would exclaim: "See! He is hiding. He hates publicity." Shaw concedes that Lawrence had made some attempts to hide himself, but they were half-hearted and no use: ". . . he was the most impish of comedians and always did something that turned up the lights again." People actually knew far less about Lloyd George and Ramsay MacDonald than about Lawrence, yet they did not regard either as a "mystery man" while persistently romancing about Lawrence.

"He was a very notable military figure; but he had the limitations of the soldier." Shaw had talked to him on every subject on which he could be induced to talk. They were many and various, but they did not include politics or religion or any other branch of sociology. For example, he never once mentioned the Russian Revolution to Shaw, in spite of the momentousness of that event, and showed no consciousness of Lenin or Stalin—or, for that matter of Mussolini or Kemal or Hitler. On the other hand, "any little chieftain who was putting up a fight" in Morocco or Syria would arouse his keen interest. Shaw continues: ". . . though . . . he suffered torments from what Ibsen called a sickly conscience, he was always a law to himself and never connected his conduct with any form of belief." Shaw cites other qualities: Lawrence's interest in technical subjects, in art, literature and music; his "immense store of knowledge," sometimes on most unexpected subjects; his skill as a mechanic: ". . . but he will be remembered as a guerrilla general and as one of the greatest descriptive historians in English literature."

The final paragraph debunks the idea that Lawrence was a shy man and dwells on some of his oddities. He went where he wanted and spoke to whomever he wished. "He was a very strange fellow, a born actor and up to all sorts of tricks; you never knew where to have him. The very curious arrest of his physical development was puzzling; at forty he still had the grinning laugh and artless speech of a schoolboy; and powerful and capable though his mind was I am not sure that it ever reached full maturity. But I must not talk any more about him. I must catch my train for Cape Town and England."

The last remark may have been literally true because the article appeared on the day Shaw and Charlotte left Durban, on Wednesday, 22 May. Their journey took them several hundreds of miles into the interior—there being no direct coastal rail link between Durban and Cape Town—on to the semi-desert plateau of the Karoo, and then southwest in slowly descending steps to the coastal plain and eventually, after two days on the train, Cape Town. Three reporters boarded the train shortly before it reached its destination at the docks and gained a final interview from a genial, welcoming Shaw in his compartment. He told them he had just passed through a "medieval land."[60]

As usual, he was prepared to talk about almost anything. He was reminded that views he had expressed on his previous visit had been described as "irresponsible babble." Shaw replied that such critics were unintelligent and illiterate. He was not irresponsible; he could not afford to be. "Unlike Mussolini, I have not got a parliament to blame if I make a fool of myself." He repeated his criticism of the "Dutch" (as he called them): "A fine people physically—but I must say they keep running away from civilization. . . . I wish someone would make them realise that the Bible is an exceedingly well-written book, but that it should be supplemented by Whittaker['s Almanac]. As a matter of fact, I wrote *The Adventure of the Black Girl in Her Search for God* purely for the advantage of the Boer." He spoke at large about the "natives" and the whites, recommending the introduction of racial fusion and the abolition of legislative barriers between the races and the vote. "If the native were more intelligent he would see that it was no good fighting for the vote. He should be more concerned in seeing that the white vote should go. If it takes you years to do what could be done in thirty minutes, you may find yourself in the position one day of having to do in thirty minutes what you should have done in thirty years. And that will entail a lot of bloodshed and cutting of throats. . . . I can see you people in a pretty mess before you get everything cleared up." He praised Hitler's anxiously awaited speech of 22 May to the *Reichstag*: ". . . a particularly truthful, sensible, straightforward and intelligent speech"; and discussed Mussolini's designs on Abyssinia: "It would be very nice if Mussolini appealed to the League of Nations for a mandate, whatever that is, but that is where you come in with the cry of 'Africa for the Africans.'"

The train drew in alongside the *Winchester Castle*; Charlotte entered the compartment and took charge of her husband. The interview was over. It was Friday, 24 May. The second visit to South Africa had lasted just under four weeks.

Notes

Thanks and acknowledgments are due to Martin Burns for preparing the map and to the editors of the following newspapers, from which virtually the entire account of Shaw's visits has been abstracted:
The Cape Times (Cape Town)—thanks as well for permission to reproduce the photographs which appear with this account
The Cape Argus (Cape Town)
The Daily News (Durban)
The Natal Mercury (Durban)
The Natal Witness (Pietermaritzburg)

1. "A London Letter," by G.O., *The Cape Times*, 5 Jan. 1932, 8:5–7.
2. *The Cape Argus*, 11 Jan. 1932, 10:4. The Australian cricketer Donald (later Sir Donald) Bradman was hitting century after century off a touring South African side in the summer of 1931–32.

3. The word "native" denoted the indigenous peoples of South Africa, i.e., the blacks. Shaw queried this usage at the conclusion of his second visit, pointing out that most of the whites were as "native" to the country as the blacks (*The Cape Times*, 25 May 1935, 12:6). The answer to Shaw's question on board the *Carnarvon Castle* about black trade unions would have been a qualified "No." The answer became a qualified "Yes" in 1978.

4. The references are to Frank Harris's "unauthorised" biography, *Bernard Shaw* (London: Gollancz, 1931). Characteristically, Shaw does not mention that he contributed to, and thus promoted, the book because Harris's widow was in need of money.

5. This "book," which is not much more than a preliminary incursion into the subject (it consists of a preface and one chapter), survived in typescript and is now among the Shaw papers in the British Library (Add. 50677). Harry M. Geduld, in his introduction, says (p. 9) that this piece was "written in South Africa during 1932" and was "an indirect outcome of Shaw's unexpectedly protracted vacation in South Africa. . . . Shaw occupied the time [in Knysna, where Charlotte was recuperating after their motor accident] by writing *The Black Girl in Search of God* and 'The Rationalization of Russia.'" In fact, as Shaw's remarks on board the *Carnarvon Castle* attest, he wrote "The Rationalization of Russia" during the voyage from Southampton to Cape Town and appears to have abandoned it after his arrival. This is not an important issue in itself. What is interesting and to the point is that the ideas and arguments that went or were to have gone into "The Rationalization of Russia" colored and often directed the trend of Shaw's comments on South Africa during his visit. Indeed, the address in the City Hall on 1 February, given under the aegis of the Cape Town Fabian Society, was advertised as "the Rationalization of Russia."

6. The foregoing account is from *The Cape Argus*, 11 Jan. 1932, 11:1–3.

7. *The Cape Times*, 12 Jan. 1932, 9:1–2; 10:2–1.

8. General J.B.M. Hertzog, the founder of the National Party, was Prime Minister in 1932.

9. Commander C.P. Newton was the Shaws' escort during the visit. An official escort would have been provided to such "V.I.P." visitors even if they had not been in their mid-seventies.

10. A replica of this statue is in Kensington Gardens, London.

11. This talk was not reported in the press. It seems that Shaw spoke about the food he liked best.

12. *The Cape Argus*, 13 Jan. 1932, 13:1–2.

13. *The Cape Times*, 14 Jan. 1932, 4:5–6.

14. The account that follows is taken from *The Cape Argus*, 13 Jan. 1932, 11:8.

15. "Boer" means "farmer." The term was used to denote the people of predominantly Dutch descent who took up arms against the British in the wars of 1881 and 1899–1902.

16. The university town of Stellenbosch is some thirty miles inland from Cape Town. "Dagbreek" is literally "daybreak"—the break of day.

17. *Die Burger* ("The Citizen"), the Cape Town Afrikaans newspaper, 21 Jan. 1932, 8:1.

18. Muizenberg, a southern extension of Cape Town, is on False Bay. It is famous for its beach. Kipling's lines "White as sands of Muizenberg/ Spun before the gale—" ("The Flowers") were its one small claim to literary fame before Shaw waded into its surf.

19. This is the original version. Re-told in the Johannesburg *Star* after Shaw's death, it shows how myth and the devaluation of money can inflate an already good story: the amount wagered had increased to five shillings and an amused Shaw gave the boy a further five shillings in recognition of his "bravery."

20. *The Cape Argus*, 22 Jan. 1932, 15:3.

21. Father O.R. Vassall-Phillips, C.SS.R. (1857–1932), arrived in Cape Town from England on 10 January to deliver a series of sermons. He was by no means a negligible opponent. I am greatly indebted to Father O. Conroy, C.SS.R. of the Monastery, Bergvliet, Cape Town, for providing me with the following information on Vassall-Phillips. He was born

in England in 1857, was converted to Catholicism in his youth and became a Redemptorist Father in 1881. He founded the Parish in Bishops Stortford, England, where, coming from a well-to-do family, he built a fine church. He specialized in apologetics, giving lectures throughout Britain. His books—*Apostolic Christianity* and *Catholic Christianity*, for example—were similarly exhortatory. A better example of his scholarship is *The Mustard Seed*, subtitled "An argument on behalf of the Divinity of Christ," which provides evidence of extensive research and profound erudition. I leave it to Fr. Conroy to proceed:

> The above, I think, is sufficient to indicate that Father Vassall-Phillips was not the kind of man to be overawed by Mr Bernard Shaw's prestige, especially when the latter decided to open out in the public press, touching on religion. Vassall-Phillips was on home ground, and took him up. In Shaw's reply, he asked, "Who is this priest? He seems to forget that it was the Priests who had Christ put to death." Vassall-Phillips then picked him up on his logic, being guilty of a 'laitus hos'— there were priests of the Old Law, and priests of the New Law, apart from priests of other religions.
>
> I can remember all this, since I was ordained in the same year Fr. Vassall-Phillips died. Our Redemptorist Confreres in South Africa sent us the newspapers which we had read out in our refectory.

Vassall-Phillips's attack on Shaw in *The Southern Cross* (20 Jan. 1932, 10:4, 11:5–6) is not as intemperate as the report in the *Argus* suggests. There are strident passages, but the general effect is of a devout man disturbed and distracted by what he interprets as Shaw's anti-Christian utterances. Vassall-Phillips died at sea in May 1932, when on his way back to England from South Africa. (See also the London *Times* of 10 May 1932 for a brief report.)

22. *The Cape Argus*, 23 Jan. 1932, 11:4.

23. *The Southern Cross*, 27 Jan. 1932, 1:3–4.

24. Shaw's first flight was in 1916 at Hendon. The Cape Peninsula flight was Charlotte's first. She wrote ecstatically to Blanche Patch: "Last Saturday we flew! It was glorious! A perfect day. We flew over two oceans, and back over a chain of mountains—one being Table Mountain. We were about 5,000 feet up, and we went about 120 miles an hour. . . . The view was glorious. . . . I believe I shall be very sorry to leave!" Quoted in Blanche Patch, *Thirty Years with G.B.S.* (London: Gollancz, 1951), p. 73.

25. *The Cape Times*, 25 Jan. 1932, 9:8.

26. Sarah Gertrude Millin was the only South African English novelist of international standing in the 1930s. General J.C. Smuts was Leader of the Opposition in 1932. Mrs. Millin's anecdote appeared in *The Spectator* (London), 17 Nov. 1956.

27. Shaw, we may assume, was being perverse. He had himself been preaching "Off gold" since the day of his arrival. The disastrous luncheon party seems to underscore the general inadvisability of putting two great intellects (and considerable egos) together and hoping for any, let alone "historic," talk.

28. *The Cape Argus*, 2 Feb. 1932, 13:7–8.

29. *The Cape Argus*, 2 Feb. 1932, 10:6.

30. The full text appeared in the *Cape Times*, 8 Feb. 1932, 9:1–2, 10:2. The original holograph is among the Bernard Shaw papers, Humanities Research Center, University of Texas at Austin. The talk was reprinted in *The Shavian* (London), No. 16, October 1959.

31. *Thirty Years with G.B.S.*, p. 72.

32. Shaw and Charlotte stayed at the Royal Hotel, Knysna. The local newspaper, *The Knysna Advertiser*, a four-page weekly, featured Shaw in one long article, in which the author made a good deal of not telling his readers what had caused Shaw and Charlotte to remain in Knysna. He promised a second article for the following week, but failed to produce it. Shaw may well have prevailed on him to refrain. The other country newspaper, *The George and Knysna Herald* (produced in George), carried brief weekly reports on the

Shaws—Charlotte, for example, was up and about by early March—and one or two articles, but like its Knysna counterpart respected Shaw's desire for privacy. Legend provides the most entertaining titbits: a manifestly unclad Shaw was observed every morning striding back and forth in front of his open hotel window—to the mingled awe and delight of the local populace. His daily dip in the Knyna lagoon—a short walk from the hotel—was similarly revealing.

33. *The Cape Times*, 22 Feb. 1932, 9:6. The Mossel Bay correspondent's report of the accident to *The Cape Times*, whence it went out to the world, was criticized in *The George and Knysna Herald* as being both inaccurate and indiscreet. Quite a tiff ensued.

34. Preface to *The Black Girl in Search of God* (London, Constable, 1934; repr. 1954), p. 1.

35. *The Black Girl in Search of God*, p. 56.

36. An "African experience" at second hand (in 1928) is worth citing. In that year Shaw wrote a letter to a Miss Mabel Shaw (no relation) in which he expressed reservations about organised religion and missionary Christianity in Africa. Shaw described Mabel Shaw to Nancy Astor (12 May 1930) as "a woman with a craze for self-torture, who broke off her engagement with a clergyman (he died of it) to bury herself in the wilds of Africa and lead negro children to Christ." Mabel Shaw was obviously Shaw's model for the missionary, the "small white woman" who converts (and thoroughly confuses) the Black Girl (*The Black Girl in Search of God*, pp. 21–22).

37. *The Cape Times*, 12 Jan. 1932, 9:1–2.

38. *The Black Girl in Search of God*, pp. 46–55.

39. To Emery Walker, 15 Jan. 1932. Bernard Shaw Papers, Humanities Research Center, University of Texas at Austin.

40. By "Dutch" Shaw means the Afrikaners. The tendency to refer to them as the "Dutch" fell away after their language, Afrikaans, had won official sanction in 1926.

41. *The Cape Argus*, 18 Mar. 1932, 11:8.

42. *Thirty Years with G.B.S.*, p. 98. The detail about the noisy ports comes from a comment in a Durban newspaper.

43. The account that follows combines the reports of the two Durban newspapers, the morning *Natal Mercury* (29 Apr. 1935, 11:6; 15:5) and the evening *Natal Advertiser* (now the *Daily News*) (29 Apr. 1935, 10:7–9).

44. These phrases are from an appreciation of Shaw, "Impressions of a Distinguished and Charming Visitor," the *Natal Witness* (Pietermaritzburg), 24 May 1935, 6:6–7. The author of this article, Maurice Webb, seems to have been Shaw's host and escort on a number of occasions. An architect, he was a prominent figure in cultural circles.

45. *The Natal Mercury*, 1 May 1935, 13:3.

46. The talk was broadcast countrywide. The Johannesburg *Star* commented: "Then Mr Shaw spoke. And the voice which assailed the ears of thousands of listeners was a soft, melodious Irish brogue compelling attention by its charm and culture" (1 May 1935, 15:1).

47. *The Natal Mercury*, 1 May 1935, 11:3.

48. There is a third "interview." It exists in typescript in the British Library (Add. 50698 of the Bernard Shaw Papers). The heading, in Shaw's hand, is "Durban 1935"; the occasional corrections are also in Shaw's hand. The theme of the piece is the exploitation of Africa by "Imperialist Europe," with particular reference to Mussolini and Abyssinia, and the need for the nations of Africa, white as well as black, to rally under the slogan "Africa for the Africans" and turn out the "greedy dogs of Europe." A search through the leading South African newspapers of the time has not brought this "Interview" to light. One may conclude that it was not printed and that Shaw wrote it in anticipation of events in Abyssinia which did not come about during his stay in Durban. A significant number of phrases from this piece crop up in his last press interview (24 May 1935) before leaving South Africa. I am indebted to Professor Dan H. Laurence for telling me about this typescript.

49. *The Natal Witness*, 24 May 1935, 6:6–7.

50. *The Natal Witness*, 7 May 1935, 7:5.

51. *The Natal Mercury*, 22 May 1935, 11:1.

52. *The Natal Advertiser*, 10 May 1935, 8:4–5.

53. Pietermaritzburg, the capital of the province of Natal, is some sixty miles inland from Durban. Charlotte was delighted with the town (*Thirty Years with G.B.S.*, p. 98.).

54. The first of these leaders (11 May 1935, 10:5–6) somehow manages to relate Shaw's visit to Pietermaritzburg to the town's eyesores. The second (16 May 1935, 6:3–4) reacts to and appreciates Shaw's article on the Silver Jubilee, which appeared on 15 May. The entry on the children's page (18 May 1935) is a photograph of Shaw with two toddlers on his lap. The comment under the photo is: "You have all heard your parents speak of Bernard Shaw. He is a very great writer—probably as great as Shakespeare or some of the famous Greek dramatists, and his plays are known and acted in many countries. He not only writes plays but does many other interesting things, and he is well-known for his original opinions. . . . Despite his greatness, he is very fond of children, and always has time to talk to them. And children all seem to like him and go straight to him without shyness. In this photograph he is seen with a little girl and boy who live in Matritzburg."

55. *The Natal Witness*, 10 May 1935, 1:6; 9:6.

56. No mention of Beatrice! The book referred to was probably *Soviet Communism*, published in 1935.

57. *The Natal Witness*, 15 May 1935, 6:6–8.

58. *Thirty Years with G.B.S.*, p. 87.

59. *The Natal Advertiser*, 22 May 1935, 9:7–8. According to Janet Dunbar in *Mrs G.B.S.* (London: Harrap, 1963), Shaw was unaware of the intense spiritual relationship between Charlotte and Lawrence.

60. This account is abstracted from reports in *The Cape Times*, *Die Burger*, and the *Star* of 25 May 1935.

Valli Rao

SEEKING THE UNKNOWABLE: SHAW IN INDIA

In January 1933, when Shaw was seventy-six years old, he made a brief visit to India as part of his world cruise aboard the *Empress of Britain*. Unwilling to be a conventional tourist visiting typical tourist spots around India, he sought out for himself temples in and around Bombay that he appears to have observed very carefully. Shaw's reactions and movements in Bombay are understandable in the light of his previous interest in and familiarity with the civilization of India, particularly the religious environment. In their turn, his reactions and movements in Bombay help to interpret certain crucial ideas that recur systematically in his late plays. The purpose of this essay is to trace briefly Shaw's earlier knowledge of India, the details of his stay in Bombay, and the way in which the latter could be used to explain the keynote of one late play in particular: *The Simpleton of the Unexpected Isles*.

From his formative years as a writer, Shaw had looked for a credible religion that would satisfy his needs. Works as early as the unfinished *Passion Play* (1878) and *The Quintessence of Ibsenism* (1891) provide indications of his distrust of established orthodox religion, and of a consistent skepticism towards both the empty mysticism of orthodox religion as well as the materialism inherent in the secularism that attracted many of his contemporaries. The author of *The Quintessence of Ibsenism* saw the curious "correlation" that exists between the rationalism found in orthodox religion and the rationalism found in materialism, arising in the former case from reasoning about the "hollowness of materialism" and in the latter case from a vehement rejection of the existence or importance of things of the spirit.[1] Neither the religion of the spiritual rationalist nor that of the material rationalist satisfied Shaw, whose attempt was to find a religion with a balanced content of the material and the spiritual, the natural and the supernatural. His religion, as *The Simpleton of the Unexpected Isles* evidences, had eventually to be one that would despise neither matters of spirit nor of flesh, and that would struggle to understand the crucial connections between the Word and the Flesh. As he continued his search, he followed with interest the religious explorations of some of his colleagues and friends, explorations that are of relevance here insofar as they concern India. One of the most unusual adventures was undertaken by Annie Besant, a close colleague in the Fabian movement. Arthur H. Nethercot's account in *The First Five Lives of Annie Besant* and *The Last Four Lives of Annie Besant* gives us clear and fascinating details of Dr. Besant's plunge from western materialism into eastern mysticism after reading Madame H.P. Blavatsky's *The Secret Doctrine* (1888). Shaw admired the strength that the change brought in her.[2] He was, nevertheless, strongly aware of the opposition of his own brand of religious realism, which he revelled in, to the idealism of the theosophist position, which he regarded as escapist.[3]

Another friend was Florence Farr, who had a strong interest in occultism and who eventually, in Ceylon, proclaimed herself as a Vedantist. Shaw had a strong degree of skepticism. In 1895, he thought her a woman "who has no religion at all" (*CL* 1, 504–5) and saw her chief weakness as her inability for hard professional work, which he tried to inculcate in her: "but her early life had been too easy. I failed, and had to give up worrying and discouraging her. She found the friend she needed in Yeats. What she called 'cantillating' for him was within her powers."[4] Shaw thought little of such cantillating and did not hesitate in telling her so. He wrote to her that she should concentrate on clear articulation and on the meaning of her words instead of being exclusively absorbed in the manner of her recitations. He concluded that "Yeats is heaping fresh artificialities and distractions and impertinences on you instead of sternly nailing you to the simple point of conveying the meaning and feeling of the author" (*CL* 2, 275). Shaw was also unsympathetic to Miss Farr's attempts at translating the Rig Vedas:

> All I can say about these Rig-Vedas is that those who advise you to throw them into narrative form are, as might be expected, dolts. They will interest nobody but the people who have taken up this particular craze; and the dialogue form will be more convenient for them than a nonsensical attempt to adapt it to the Strand Magazine people. . . . Do not be misled by the sloppy-minded lunatics; if you want to write popular books, write them: if you want to write mystic gospels, write them; but in the name of commonsense dont try to popularise your mysticism or to mystify your popular readers.[5]

Part of Shaw's antagonism to empty mysticism of this sort, as he viewed it, arose from an impatience toward superstition that he shared with material rationalists like William Archer. In a note that acts as a preface to three of Archer's plays, Shaw expressed, at some length, his agreement with Archer's realistic and skeptical look at India, an attitude very different from the Theosophical and Vedantist outlook. Of the book that resulted from Archer's visit to India, Shaw wrote

> At that time it was the fashion for literary European travellers returning from Asia to display their susceptibilities to the call of the East by depicting an India of boundless and magical fascination lit up with Bengal lights, saturated with the charm of Pierre Loti's romances, adorned with the temples of a living religion more profound than our own, and inhabited by Rabindranath Tagores and dark eyed enchantresses, with Mahatmas in the mountain background. These enthusiasts were more Indian than any Indian; and their readers, who had never been in India, began where they left off, and went much further into an imaginary east. Archer went to see for himself, and instantly and uncompromisingly denounced the temples as the shambles of a barbarous ritual of blood sacrifice, and the people as idolaters with repulsive rings through their noses. He refused to accept the interest of Indian art and the fictions of Indian romance as excuses. He remained invincibly faithful to Western civilization, and told the Indians flatly what a civilized western gentleman must think of them and feel about some of their customs. . . . It is certain that if . . . the Indians are ever to say "It was a good thing for us that the westerners came and taught us something," it will be because the English criticism of India was Archer's criticism, and not that of occidental renegades who swell the heads of our Indian students by assuring them that we are crude barbarians compared to them. Archer would have been the last man to deny that we are shocking barbarians. . . . All the same, the Fundamentalist does not sacrifice his daughter or even his calf and would send anyone who did to the electric chair or the lunatic asylum; and the eastern toleration of noserings is not justified by the western toleration of earrings. People who make the one an excuse for the other will never do anything to lighten the load of human superstition; and as this was really Archer's appointed task in life he wrote one of the most useful because one of the most resolutely unsympathetic books on India produced in his generation.[6]

Shaw understood very well the attitude of the material rationalist who wanted to fight superstition, particularly in spiritual matters. The chief reason why he seems uninterested in the superficial exoticism of India is not the negative one of disliking superstition; it arises rather from a more positive diversion of energy and attention to getting at the true essence that Indian religion has to offer. Shaw could identify his own religious instincts, for instance, in a personage like the Indian leader Mahatma Gandhi. The reader of *Man and Superman* will have no trouble in realizing that when Shaw in a note to Henry Salt equates "Superman = Mahatma" (*CL* 2, 349), the qualities he has in mind are the Gandhian and positive qualities of hard work, discipline, and self-control

(the greatest virtue that belongs to the Creative Evolutionist). To Shaw,
Gandhi was also an example of the natural leader, the born boss of his
later plays, an inspired ruler like King Magnus of *The Apple Cart*. When
in 1945 Gandhi was attacked on grounds of being out of date and was
asked to retire in favor of Nehru, Shaw, as D. G. Tendulkar relates,
"stepped in to defend Gandhi: 'Gandhi's politics is half a century out of
date. His tactics like all tactics are subject to error and readjustment, but
his strategy is sound, as it was fifty or five million years ago.' As for
Gandhi's retiring, he added: 'Retire from what? His position is natural,
not official. The Mahatma cannot hand over anything. Leadership is not
a plug of tobacco that can be passed from one man to another.'" [7]

Shaw met Gandhi in London in November 1931 when Gandhi was
there to participate in the Round Table Conference. The meeting appears to have left them mutually satisfied. Among other comments to a
group of journalists before he left London, Gandhi remarked of Shaw
"I think he is a very good man. . . . I think he is a very witty man, a lover
of epigram and paradox, with a Puck-like spirit and a generous ever-
young heart, the Arch Jester of Europe." [8] Gandhi, who had read various
books by Shaw including *Man and Superman* and *The Black Girl in Her
Search for God*, was one of the few contemporary readers of Shaw who
was thoroughly convinced of the religious content of Shaw's work.
Countering Vincent Sheean's doubts regarding Shaw's religion, Gandhi,
"still smiling almost playfully at the thought [of Shaw having no reli-
gion], said with his slow, careful enunciation: 'I was just about to say that
it would be difficult for anybody to say that Bernard Shaw had no religion. In everything of his that I have read there has been a religious
centre." [9] At the meeting in London, Gandhi and Shaw seemed to understand each other extremely well. During their hour-long conversation
Shaw questioned Gandhi on "a bewildering variety of topics—ethno-
graphical, religious, social, political, economic," and he also remarked,
"I knew something about you and felt something in you of a kindred
spirit. We belong to a very small community on earth." [10]

When Shaw visited Bombay in 1933, it was the kinship he felt with
Gandhi that prompted his responses to queries from journalists about
his opinion of the Indian leader. In 1933 my father was starting his
journalistic career as an apprentice with *The Times of India*. He accompanied a senior journalist who interviewed Shaw for about half an hour
one afternoon, and towards the end of the interview the young apprentice shot out his timid question: "What do you think, sir, of Mahatma
Gandhi?" Shaw, "with a twinkle in his eyes" as my father always recalls,
replied, "Mr. Gandhi is the second greatest man in the world!"

Shaw's visit to Bombay was widely publicized by the Indian press. The
newspaper-reading, educated Indian middle classes did not, any more

than their British counterparts, understand the depth of Shaw's religious quest; but they had always liked Shaw for his humor and wit, and his ability to supply appropriate epigrams for any occasion. They enjoyed reading of his visit and the interviews he gave. Typical of press response is the article on page 3 of *The Times of India*, dated Monday 9 January 1933.[11] Under the heading "India is the Centre of the British Empire" and the sub-heading "It takes Mr. Gandhi very long to find the world is not like him," the report summarizes Shaw's interview with a group of Indian journalists the day after his arrival in Bombay. Shaw discussed a variety of subjects, as the report informs us in the opening paragraph. "Casting off all reserve and sparkling with wit and humor, he apparently enjoyed the heckling to which he was subjected by his interviewers on every conceivable subject. Disarmament, the future of Indo-British relations, untouchability, and the prospects of the next world war were some of the subjects upon which Mr. Shaw discoursed."

A couple of comments remind us of situations Shaw was to envisage in *The Simpleton of the Unexpected Isles*. Talking of dominion status and the future of the British Empire, Shaw said, "We were told in a lecture the other day on board that the population of India was 315,000,000. It is a formidable figure. Taking things as a whole, therefore, India is the centre of the British Empire. . . . Consequently the British Empire is not a Christian Empire; it is more a Hindu or a Mohamedan Empire. It is quite possible in the future, Indian institutions will develop and if the population becomes more educated, instead of India wanting to be separated, a time will come when England may make a desperate struggle to get separated from you, and you will decline to allow it." Pra in Act II of *The Simpleton* mentions how "since India won Dominion status Delhi has been the centre of the British Empire" (*BH* 6, 807). And a few pages later, in the same act, the four siblings read their news from newspapers:

KANCHIN. The land that brought forth Iddy begins the apocalypse.

HYERING. What do you mean? Has anything happend in England?

KANCHIN. England has broken loose. . . . [*reading the headlines*] Dissolution of the British Empire.

JANGA [*reading*] Withdrawal of England from the Empire.

KANCHIN. England strikes for independence.

JANGA. Downing Street declares for a right little tight little Island.

KANCHIN. The British Prime Minister cuts the cable and gives the new slogan.

JANGA. Back to Elizabeth's England; and to hell with the empire!

KANCHIN. Ireland to the rescue!

JANGA. Free State President declares Ireland cannot permit England to break the unity of the Empire. Ireland will lead the attack on treason and disruption.

[BH 6, 813–14]

The germ of these ideas may be seen to originate in Shaw's press interview in Bombay.

The comments on Gandhi made by Shaw at the interview are consistent with his admiration for him as an exceptional human being, morally as superior to his contemporaries as Pra and Prola in *The Simpleton* are to those around them:

> "I have not seen very much of the population of India yet, but I have noticed that every man I see in Bombay is not a Gandhi. . . . He is, of course, the sort of man who occurs once in several centuries. It is very hard for you to understand him. The result is he always gets tired of you and threatens to fast and kill himself. If I saw him I would simply say, 'Give them up; it is not your job.' It takes him very long to find out that the world is not like him."
>
> It was, however, encouraging to know, he went on, that there was such a person as Mr. Gandhi, because there might come a future when the whole population of India would be much more like Gandhi than they were at present.

Perhaps the compromise of Pra and Prola with the other couples in *The Simpleton* and with the eugenic experiment may be seen in terms of the necessity or otherwise for the involvement of the superior moral and religious force with the commonplace, and the whole compromise seen in terms of Shaw's understanding, when he writes *The Simpleton*, of why Gandhi could not "give them up" as not being his job.

The report in *The Times of India* indicates that most of the 300 passengers on board the ship planned to divide into three parties for tours into India. About half the number were to leave on the night of the 9th of January for visits to Delhi and Agra. Others planned to make even more extended tours of the country. Shaw and his wife did not intend to make any trips outside Bombay. "It is suggested that I should make an extensive tour of India, but on examining the map I find that I should hardly see anything except the inside of a railway carriage, the country is so vast," remarked Shaw to the reporters. Further, his attitude as a traveller appears to coincide with that of Peter Keegan in *John Bull's Other Island* who thinks that the wonders of all countries are the same in essence, if the traveller could but look with the "eyes in his soul as well as in his head" (*BH* 2, 929). "You must understand," Shaw told the journalists, "that I do not look upon Indians as unlike Englishmen." This remark, incidentally, is the strong undercurrent that informs an article on India

that Shaw wrote in 1914 for *The Commonweal,* the journal started that
year by Annie Besant for the Theosophical Society in Adyar, Madras.[12]

Comments such as those quoted above at the interview in Bombay are
scattered through the article, the point of which appears to be that in
order to throw off the yoke of the British as a foreign power, Indians
should train their children not to be submissive to their elders but to be
free to assert their freedom to be themselves, to fight anybody (whether
it be their elders or the British) who tries to keep them "quiet, silent,
obedient, respectful." Shaw writes:

> One man is very like another . . . one nation is very like another. . . . The
> truth is, all nations have been conquered; and all peoples have submitted
> to tyrannies which would provoke sheep or spaniels to insurrection. I
> know nothing in the history of India that cannot be paralleled from the
> histories of Europe. . . . It is not a matter of national character at all
> [whether a country's people are cowards or whether they are brave]. Eng-
> lish soil is like Indian soil: you reap what you sow, in the animal world as
> in the vegetable. . . . The Indian who admits that they [the virtues of
> being brave] are any less characteristic of eastern human nature than of
> western human nature is, if I may be so blunt, a fool.

The superficial difference between the British and the Indian does not
impose on Shaw anymore than the exotic out-of-the-way wonders that
the average tourist might wonder at. But that does not mean that Shaw
was uninterested in India. As the report in *The Times of India* observes,
"Throughout the conversation Mr. Shaw kept questioning his question-
ers, obviously trying to gather something about conditions in India."
And Shaw wrote to Rabindranath Tagore, as reported in a news item in
The Hindu of 19 January 1933: ". . . the ship in which I am going round
the world to get a little rest and do a little work has to put in at Bombay
and Colombo to replenish her tanks and on such occasions I step ashore
for a few hours and wander about the streets and such temples as are
open to European untouchables." During the week's stay in Bombay he
visited local Jain temples and the Elephanta caves, places of worship he
sought for himself. His escort on the visits to two of the Jain temples,
Hiralal Amritlal Shah, gives us an interesting account of the afternoon
on which the visits were made and of the following day when he took
his collection of photographs (of temples like the Delwada temples on
Mount Abu) for Shaw to examine, which he was able to do in detail with
the aid of a magnifying glass.[13]

The temples to which Shaw was escorted were the Jain temple dedicated to the deity Shri Godi Parshwanathji, in the suburb of Pydhunie,
and the Babu's Jain marble temple, built on a hilltop in Walkeshwar hills.
The central marble image (Fig. 1) in the latter temple, along with the
various small images surrounding it (Figs. 2, 3, and 4) provided much

FIG. 1. The main deity in the Walkeshwar temple: Shri Adinathji, meditating in the Padmasana posture.

food for thought for the votary of Creative Evolution. Before we examine the influence of these scenes on Shaw's thinking, let us recall Hiralal Amritlal Shah's record of them:

> We proceeded to the Walkeshwar Hills to see the Babu's Jain Marble Temple, built on a hilltop. Mr. Shaw expressed delight at the panoramic view that spread before his eyes. Inside, in its sanctum, stood the huge central marble image of Tirthankara (Prophet), and Mr. Shaw was able to observe it at close range. I explained to him how the image showed the expressions of Yogi in *Dhyana* (meditation), seated cross-legged in *Padmasana* posture (that is, each leg resting on the other thigh, the palms of the hands opened out and resting one on the other in the center, above the legs; the gaze of the eyes fixed on the tip of the nose; the body remaining perfectly erect and in a sitting position, while controlling the breath).
>
> Around the central shrine, in the surrounding walls, in individual niches, there were numerous small images of various gods and goddesses. Mr. Shaw then directed his attention to the details of these images and observed them intensely, putting several queries to me. I explained to him the different characteristics of these images and of such other types as the God "Harina Naigameshi," etc. "When the people see these sculptured images," he asked, "do they accept them, in their beliefs and

FIG. 2. Images in individual niches: Gow-mukha Yaksha, the god with the face of a cow.

FIG. 3. Images in individual niches: Shri Magibhadravir

FIG. 4. Images in individual niches: Shri Parshva Yaksha, the elephant-headed god who, the Jains claim, is akin to but not to be confused with the Hindu god Ganesh.

in their thoughts, conceived as such, in concrete form and shape?" I affirmed this.

We learn from allusions in Shaw's writings that the stark contrast between the ideal that the Jain religion contains and the reality to which it
had accommodated itself, impressed itself strongly upon Shaw's mind.
Again and again, in the years to come, he returns to the message implicit
in the Jain images, in an attempt to understand the fall of man when
viewed as a fall from true religion into idolatry, from what in the Blakean world is a fall from the spiritual to the material, from an imaginative grasp of reality to an effort at a literal hold of apparent reality. The
attempt to understand man's fall in terms of a fall from true religion to
idolatry may indeed be seen as forming a major impulse in the make-up
of *The Simpleton of the Unexpected Isles*.

The most widely applicable philosophic conclusions are drawn in the
Preface to *Farfetched Fables*, written in 1948–49:

> . . . all the established religions in the world are deeply corrupted by the
> necessity for adapting their original inspired philosophic creeds to the
> narrow intelligences of illiterate peasants and of children. Eight thou-
> sand years ago religion was carried to the utmost reach of the human
> mind by the Indian Jainists, who renounced idolatry and blood sacrifice
> long before Micah, and repudiated every pretence to know the will of
> God, forbidding even the mention of his name in the magnificent
> temples they built for their faith.
>
> But go into a Jainist temple today: what do you find? Idols everywhere.
> Not even anthropomorphic idols but horse idols, cat idols, elephant idols
> and what not? The statues of the Jainist sages and saints, far from being
> contemplated as great seers, are worshipped as gods.
>
> For such examples it is not necessary to travel to Bombay. The articles
> of the Church of England begin with the fundamental truth that God
> has neither body, parts, nor passions, yet presently enjoin the acceptance
> as divine revelation of a document alleging that God exhibited his hind
> quarters to one of the prophets. . . .

Shaw is not an idealist of the sort who necessarily or merely condemns
the deep corruption that occurs in a religion as it is adapted to the needs
of a people. His foremost concern is to understand the problem clearly,
as his treatment of it in two instances makes clear. One instance occurs
in chapter 43 of *Everybody's Political What's What?* in the section titled
"Religious Summary":

> Anthropomorphic Deism will remain for long as a workable hypothesis
> not only for children but for many adults. Prayer consoles, heals, builds
> the soul in us. . . . But there are all sorts of prayers, from mere beggars'
> petitions and magic incantations to contemplative soul building, and all
> sorts of divinities to pray to. A schoolboy who witnessed a performance

of my play St Joan, told his schoolmaster that he disliked Jesus and could not pray to him, but that he could pray to Joan. [The schoolmaster wisely] told the boy to pray to Joan by all means: it is the prayer and not the prayee that matters. To the Franciscan, Francis and not Jesus is the redeemer; and to countless Catholics and not a few Anglicans Our Lady is the intercessor. To the Jains God is Unknowable; but their temple in Bombay is full of images of all sorts of saints, from nameless images of extraordinary beatific peace to crude elephant-headed idols. . . . Every Church should be a Church of All Saints, every cathedral a place for pure contemplation by the greatest minds of all races, creeds and colors.

The other instance dramatically and tellingly impresses on us the necessity of admitting the reality of the fallen world, and of religion in such a world being manipulated to a large extent by the Devil. Shaw wrote the film version of *Major Barbara* in 1940,[14] and in it he uses his experience in the Jain temples to underscore his point about the corruption of religion. The second half of the last act of *Major Barbara* shows us Undershaft's town of Perivale St. Andrews, where his employees live and where the Undershaft weapons are manufactured. In the film version, Shaw takes the opportunity, as Undershaft guides his family on a tour through his city, to elaborate on the connection between orthodox religion and war. As Undershaft points out the various sights of his town, one of the places he halts at is "The Meeting Place of all Religions," also called "Piety Square." His idealistic daughter Barbara, in the process of being converted from religious idealism to an appreciation of her father's realism, ponders curiously: "Is the real meeting place of all the religions a cannon foundry?" Undershaft invites them to have a closer look at the various religious buildings, and they go into a Jain Temple. They "stop before one of the shrines, in which is a seated image" much like the central image in *Padmasana* posture that Hiralal Amritlal Shah describes as the one Shaw saw in Bombay. The image fascinates the party:

> BARBARA. How utterly wonderful! Perfect peace! Perfect beauty! I think I shall become a Jain too. What god is it?
>
> UNDERSHAFT. It is not a god. It is supposed to be only a wiseacre of some sort; but it is really a symbol. I am afraid it is worshipped and prayed to as a god, though the Jains hold that God is something beyond us with which they dare not meddle.

Even Lomax, the frivolous Church of England conformist, is impressed as he asks Undershaft whether the peace generated in the temple would not be "bad for the cannon trade." But Undershaft tells them the brutal truth, which the idealistic Cusins finds difficult to digest, that the image was made in Undershaft's town, and that it is a by-product of the cannon trade:

UNDERSHAFT. One of our troubles here used to be the waste of good gunmetal involved in making cannons. This went on until I had to visit India on business. I was greatly struck by these figures, especially as they were quite new; for I had enough waste metal here to supply all India with them. I found they were made in a certain place by a certain set of native workmen, and nowhere else. I went to that place and bought up the whole concern, workmen and all. The wages I offered were of course far beyond anything they had ever dreamt of. I promised them a temple as well: you are now in it. Sometimes, when my nerves are overwrought I come in here and sit for an hour before this shrine while a priest recites prayers in a language of which I do not understand one word. It soothes me as nothing else does. This Jain religion is far ahead of anything we have in the west.

And thus the Jain religion is seen as depending on, and catering to, Undershaft-Mammon, even as the various other religions in Piety Square do. It seems appropriate that some of the wealthiest business-men and tradespeople in India today are Jains.

Shaw's impressions of India, and her religious spirit, are recorded in detail by him in a letter dated 4 February 1933, written at sea in the Gulf of Siam. He wrote to Ensor Walters about Hinduism as the most tolerant of religions and as one that accommodates all manner of believers. Shaw reproduced this letter in chapter 25 of *Everybody's Political What's What?* when he wrote about architecture as a world power:

The apparent multiplication of Gods is bewildering at the first glance; but you soon discover that they are all the same God in different aspects and functions and even sexes. There is always one uttermost God who defies personification. This makes Hinduism the most tolerant religion in the world, because its one transcendant God includes all possible Gods, from elephant Gods, bird Gods, and snake Gods, right up to the great Trinity of Brahma, Vishnu and Shiva, which makes room for the Virgin Mary and modern Feminism by making Shiva a woman as well as a man. Christ is there as Krishna, who might also be Dionysos. In fact Hinduism is so elastic and so subtle that the profoundest Methodist and the crudest idolater are equally at home in it.

Islam is very different, being ferociously intolerant. . . . The main dif-ference between the opposition of Islam to Hinduism and the opposition between Protestant and Catholic is that the Catholic persecutes as fiercely as the Protestant when he has the power; but Hinduism cannot perse-cute, because all the Gods—and what goes deeper, the no Gods—are to be found in its Temples. There is actually a great Hindu sect, the Jains, with Temples of amazing magnificence, which excludes God, not on ma-terialist atheist considerations, but as unspeakable and unknowable, tran-scending all human comprehension.

So far, it is all simple enough for anyone with religious sense. When you are face to face with the Temples and the worshippers, you find that before Mahomet and the founder of the Jains were cold in their graves, the institutions and rituals they founded began to revert to the more popular types, and all the Gods and no Gods became hopelessly mixed up, exactly as the Apostles backslid when Jesus was killed. In the Jain Temple you find shrines and images, and baths where you must wash all over before you may enter the shrine and adore the image. If you can find an intelligent Priest who is a real Jain theologian, you say "How's this? A God in the Jain Temple!" He explains to you that the image is not a God but a portrait of one of their great Saints; and that the man just out of the bath prostrating himself is not worshipping but expressing his respect for the memory of the late eminent Ensoramji Waltershagpat. But it is like Dean Inge trying to explain away St. Paul. It is perfectly plain that the image is a super refined Buddha, and that Jainism and Buddhism have got hopelessly mixed. Jain Buddha is attended by sculptured elephants. You ask what they mean, and are told they are purely ornamental works of art. Then your eye lights on an image of Ganesh, the Hindu God with the head and trunk of an elephant. On the point of exclaiming "*Que diable fait-il dans cette galère?*", you remember that you must not put your courteous host in a corner, and politely hold your tongue, but think furiously.

It is always the same. Outside the few who have religious sense, and who are equally at home and equally estranged in all the temples of all the faiths, there is the multitudinous average man. What he demands from the founder of his faith is, first, miracles. If, like Mahomet, you rebuke him and tell him that you are not a conjurer, or like Jesus, turn on him angrily with "An evil and adulterous generation seeketh after a sign," you will waste breath; for when you have become famous through your preaching, and cured the sick by healing their minds and thereby curing their bodies, your average man will invent miracles enough for you to eclipse Saint Anthony of Padua. Then he will make you his God, which means that he will beg from you, and, when he is properly frightened of you, make sacrifices to propitiate you, even to the extent of killing his daughter (Iphigenia or Miss Jephtha) to please you; but he will soon begin to cheat by substituting a ram for his son (Isaac) and making the sacrifice purely symbolic and imaginary. And so finally it is not through the authentic principles of the founder of his faith that you must get at him if you are to make a decent human being of him. You must govern fools acording to their folly. In Jamaica and Rhodesia all the good negros and their great ministers and leaders are Fundamentalists. If you rubbed Bradlaugh and Ingersoll into them, you would probably not only shock but demoralize them. You find the same thing in our mining villages.

Shaw concluded, "It is clear from my letter to Ensor Walters that a freethinking westerner can feel as much at home in the temples of the farthest east as in a British or foreign cathedral. The dozens of personifications by which the manifold nature of the Life Force is represented trouble him no more than the three persons of the Trinity, plus the Virgin Mother goddess, to say nothing of a host of minor gods called saints."

In *The Simpleton of the Unexpected Isles*, Shaw gives us an example of an unenlightened person of the sort who does not feel at home with the personifications by which the manifold nature of the Life Force is represented. She is Lady Farwaters, known to us at first as an English lady tourist, a Christian missionary who is trying to identify the various images around her in scene 3 of the Prologue to *The Simpleton*. The scene is set in the cave temple of Elephanta, as Shaw informed Floryan Sobieniowski when discussing the Polish translation of the play: "the third scene of the prologue is taken from the caves of Elephanta, an island near Bombay. The giant figures are of Indian deities. It is impossible to describe them."[15] It is here that Shaw had seen the figure of Ardhanarisvara, Shiva as half male and half female, to which he referred in the letter to Ensor Walters as making room for the Virgin Mary and modern Feminism. In *The Simpleton*, the recruits for the ensuing eugenic experiment gather in this magic cave. An introductory dialogue ensues between Lady Farwaters as the Lady Tourist, Pra as the Priest, Prola as the Priestess, and Mrs. Hyering as the Young Woman.

> THE L.T. Excuse me; but can you tell me which of these figures is the principal god?
>
> THE PRIEST [*rising courteously*] The principal one? I do not understand.
>
> THE L.T. I get lost among all these different gods: it is so difficult to know which is which.
>
> THE PRIEST. They are not different gods. They are all god.
>
> THE L.T. But how can they be? The figures are different.
>
> THE PRIEST. God has many aspects.
>
> THE L.T. But all these names in the guide book?
>
> THE PRIEST. God has many names.
>
> THE L.T. Not with us, you know.
>
> THE PRIEST. Yes: even with you. The Father, the Son, the Spirit, the Immaculate Mother—
>
> THE L.T. Excuse me. We are not Catholics.
>
> THE PRIESTESS [*sharply*] Are your temples then labelled "For men only"?
>
> THE L.T. [*shocked*] Oh, really! So sorry to have troubled you. [*She hurries away*]
> . . . .
> THE PRIESTESS. I find these heathen idolaters very trying. Is it really kind to treat them according to their folly instead of according to our wisdom?
>
> THE Y.W. Here! Steady on, you. Who are you calling heathen idolaters?

Look at all those images. I should say, if you ask me, that the boot is on
the other leg.

THE PRIEST. Those images are not idols: they are personifications of the
forces of nature by which we all live. But of course to an idolater they
are idols.

(*BH* 6, 776–77]

Shaw commented on the meaning of this passage and tried to explain
the idea of the unity of God in the midst of a variety of images, an idea
that flashed home to him in the Jain temples, in a letter to Dame Laurentia McLachlan. The Benedictine nun was the Abbess of Stanbrook
with whom Shaw carried on extensive (and intensive) correspondence.
They called each other Sister Laurentia and Brother Bernard, and she
had asked for and received a copy of *The Simpleton*, as yet unpublished.
This was in January 1935. She discovered the divinity under the profanity, as Shaw had said she would. She also objected strongly to some of
the profanity, and commanded him to "omit the allusion to the Immaculate Mother. . . . You know, as well as I do, that we do not worship her
as God," and wanted him to say a Hail Mary in penance. Shaw replied
promptly, from the east coast of Africa where he was travelling, and
wondered why Dame Laurentia should "fly out at me when I devoutly
insist that the Godhead must contain the Mother as well as the Father."
In typical unrepentant fashion he took the opportunity to remind Dame
Laurentia that he was "always saying Hail Mary! on my travels. Of
course I dont say it in that artificial form which means nothing. I say it
in my own natural and sincere way when She turns up in the temples
and tombs of Egypt and among the gods of Hindustan—Hallo, Mary!
For you cannot really get away from Her. She has many names in the
guide books, and many disguises. But She never takes me in. She fa-
vours Brother Bernardo with special revelations and smiles at his delighted 'Hello, Mary!' When I write a play like *The Simpleton* and have to
deal with divinity in it She jogs my elbow at the right moment and whis-
pers 'Now Brother B. dont forget *me*,' and I dont."

He goes on to analyse the various Marys of Raphael as too human
("highly respectable Italian farmers' daughters") and, on the other
hand, the giantess-goddess of Cimabue as having "just a little too much
of the image and too little reality," and he concludes with a reference to
the Jain temples he visited in Bombay:

> In short, the Christian Maries are all failures. This suggests that the Jains
> were right in excluding God from their ritual as beyond human power
> to conceive or portray. At least that is their theory; but in practice they
> have in their shrines images of extraordinary beauty and purity of design
> who throw you into an ecstasy of prayer and a trance of peace when they
> look at you, as no Christian iconography can.

I said to the pundit who showed me round "Those images are surely
gods, are they not?" "Not at all," he said, "they are statues of certain very
wise men of the Jains." This was obvious nonsense; so I pointed out that
man kneeling in the shrine (having first washed himself from head to
foot) was clearly praying to a god. "Pooh!" said the pundit with enormous
contempt, "he is only a heathen idolater."

It is in these temples that you escape from the frightful parochiality of
our little sects of Protestants and Catholics, and recognize the idea of
God everywhere, and understand how the people who struggled hardest
to establish the unity of God made the greatest number of fantastically
different images of it, producing on us the effect of crude polytheism.[16]

A major concern of *The Simpleton* is indicated in the conversation between Pra and Prola and Lady Farwaters: the gulf between two different
ways of viewing God, one involving an appreciation of the life-force,
which evokes artistically worthwhile images of God (such as those Shaw
found in the Elephanta caves), the other involving an adoration of the
physical without the spiritual: the first may be defined as true religion,
the second as idolatry. As Pra observes the same image may give scope
to both ways of looking at it: "Those images are not idols: they are personifications of the forces of nature by which we all live. But of course
to an idolater they are idols." It is, as Shaw observed to Ensor Walters,
the prayer and not the prayee that makes the crucial difference. And
when the prayer reaches the nadir of idolatry, then a Last Judgment is
triggered, with the irresponsible idolaters classed as dispensables to be
liquidated and the responsible, self-respecting worshippers of the Life
Force recognized as indispensable helpers in the struggle of life towards
further evolution. The movement of *The Simpleton* leads us from the
pure religious and spiritual force that inspires Pra and Prola at one end,
through the simple Adamic trauma of Iddy caught between the spiritual
and the material, to the mocking materialism and idolatry of Maya and
her siblings at the other end, the whole movement culminating in the
Judgment that destroys the idolaters.

In what ways may we trace the basic inspiration for the movement of
the play to Shaw's various encounters with India, particularly the contrast between true faith and idolatry that the Hindu and Jain temples
brought home to him? Also how far do Gandhian ideas of responsibility
and self-judgment dominate the play more than the Russian ideal that
Shaw defends in the Preface, of a tribunal of human judges exterminating those around them?

The Preface does not give a hint of the play's connection with India:
It advertises the play as being directly inspired by the Russian change-
over to communism and the role of the Cheka in exterminating the idle
and the socially useless. Even in the Preface, though, an attempt is made

to give a universal and a religious dimension to the political change in Russia. There is the unusual linking of Communist Russia with early Christianity, with the "communist principles of Jesus, Peter and Paul," a connection that allows for the association, later in the Preface, of the Russian Cheka with the Apocalyptic judgment and of Djerjinsky with the Angel who appears in the play. The play itself contains very little allusion to Russia, the only direct mention being when Wilks applies "the Russian touch" in shooting himself in the back of the head and when Pra hears on telephone about the "Russian plot" to destroy valuable citizens as the Last Judgment flourishes.

F.P.W. McDowell, in one of the most perceptive analyses of *The Simpleton*, commented on the difference of emphasis in the play and the preface: "Shaw's thesis that the socially undesirable should be eliminated has its most valid projection in the allegory of this play, which has a tentative, experimental and 'as if' flavor about it. The imaginative toying with the ideas of a last judgment in which the wages of social indifference is death is far more satisfying than the explicit exposition of such views in the preface to the play."[17] In this context, it is worth pursuing the means Shaw used to universalize the Russian case, keeping in mind Shaw's hint to Hesketh Pearson that

> "I have been something of a globe-trotter since I married a nomadic wife; but I dont think it has left much mark on any of my plays except the Simpleton of the Unexpected Isles, which you dont appreciate. I could not have written it exactly as it is if I had not been in India and the Far East, though almost all my life as a playwright I have hankered after a dramatization of the Last Judgment."[18]

The Last Judgment that occurs in the play has not only biblical overtones but Hindu overtones, and Gandhian overtones, attached to it. Correspondingly, Pra and Prola have the strength and integrity that they share with other Christ figures in the Shavian oeuvre, such as Dick Dudgeon, Barbara, and Joan; they also have substantial components in their nature of a Gandhian sense of responsibility, as well as of the superior terrifying and judgmental aspect that belongs to Hindu divinities like Shiva and Parvati.

The ancient cave temples of Elephanta are dedicated to Shiva and his consort Parvati and feature sculptures of Shiva in various moods and forms, most of them carved out in the fifth or sixth century. Many of the sculptures are in a partially damaged condition now, but what remains is still magnificently impressive. There are joyous life-celebrating forms such as Shiva Lalita (Shiva as the lord of dance, engaged in the dance of creation), Kalyanasundara (the marriage of Shiva and Parvati), Gangadhara (Shiva channelling the energy of the sacred river Ganga through his hair so that it does good and not harm to the world as it rushes down from heaven), and Yogisvara (Shiva the great Yogi, meditating in the *Padmasana* posture on a lotus seat). There are also terrifyingly destructive forms such as that which shows Shiva's slaying of the demon Andhaka. The co-existence of the life-giving with the life-destroying forms finds its epitome in Sadasiva, the central bust of Shiva which portrays three heads; to the left the creative, beautiful, and feminine aspect of Vamadeva, to the right the death-dealing aspect known as Aghora, and in the middle the face of Shiva as Tatpurasha, in which all manifestations of Shiva are merged. The overwhelming message of the three-headed bust is the recognition of the necessity of both creation and destruction in the life process. It could be seen as confirming for Shaw the rule he had upheld at all times, that life is not always and automatically sacred: capital punishment, Djerjinsky's schemes of liquidation, and similar devices for taking a citizen's life are universalized by being given divine sanction, and made a way of reckoning with what Shaw in the Preface to *The Simpleton* identifies as "the instinctive shrinking from outright killing which makes so many people sign petitions for the reprieve of even the worst murderers, and take no further interest if a reprieve decrees that their lives shall be taken by the slow torture of imprisonment" (p. 761). And again, "We need a greatly increased intolerance of socially injurious conduct and an uncompromising abandonment of punishment and its cruelties, together with a sufficient school inculcation of social responsibility to make every citizen conscious that if his life costs more than it is worth to the community the community may painlessly extinguish it" (p. 762).

The existence side by side of life-giving and death-dealing aspects in the image of Sadasiva may be seen to have inspired the idea of the proximity of the cliff of death and the cliff of life in *The Simpleton*. As the Emigration Officer (later Hugo Hyering) makes for the edge of the cliff to hurl himself into the sea, his path is barred by Pra, the handsome priest:

> Pardon, Son of Empire. This cliff contains the temple of the goddess who is beyond naming, the eternal mother, the seed and the sun, the resurrection and the life. You must not die here. I will send an acolyte to guide you to the cliff of death, which contains the temple of the goddess's brother, the weeder of the garden, the sacred scavenger, the last friend on earth, the prolonger of sleep and the giver of rest. It is not far off: life and death dwell close together. . . . [p. 773]

This theme of the free choice between life and death runs as an important thread through the play. Pra, who in matters of practical wisdom is a total contrast to the unworldly Lama in Kipling's *Kim* (and it seems to me that their creation reflects the respective attitudes of their authors towards India), comments on the Emigration Officer's desire for death:

> they [Englishmen] play games with balls marvellously well; but of the great game of life they are ignorant. Here, where they are in the midst of life and loveliness, they die by their own hands to escape what they call the horrors. We do not encourage them to live. The empire is for those who can live in it, not for those who can only die in it. [p. 774]

Iddy's infatuation for Maya and Vashti is sealed with the kiss of death practically from its inception. He declares he would die for Maya ten times over, and is made to admit that he would also die a thousand times for Vashti, and a million times for either of the sisters:

> IDDY. Yes, yes. I would die for either, for both; for one, for the other—
> MAYA. For Vashti Maya?
> IDDY. For Vashti Maya, for Maya Vashti.
> VASHTI. Your lives and ours are one life.
> MAYA [*sitting down beside him*] And this is the Kingdom of love.
> *The three embrace with interlaced arms and vanish in black darkness.*

Their love ends in the death and nothingness into which Maya and Vashti dissolve, foreshadowed by the black darkness into which they, like the ancient Egyptian god Ra in *Caesar and Cleopatra*, disappear. Theirs is the attitude that asserts, with Kanchin, that "Without death there can be no heroism" (p. 831).

The use of the Elephanta caves as the location for the temple scene in the Prologue involves a characteristically audacious reinstatement of original values on Shaw's part. The reality of Elephanta in 1933, as to-day, is described neatly by Gandhi when he laments the degeneration of places of worship:

> To my mind, a model temple means an ideal priest. Bricks and mortar do not make model temple. If the priest is good, even a rough hut will shine forth and earnest devotees will find solace there. And when there is no such priest, even a marble temple inlaid with mosaic would be a desolate structure. There are today a number of such famous ruins in India. . . . The caves of Karla, Ajanta and Gharapuri [Elephanta] were temples once. God has disappeared from there because of want of the priest and instead of devotees connoisseurs of art go there to see the works of art. . . . These days most of the temples are lifeless.[19]

Shaw makes such a place come alive again, and ensures that art is an expression of religion, as it is meant to be in temple architecture in India, by endowing his temple with Pra and Prola, who give the play's meaning a symbolic richness. They act as the representatives, or human aspects, of Shiva and Parvati. And they represent not only the destructive side but also the creative side of Shiva and Parvati: Thus while *The Simpleton* deals with death and extermination (as the Russian Cheka did), it is nevertheless preoccupied with life and the value and courage of living responsibly. Pra is a priest with an air of religion, purpose, and calm strength; Prola, married and with children to complete her experience as a mother, is a priestess with as much power and strength as her male counterpart. In their equality they represent the male-female relationship in its ideal state (much as Shaw saw the Ardhanarisvara aspect of Shiva making room for the equality of women with men), with respect on both sides, and no discrimination or subjugation on either side. Prola's state may be seen to represent the state of women in ancient India when, according to the writings of Panini and Badarayana, they had as much right as men to spiritual knowledge of the scriptures and to being learned teachers. How and when later inhibitions and taboos crept into modern social customs and forced women to be passive, and to depend on their sexual power and the desire of men like Iddy to idolize them, is an interesting question which *The Simpleton* may be seen as tackling in the contrast it shows between the learning and behavior of Prola on the one hand and Maya and Vashti on the other hand.

In the attempt to be representative of the creative aspect of Shiva and Parvati, Pra and Prola represent not only spiritual power but the bodily attraction of the sexes for each other. An archetype for the attraction of male and female towards each other may be found in essential form in the representation of Shiva as linga and Parvati as yoni, symbolic representations of the phallus and the womb, and in an attendant Hindu myth that the material world began with a gigantic act of copulation on the part of Shiva and Parvati. There is an impressively large linga in the central shrine, the garbhagrha (literally, the womb-house) at the western entrance to the Elephanta caves. The linga and yoni are typical symbols in Hinduism of divine procreative energy, which acts as the bridge between the spiritual and the material. The Prologue to *The Simpleton* shows us one attempt at the fusion of the spiritual with the physical and material, in the setting afoot of the eugenic experiment. Shaw provides a contrast to the varied philosophies of Annie Besant the Theosophist, Florence Farr the Vedantist, and William Archer the Secularist, whose outlooks tended to view the spiritual and the material as being in separate watertight compartments and unable to relate to each other. In scene 3 of the Prologue the emphasis is on the connection between the spiritual and the physical. We are reminded of this connection right from the beginning, when the Young Woman learns, to her amazement, that Prola is married, although a priestess: "I could not be a priestess if I were not married. How could I presume to teach others without a completed human experience? How could I deal with children if I were not a mother?" (p. 776). Pra can initially reach the soul of the lady tourist (Lady Farwaters) "only through the flesh, and accordingly he makes love to her. The male tourist—who is her husband, Sir Charles Farwaters, and later governor of the Isles—is simultaneously instructed in the same manner by Prola to a realization that a realm of life-giving values exists beyond those generally accepted by the British aristocracy."[20] Prola involves the Young Woman and the Emigration Officer (later Mr. and Mrs. Hyering) too in the eugenic experiment, indicating that she and the Young Woman could "share" the Emigration Officer, and that the Young Woman should not think of running away from the situation arising in the cave. The reader might well wonder why Pra and Prola take so much initiative and trouble in their attempt to compromise with people obviously less evolved than themselves, when it appears more sensible to "give them up; it is not your job" as one may proclaim in echo of Shaw's advice to Gandhi at the press interview in Bombay. Pra and Prola have a purpose, of course, which is to blend "the flesh and spirit of the west with the flesh and spirit of the east" (p. 794) in an attempt to breed better children. This attempt at procreation with a purpose, as opposed to sexual fulfilment for its own sake, is itself Gandhian in concept, and may also be seen in terms of Gandhi's eveready compromise of his high religious and political ideals with the practicalities of political necessity, in his attempt to create an independent and better modern India. The result may or may not justify the attempt and the experiment, but that is immaterial, as Pra and Prola (in opposition to the Shaw whose advice to Gandhi would be to "give them up") conclude at the end of *The Simpleton*. The message at the end of the play may be interpreted as indicating that the rest of the world may not live up to the standards of Pra and Prola, or of Gandhi, but that is no valid reason for their giving up the good fight to improve the world:

> PROLA. Remember: we are in the Unexpected Isles; and in the Unexpected Isles all plans fail. So much the better: plans are only jigsaw puzzles . . . we are not here to fulfil prophecies and fit ourselves into puzzles, but to wrestle with life as it comes. And it never comes as we expect it to come. . . . I tell you this is a world of miracles, not of jigsaw puzzles. For me every day must have its miracle, and no child be born like any child that ever was born before. And to witness this miracle of the children I will abide the uttermost evil and carry through it the seed of the uttermost good. [p. 839]

"Uttermost evil" and "a precious mess" (p. 838) might seem to be the result, in the short run, of the eugenic experiment as well as of Gandhi's attempts to achieve a free, independent, and godly generation in modern India, but the experiment and the attempt must nevertheless *still* be made, as we understand when we view the process as taking its cue from the attempt to fuse the spiritual and the material that is symbolized in the representation of Shiva and Parvati as linga and yoni. Why should commandingly superior religious strength such as that obvious in a priest like Pra, a priestess like Prola, and a mahatma like Gandhi, move to compromise with the physical and the material? Because life is one, because there can be no rigid barrier between the spiritual and the material, the spirit and the flesh, as the author of *Back to Methuselah* believed wholeheartedly when he elaborated on the attempts of fallen man to transform matter and flesh into thought and spirit. The myth of the fall of man itself, in this Blakean view of the universe, refers to a fall from spiritual wholeness into materialism, a happy and necessary fall in that the fall into matter saves man from a deeper and totally disastrous fall into chaos and, farther, into nonentity. The compromise between the spiritual and the material is justified in this light, and indicates a kinship of the two in an attempt to safeguard against further deterioration. It is also a fall fraught with danger, because one important consequence of such a compromise is that it could become easy to lose sight of the spiritual in our involvement with the material, the physical appearance, to forget the essential reality in the pursuit of appearance and illusion, what the Hindus label *maya*. Shaw's attempt in *The Simpleton* may be seen to be an attempt to explore the relationship between the spirit and the flesh, how the spirit must compromise with the flesh, but also how avoid the danger of being totally overwhelmed by the flesh, to the point of idolatry. From Shaw's references to the Jain temples that we have looked at, it is clear that he could sense in modern Indian religious practice a loss of true faith and vision, exchanged for idolatrous worship of the physical image adorned with flowers and ornaments and finery of dress.

Such a fall into materialism and idolatry is elaborated on in the first act of *The Simpleton*. The scene is set by the shift in location and mood that occurs between the Prologue and Act I, the two serving as bases for the unfallen and the fallen world—paradise and earth, respectively— and exploring two powerful areas which appear to be connected as off- spring are to parents and which yet show the clash of apparently oppo- site forces. The location shifts from the ancient caves of Elephanta to a tropical island in the Pacific Ocean, and correspondingly there is a shift away from an emphasis on the spiritual to an exclusive emphasis on the physical, from concerns of the good life to romantic dalliance with death, from spiritual strength to sensual weakness, from the represen- tation of Woman (as seen in Prola) as the Blakean emanation and help- mate of man to the representation of her (as seen in Maya and Vashti) as the Blakean Female Will keeping the worshipping and mindless Adam in her clutches: "Strive not, beloved: I will keep thy soul for thee," Maya sweetly informs the adoring and vacillating Iddy (p. 790).

Iddy, like his namesake Iddy Toddles the Elderly Gentleman in *Back to Methuselah*, is fallen Adam, and like the Elderly Gentleman he too is capable of redemption because he can face facts courageously and change when necessary, as he proves at the critical point when Maya disappears. The progressive enlightenment of Iddy in the play may be seen in terms of the journey of the human soul towards recognition of God and his own true self, away from the non-enlightened stage where he is, as the Vedânta-sûtras explain,

> unable to look through and beyond Mâyâ, which, like a veil, hides from it its true nature. Instead of recognizing itself to be Brahman, it blindly identifies itself with its adjuncts (upâdhi), the fictitious offspring of Mâyâ, and thus looks for its true Self in the body, the sense organs, and the internal organ (manas), i.e. the organ of specific cognition. . . . That student of the Veda, on the other hand, whose soul has been enlightened by the texts embodying the higher knowledge of Brahman, whom passages such as the great saying, "That are thou," have taught that there is no difference between his true Self and the highest Self, obtains at the moment of death immediate final release, i.e. he withdraws altogether from the influence of Mâyâ, and asserts himself in his true nature, which is nothing else but the absolute highest Brahman.[21]

Whether Iddy lives or dies after his final speech of great sadness and wisdom is never made explicit. What is certain is that, as in the Elderly Gentleman's in *Back to Methuselah*, his death as an individual will in no way jeopardize the survival and spiritual enlightenment of the Adamic race of whom he is representative. In this respect, he is the hero of the play.[22]

Maya and her siblings, in contrast to Iddy, are static and decadent, incapable of change. Their physical health is perfect (p. 796), they have artistic consciences, but "they have not between the whole four of them a scrap of moral conscience" (p. 795). In their exclusively physical perfection, the "two girl-goddesses" and the "two youthful gods," all "magically beautiful in their Indian dresses, softly brilliant," are a sharp contrast to the physical *and moral* handsomeness of Pra and Prola, and a parody of the concept put forward in the Prologue about the various images in the Elephanta caves which represent not different gods, not idols, but various aspects of God, and personifications of the forces of nature by which we all live. The unity that Pra and Prola sense in the various images is echoed in the hideous oneness of the siblings: ". . . they hit out for themselves the idea that they were to be one another" (p. 799), which means that they are equally superficial in their beauty and hollow in substantial worth. That the carefully planned progeny of Pra and Prola can be so utterly devoid of moral conscience is to be pondered on, and perhaps one way of understanding the process may be to connect their materialism with that of the majority of middle-class Indians that Shaw saw in Bombay and elsewhere, the potential inheritors of independence through the efforts of Gandhi who nevertheless, in their materialistic concerns (including the worship of the physical image in the temples), represent the irreligion of idolatry that Gandhi defines as the attempt to "see something through one of the five senses."[23]

The atmosphere in Act I of *The Simpleton* is one of disillusionment, beneath the initial references to gods and enchantment, idols and consecrated ground. This could be seen as Shaw's disillusionment with modern Indian religion, as meaningless as he found contemporary churchgoing in Britian. *The Simpleton* could then be seen as a moral fable particularly for Indians, for whom it could deliver a relevant and useful message about the Gandhian heights to which true religion could aspire and, in contrast, the nothingness into which shallow pursuit of the exclusively material could plunge mankind. This contrast is hinted at in Hiralal Amritlal Shah's recording of the afternoon when he escorted Shaw to the Jain temples. After their visit to the impressive temples, Shaw invited Shah to accompany him to the next item in his itinerary, a visit to a

> red-painted bungalow with a crescent mark on the gates. The Shaw couple were to get a reception there, sponsored by the "Three Arts Circle." Chief among its sponsors was a lady called Atiya Begum. When we arrived, we were taken to the terrace at the rear of the house, which commanded a fine view of Bombay and its sea-face. Here tea, drinks and light refreshments were set out on tables, and everyone partook while mingling with music and dances. Enthusiastically, they took us to the inner hall, switched off the lights, and let the entertainment begin. It did not take long before I saw that Mr. Shaw had taken out his pocket watch. It was a dull affair, a jumble which reached a low grade in artistic taste, and was exceeding both the time limitations and the patience of the guests. The more the show dragged along, the more Mr. Shaw became restive. He whispered to me that it was 4:30 P.M., and that he wanted to leave for his ship by the early evening ferry.
>
> He stood up and told one of his hosts that his time was up and that he had to go, but the host took it rather lightly assuming that, out of courtesy, his guest would remain. But Mr. Shaw made straight for the portico, walking fast, his tall figure taking long strides. We had to run after him.
>
> We were all rather silent in the car at first, until Mr. Shaw remarked, "There was nothing in that show. Such things and such people are met at every port in every country. My time has been wasted."

Beneath the superficial glamor and fine elegance, there is revealed a degree of vapidity and nothingness that is the characteristic of Maya and her companions, and which is in total contrast to the meaningful commitment shown in the architecture of the Jain Temples and the Elephanta caves, in Pra and Prola, in Gandhi.

The climax of *The Simpleton* occurs in Act II of the play, when Maya and her siblings indulge in a hysterical, trance-like worship of war and death (much as the inhabitants of *Heartbreak House* do), leading up to a compulsive deification of Prola, which earns them her total contempt.

KANCHIN. We have made this house a temple.

JANGA. We have made Prola its goddess.

MAYA. We have made it a palace.

VASHTI. A palace for Queen Prola.

KANCHIN. She shall reign.

JANGA. For ever and ever.

VASHTI AND MAYA [*in unison*] Hail, Prola, our goddess!

KANCHIN AND JANGA [*in unison*] Hail, Prola, our empress!

ALL FOUR [*rushing down to the lawn and throwing themselves on their knees before her*] Hail!

PROLA. Will you provoke me to box your ears, you abominable idolators. Get up this instant. Go and scrub the floors. Do anything that is dirty and grubby and smelly enough to shew that you live in a real world and not in a fool's paradise. If I catch you grovelling to me, a creature of the same clay as yourselves, but fortunately for you with a little more common sense, I will beat the slavishness out of your bones.

MAYA. Oh, what ecstasy to be beaten by Prola!

VASHTI. To feel her rule in the last extremity of pain!

KANCHIN. To suffer for her!

JANGA. To die for her!

PROLA. Get out, all four. My empire is not of such as you. Begone.

MAYA. How lovely is obedience! [*She makes an obeisance and runs away through the garden*].

VASHTI. Obedience is freedom from the intolerable fatigue of thought. [*She makes her obeisance and sails away, disappearing between the garden and the house*].

KANCHIN. You speak as an empress should speak. [*He salaams and bounds after Maya*].

JANGA. The voice of authority gives us strength and unity. Command us always thus: it is what we need and love. [*He strides away in Vashti's footsteps*].

PROLA. An excuse for leaving everything to me. Lazy, lazy, lazy! Someday Heaven will get tired of lazy people; and the Pitcairn Islanders will see their Day of Judgment at last.

[pp. 819–29]

Idolatry, with all that it implies of laziness, inaction, and irresponsibility, is shown as having reached a climactic point—a comment relevant to many societies and many religions, which does not decrease its significance in the context of the modern Indian worship of temple idols as well as of nominal subscription to Gandhi as the spiritual Father of the Nation. Concurrent with this nadir of idolatry is the occurrence of Judgment Day, symbolically shown by the appearance of the judging Angel. The Angel is meant to represent the Russian Djerjinsky, the designer of the Cheka, which liquidated people it considered to be not worth their salt to society. The Angel tells his audience, in echo of Jesus's words in the gospel of St. Matthew, "We angels are executing a judgment. The lives which have no use, no meaning, no purpose will fade out. You will have to justify your existence or perish. Only the elect shall survive. . . . The Day of Judgment is not the end of the World, but the end of its childhood and the beginning of its responsible maturity" (p. 825). It is educative, and relevant in the Indian context, to see how Pra and Prola in their maturity take the responsibility of judgment away from the Djerjinskian Angel and towards themselves: they take charge and make it an affair of self-judgment rather than arbitrary judgment by an outside force, however angelic or otherwise it might appear to be. Towards the end of Act II, Hyering resigns himself passively to the fact that "The angels are weeding the garden. We here are awaiting our own doom." But Prola elaborates on the theme of judgment by the angel, qualifying it so that it gives way to self-judgment:

> The lives which have no use, no meaning, no purpose, will fade out. We shall have to justify our existences or perish. We shall live under a constant sense of that responsibility. If the angels fail us we shall set up tribunals of our own from which worthless people will not come out alive. When men no longer fear the judgment of God, they must learn to judge themselves. [p. 835]

Pra and Prola judge themselves:

> PRA. . . . We are awaiting judgment here quite simply as a union of a madwoman with a fool.
>
> PROLA. Who thought they had created four wonderful children. And who are now brought to judgment and convicted of having created nothing.

They discuss the uselessness of the children and Pra sums up: "The coming race will not be like them. Meanwhile we are face to face with the fact that we two have made a precious mess of our job. . . . We are failures. We shall disappear." They recognize, and judge themselves for, the mistake they have made, much as Gandhi recognized and judged himself for his "Himalayan blunder" in 1919, when he blamed himself for the violence that erupted in the wake of the *hartal* or general strike he had called as a protest. He felt he had underrated the forces of evil in Indian society and expected his countrymen to show a strength of nonviolence, self-purification, and prayer of which they proved incapable. The self-judgment of Gandhi, and Pra and Prola, is different from the arbitrary external judgment of the Djerjinskian Angel, in that mistake-makers still survive. They do not disappear, as Prola convinces Pra, when she judges herself:

> I do not feel like that [that she and Pra will disappear]. I feel like the leader of a cavalry charge whose horse has been shot through the head and dropped dead under him. Well, a dead hobby horse is not the end of the world. Remember; we are in the Unexpected Isles; and in the Unexpected Isles all plans fail . . . in the Unexpected Isles there is no security; and the future is to those who prefer surprise and wonder to security. I, Prola, shall live and grow because suprise and wonder are the very breath of my being, and routine is death to me. Let every day be a day of wonder for me and I shall not fear the Day of Judgment. [*She is interrupted by a roll of thunder*]. Be silent: you cannot frighten Prola with stage thunder. The fountain of life is within me. [pp. 839–40]

There is a certain sense of humor, and putting things into proper perspective, in such a speech, and these are qualities, one sometimes feels, that are missing in the world of Stalinist values. No external judgmental force can frighten man's soul as represented in Pra and Prola, and in such people as Gandhi who are capable of self-judgment, but who in the process still ensure that the spirit and the pride of mankind are not broken down, as one suspects they are liable to be in a closed and determinist society such as operates in Russia. In *The Simpleton*, the pervasive Indian influence thus counteracts Shaw's Russian infatuation and makes the play a sensible one, with a serious message to the world, that it should wake up to the folly of idolatry and to the potential power of true religion. I believe it is a Gandhian ideal, rather than a Stalinist ideal, that gives the play's ending the quality of unexpectedness and fearless experimentation that is the characteristic hallmark of the Shavian view of social and spiritual evolution.

Notes

1. In *Major Critical Essays*, vol. 18 of the Standard Edition of the works of Shaw (London: Constable, 1931–1950), pp. 21–22.

2. See Dan H. Laurence, ed., *Bernard Shaw: Collected Letters* (London: Max Reinhardt,

1965–1972), vol. 1, pp. 431, 505. See also Nethercot, *First Five Lives of Annie Besant* (Chicago: University of Chicago, 1960), p. 283.

3. *First Five Lives*, pp. 328–29.

4. Clifford Bax, ed., *Florence Farr, Bernard Shaw, W. B. Yeats: Letters* (London: Home and Van Thal, 1946), p. x.

5. 15 September 1903, in Clifford Bax, ed., *Florence Farr, Bernard Shaw, W. B. Yeats: Letters*, pp. 17–18.

6. William Archer, *Three Plays. With a Personal Note by G. B. Shaw* (London: Constable, 1927), pp. xxxvi–xxxviii.

7. D. G. Tendulkar, *Mahatma—The Life of Mohandas Karamchand Gandhi* (New Delhi: Publications Division, Ministry of Information and Broadcasting, Government of India), vol. 7 (1945–1947), p. 4; quoted in *The Collected Works of Mahatma Gandhi* (New Dehli: Publications Division, Ministry of Information and Broadcasting, Government of India), vol. 53 (25 April–16 July 1945), pp. 65–66.

8. *Collected Works of Gandhi*, 48 (September 1931–January 1932), p. 353.

9. Vincent Sheean, "Tribute: From 'a Last Disciple,'" a recounting of Sheean's interviews with Gandhi on 27 and 28 January 1948, in Norman Cousins, ed., *Profiles of Gandhi* (New Delhi: India Book Company), pp. 75–82.

10. Gandhi's interview with Shaw, recorded in Sgt. Mahadeo Desai's Diary and published in the 19 November 1931 issue of the weekly *Young India*. There is an extract from the original publication in *The Collected Works of Gandhi*, 48, 272–73.

11. Reports substantially the same may be found in *The Hindu* (Madras) *Daily Herald*, *The New York Herald Tribune*, and *The New York Times*, all dated 9 January 1933.

12. A. H. Nethercot in *The Last Four Lives of Annie Besant* commented on the article, with its ironic title of "Indian Cowardice and English Pluck," and the article itself is reprinted in the *Independent Shavian*, 6 (Winter 1967), pp. 1–3.

13. "Bernard Shaw in Bombay," *Shaw Bulletin*, 1, no. 10 (November 1956), pp. 8–10. The article is adapted from Shah's translation of his reminiscences, first published in Gujrati in 1950.

14. The film was produced by Gabriel Pascal in 1941 and the film version of the play first published in 1945 by Penguin Books.

15. As quoted in Dan H. Laurence, ed., *Shaw: An Exhibit* (Austin, Texas: Humanities Research Center, 1967), exhibit 471.

16. Benedictine Nuns of Stanbrook, *In a Great Tradition* (New York: Harper and Row, 1956), pp. 268–72. For other references in Shaw to Jainism and the Jain temples, see "If I were a Priest," Shaw's article on Dean Inge in *Atlantic Monthly*, 185 (May 1950), pp. 70–72; and Blanche Patch, *Thirty Years with G.B.S.* (London: Victor Gollancz, 1951), pp. 107, 186.

17. Frederick P. W. McDowell, "Spiritual and Political Reality: Shaw's *The Simpleton of the Unexpected Isles*," *Modern Drama*, 3 (September 1960), 207.

18. *G.B.S.: A Postscript* (New York: Harper, 1950), p. 62.

19. *Collected Works of Gandhi*, 55, April 1933.

20. "Spiritual and Political Reality."

21. The quotation is from pp. xxvi–xxvii of the Introduction to the Vedanta Sutras of Badarayana, with the commentary by Sankara (translated by George Thibaut), published as volume 38 of the series, "The Sacred Books of the East" (ed. F. Max Müller). That Shaw had read the Vedanta Sutras seems a reasonable guess since it was in his study library at Ayot St. Lawrence.

22. Iddy's role as the "humming center of the play" and his spiritual movement are analyzed in detail by Daniel Leary in "About Nothing in Shaw's *The Simpleton of the Unexpected Isles*," *Educational Theatre Journal*, 24, no. 2 (May 1972), 139–48. For a discussion of

the Elderly Gentleman as the representative hero of the Adamic race, see my article, "*Back to Methuselah*: A Blakean Interpretation," in Charles A. Berst, ed., *Shaw and Religion* (*SHAW: The Annual of Bernard Shaw Studies*, 1 [1981]).

23. *Collected Works of Gandhi*, 48, p. 397.

Piers Gray

HONG KONG, SHANGHAI, THE GREAT WALL: BERNARD SHAW IN CHINA

Hong Kong

Shaw's descent upon Hong Kong on Saturday, 11 February 1933, was given extensive coverage by the local press. A small insecure territory ruled by a group holding the values of the British middle-class ("attitudes to the Chinese were close to middle-class attitudes to servants in Britain")[1] offered a multitude of chances to be *terrible*. The visit got off to a good start with Shaw refusing to speak to the Rotarians: he reasoned it thus to reporters who interviewed him on board the *Empress of Britain*: "I remember the beginning of Rotary. . . . It was a movement to induce captains of industry to take their business more scientifically and to raise business men to the professional rank." But now, "Rotary Clubs are merely luncheon clubs, which as a general rule know as much about the aims and objects of Rotary as a luncheon of Church of England members knows about the 39 Articles. . . ."[2]

The Rotarians' Vice-President, P. S. Cassidy, attempted to respond to this snub in what he presumably took to be the Shavian spirit: "I am sure it is his loss." Unfortunately, his comrades lost their nerve and at the Shawless meeting of February 14th, the hapless Cassidy retracted his comment: "In case a reflection is cast on the Rotary Club as a whole I would like to make it quite clear that no criticism was intended. The remark was meant to be humorous. . . . I am a great admirer of Mr Shaw and have benefitted intellectually from reading his works."[3] Alas, poor Cassidy.

Shaw's brief stay in Hong Kong seemed, at first, doomed to arouse only the most facetious and trivial of controversies. Not that Shaw himself was avoiding the seriousness of the East. His journey into China would be taking him towards the first struggle, in effect, of the Second World War—the Japanese invasion of Manchuria, of which he had this to say:

> Japan is going to take Manchuria. . . . But hasn't she behaved very correctly over it all? She pledged herself to the League of Nations that she would not declare war on anyone. Consequently she has not declared war on China, but has contented herself with fighting—all so legitimately.
> What does China expect the League to do? An economic boycott? But the League has funked the issues. And now it is gradually ceasing to exist. Japan has smashed the League, or, let me put it this way, Japan has called the League's bluff.

And he was able to add the observation that through disarmament

> [the Great] Powers want to come to some arrangement by which they can fight more cheaply. They hold meetings and say to each other "if you disarm, we'll disarm," and the result is deadlock.
> The greatest satisfaction to us is that in the next war we will be knocked by a ten inch shell and not a sixteen inch shell.[4]

Although the newspaper's subheading to this interview was "Satire is the keynote," there was really no threat—*pace* the Rotarians—to home and hearth. But he was not done yet. Imagine the sheer folly of *not* exploiting Shavimania while the Hong Kong press were spanieling at his heels. Consider: Reports were coming through of excited students at Sun Yat-sen University in Canton desperate to see him and of enlisted men in Hong Kong being read to from the Preface to *The Apple Cart*. Editorials greeted him as the greatest man ever to visit the place. Photographs immortalized him clowning on the deck of the *Empress of Britain* as a sea-dog gazing out toward some mythical horizon. Reporters reported everything they could scrounge up. They told of his eccentric clothes, his funny hat, his white beard, his "twinkling eye." And when tired of his appearance, they told of his opinions, however satirical. And when tired of his appearances and opinions, they told of his movements. Thus:

> In the afternoon [of Saturday, 11 February] a party on a ramble organized by the Sailors' and Soldiers' Home, in Wanchai, having visited several old landmarks of the Colony in the Pokfulam neighbourhood, had the pleasure of seeing one of the world's landmarks, Mr Shaw, who was returning from a drive round the island under the guidance of Professor R. K. Simpson of Hong Kong University.[5]

And what could be more appropriate than an afternoon spin with the Professor of English? Perhaps it was completely innocent but one would like to believe—with hindsight—that the academic (who was to be succeeded, after the war, by Edmund Blunden) and the playwright were whispering conspiracy as they pottered through Pokfulam.

Yet events unfolded decorously enough: on Monday, 13 February, Shaw, accompanied again by Professor Simpson, took "tiffin" at the residence of Sir Robert Ho Tung—perhaps Hong Kong's most intriguing resident and certainly one of its university's greatest benefactors. Widely known as the "Grand Old Man," Ho Tung—who was six years Shaw's junior—had risen dramatically from poverty to become, via the Maritime Customs in Canton, the Manager of the Chinese Department of Jardine, Matheson and Company, erstwhile purveyors of opiates, now mightiest of hongs. As Woo Sing Lim in *The Prominent Chinese in Hong Kong* (1938) observed—somewhat laconically, perhaps—"Sir Robert soon multiplied the business returns and connexions of the firm." Indeed, by the age of thirty Ho Tung was a millionaire and

> associated with every important business enterprise in the Colony. When he resigned his compradoreship in 1900 (at the early age of 38) Sir Robert Ho Tung was already known as the leading expert and merchant in Hongkong in property, insurance, shipping, and [the] import and export business, with agencies in Java and the Philippines. From 1900 and onwards one company after another invited him to serve on its Board of Directors, until to-day he is a Director of 18 of the leading companies in Hongkong and Shanghai as well as being Chairman and largest shareholder of a number of them.[6]

The meeting in Hong Kong certainly seemed to grip Shaw's imagination. Above all, the Eurasian millionaire of obscure origins and astounding ascent had a very sharp self-image. "Sir Robert adopted the manners, deportment, and costume of a Chinese gentleman and did not seek to pass as a European nor to enter European society. 'Sir Robert,' a contemporary wrote, 'takes a keen interest in all matters relating to Chinese life.'"[7]

That "Chineseness" appealed to Shaw. The interior of the Ho Tung residence, "Idlewild," made a significant impression: he was to use the private temple as a setting for Act III of *Buoyant Billions* and to recall it elsewhere in an article on "Aesthetic Science" in 1946:

> When I was in Hong Kong, I was entertained very agreeably indeed by Sir Robert Ho Tung. We were both of the age at which one likes a rest after lunch. He took me upstairs into what in England would have been a drawing room. It was a radiant miniature temple with an altar of Chinese vermilion and gold, and cushioned divan seats round the walls for the worshippers. Everything was in such perfect Chinese taste that to sit there and look was a quiet delight. A robed priest and his acolyte stole in and went through a service. When it was over I told Sir Robert that I

had found it extraordinarily soothing and happy though I had not understood a word of it. "Neither have I," he said, "but it soothes me too." It was part of the art of life for Chinaman and Irishman alike, and was purely esthetic. But it was also hygenic: there was an unexplored region of biologic science at the back of it.[8]

Although Ho Tung had several residences in Hong Kong—as well as houses in Macao, Shanghai and London—and although the Hong Kong houses were literally above those of almost all his fellow Chinese, "Idlewild" was clearly something special. Irene Cheng, Ho Tung's daughter, describes its physical and spiritual significance:

> "Idlewild" was a large, well-known house, with an excellent view of the harbor and with gardens on several levels linked to each other by flights of steps and pathways, two cement tennis courts (which were used as a nursery for plants instead of for tennis), and a large vegetable patch on the highest level. Several of the older Ho Tung children were born in "Idlewild."
>
> Many happy events occurred there . . . when Father celebrated his sixtieth, seventieth, and ninetieth birthdays. In 1920 he commemorated his Silver Wedding Anniversary with Mamma and in 1931 his Golden Wedding Anniversary with Mother. . . . "Idlewild," sadly, was also the scene of several funerals, including Father's in 1956. . . .[9]

And so Shaw was indeed being honored.

Yet if they agreed on spiritual health, there was surely some intellectual distance between them on the international body politic and its well-being. Ho Tung was a committed supporter of Chiang Kaishek. And Chiang Kaishek and the Kuomintang (Nationalists) were committed, in turn, to the suppression of—above all—Communism. So one wonders, therefore, what Sir Robert made of his guest's performance down the hill that afternoon at the university to which he had given so much support. On Tuesday, 14 February, the *South China Morning Post*, reported as follows:

BRILLIANT ADDRESS
GEORGE BERNARD SHAW
BREAKS RESOLUTION
ADVISES UNIVERSITY STUDENTS
TO BE COMMUNISTS
EDUCATION DENOUNCED

It is one thing to ignore the Rotarians; it is quite another to urge a group of young Chinese to become radicals. The university, after all, was a focus of Colonial contradictions: a "British University on Chinese soil."[10] Here is the version of that paradox in the words of its founder and first chancellor, Sir Edward Lugard:

It is open to all races and creeds, and its matriculation and degree ex-
aminations will be maintained at a standard equal to that of English Universities. Its medium of instruction will be English so that those who
graduate may be able to read for themselves the works in English dealing
with the subjects they take up, and British influence in the Far East may
be extended.[11]

It could hardly help to spread that influence if very famous people like
Shaw advised students to become Communists. Nor should one under-
estimate the important position universities had gained in Chinese societies: the uprising of May 4th, 1919, in China, against ratification of
the Treaty of Versailles, was inspired and led by university students in
Beijing. The consequences of this protest were profound; the May 4th
Movement "had an incalculable effect on education, on labor organiza-
tions, on the attitudes of intellectuals toward their country and toward
themselves."[12] Indeed, the founder of the Chinese Republic, Dr. Sun
Yatsen, "had tried out his wings in an attempted armed occupation of
Canton in 1895, only three years after graduating from the University
of Hong Kong's own forerunner, the Hong Kong College of Medicine
for the Chinese, a hotbed of young revolutionaries."[13]

That afternoon, the Great Hall of the University was packed with students and distinguished guests; but before Shaw could rouse the young
he had to negotiate another round of grovelling from the Rotarians.
Clearly tenacity and ubiquity were essential to their nature. The *South
China Morning Post* reported it with a degree of malicious pleasure:

> When Mr Shaw was accompanied to the dais by the Vice-Chancellor, Sir
> William Hornell, there was a terrific out-burst of cheering. Sir William
> introduced Mr Shaw collectively and then individually to the vistors.
>   The pair stopped before the Press representatives. "I have met them
> already," commented G.B.S.
>   "And this is Mr M. F. Key, formerly of the Press," said Sir William.
>   "Yes," said Mr Key, "But now secretary of the Rotary Club. I want to
> tell you, Mr Shaw, that you were quite right in all you said about the
> Rotary Club the other day."
>   Sir William interjected, "But Mr Shaw said that the Hongkong Rotary
> Club was probably an exception."
>   "I had to be polite" was the dry comment of the famous man.

Thus warmed up for the task ahead, Shaw set about his audience with
enthusiasm: "I am here as a guest of the University. I have a very strong
opinion that every University on the face of the earth should be levelled
to the ground and its foundations sowed with salt." Further:

> There are really two dangerous classes in the world—the half-educated,
> who half-destroyed the world, and the wholly-educated who have very
> nearly completely destroyed the world. When I was young—an incalcu-

lable number of years ago—nobody knew anything about the old, old civilizations. We knew a little about Greece and Rome and we knew that Rome somehow or other collapsed and was very ably replaced by ourselves. But we had no idea how many civilizations exactly like our own had existed. They almost all collapsed through education.

And the response to this demagoguery? "Laughter." Or a little later—banter:

> "What are you going to do? I don't know. You may say 'Shall I leave the University and go on the streets?' Well, I don't know. There is something to be got from the University. You get a certain training in communal life which is very advantageous. If I had a son I should send him to the University and say 'Be careful not to let them put an artificial mind into you. As regards the books they want you to read, don't read them." (Applause)
> Professor Brown: "They never do." (Laughter)
> Shaw: "Well, that's very encouraging."

This was the spirit of the assembly: laughter, applause, cheerful backtalk. "We like it" one student shouted out when Shaw asked if he should continue. So where was the Communist menace?

> If you read, read real books and steep yourself in revolutionary books. Go up to your neck in Communism, because if you are not a red revolutionist at 20, you will be at 50 a most impossible fossil. If you are a red revolutionist at 20, you have some chance of being up-to-date at 40. So I can only say, go ahead in the direction I have indicated.

And although the exhortation immediately following this assertion—always argue with your teacher—was again greeted with laughter, one wonders what these students really thought about Shaw's political advice. In China, the Kuomintang and a host of warlords were shooting and beheading, among other things, Communists.

Whatever the individual's response to this argument, the mass greeted Shaw's peroration with "Prolonged applause":

> The thing you have to remember is valuation. Remember all you have to forget or you will go mad. Keep and stick to your valuation. You may be wrong but you must make up your mind. Being human and fallible you may come to wrong opinions. But it is still more disastrous not to have opinions at all.
> I hope you are properly edified and will not regret having made me break my promise not to make a speech while in Hongkong.[14]

One imagines that the audience was indeed edified—in several ways. First, there was the metaphysical defiance of the man: Shaw rampant, time couchant. In a sense what he said mattered less than the *fact* of being able to say it—still. Hence the second and related aspect of the performance: its theatricality. The students were clearly overwhelmed by the brio, the iconoclastic gaiety, the reckless comedy of it all, the sense of liberation from the solemnity of institutionalized thought. The burden of two cultures, two sets of tradition, two languages of instruction and correction, can be felt even today. And thus we come to the third aspect of that speech: How far can we see a real political gesture in it? How much trouble *did* Shaw wish to stir up among these students? Certainly he was firm about Colonies; in the Preface to *John Bull's Other Island*, he had written of "the truth formulated by William Morris that 'no man is good enough to be another man's master'" (*BH* 2, 870). But that is not necessarily a preliminary for the advocacy of Communism. Here we can turn to another Preface, that of *On the Rocks*, written immediately after his return to Britain.

> I went round the world lately preaching that if Russia were thrust back from Communism into competitive Capitalism, and China developed into a predatory Capitalist State, either independently or as part of a Japanese Asiatic hegemony, all the western States would have to quintuple their armies and lie awake at nights in continual dread of hostile aeroplanes, the obvious moral being that whether we choose Communism for ourselves or not, it is our clear interest, even from the point of view of our crudest and oldest militarist diplomacy, to do everything in our power to sustain Communism in Russia and extend it in China, where at present provinces containing at the least of many conflicting estimates eighteen millions of people, have adopted it. [*BH* 6, 607]

Of course, this is a familiar Shavian rhetorical ploy: induce consternation amongst the opposition by turning its world upside down; what you fear most you should actually fear least. International Communism will keep the world safe for international Capitalism. It is an interesting argument and one that can be pondered today. Was Shaw right? Does the world paradoxically *need* two apparently conflicting—hostile, even—systems in order to remain balanced and stable? Certainly, one world war and two atomic bombs later, great nations are having to consider the implications of a Capitalist Japan and a Communist China.

But to what extent are we now peering into an unholy nest of contradictions? On the one hand, here is Shaw, having lunched with one of Hong Kong's great entrepreneurs, sallying forth to incite Chinese students (who were directly benefitting from Sir Robert's financial skills) to overthrow the shackles of Colonialist Capitalism. On the other hand, there is the puzzle as to how he thought the students were actually to benefit from this advice: according to the argument of the Preface to *On the Rocks*, a Communist China would be of advantage to Britain and its Capitalists. What then was Shaw's position in the whole reckless adventure? Consider again the Preface to *On the Rocks* and its concluding remarks:

> Now I was not physically prevented from saying this, nor from writing and printing it. But in a western world suffering badly from Marxphobia, and frantically making itself worse like a shrew in a bad temper, I could not get a single newspaper to take up my point or report my utterance. When I say anything silly, or am reported as saying anything reactionary, it runs like wildfire through the Press of the whole world. When I say anything that could break the carefully inculcated popular faith in Capitalism the silence is so profound as to be almost audible. I do not complain, because I do not share the professorial illusion that there is any more freedom for disillusionists in the British Empire and the United States of North America than in Italy, Germany, and Russia. I have seen too many newspapers suppressed and editors swept away, not only in Ireland and India but in London in my time, to be taken in by Tennyson's notion that we live in a land where a man can say the thing he will. There is no such country. [*BH* 6, 607–8]

But this—surely?—is manifestly untrue. It was indeed the Western press *within* the Empire that was lavishing attention upon his most provocatively anti-Capitalist utterances. "When I say anything that could break the carefully inculcated popular faith in Capitalism the silence is so profound as to be almost audible"—to have written those words demands some explanation. Was Shaw's memory impaired? It would seem not; had he not complete recall about Sir Robert Ho Tung's domestic temple? Perhaps then we should argue from the other extreme. He knew exactly what he was saying in his revision of the narrative: he was speaking as playwright/manager of the comic's past performance. In that case, it is necessary, above all, to keep the house open, not to let the theater of the self "go dark." Thus what may matter is the understanding that a speech once made—a performance—needs to be kept alive within the series of further performances it can generate.

Contrary to Shaw's own account then, there was an immediate response to reports of his speech: the front page of *The Hong Kong Telegraph* carried, in its first column, the following letter:

> Sir—Allow me to congratulate the Vice-Chancellor of the Hongkong University on his enterprise in securing the attendance of Mr Shaw at a tea-party held there yesterday afternoon. Sir William Hornell's [the Vice-Chancellor] distinguished supporters are also to be thanked, many of whom will no doubt treasure the newspaper account of the affair.
>
> Mr Shaw's student listeners had the treat of their lives. They, really, quite understood that the famous author was but talking with his tongue in his cheek. The Chinese have such a keen sense of humour!
>
> Seriously, I trust that all concerned in yesterday's farce now see their

mistake. I can appreciate the misgivings of those responsible if a lesser light of theirs had raved half so rantingly in a lecture-room of our University.

We can also realise how difficult it will be for those in authority to deal with any mild outbreak of "Bolshevism" which may occur at our principal seat of learning.

After the wise counsel given yesterday, I can, in addition, appreciate the confusion in the minds of students when next they hear that one [of] their countrymen has been gaoled for preaching "revolution" in our streets.

Yours etc. . . .[15]

Fair enough: what indeed if the students had taken to the streets or stormed the library chanting Bolshevik slogans? Had not authority already compromised itself? And had not Dr. Sun Yatsen, founder of the Chinese Republic, stated, just ten years earlier at the same University, as he addressed the Students' Union, that "I got my revolutionary ideas in Hong Kong?"[16]

Whatever the outcome of the speech, Shaw had pitched his audience (both Chinese and European) back into history, into thinking about the world that was grinding itself into very small pieces indeed. The correspondence that followed suggests as much. There was, true, a leader from the *South China Morning Post* which put up a fair imitation of judicious, even-handed assessment, to begin with. On the one hand:

> Reactions to Mr G.B. Shaw's visit are mixed. His ardent admirers stand staunchly by him and dilate upon the brilliance of his utterances, while the mischievous chuckle to see the pained expressions on the faces of the eminently proper. Outrageous! The average person, perhaps, has been surfeited and, not a few disappointed, having in their dullness expected something far better from the oracle. In fairness, it must be said, however, that no criticism attaches to Mr Shaw. He was on holiday and with no desire to speak or to be interviewed.

On the other:

> Having been pestered [by Professor Simpson? by Sir Robert Ho Tung? by the Vice-Chancellor?], he responded naturally and with Shavian malice aforethought, setting himself out to be deliberately outrageous, by way of reprisal and as though to teach us that stinging plants and insects are best left alone.

The editor can only abuse Shaw since, as he somewhat testily concedes, despite being the kind of venomous toad he is, the man cannot actually be "blamed" for the debacle:

> Exception has been taken to his remarks to the University students, and it is being said that no explaining may remove all of the harm that may

have been done thereby. Nevertheless the position remains that upon his hosts falls the responsibility of justifying Mr Shaw's irresponsibility. Himself would offer no apology: and his disciples deny that his satires can have been misunderstood, or, in any event, that any harm can come from candour. The discussion thus ends in impasse or else is ruled out as unnecessary and the episode to be forgotten.

It is a pity the editor couldn't have stiffened his sinews for a crusade and demanded, for example, a naming of names, since the piece tails rather sadly away, as if—suddenly—the world of Hong Kong was seen as forever on the outside of somewhere really important:

> There is only one Shaw, and that he should grace Hongkong but once in his lifetime is an historical event, to be appreciated in all humility. In comparison, what matters? If in fact the Shavianism has been overdone, having acquitted Shaw of blame it can only be pleaded that seldom does a fish worth baiting come this way. . . . As we are, Shaw has come and Shaw has gone; and so back into our narrow beds creep and let no more be said.[17]

It is a relief to discover, therefore, that some of the journal's readers were made of sterner stuff. "Graduate," for example:

> Actually Shaw himself is an example of the tragedy of a mind undisciplined by a University education. Nobody can deny his genius; everybody is made to laugh by his humour; but on reflection anyone might also weep that such a genius has done so little, if any, constructive work. . . . Few people in Britain take Shaw's social or political views seriously and it is unfortunate that any of the British in Hong Kong should have done so. . . .

And P. H. Larkin:

> You have absolutely spoilt him! You have credited him with a power greater than the Creator! You have placed him on a pedestal so high that he fears to fall, lest his fall would be disastrous; hence his attempt to justify his omnipotence by clinging fast to the top, daring not to look down on the ground from his dizzy height! And what do we, mere men in the street, get from this man-made god? Trash! Absolutely undiluted trash! Shaw is first and last an egoist, and the way he babbled about the affairs of the world as if he knew all, escaping nothing, plainly shows this self-patting of him. For the love of Mike give us less of Shaw and more of the saner men![18]

And so on. Except that the point was being missed. These critics wrote as if they were back in the genteel suburbanity of London's Metroland; but Shaw had made his gesture with great calculation: ignore the Europeans, speak to the Chinese. That allowed him to delight and offend simultaneously. And it raised a nagging doubt for the European mind:

what would the Chinese make of this provocation? Could they—unlike the British in Hong Kong—take him seriously? And this, as "Pro and Anti-Shavian" observed, is what really mattered:

> In the welter of correspondence on G.B.S.'s famous lecture, it appears to me that most of your correspondents, Shavian and anti-Shavian alike, ignore the main point. I mean the effect that such an open support of Communism will have on the lower social strata of our Colony. I know nothing of the student body of the University, but am willing to take it as read, that they will be able to place such advice in its proper perspective. I take it that representatives of the Chinese press were in attendance at the lecture, and I would like to know how it appeared in their papers, and what the average Chinese would make of it.[19]

Indeed: what *was* the reaction of the Chinese press? In the first instance—none. The Hong Kong Government Secretariat for Chinese Affairs was not enthusiastic about Shaw "preaching" to the natives. And so the Chinese papers were discouraged from meeting him on the day of his arrival. As a result, there was the following exchange, quoted in the Shanghai *North China Herald*:

> Mr. Shaw greeted the correspondents with the words: "You do not look very much like Chinese" and expressed surprise at the entire lack of Chinese pressmen. "Where are the Chinese," he asked with his usual genial impertinence. "Are they so primitive that they have not heard of me?"[20]

What seems a gratuitously offensive remark made a point, then, about government by ignorance.

On the other hand, the *South China Morning Post* heard Shaw somewhat differently:

> On Saturday there were only six reporters present when G.B.S. strolled in. We watched him anxiously, but our fears were groundless. G.B.S. was at peace with the world.
> "Hullo, only six of you? Where's the rest?" were his first remarks. Someone explained that all the Hongkong newspapers were represented.[21]

Well, all the *English* language papers, that is.

Thus Shaw's remarks in the Preface to *On the Rocks* turned out to be half-true. A silence *was* imposed where it mattered. The Colonial Government was reacting to Shaw with, no doubt, the student uprisings in China of 4 May 1919, the Hong Kong seaman's strike of 1922, and the General Strike in Canton of 1925—the subject of Malraux's first China novel, *Les Conquérants* (1928)—on their minds. The unions and radicals had shown their potential in that last uprising; Hong Kong had been severely affected:

A boycott of British goods and a general strike were immediately declared [in response to the machine-gunning by British and French troops of fifty-two demonstrators in Canton]. Hong Kong, fortress of British imperialism in China, was laid prostrate. Not a wheel turned. Not a bale of cargo moved. Not a ship left anchorage. More than 100,000 Hong Kong workers took the unprecedented action of evacuating the city and moving *en masse* to Canton.[22]

The times in China had been and still were interesting. Thus tight censorship over the local Chinese press's reporting of Shaw's speech to the University was deemed mandatory. The day after he spoke, it appears that no Hong Kong Chinese newspaper reported his Communist exhortations; yet ironically enough, Shanghai itself was aware of these events. A large number of the bigger papers' Hong Kong correspondents were there and telegraphed the text of the speech back to their editors.[23] Indeed, for one of the Chinese language papers there—*Shen Bao*— Shaw composed "A Message to the Chinese People," the last words of which offered the following advice:

> Europe can give no counsel to Asia except at the risk of the rebuff "Physician, heal thyself." I am afraid I have like-wise nothing to say in the present emergency except "China, help thyself." With China's people united who could resist her?[24]

But how could the Chinese people unite themselves? The crisis into which this most ancient of civilizations was being dragged would not be resolved with the (far from simple) defeat of the Japanese. The whole history of China involved, in 1933, not just the contradictions of the European and Japanese occupations, but also the internal conflicts of the Chinese themselves—the sum of which Trotsky called "historical backwardness." Not just colonialism, then, nor the exploitation of the urban proletariat was sufficient to explain the tragedy of China. Above all it was necessary to get at the very roots of a profoundly degrading poverty. Trotsky again offers the analysis:

> In agrarian relations backwardness finds its most organic and cruel expression. . . . Half-way agrarian reforms are absorbed by semi-serf relations, and these are inescapably reproduced in the soil of poverty and oppression. Agrarian barbarism always goes hand in hand with the absence of roads, with the isolation of provinces, with "medieval" particularism, and absence of national consciousness. The purging of social relations of the remnants of ancient and the encrustations of modern feudalism is the most important task. . . .[25]

As the *Empress of Britain* pulled out of Hong Kong harbor on 15 February, one eager commentator, aware of the events which had just taken place, was already committing his thoughts to print in Shanghai. "In

Praise of Bernard Shaw" appeared in *Shen Bao*, two days later, under the signature He Jiaqin. This was just one of the numerous pseudonyms used by China's greatest analyst and ironic narrator of its appalling "historical backwardness"—Lu Xun, itself an alias. Here is the piece, hitherto untranslated into English. Let it serve to introduce the man Shaw was to meet, on 17 February, in Shanghai.

"In Praise of Shaw"

Before Shaw came to China, the newspaper *Dawanbao* expressed the hope that the Japanese military activities in the north would be suspended because of his visit, and it called Shaw "the peace-making old man."

After Shaw arrived in Hong Kong, the press translated the Reuters dispatch on Shaw's address to the youths of Hong Kong, and titled it Communist Propaganda.

Shaw told the Reuters reporter that the latter didn't look Chinese, and that he was surprised at the fact that not a single Chinese journalist had come to interview him. He asked,

"Are they so ignorant that they don't even know who I am?"

On the contrary, we are all very sophisticated and well-informed. We know all about the benevolence of the Hong Kong Governor, the regulations of the Shanghai Ministry of Administration, the latest news about which celebrity is a relative of which, and who has now become an enemy of whom. We even know which day of the year happens to be the birthday of whose wife, and what her favourite dish is. But as for Shaw, well, alas, all we gather of him is the three or four translations of his works.

Therefore, we cannot know of his thoughts before and after the war, nor can we understand profoundly the way he thinks after his visit to the Soviet Union. But still, his greatness can be seen from his very words of address to the students in the University of Hong Kong, as reported by Reuters on the 14th:

"If you don't become a red revolutionary at the age of twenty, you will become a hopeless fossil when you're fifty. If you try to become a red revolutionary when you're twenty, then you may have the chance of not falling behind the times when you get to forty."

What I meant by greatness does not lie in his urging our people to become red revolutionaries. For, our country does have "special national conditions"—you don't have to be red, just become a revolutionary and you will lose your life tomorrow, without the chance of ever reaching forty. What I meant by greatness lies in the fact that he had even thought about the day when our youths of twenty turn forty or fifty, while not losing sight of the present either.

The rich can take their money into foreign banks, take planes to leave the land of China, or lament that Politics is like the whirling wind, and the people hunted like wild deer. The poor can't even afford to think about tomorrow—they are not allowed to and neither do they dare to anyway.

So how can we talk about twenty or thirty years from now? What Shaw said was nothing unusual, but it is an evident sign of his greatness nevertheless.

That is why this man is called Bernard Shaw.[26]

These contradictions were to haunt Lu Xun after his encounter with their master in Shanghai. The metropolis was a bizarre and grotesque cosmopolitan *point d'appui* for all kinds of barbarism. In Shanghai, Japanese, Colonialists, War Lords, Nationalists and Communists were converging for the end. Their bitter struggle was, in effect, the logical conclusion to the nightmare of China's history. Lu Xun saw it clearly enough:

> Our vaunted Chinese civilization is only a feast of human flesh prepared for the rich and mighty. And China is only the kitchen where these feasts are prepared. . . .
>
> Because the hierarchy handed down since ancient times had estranged men from each other they cannot feel each other's pain; and because each can hope to enslave and eat other men, he forgets that he may be enslaved and eaten himself. Thus since the dawn of civilization countless feasts—large and small—of human flesh have been spread, and those at these feasts eat others and are eaten themselves; but the anguished cries of the weak, to say nothing of the women and children, are drowned in the senseless clamour of the murderers.[27]

Shanghai

In Shanghai there was little to suggest the millenium. And yet a kind of fantasy also seemed to be true to the city's animus. Or rather fantasy was one way in which the realities of history could be "translated." Christopher Isherwood's prose account of 1938 suggests exactly how far the European world of Shanghai then challenged reality:

> You can buy an electric razor, or a French dinner, or a well-cut suit. You can dance at the Tower Restaurant on the roof of the Cathay Hotel, and gossip with Freddy Kaufmann, its charming manager, about the European aristocracy or pre-Hitler Berlin. You can attend race-meetings, baseball games, football matches. You can see the latest American films. If you want girls, or boys, you can have them, at all prices, in the bathhouses and the brothels. If you want opium you can smoke it in the best company, served on a tray, like afternoon tea. Good wine is difficult to obtain in this climate, but there is enough whisky and gin to float a fleet

of battleships. The jeweller and the antique-dealer await your orders, and their charges will make you imagine yourself back on Fifth Avenue or in Bond Street. Finally, if you ever repent, there are churches and chapels of all denominations.[28]

And then there was the "real" world, the world which offered little hope of escape—*la condition humaine*:

> Within the International Settlement, the two extremes of the human condition almost touched each other. Here were the mansions and the banks, the elegant shops, the luxury restaurants and the night-club at the top of a tower, from which guests had watched the Japanese attack on the outer city, a few months earlier. And here were the refugee camps and the dozens of factories in which children were being literally worked to death by their employers. The refugees were packed into huts with triple tiers of shelves; one shelf for each family to cook, eat and sleep on. The perimeter of the Settlement was guarded by a mixed force of foreign troops, confronting the Japanese troops who guarded their conquered territory of deserted ruins. . . . Misery in Shanghai seemed more miserable than elsewhere, because its victims were trapped between their western or Chinese exploiters and their Japanese conquerors, without any apparent hope of escape.[29]

That nightmare was remorselessly enveloping Shanghai when Shaw arrived.

In one sense, then, the famous man's day-trip to such a world (the number of foreigners in Shanghai—50,000—equaled the number of dead babies left on the streets in any one year in the 1930s) becomes an "historical" moment which almost refuses to let itself be taken imaginatively: a Dante is needed to guide our spirits through this Inferno. Nevertheless, Shaw—a diabolical enough spirit—did indeed have an extraordinary gift for creating significant moments; a kind of moving negative capability. Thus in Shanghai, on 17 February 1933, he, the cynosure, created a conversation piece: in the attention focused upon Shaw, a *moment* in China, in this disastrous decade, was distilled. History is process, yes, but we return in this "photographic world" to the ideal (perhaps fallacious) of the frozen frame; the "images" *in* time are the "images" *of* a time. Certain photographs were taken.

A useful initial focus on these "images" is found in Harold Isaacs's Introduction to *Straw Sandals: Chinese Short Stories 1918–33* (with a foreword by Lu Xun). Apart from eventually completing the classic account of Stalin's betrayal of the Chinese Communist Party in 1927, *The Tragedy of the Chinese Revolution* (with a foreword by Trotsky), Isaacs also published highly critical accounts of the Kuomintang Shanghai terror in the *China Weekly Review*, of which he was the founding editor. Furthermore, in his Introduction to *Straw Sandals*, Isaacs recalls not only the violence directed against writers and intellectuals in the thirties, but also the courage of those "visible important Chinese"[30] who opposed it. In particular, three people stood out. First, Lu Xun, whose "prestige as China's foremost writer protected him from arrest, if not suppression of his work and repeated anonymous threats against his life."[31] A second figure was Cai Yuanpei, a man "beyond reach of any ordinary attack"[32] because he had shown great moral courage during the May 4th period in 1919 when, as Chancellor of Beijing National University, he had supported the students in their demands for freedom of expression. Now he was active in the League for Civil Rights (of which he was a cofounder), the organization which was acting as Shaw's host in Shanghai.

The third major figure Isaacs mentions is Soong Chingling, widow of Dr Sun Yatsen—founder of the Republic—sister of Madame Chiang Kaishek and T. V. Soong, Chiang's Financial Advisor. Repudiating her family, this formidable woman—Madame Sun—had moved to a radically critical attitude towards Kuomintang policies. As Cai Yuanpei's cofounder of the League for Civil Rights, she was prepared to speak directly about the state of affairs:

> The Shanghai International Settlement, which the imperialists describe as an "Island of security and justice," is also a paradise for imperialist enemies, traitors and betrayers of the Chinese people, opium traffickers and gangsters. Indeed, the foreign settlements are the headquarters for the auctioning off of China, and one of the chief bases of activities against the Chinese people and the existence of the Chinese nation. In this city now come and go, in absolute freedom and with official recognition and honor, representatives of Japanese imperialism that has invaded, conquered and annexed four of our provinces. Here representatives of the Chiang Kaishek Government and of the invaders of our territory, make official and friendly calls to prepare for the secret treaty that will turn our territory and millions of our people over to a foreign imperialist conqueror. While this goes on, members and leaders of the Chinese revolutionary workers' and peasants' movement who are struggling against the dismemberment and subjection of China, suffer imprisonment, torture, death and a living death in mediaeval prisons.
>
> These iniquitous conditions must be brought to an end by the united, determined struggle of the broad masses of the Chinese people. They can be terminated forever only when we take our fate in our own hands, free the country from imperialists, and establish our own courts and other institutions of a free people.[33]

It was at this woman's house (in the aptly named Rue Molière) that Shaw was the guest of honor for lunch. Also present were Lu Xun, Cai Yuanpei, Harold Isaacs (in a manner of speaking) and three figures who are new to the narrative: Agnes Smedley, Lin Yutang and Yang Xingfo. Yang Xingfo will take up an enigmatic role in this lunch—the image of which offers us an ironic example of our historical interpreted world—while in their separate ways Isaacs and Lin Yutang force us to recognize the truth of F. H. Bradley's observation that

> history stands not only for that which has been, but also for that which is; not only for the past in fact, but also for the present in record; and it implies in itself the union of these two elements: it implies, on the one hand, that what once lived in its own right lives now only as the object of knowledge, and on the other hand that the knowledge which now is[,] possesses no title to existence save in right of that object, and, though itself present, yet draws its entire reality from the perished past.[34]

Lin Yutang's presence should seem clear enough. The soon-to-be-celebrated explicator of things Chinese in *My Country and My People* (1935) was Shanghai's leading *belle lettrist* and literary editor (his journal *Lun Yu* [*Analects*], was to publish a "Special Issue on Bernard Shaw" in March 1933) and yet, as we shall literally see, despite his written testimony about the lunch, he was to suffer a most bizarre obliteration as an *object* of historical knowledge. Likewise Harold Isaacs.

Agnes Smedley, on the other hand, seemed to create an inviolable historical presence *with* her life. An *élan vital* (if ever such a thing were to exist) seemed to possess her soul. In their introduction to a selection of her reportage from this period, *Portraits of Chinese Women in Revolution*, Jan and Steven MacKinnon give us a brief life:

> She exposed prison conditions in the United States; worked to establish birth control clinics in Germany, India and China; raised funds and helped organize the Indian revolutionary movement against the British; defended Chinese writers against persecution by Chiang Kaishek; became a war correspondent of international stature; raised funds for Chinese war relief; nursed wounded guerillas of the Chinese Red Army; and at the end of her life fought McCarthyism in the United States.[35]

Smedley had come to Shanghai via Germany (the *Frankfurter Zeitung* had serialized her autobiographical novel *Daughter of Earth* in 1928–29) and, not surprisingly, the worst of what she found in China appalled her. In *Chinese Destinies* (1933), *China's Red Army Marches* (1934), and *Battle Hymn of China* (1943), she reported the struggle of China to escape from its medieval nightmare. Equally, as the titles suggest, her sympathies were manifest—she was unreservedly pro-Communist; her last major work (published posthumously) *The Great Road: The Life and Times of Chu Teh* (1956) emphasized the extent of that commitment. On the other hand, it would be a mistake to confuse that conviction with fanaticism, with a Yeatsian "excess of love." If her work suggests an obsession with death, with cruelty and degradation, that is so because it was true of the place and the time. There is, however, her equal insistence upon the extraordinary *intensity* of Chinese life; its potential for delight, for pleasure. In her intellectual sympathies, she was able to extend respect to Lin Yutang while not only being an admirer of Lu Xun (who did not hold Lin Yutang in high regard) but also a translator of his work (as he was of hers) and a co-editor. In her own writing, she sought to resolve the apparent conflict between journalism and fiction, "to write with the factual truth of journalism and yet produce writing that will live beyond its first appearance."[36] She looked for artful truth.

There is, however, one further fact to note about this remarkable woman. In 1949, Smedley was accused by the United States Army of having been part of a Soviet spy ring in Shanghai. She went to court and forced the accusations to be retracted; nevertheless Chapman Pincher, in *Their Trade is Treachery*, asserts that there is "no doubt that she was a dedicated agent of the Comintern, promoting world revolution, and was deeply involved with several Soviet spy rings in Shanghai which, at that time, was a major centre of the Comintern conspiracy."[37] Pincher further alleges that Smedley was friendly with Roger Hollis, then employed in the advertising department of British American Tobacco, later to become the knighted Director General of MI5—Britain's intelligence bureau—and, according to Pincher, along with Burgess, MacLean, Philby and Sir Anthony Blunt, a Soviet agent: a spy. History has many cunning passages: that much we *can* claim to know.

Thus the lunch group: Shaw, Madame Sun, Lu Xun, Cai Yuanpei, Harold Isaacs, Lin Yutang and Agnes Smedley. And Yang Xingfo. But first, there were or rather were not the Rotarians. Lin Yutang puts it in perspective:

> Bernard Shaw once looked in at Shanghai and looked out again. On the morning of his arrival, the papers reported that the local Rotary Club had decided to snub Shaw by letting him "pass unnoticed." The apparent implication was, of course, that Shaw would suffer such terrible disgrace from being passed unnoticed by the local Rotarians that he would never be able to recover his reputation. That was, of course, very intelligent on the part of the Shanghai Rotarians in view of the fact that the Hong Kong Rotarians had been worse than snubbed by Bernard Shaw. But it would have been still more intelligent to decide not to read Shaw altogether. Shaw had aroused, besides, such a scare among the Shanghai respectable society by urging the Hong Kong students to study communism that the entire Shanghai foreign press was in hiding that morning for fear of coming into contact with him. The attitude of the Rotary Club was but typical. The only thing, however, that will go down to posterity about the Shanghai Rotary Club is that on the day preceding Shaw's arrival, these Rotarians, or by Shaw's definition, these people who "keep in the rut," called Shaw "Blighter," "Ignoramous," "Fa Tz" and "Baka-yaro."[38]

Enough: *pace* Rotarians; there are, after all, those people Shaw *did* meet who now demand our attention.

The day, it seems, can be divided into five phases. Of the first and the last we have an extended record in Lin Yutang's magazine *Lun Yu*. Madame Sun apparently met the *Empress of Britain* at five in the morning and secretly took Shaw into Shanghai by tender. Although Lin Yutang accused the foreign press of hiding from Shaw, the reporter from *The North China Herald* had a different story: "With a touch of his characteristic contrariness, Mr. G. B. Shaw contrived to disappoint such people as were interested in his arrival at Shanghai . . ."[39] namely reporters from the foreign press who were left cooling their heels at the Customs jetty while Shaw chuntered about with the people he had gone out of his way *not* to disappoint:

> Before he left Hong Kong, Shaw sent a cable to Madame Soong Ching-ling [Madame Sun] informing her that he would pay her a visit. Madame Sun, considering Shaw's age and the fact that this was his first trip to China, went all the way to meet him . . . accompanied by two friends. Shaw said he would have had no intention of leaving the ship when it arrived in Shanghai were it not for his wish to meet Madame Sun. . . .[40]

The trip from ship to Shanghai and back again lasted for four hours— time enough for "Shaw, the outspoken conversationalist, to comment on a wide range of topics wittily."[41] The major concern was politics, specifically the example of Soviet Russia. In the *rapporteur's* words, "during the four hour conversation, Shaw never stopped discussing this."[42] Alas, there was, moreover, the usual discourse on Stalin:

> What is freedom? The British give the Indians a free trial by jury, in which the judge would go back on the verdict if the jury decided that the accused should be released, and send him to jail. This is the so-called free system of the British. And what about the freedom of speech in various countries? Only a privileged few have the right to say a few words. The freedom of speech or democracy that is truly valuable should give to peasants and workers the freedom to cry aloud when they are hurt, and improve their conditions subsequently. This is the freedom that the Russians have.
>
> I paid close attention to Stalin. When we were talking to him, everyone thought that we had only talked for twenty-five minutes, but actually we had been talking for two and a half hours already. He seemed to pay little attention to theory. He is a practical man. He finds solutions to problems by experiments, and calls all successful projects Marxism. . . . He values the objective and not the theory. He may be unscrupulous in trying to reach his goal, but in the end, he manages to reach it.[43]

Of course, the Russian "experiment" was of considerable interest to Shaw's audience. In central China, the Soviet in Jiangxi Province was seen by Madame Sun's brother-in-law, Chiang Kaishek, as a greater menace than the Japanese in Manchuria: in 1935 his encirclement of the center of Chinese Communism necessitated the Long March and, ironically, his own defeat. For Madame Sun herself the issue was clear and her loyalties manifest. In conversation again:

> SHAW: The Peace Conference cannot stop the war, and neither can we end a war by starting another war. Only when all nations are determined to have peace can the war be ended. The people themselves do not want war. After the European War, all the nations that took part discovered that they were worse-off than before. Everyone was destroyed. Facts like these can make people weary of war. The League of Nations has a tool called the International Committee of Intellectual Cooperation. If all the Intellectuals in the world can make use of this tool, it may be more effective than forming another conference.
>
> MADAME SUN: . . . The only effective way to eliminate wars is to eliminate the system which gives rise to wars—the capitalist system.
>
> SHAW: But aren't we all capitalists? I admit that I am—to a certain degree. Aren't you?
>
> MADAME SUN: No. Not entirely.[44]

And so we move to the day's second phase—and the narrative's crux—lunch at Madame Sun's house on Rue Molière. Of that event there are cheerfully unsensational memories by guests Cai Yuanpei and Lin Yutang. But for Lu Xun there was, as one might expect, a dimension of complexity in this meeting. It is the ordinariness, the sanity of the man, with which Lu Xun plays. In his essay "Who is the Paradox?" he teases out the contradictions which Shaw excites, shifting the balance of perceptions in order to create a point of view:

> He tells the truth, yet they say he is joking, laugh loudly at him and blame him for not laughing at himself.
>
> He speaks frankly, yet they say he is satiric, laugh loudly at him and blame him for thinking himself intelligent.
>
> He is not a satirist, yet they insist on calling him one, though they despise satirists and use futile satires to satirize him.
>
> He is not an encyclopaedia, yet they insist on treating him as one, questioning him about everything under the sun. And when he has answered, they grumble, as if they knew more themselves.
>
> He is on holiday, yet they force him to expound general principles. And when he has said a little they are annoyed, and complain that he has come to "spread communism."
>
> Some despise him for not being a Marxist writer. But if he were one, those who despise him would not look at him.
>
> Some despise him for not being a worker. But if he were one, he would

never have come to Shanghai and those who despise him would not be able to see him.

Some despise him for not being an active revolutionary. But if he were one, he would be imprisoned . . . and those who despise him would not mention him.

He has money, yet insists upon talking about socialism. Refusing to work, he insists upon taking pleasure cruises. He insists on coming to Shanghai, insists on preaching revolution, insists on talking about the Soviet Union. He insists upon making people uncomfortable.

So he is contemptible.[45]

Watching those who watched Shaw, Lu Xun was alert to a grotesque sense of (perhaps) unpurgeable universal bad faith. No one could actually tolerate Shaw (rightly?) for what he was:

So everybody hopes for different things. The lame hope he will advocate using crutches, those with scabies hope he will praise hat-wearing, those who use rouge hope he will taunt sallow-faced matrons, and the writers of nationalist literature are counting on him to crush the Japanese troops. But what is the result? You can tell the result is not too satisfactory by the great number of people who are complaining. Herein, too, lies Shaw's greatness.[46]

That passage comes from the Preface to *Bernard Shaw in Shanghai*, a volume of pieces (mainly journalistic) about the visit. Lu Xun edited it with a young poet, critic, and teacher called Qu Qiubai; it is not strictly digressional or tangential to introduce his brief life now.

In *The Gate of Heavenly Peace*, Jonathan Spence pays considerable attention to Qu Qiubai. Qu had spent several years in Moscow learning Russian and becoming, in his own way, a Marxist and a member, in 1922, of the Chinese Communist Party. In Shanghai, he became a central Communist Party figure, and, in 1927, its "de facto head . . . at the age of twenty-eight."[47] His allegiance to Stalin's orders led to a sequence of disastrous insurrections against Kuomintang armies; as a result—in the stupifyingly cynical discourse of Stalinism—he was stripped of power for "left-wing opportunism" by Moscow. In late 1933, he joined Mao Zedong in the Soviet at Jiangxi; when Chiang Kaishek's encircling armies forced Mao and 100,000 other Communists to start the Long March, Qu Qiubai—a sickly man—attempted to get back to Shanghai. He was captured by Nationalist soldiers. Jonathan Spence—whose account of this life is engrossing—quotes his final testament:

In short, this burlesque show has come to an end; now the stage is completely empty. What difference does it make anyway even if I were reluctant to leave? What I will have is a long, long rest. I do not even have any say as to how my body should be disposed of. Farewell, all the beautiful things in the world!

FIG. 1 At the home of Madame Sun in Rue Moliere, Shanghai, 17 February 1933. Two people are missing. (left to right) Agnes Smedley, Shaw, Madame Sun, Cai Yuanpei, and Lu Xun. (Source: *Lu Xun, 1881–1936* [Beijing, 1976], p. 78)

> *The Life of Klim Samgin* by Gorky, *Rudin*, by Turgenev, *Anna Karenina* by Tolstoy . . . *The Dream of the Red Chamber* by Cao Xueqin—these are all worth reading. The Chinese bean curd is the most delicious food in the whole world. Good-bye and farewell![48]

This collator and editor of Shaviana was executed by firing-squad on 18 June 1935. Consider now his collaborator Lu Xun having to defend his defense of Shaw's Hong Kong performance:

> As for my defense of Shaw . . . it started with his speech at the University of Hong Kong which is a typical institution of slave education. No one dared to throw a bomb at it before. Shaw did it. He is the only person who dared. And yet the Shanghai press detested him exactly because of that. That was why I had to give him support. For to attack him that time was to promote slave education.[49]

Perhaps now we are able to contemplate the images which have survived of that day: the photographs taken at Madame Sun's house. There were two occasions at which these could have been taken; first at the lunch, before the Pen Club meeting; second immediately after it. Or at both; thus the first enigma. Of the photographs themselves there is a

Fig. 2. The picture restored with Harold Isaacs and Lin Yutang. (Source: *A Pictorial Biography of Lu Xun* [People's Fine Arts Publishing House, 1981], p. 95).

further mystery: compare the two versions of the "same" picture reproduced above. Figure 1, from *The Gate of Heavenly Peace*,[50] shows the luncheon group—except that it doesn't. Figure 2 shows us the "true" image of the gathering. Here we could do with an explanation, and the editors of *A Pictorial Biography of Lu Xun* have provided one:

> In commemoration of the centenary of Lu Xun's birth we think it important to publish the album *A Pictorial Biography of Lu Xun* to document his life truthfully. The idea came to us when we saw the photos [of] Lu Xun [taken] . . . on February 17, 1933 with George Bernard Shaw, Cai Yuanpei, Soong Chingling, Agnes Smedley, Lin Yutang and Harold Isaacs. In some previous publications, Lin Yutang and Harold Isaacs had been either blocked out and replaced with stones and grass or simply cut out completely as if they had never been present. We felt it absolutely necessary to restore the truth.[51]

The irony of History: the more the object of knowledge seems present—look, *there*, the image—the greater the chance for deception. Isaacs and Lin Yutang presumably disappeared because of their critical attitudes (from different positions) towards the Chinese Communist Party. Our trust in the evidence is utterly dependent upon good faith.

True images? Truer images? Then where is Yang Xingfo? Lu Xun, in his diaries, mentions Yang Xingfo's presence at the lunch table; further- more as a member of the executive of the League for Civil Rights and Cai Yuanpei's chief assistant, he would have been one of the afternoon's organizers. But, unlike the others, he had no reputation to afford him protection. He was, apparently, a careful, crafty man, fully aware of the dangers around him. But not careful enough: four months later, on 18 June 1933, as Yang climbed into his car outside an Academica Sinica office in Shanghai, a group of unidentified gunmen opened fire. He was killed instantly.[52]

It is, therefore, further ironic to move away from Rue Molière[53] to the Pen Club (the third phase) and the unambiguities of recorded speech as Shaw held forth before a "distinguished group of matrons and debutantes"[54] and the disgruntled reporter from *The North China Herald* who managed, at last, to record these questions from Shaw:

> "Will you please tell me how a Chinese actor can do anything in the midst of such infernal uproars as one hears on your stage? In our theatre, they put a man out if he sneezes. But you have gongs and symbals [*sic*] and the competition of half the audience and innumerable vendors. Don't you object?"[55]

One answer to these brusque questions is reported in the biography of their recipient, Mei Lanfang, founder of The Left Theatre Club in Shanghai and the most celebrated performer of Peking Opera in this century. The noisy drums and gongs were necessary, he said, "because the opera was a folk art first performed in the open air and the drums and gongs were then used to attract people to the show and the tradition has been kept to this day."[56] A much livelier and more comprehensive account of the Pen Club meeting appeared in the Chinese language pa- per *Shen Bao*, which was reprinted in *Xiaobona zai Shanghai [Bernard Shaw in Shanghai]*. Here we read of Shaw's ironic dissertation upon culture, in the most aggressively ameliorist fashion:

> China and the East don't have much culture worth speaking of. Culture, by scientific definition, is all those human activities which enable human beings to control nature. In China, except for the little culture that can still be found in the farms, there isn't any culture to speak of. China is now importing from Western Europe, a lot of so-called 'cultural ideas' which have long ceased to be effective and have in fact had harmful ef- fects on the people. . . . What good will it do to bring this sort of Western culture to China?

And of his notorious speech at the University of Hong Kong:

> When I was in Hong Kong, I urged the students to start revolutions. But please don't misunderstand; I didn't ask them to go to the streets and

fight the police. When the police come to suppress revolutionaries with their clubs, the safest way is to run. You should run as fast as you can so your head won't bleed. And you don't have to get into a confrontation with the police, for policemen are like the gun in a robber's hand; of course you don't want to fight against the gun when you're robbed, nevertheless those with guns in their hands should still be beaten down. But this takes time and you cannot make it by sheer force.

And finally, of his view of the Soviet Union and international socialism:

> The international conditions of the Soviet Union both spiritually and materially are improving vastly these days. And this systematic improvement is not only to the best interests of the Russians alone. It serves as an example for all the other countries which should learn from her strong points and start imitating her. Socialism will surely be implemented in every country sooner or later. The means and process of the revolution may appear in different forms in each country, but as all roads lead to Rome so all countries will be on the same path and the same level in the end.[57]

Thus the day, 17 February 1933. Yes, talk with Madame Sun and talk at the Pen Club—that is essential to the man. But, equally, it is the cold silence of those photographs from the Rue Molière which seems to speak most hauntingly; silent forms that tease us out of thought as does eternity.

The Great Wall

As the Shaws move northwards the remaining stages of the expedition lack focus, are blurred. The experience of Shanghai, its intensity, its meaning, obscures both the memory of Hong Kong and the anticipation of Beijing. In the latter, Shaw did get to the theater (where he was most impressed by "the throwing and catching of bundles of hot towels deftly performed at great distances in the auditorium by the ushers")[58] and he did manage to visit A. C. Arlington, author of *The Chinese Drama* (1930); but there is, quite distinct from Shanghai and even Hong Kong, a fragility to this conclusion in China. Charlotte came down with some germ Shaw had picked up, while "he slipped and hurt his leg."[59] And there was the simple fact that Biejing was another world where the academics and intellectuals were simply not terribly interested:

The press only gave brief accounts of his activities during his stay and the remarks about him were often quite harsh. Shaw's comment that China had no culture had repelled people here, for they found it really rather insulting that China had been derided. . . .[60]

Besides, for people in Beijing the mind was being focused wonderfully by events at the Great Wall, just to the north. Shaw, who had said that the main reason he had for visiting China was to see the Great Wall, saw them too:

> On her recovery, Shaw insisted that Charlotte should go with him to see the Great Wall of China. The best way to see it, he decided, would be from an airplane which would reveal the vast expanse of the wall. . . . The plane was one of the early biplanes, their seats were open to the sky. As the plane flew low over the Great Wall, Shaw was horrified to see a fierce battle in progress just below them between the Chinese Army and a horde of armed Japanese. . . . Shaw frenziedly jabbed the shoulder of the pilot in front. "Turn back! Turn Back!" he shouted. "I don't like wars. I don't want to look at this."[61]

Apparently they flew back to Beijing in silence.

Notes

I would like to acknowledge with gratitude the assistance of colleagues in the University of Hong Kong. Particular thanks are due to Anita Chan for her original translations of Chinese texts. In addition, I would like to record the help of Mimi Chan, Lawrence Wong, and Louis Wong of the Department of English Studies and Comparative Literature; and of Elizabeth Sinn and Alan Birch of the Department of History.

1. H. J. Lethbridge, *Hong Kong: Stability and Change* (Hong Kong: Oxford University Press, 1978), p. 167.

2. *The Hong Kong Telegraph*, Saturday, 11 February 1933, pp. 1, 9.

3. *The China Mail*, Tuesday, 14 February 1933, p. 1.

4. *South China Morning Post*, Monday, 13 February 1933, p. 16.

5. Ibid.

6. Woo Sing Lim, *The Prominent Chinese in Hong Kong* (Hong Kong, 1938), p. 3.

7. Lethbridge, *Hong Kong: Stability and Change*, p. 176.

8. George Bernard Shaw, "Aesthetic Science," *Design '46*, The British Council for Industrial Design, p. 143–44. See also: Stephen Winsten, *Days with Bernard Shaw* (London, 1951), pp. 232–33.

9. Irene Cheng, *Claro Ho Tung: A Hong Kong Lady, Her Family and Her Times* (Hong Kong: Chinese University Press, 1976), pp. 29–30.

10. Bernard Mellor, *The University of Hong Kong: An Informal History*, 2 vols. (Hong Kong University Press, 1980), I: 37.

11. Ibid.

12. Jonathan D. Spence, *The Gate of Heavenly Peace: The Chinese and their Revolutions 1895–1980* (Harmondsworth, Middlesex, 1981), p. 159.

13. Mellor, *The University of Hong Kong*, p. 12.

14. *South China Morning Post*, Tuesday, 14 February 1933, p. 10.

15. Letter from Robt. McWhirter in *The Hong Kong Telegraph*, Tuesday, 14 February 1933, p. 1.

16. Brian Harrison, ed., *The University of Hong Kong, the First 50 Years: 1911–1961* (Hong Kong University Press, 1962), p. 52.

17. *South China Morning Post*, Thursday, 16 February 1933, p. 10.

18. Ibid.

19. *South China Morning Post*, Saturday, 18 February 1933, p. 11.

20. *The North China Herald*, Thursday, 16 February 1933, p. 5.

21. *South China Morning Post*, Monday, 13 February 1933, p. 16.

22. Harold R. Isaacs, *The Tragedy of the Chinese Revolution*, with an Introduction by Leon Trotsky (New York, 1938), p. 76.

23. Lu Yan, *Xianggang zhanggu*, vol. 3 (Xianggang, 1981), pp. 153–66.

24. Requoted, *inter alia*, in English in *Xianggang zhanggu*, p. 162.

25. Leon Trotsky, Introduction to *The Tragedy of the Chinese Revolution*, pp. xv–xvi.

26. He Jiagin (Lu Xun), "In Praise of Shaw" (trans. Anita Chan), in *Shen Bao*, 17 February 1933; repr. in the 16-volume *Lu Xun quanji* (Beijing, 1981), 5: 32–33.

27. Lu Xun, "Some Notions Jotted Down By Lamplight," in *Selected Works* (in four volumes), trans. Yang Xianyi and Gladys Yang (Beijing, 1980; 3rd ed.), 2:156.

28. Christopher Isherwood (with W. H. Auden), *Journey to a War* (London, 1939; rev. 1973), pp. 227–28.

29. Christopher Isherwood, *Christopher and His Kind, 1929–1939* (London, 1977; repr. 1978), p. 229.

30. Harold R. Isaacs, Introduction to *Straw Sandals: Chinese Short Stories, 1918–1933*, ed. H. R. Isaacs, with a Foreword by Lu Hsun (Lu Xun) (Cambridge, Mass., 1974), p. xxxiv.

31. Ibid.

32. Ibid., p. 45.

33. Soong Chingling (Madame Sun Yatsen), "A Call to Rally to the Protection of Imprisoned Revolutionaries, Shanghai, April 1, 1933," in *The Struggle for New China* (Beijing, 1952; repr. 1953), p. 55.

34. F. H. Bradley, "The Presuppositions of Critical History," in *Collected Essays* (Oxford: Clarendon Press, 1935), I: 8.

35. Jan MacKinnon and Steve MacKinnon, eds., *Agnes Smedley: Portraits of Chinese Women in Revolution*, with an Introduction by J. and S. MacKinnon and an Afterword by Florence Howe (Old Westbury, New York: Feminist Press, 1976), pp. ix–x.

36. Florence Howe, Afterword in *Agnes Smedley: Portraits of Chinese Women in Revolution*, p. 174.

37. Chapman Pincher, *Their Trade is Treachery* (London, 1981), p. 39.

38. Lin Yutang, "A Talk with Bernard Shaw," in *With Love and Irony* (Garden City, New York, 1945), pp. 237–38.

39. *The North China Herald*, 22 February 1933, p. 294.

40. "Bernard Shaw's Conversations During His Stopover in Shanghai" (trans. Anita Chan), as recorded in *Lun Yu [Analects]* (Shanghai, 1933), I(13): 391.

41. Ibid.

42. Ibid., p. 393.

43. Ibid., p. 395–96.

44. Ibid., p. 394.

45. Lu Xun, "Who is the Paradox?" in *Selected Works*, 3: 247–48.

46. Lu Xun, "Preface to *Bernard Shaw in Shanghai*" in *Selected Works*, 3: 256.

47. Jonathan D. Spence, *The Gate of Heavenly Peace*, p. 248.

48. Ibid., p. 293.

49. Lu Xun, Letter to Wei Mengke, 5 June 1933 (trans. Anita Chan), in *Lu Xun quanji*, 3: 339–41.

50. Jonathan D. Spence, *The Gate of Heavenly Peace*, illustration no. 45.

51. Editors' Note, *A Pictorial Biography of Lu Xun* (Peoples' Fine Arts Publishing House, 1981), p. 173. Figure 2 was published on p. 95 of this volume; Figure 1 appeared on p. 78 of *Lu Xun, 1881–1936* (Beijing, 1976), another pictorial biography with Chinese text.

52. John King Fairbank, *Chinabound: A Fifty-Year Memorial* (New York: 1982). On p. 74n Fairbank reveals that an account by Isaacs of the reasons for the deletion from the picture is forthcoming.

53. See also "Shaw in Japan," which follows immediately in this volume, for another account, by a Japanese reporter, of Shaw's visits to Shanghai and Beijing.

54. The Little Critic (author of an otherwise-unsigned column), "On Bernard Shaw," in *The China Critic*, 2 March 1933), 6(9): 238.

55. *The North China Herald*, 22 February 1933, p. 294.

56. Wu Zuguang, Huang Zuolin, and Mei Shaowu, *Peking Opera and Mei Lanfang* (Beijing: New World Press, 1981), p. 5.

57. "What Shaw Really Said" (trans. Anita Chan), as recorded in *Xiaobona zai Shanghai* (Shanghai, 1933), pp. 106–23, *passim*.

58. S. Hsiung, "Through Eastern Eyes," in *G.B.S. at 90: Aspects of Bernard Shaw's Life and Work*, ed. S. Winsten (London, 1945), p. 198.

59. Blanche Patch, *Thirty Years with G.B.S.* (London, 1951), p. 95.

60. Li Jinming, "Bernard Shaw in Beijing and Tianjin" (trans. Anita Chan), in *Shen Bao*, June 10, 1933.

61. R. J. Minney, *Recollections of George Bernard Shaw* (New York, 1969), pp. 133–34.

Sidney P. Albert, with Junko Matoba

SHAKING THE EARTH:
SHAW IN JAPAN

March 1933 brought to Japan a major earthquake with destructive tidal waves, a thunderous eruption of a long-dormant volcano, Mount Aso on Kyushu, and—at the nearby hot spring spa of Beppu—Bernard Shaw.[1] A nation accustomed to periodic geological upheavals, and the storm center of world disapproval over its annexation of Manchuria, its incursions into China, and its defiance of the League of Nations, cautiously prepared for his arrival. In literary and dramatic circles and among labor leaders the news of Shaw's imminent arrival generated an ambivalent mixture of curiosity and apprehension about the possible shocks and jolts this unpredictable world personality might have in store for them.

Initially skeptical that Shaw would ever set foot on their soil, Japanese newspapers had paid scant attention to his travels. A belated account in the *Osaka Asahi* newspaper on 26 January quoted Shavian barbs in Naples about the ruins of Pompeii, and told of his secluding himself in his cabin aboard ship in order to work on a new play. Then on 6 February it printed some of his replies to reporters' questions in Bombay.

Word of Shaw's arrival in India aboard the *Empress of Britain* stirred the press into action. A few background articles on him, by writers acquainted with his work, began to appear. They dealt with him as playwright, artist, man of ideas, and champion of the concerns of women, and recalled his introduction to the literary world of Japan early in the century by Hogetsu Shimamura, poet and critic. Readers were also reminded that Shaw's literary reputation grew as a result of the critical expositions of his work by the eminent Shakespearean scholar Professor Shōyō Tsubouchi of Waseda University.[2]

Editors found themselves faced with a knotty problem: whom could they use as qualified correspondents? None of the regular reporters had the requisite linguistic skills. Even those who could speak English felt unequal to the task of understanding and interpreting Shaw's ideas; and they were not eager to expose these failings. On the other hand, literary critics competent to comprehend Shavian subtleties were not only untrained in journalism, but would consider it degrading to serve as reporters.

One ostensibly suitable candidate for the assignment emerged: Ki Kimura, an active free lance writer who had lived in Europe and was well versed in English literature. Kimura, who had written one of the early background pieces on Shaw (for the *Yomiuri Shimbun*) was sought after by all. The liberal magazine *Kaizo* and the newspaper *Jiji Shimpo* managed to engage him as special correspondent.

He set off for China to meet Shaw in advance of his arrival in Japan. Armed with a letter of introduction from Sōbei Mogi, an industrialist who had lived in London for ten years and knew Shaw, and with instructions from the president and proprietor of *Kaizo*, Sanehiko Yamamoto, Kimura reached Shanghai shortly after Shaw did. With the assistance of Kanzō Uchiyama, manager of a Japanese bookshop in Shanghai (whom he had telegraphed from Tokyo to arrange a meeting between Shaw and Lu Xun) and more directly of Lu Xun, Kimura met Shaw at the home of Madame Sun Yat-sen. There he observed a Shaw interview with a group of selected reporters. His version of this hour-and-a-half press interview appeared in his article, "Bernard Shaw and the Orient," which was published in *Kaizo*.[3] A long, rambling narrative, it recounted the earlier itinerary of the Shavian cruise and what Shaw had to say in Bombay and Hong Kong. Informed that a special Shaw edition of *Kaizo* was being planned, Shaw laughingly retorted, "Oh, that is bad journalism!" Refusing a request at the time to write something for *Kaizo*, he granted permission for the translation of his pamphlet on Russia, and pointed out that under international copyright, no royalty payments were necessary.

Continuing on the trail of Shaw, who had gone by ship to Chinwangtao and thence to Beijing, Kimura ventured to that city on a train trip that was for a Japanese in those tense times as risky as it was long. Arriving too late to cover Shaw's meeting with the press and subsequent conversation with Chang Hsüeh-liang, the commander of the Manchurian army, the correspondent drew upon other press coverage for his own report. He did, however, chance upon Shaw, unexpectedly alone in the lobby of his hotel, reading a volume of Trotsky's *History of the Russian Revolution*.

Kimura was flattered to find that Shaw remembered both him and his magazine by name. The encounter took Shaw by surprise. Concerned for Kimura's safety, Shaw urged him to leave the city, which then was a dangerous place for anyone Japanese. Before heeding the warning, Kimura asked instead whether Shaw was planning to take in any theater in Japan. The answer: "Yes, of course, I shall want to see a play, but only from a technical point of view. If I find the directing bad, I shall teach you a lesson about it." Kimura judged his brief interview a success, and felt that he had won Shaw's confidence.[4] He wired Shōō Matsui (playwright, director [of *Man of Destiny*], and translator, who had been a guest at the Shaws' in London in 1919) in Tokyo to make the necessary theatergoing arrangements, and sent a similar message to the *Osaka Mainichi* newspaper.

Meanwhile, in Japan a spate of Shavian articles were published late in February, including a four-part series "On Welcoming Shaw" in the *Tokyo Asahi*. Many of these appeared in the "Culture Column" of newspapers, and they bore such varied headings as "Impressions of Bernard Shaw," "The Rare Visitor Who Has Conquered the World," "His Ironical Views of Parliamentarianism," "Shaw, the Vegetarian," "Shaw and Ellen Terry," "The Tangoist Shaw" (about his learning to do that dance at age 70), "On His Cynicism and Humor," "Bernard Shaw and Journalism Literature," "G.B. Shaw and Japan" (in a Tokyo English newspaper), and "Tsukiji Small Theatre and Shaw" (by Ryōichi Nakagawa, a translator of Shaw plays and later the President of the Shaw Society of Japan). Readers were reminded that Japan had previously played host to such visitors as Einstein, Russell, and Tagore, but as yet to no one in literature of comparable stature. The most reiterated characterization of Shaw was as a satirist who hurls "sharp irony." A number of writers of these columns had met Shaw in London at various times, among them Yonejirō Noguchi, Kichizō Nakamura, Shinzaburō Miyajima, and Hisao Homma.[5] Nakamura colorfully lauded Shaw "in the Japanese way" as "the old man of literature who is a superman flying the high skies." Some remarked, as did Kimura in *Kaizo*, on the paradox of a wealthy socialist touring the world on an ultraluxurious liner in the company of people he held in low regard and studiously avoided. Most voiced a piquant curiosity and interest in what this ironist would have to say about Japan, and several writers expressed an earnest desire to get to know him better.

The *Empress of Britain*, with its renowned passenger, dropped anchor at Beppu, one day ahead of schedule, on Tuesday, 28 February, at 8 o'clock. An hour later Shaw entered the ship's smoking room. There, awaiting him, were about thirty newsmen, whom the press representative of the Canadian Pacific Steamship Lines had forewarned: "For goodness sake be careful; Mr. Shaw hates to be misquoted." They were immediately struck by his cheerfulness and, for a man of 77, his remarkably youthful appearance: the beautiful silver hair and beard, healthy-looking pink cheeks, keen eyes ("like an airplane pilot"), and straight, unbent back. His attire, too, contributed to the impression of youthfulness: green shirt, short necktie, two sweaters, and white tennis shoes.

Asked whether he was afraid when he flew over the Japanese army in China in Chang Hsüeh-liang's plane, he answered that he was not, because the Japanese were not prone to fire indiscriminately. Rather, he jocularly told them, he was more frightened on the return flight because there was no telling what the Chinese might do. More seriously, he declared that Japan had demonstrated the impotence of the League of Nations: "As soon as you started to fight China, as soon as you broke the Covenant, they should have done something. They should have boycotted you straight away. But they didn't do anything, they didn't try to do anything. Instead they started to sell munitions and arms to China and Japan, and they are still selling them."[6]

The war the Japanese have ventured on "won't be won by courage or Bushido; it will be won by machinery." The claim that the fighting was in self-defense he scouted roundly: "All wars are fought in self-defense." In not declaring war they had behaved correctly, but "if you are going to be allowed the power to kill, and destroy, and murder as long as you don't declare war, then what's the use of the League?" He went on to lecture his interviewers on the evils of nationalism, but contended that putting it down—as England had tried to do with Ireland, and as Japan would be faced with doing in China—would be like sitting on the head of a horse that had slipped and fallen. It could occupy their attention and energies for as long as a hundred years, and prevent any other work being done. Shaw suggested that they reprint "Common Sense About the War," simply changing the names of the statesmen, since all wars are the same. But then, he added, whoever did so would probably be shot for it.

Commenting on his age, he said that some regarded him as not playing the game by having exceeded the allotted life span and living on to an indecent age. Yet being old did allow him to be quite reckless and candid.

A query about his attitude toward sports evoked a vehement reaction from the former amateur athlete: "I loathe sport. It creates bad feeling, bad manners, and war. All athletes hate and loathe one another. If an Englishman is beaten by a Japanese in a race he begins to feel that only a war can wipe it out." More conciliatory was his qualified approval of the talking film.

The books of Lafcadio Hearn, of which he had read "one or two," Shaw dismissed as describing the East not as it really is, but as the West would like to regard it. As for Kipling, his dichotomy of East and West was rubbish, there being no real difference. Reporting the receipt of a six-page letter in Japanese that morning, he protested that he knew the meaning only of "yen" and, when reminded, "Bushido." If Bushido is patriotism, "a patriot is a man who makes himself and his country ridiculous" and "generally has to be shot."

Shaw had some questions of his own. "What's your religion? Being newspapermen you haven't any, but what are the people in Beppu? Are they Buddhists, Shintoists, or what?" Sounding very much like Adolphus Cusins in *Major Barbara*, he went on merrily: "You see I collect religions. I am very curious about them. There is a portion of truth in all of them, and so I believe in all of them. Yet all religions are corrupt. Buddhism, here, for instance, is not true Buddhism. You have merely set up an Indian god to cheat, and to beg to."

What did he want to see in Japan? "Nothing. I don't want to see anything. I'm only here by accident. I wanted a long voyage, so I got on the ship and the ship has happened to come here. I can't help it. I'm writing another play in comfort. That's my business, writing plays, just as a cobbler's business is making shoes."

Japanese music and Kabuki theater did arouse Shaw's interest, subject to the proviso that the drama have more natural acting and voice projection than the Chinese. When asked if he had any message for Japanese women, he had none; besides, any "messages" would only kill their newspapers. When another large contingent of newspapermen then came on board to join the others, he decided to end the hour-long interview. Rising, and bidding them goodbye, he strode off quickly to his cabin, where a special guard was stationed at the door to assure his privacy.

Shaw had refused to divulge either the title of the play he was writing or its content, saying that he would not know what it was about until it was completed. He had already written *Village Wooing* during the month of January, finishing it on the 27th in the Sunda Strait. *On the Rocks* was begun soon thereafter on 6 February. Four days later he requested his secretary, Blanche Patch, to inform Sir Barry Jackson, in strictest confidence, that he was writing a new political play, on the lines of *The Apple Cart* but with a contemporary setting.[7] Only the first and last leaves of the manuscript (with their dates) survive, so it is impossible to determine what point in the composition he had reached upon landing in Japan.

One correspondent, impressed by Shaw's uninhibited onslaught on capitalism, politicians, imperialistic patriotism, and England, marveled at the English for permitting such persistent attacks. "Japan's conditions," he observed, "are good material for his ironies and he has no scruples about being politely quiet. I would like such a man to live in Japan and give sharp comments on current problems."[8] A more detached and ironic commentator, H. Vere Redman (writing in an English

language periodical), deplored Shaw's apparent disinterest in his surroundings: "Before him lay the Bay of Beppu, one of the most striking
views in a region famous for its beauty, the Japan Inland Sea. But with
one of his characteristic gestures, which seem to involve his whole anat-
omy, he dismissed the landscape. . . ."[9] Shaw did, however, briefly stroll
through the streets of Beppu, with photographers inevitably in tow.

The next day, the first of March, the *Empress* moved on to Kobe, remaining there until the 5th. That night Shaw "stayed cooped up in his
cabin like a snail withdrawing into its shell," as the *Osaka Asahi* notified
its readers (on 3 March). The following morning, after a half-hour solo
walk along the pier, he returned to the ship, where an even larger
throng of newsmen than at Beppu lay in wait. In high spirits, he opened
the collective interview by asking them for news, in particular about the
war in Manchuria. From then on he held forth for an hour, ranging
over a wide variety of topics with his customary candor.

Addressing the contention that Japan's population problem was ag-
gravated by the barring of Japanese immigrants in many parts of the
world, he defended that policy of exclusion by the British, Americans,
and Australians. "There is no prejudice against the vices of the East," he
told them. "What they object to are your virtues." The industry of the
Japanese worker, his sobriety, frugality, and willingness to work twice as
long for half the wage, made it impossible for the laborers in other
countries to compete with him and posed a threat to the standard of
living and level of civilization in those nations. Would not Japan do the
same if its living standards were similarly threatened by the influx of
immigrants from India or China?

The replies to his inquiries about factory legislation, child labor, and
industrial working hours he found shocking. "A ten or twelve hour day
is monstrous," he admonished. "I wonder Fuji doesn't erupt and cover
you with fire." The enforcement of factory legislation, admittedly difficult, had been accomplished in England. All the same, salvation would
come for the Japanese laborer, he prophesied. By adopting Western civilization, Japan had changed her feudal system. Were they ready for the
next change? Thus introducing the subject of communism and Russia,
he proceeded to his familiar praise for the changes occurring in Russia
under Stalin, and his corresponding derogation of parliamentary government, in which system Japan was following the English and American systems. Finally, he issued a warning to Japan against the dangers
of another world war, pointing to the unforeseen consequences of
the last one: the destruction of the empires of the imperialists who
launched it.

G.B.S. brought the session to a close by observing, "I have given you
enough to fill your newspapers for three months—if you care to print

it." But his reproofs were in large part lost on those present, a volunteer interpreter having found the political concepts beyond his ken. Still, if his ideas floated over many of their heads, they were at least able to pay homage to the sheer flow of Shavian eloquence.[10]

Going ashore, Shaw drove round Kobe, dropping in at the office of the *Japan Chronicle*, where he met its editor, A. Morgan Young, whose geniality in person and fierceness in print made him kindred in spirit to his illustrious caller.[11] Other stops were a local English bookshop and the Eifukuji Temple. Recognized at various places along the way, Shaw found it necessary to fend off importunate autograph hunters.

Late in the afternoon he was taken to Osaka by representatives of the *Osaka Mainichi* newspaper to see some of the sights and to attend a Kabuki performance. Shaw sought, but was denied, admission to several factories in Osaka.[12] Arriving at the theater at 6 P.M., in the interval between the first and second numbers on the program, he took a seat in the balcony, accompanied by the theater manager. There his white beard made him conspicuous, and soon cameras were being aimed at him. He seemed to chafe at the length of the intermission. While waiting for the next presentation, *Takatoki*, he elicited from the manager information about the highest salary then paid Japanese actors (10,000 yen a performance), which he judged far too low by English standards.

A chance visitor, Glenn Shaw, came and sat next to the playwright, presumably during the same intermission. Relating the episode in a jaunty column for the *Osaka Asahi* of 3 March, the writer—actually a professor at the Osaka School of Foreign Languages and author of a book, *Osaka Sketches*—engaged in some word play on "Shaw" and "shō," which are pronounced alike in Japanese, saying that "'Shaw' (Shō) means anything for 'show' (shō)." To his "uncle" he explained that "Kabuki" meant "an art of songs and dances," and one that had a long tradition. After they talked about the playwright's own plays, Shaw was exhorted by his "relative" Glenn to do something to improve film making in Hollywood when he reached there. Laughing, "Uncle Bernard" replied, "That's interesting. But I plan to take a plane of Mr. Hearst's to his villa and then fly back to Los Angeles to board the *Empress of Britain*. I'm afraid that I will be unable to have time enough to reform Hollywood."[13]

Once the performance of *Takatoki* began, G.B.S. watched intently through his opera glasses. Afterward he found the venerable actor Ganjiro waiting in the lobby to shake his hand. Learning that the actor was 72, Shaw marveled at his on-stage appearance and congratulated him on his skill in make-up. The two posed for a newspaper photographer before Shaw left the theater.

Shōō Matsui was sorely distressed by Kimura's request to make arrangements for Shaw's theatergoing in Tokyo. It would appear that he had grounds for his misgivings. From his acquaintance with Shaw in London, Matsui was convinced that the playwright would be unimpressed with the performing arts in Japan, and expected nothing positive to result from showing him Kabuki and puppet shows.

Most of the next two days were given over to sightseeing. On Friday, Shaw joined a party of other passengers from the ship for a train trip to Kyoto, the former capital of Japan. There he went independently by taxi to a number of places, including the Buddhist temple, Higashi-Honganji; the Heian Shrine; the Gosho, or Imperial Palace; Chioin Temple, and Sanjusangendo (Hall of Thirty-three Bays). A close-up glimpse of G.B.S. as sightseer has been preserved for us in three vignettes by Chyōshō Yoshida, who seems to have acted as cicerone on this outing.[14]

Upon learning that the formerly clear river water of the Kamo Gawa was now polluted, Shaw asked, "Doesn't the Municipal Bureau do something about the system of sewage? Do each of the families keep barrels for it?" Just then a collector of excrement emerged from a house, balancing two full barrels on his shoulder.

At the Shinto Heian Shrine, Shaw surprised Yoshida (who recalled Shavian utterances sympathetic to the religion) by inquiring, "What do you worship in Shinto religion?" Primed for the answer—that the gods worshipped in Shintoism are their ancestors—the irrepressible critic gently quipped, "Why don't you worship your descendants?"

The many temples in Kyoto brought to mind an earlier travel experience: "When I was in Singapore, I was taken to a family whose members were praying before a beautifully decorated Buddhist altar. They were muttering words of prayer with a priest, but they said that neither they nor the priest could understand the words, because they were in Sanskrit. That is incredible. What language do you use for a Buddhist prayer? Is it in Japanese?" Yoshida responded, "Some parts are in Japanese, but we have a saying that what is most difficult to understand is someone talking in his sleep—and a Buddhist prayer. However, we think that there would be more reverence for something that is obscure." "Yes," came the Shavian rejoinder, "that is quite right. Many parts of the Bible are only understood by experts."

A number of articles in Chioin Temple moved Shaw to open admiration, including the simple lines of a huge water basin in the shape of lotus leaves, and the drawings on the paper sliding doors in the inner temple. Attracted to a huge drum in a corridor, he drummed on it with his fingers, listened attentively, and remarked, "Do you notice that this drum has a different sound between the edge and the middle? In China, the musicians knew one piece of music and could only play that one piece. I took up a drum and showed them there are many sounds to one instrument, and they were surprised. Are the Japanese players like that?"

Unwilling to enter the Sanjusangendo without shoes, Shaw was provided with acceptable shoe covers. His interest in the rows of Buddhas seems to have been confined to walking up and down counting them. Outside they passed a detail of policemen carrying red flags, tempting Shaw to inquire impishly if they were communist agitators.

At noon he lunched at the Kyoto Hotel, where he was staying temporarily. Awaiting him in the lobby, when he emerged, were Kimura, Sanehiko Yamamoto, the owner of *Kaizo*, and Professor Kanehiro of the Osaka University of Commerce, who was brought along as a more fluent interpreter than Kimura. As instructed by the *Kaizo* management, Kimura had attempted the day before to make plans for Shaw's itinerary in Tokyo. The press representative of the *Empress of Britain*, Miss Gorland, who acted as intermediary, informed him that the schedule was to be arranged by G. B. Sansom, a British consular official, but that this information should be kept confidential. She also confided that he and Yamamoto, then on his way from Tokyo, could find Shaw at lunch at the Kyoto Hotel the next day.

Sansom, who not only shared Shaw's initials but also his friendship with Granville Barker, Sidney Webb, and William Archer, had met the more famous G.B.S. in London several times. On the basis of this limited acquaintance he had telegraphed to Hong Kong an offer of hospitality in Tokyo. Expressly motivating the overture was a desire to have someone other than the Japanese serve as host to his prominent compatriot and an awareness that the British Ambassador, Sir Francis Lindley, might not take too kindly to Shaw's "preposterous statements."[15] Mrs. Shaw warmly accepted the invitation, and her husband, presumably to avoid being exploited by a single journal, had in turn requested that his prospective host undertake to arrange his Tokyo program.

"Thereupon," wrote Sansom in a diplomatic memorandum on the Shaw visit requested of him by Ambassador Lindley for transmittal to the British Foreign Office, "I received innumerable visits from all kinds of people—emissaries of Ministers of State, professors of Universities, reporters, etc.—all wanting to meet Mr. Shaw. Among the most interesting were gentlemen who came to arrange interviews with the Prime Minister and the War Minister, but were anxious not to let it seem that those personages had taken the initiative."

According to Kimura, he submitted the following agenda for Shaw's approval: 1) the Minister of War, Sadao Araki, would see him if he wished it; 2) the Prime Minister would meet with him privately; 3) he was invited to a Noh performance sponsored by *Kaizo*; 4) he was invited to Waseda University Theatre Museum, where he would receive the gift of a Noh mask. In addition, Professor Takeshi Saito, Professor of English and English Literature at the Imperial Tokyo University (the present Tokyo University) had invited him to a vegetarian dinner. As for the meetings with the Prime Minister and the War Minister, it would seem that Shaw, like they, was conducting his own diplomacy on two separate fronts. Ostensibly these converged, for Kimura declares that on the next day he went to Hakone to see the Sansoms, and "Mr. Sansom arranged everything for us."

It was at their Kyoto Hotel meeting that Yamamoto—undeterred by the dogged refusal of G.B.S. to write anything for anyone during his world tour—approached him about doing just that for *Kaizo*. Mentioning that he was editing a collection of volumes on the works of Marx and Engels, the publisher won the promise of a Shavian article on Lenin for his magazine.[16]

Also waiting in the hotel lobby since early morning, in the hope of meeting and paying homage to Shaw, were two professors of literature, Mukyoku Naruse and Shūji Yamamoto. After the *Kaizo* business had been concluded, Kimura introduced the professors to Shaw. It was a disappointing experience. Professor Yamamoto, an authority on English and Irish literature, had written a column in the *Osaka Asahi* paper on Shaw and Ellen Terry. Awed to be in the presence of the great dramatist whom he admired so much, he stammeringly asked, "Did you read my comments on you?" "I can't read Japanese," came the unexpectedly impatient reply. Professor Naruse, a poet and a German literature scholar who had lived for some time in Europe, was warmly greeted by Shaw but was bothered by Kimura's introduction of him as "one more professor." Much to the chagrin of Kimura, another man in the lobby, sought, on his own, to meet Shaw—an imposter posing as the famous Professor Tsubouchi of Waseda University.[17]

Those in Japan who were most cognizant of, most knowledgeable about, and most appreciative of Shaw's literary and dramatic art were members of the academic profession. They were the ones called upon to help acquaint the public with the accomplishments of the eminent figure visiting them. Yet they were left for the most part pathetically on the fringe—if not out in the cold—so far as opportunities to meet and talk with him were concerned.

At the opposite extreme from the diffidence, awe, and solicitude for the privacy of a literary great on holiday felt by the professors, was the relentless hounding by members of the fourth estate, with whom Shaw shared a degree of fellowship, yet with whom he was locked in perpetual combat. A striking juxtaposition of the two patterns of conduct occurred later in Tokyo, in an incident recounted by George Sansom:

> The interest taken in Mr. Shaw was really remarkable. I have never seen anything quite like it. When my wife drove him round to see the sights he was recognized by passers-by, old and young, in the remotest quarters of Tokyo. Journalists besieged my house in scores, and (as I later discovered) kept watch in shifts in the kitchen, telephoning his movements and, for all I know, his vegetarian menu to their papers. On one occasion I asked Mr. Shaw if he would cope with a crowd of reporters who were on my doorstep. He appeared at the front door, waved his arms and drove them off with objurgations. It happened that the crowd included two mild professors from one of the universities, translators of his works, who had come to pay him deep respect. They were rather astonished, but took the rebuff quite patiently, feeling that the object of their adoration had been true to form.

That he did not entirely resent the depredations of the press, Shaw indicated later during a conversation at Yokohama with Sōbei Mogi, whom he had known in England. "Everywhere I go, I am surrounded by reporters," he noted, "but they really assailed me thoroughly in Japan and Greece. I think it will be the same in America."

Equally in marked contrast to the deferential scruples of the Japanese academicians in Kyoto was the behavior of a zealous British lady, who succeeded in gaining exclusive claim to Shaw's time and attention for a two-hour period on that same day. During the afternoon he had resumed his sight-seeing, taking in Nijō Castle in Kyoto and going for a drive to Saga and Arashiyama. Returning to the hotel before the other touring passengers, he met the lady (who had sent him a letter of welcome at Beppu) in the lobby at five o'clock. A veteran major in the Salvation Army, she proposed to show him the Army Headquarters, and they walked off together. A report has it that Shaw chatted cheerfully with her about William and Catherine Booth; inevitably, about *Major Barbara* as his own Army tract and, as such, "better than your best"; and about how ignorant the Japanese were of the realities of modern war. Gallantly, he admired everything shown him at the headquarters, and when asked by the major if she might say a prayer for him, responded, "Please do," then thanked her, contributed ten shillings to the Army, and protested in leaving, "The alleluias will get me yet."[18]

That evening Shaw went to the Kyoto Za (Theater) where the Shinsei Theatre Group were performing *Aizu no Kotetsu*, a modern version of a historical drama. The impression conveyed in the *Osaka Asahi* newspaper the next day was that it was a pleasant theatrical experience, and that Shaw remained until the conclusion of the third act. Intimations that the occasion was somewhat less gratifying appeared in a subsequent brief magazine article, which mentioned that upon entering the theater Shaw cocked his hat to deter camera flashes, that he sat in the rear, and that he left abruptly near the end of the second act.[19]

What really happened is clarified by the message Shōō Matsui received in a telephone call from Kimura: "In Kyoto Mr. Shaw went to the theatre alone, but he had to get out because newspaper reporters surrounded him in less than ten minutes. He seems to long to see plays, but the reporters hinder him." Accordingly Kimura asked Matsui to arrange for Shaw to receive a free pass to the theaters in Tokyo. Matsui went further, requesting of the theater managers that when possible Shaw be allowed to view plays from "the inspector's room."

Shaw's sightseeing continued on Saturday, 4 March, with an excursion to Nara. The highlight for him there apparently came during a walk in the mist through Nara Park on the way to the Great Buddha. The resounding of the temple bell through the tall pines caused him to halt and ask, "What was that? I have never heard such a mystic sound in all my life. Could you take me to the source of that sound?" Taken to the bell, he volunteered to pay many times the five sen charged to strike it, saying he would like to spend the entire day there. He wanted someone to strike the bell for him, but when a man did so with all his might, he protested, "No, not so loud. I would like to hear its low tone." Taking the rope himself, he tapped it lightly, and listened intently. "This is wonderful. Much better than Big Ben," he announced, continuing to toll the bell and walk under it. The *Osaka Asahi* (5 March) was pleased to report that at last Shaw had found something in Japan for which he could express appreciation.

That evening Shaw returned to Kobe, and at seven the following morning sailed on the *Empress of Britain* for Yokohama, to begin the last leg of the tour in Japan. The ship arrived during a drizzle, in the early hours of Monday, 6 March.

So eager was Sōbei Mogi for his reunion with Shaw, that, though ill, Mogi set out on a tender to board the ship before it entered Yokohama harbor, and while still under quarantine. An industrialist who ran many trading companies and banks, yet also a socialist, Mogi had studied sociology at London University, and collaborated on an English book on the Far East. Ushered into Shaw's cabin, he welcomed his friend to the country and won agreement to a Tokyo meeting with Japanese socialists.

Shaw greeted Mogi warmly, but evinced surprise that the Japanese police had permitted a confirmed socialist to board the ship. Assured that socialism was legally recognized in Japan, Shaw credited Japan with showing greater respect for freedom of thought than did Italy.

The docking of the liner brought a charge up the gangplank by an even larger troop of reporters than before. Shaw began this levee jovially, but before long it was evident what was uppermost in his thoughts. Nara he liked, but Kobe and Osaka had impressed him as "very disorderly cities, nothing but chimneys, crowds of people and narrow thoroughfares, all in confusion. If attacked from the air they will become hells of fire." "Haven't your people ever heard of town planning?" he wanted to know. Evidently the sights in Osaka that made the most profound impact on him were dirty women and children in the squalor of slums, and of acrid fumes emanating from factories. His exclusion from the factories must also have rankled. Behind every factory door, he was convinced, there were women and children compelled to work under revolting conditions for twelve or fourteen hours a day.[20]

Aroused, the inveterate foe of poverty and industrial iniquity launched into a sermon not unlike those delivered in his *Man and Superman* and *Major Barbara* some three decades earlier: "I was unable to see any of the beauty of Japan of which Lafcadio Hearn speaks so much. It is as though I have entered hell. You should rebuild [each as] a new and modern city. You must observe strictly the rules of factory labor and factory management. If an owner will not observe these rules, he should be sued. Japanese cities are like our cities one hundred years ago. There is a striking paradox, and that is that the Japanese have a huge stage in their theatre compared to the little huts they live in. I suppose it is there in the theatre that they can forget about their daily hardships."

Other questions ranged from the trivial—did it not seem odd to him that Japanese people were wearing European clothes?—to the more timely: Had communism spread in China? At 77, Shaw responded, he had long been aware that people rarely dress in the traditional attire of their country; and the constitutional redistribution of private land was not communism. He wondered why the Japanese encouraged suicide, and again deplored the incompetence and impotence of parliamentary government. Commenting on the Japanese invasion of Manchuria, he described the bomb damage inflicted on London during the earlier World War and repeated his warning to Japan: "Battles are no longer what they used to be. To win a war is to be committing suicide. Modern war is fought in the air, so that there are more women killed by bombs than men dying on the battlefield. When its women die, a country will perish."

Shaw had been strolling through Nara on 4 March, the day Franklin D. Roosevelt was inaugurated as President of the United States. A question about the great American depression revealed that Shaw was keeping abreast of current developments in the next nation on his itinerary. It was wonderful, he said, to have national management of banks supplant private ownership.

According to Blanche Patch, Charlotte Shaw wrote to her from the

Pacific, "I was ill for a week, and saw nothing of Japan."[21] The first ostensible mention in the Japanese press of Mrs. Shaw and her illness is to be found in the 7 March *Tokyo Asahi* news article, which offered it as explanation for Shaw going ashore without her. After Mr. Yamamoto and Mr. and Mrs. Mogi had left the ship, Mrs. Sansom came aboard to take Shaw to Tokyo. She "discovered an old man wandering with a slightly lost look on the deck of the ship. Evidently there was no one to talk to. For when I introduced myself he at once became the sprightly Shaw one was anticipating. 'My wife isn't well,' he said, 'and can't leave her bed today. But she wants to see you.'" A steward brought Katharine Sansom to the cabin, where Charlotte thanked her for inviting them, adding "G.B.S. will love to go with you. But don't let him talk too much; he always does. And please, make him rest after lunch."

Shaw talked uninterruptedly throughout the twenty-minute drive to Tokyo. At their destination, the Sansoms' house in the British Embassy Compound, "we made our way past a horde of newspapermen up the steps to the front door, where our servants were politely awaiting us. Photographers immediately took possession of the scene—obviously to the great man's pleasure—so I tactfully began a hasty retreat. But was ordered to return and stand beside him. 'Now you must stay and be photographed too; I'm the most photographed man in the world, and I can tell you exactly how to stand and where to look.'"

At the Sansoms' vegetarian lunch, Shaw regaled his hosts with "a superb flow of talk, inspired by racy high spirits, flecked with wit, full of understanding of comic human beings. Every now and then one of us would make a slight comment, and away he would go again, throwing off laughter at his own admirable jokes." Continuing her vivid sketch of G.B.S. as guest, Mrs. Sansom described "a disquisition on music" he gave, a "gorgeously funny" performance in which he demonstrated points of instrumentation by miming with his hand the playing of trumpets, while singing aloud to this manual accompaniment.

They wanted to know if he liked touring the world. "Me? No; I'm like a tree—I should prefer to stay in one place. But you see, Charlotte is tired of servants—or perhaps of not always having them. And so she brings me travelling." The only peoples encountered on this tour who attracted him and with whom he felt the most genuine affinity were the brown folk of the tropics. "That's what your uncles and aunts and cousins essentially were," he added, "but Western civilization has spoiled them."

Obeying her promise to Charlotte, Mrs. Sansom directed Shaw to a large, comfortable chair in which to rest after lunch. "Pshaw," he protested, "Charlotte would like to keep me in a cradle." But before she was out of the room he was asleep.

At four-thirty in the afternoon Shaw was taken to the gathering to which Mogi had invited him, a tea party at the headquarters of the Japan Federation of Labor. Assembled there were approximately thirty labor leaders, members of the Socialist People's Party and of various trade unions. These labor notables were impressed by Shaw's vigor and height (one thought him nearly seven feet tall) and were surprised to find him warm, jovial, and friendly—indeed, "a lovable old man," who had not the slightest appearance of being a revolutionary. Even when he demanded that all journalists be sent away or he would refuse to speak, his demeanor was neither unpleasant nor domineering.

Following the departure of the photographers and reporters, Mogi introduced Shaw, who declared that he felt as if he were meeting once again the militants in England's labor movement of thirty years past. Characteristically, his free and uninhibited responses to their questions evolved into a speech, lasting an hour and a half. Notwithstanding the agreement of the participants not to divulge what he said to them, it is not very difficult to glean from accounts of the meeting the tenor of his message. One of those present asserted that its outlines could be inferred from reading news reports of his press interview in Yokohama; another touched on several of his topics. It is clear that he repeated his familiar themes: England's deficient parliamentary system and Labour Party, the five-year plan of the Soviet Union, factory hours, autocratic rule, and the Manchurian conflict. On the last he is quoted as saying, "If Japan were to swallow up Manchuria, would she not suffer from poisoning?"

Shaw obviously charmed and entertained his Japanese fellow socialists, but moved their minds minimally. The judgment of Isoo Abe—characterized by Mogi as the leader of Japan's socialists and of its labor movement—may be taken as a fairly representative reaction to the talk: "We were touched by his humor, irony, and epigrams, but we were not impressed by his political opinions. He is a leading figure of literature, but not of politics."

As had happened elsewhere and so often before, Shaw's most earnest striving to sway with ideas ironically served only to convince his audience of the brilliance of his wit and art—and of the idiosyncrasy of his thought. For the moment, though, he seemed pleased with the meeting, reiterating to Mogi on their return trip to the ship how interesting he had found it. To George Sansom he confided later that he found the labor leaders to be of exactly the same type as the old-fashioned English trade unionists; he thought them earnest and agreeable, but seemed none too impressed by them.

The program the consular G.B.S. had arranged for his distinguished guest was, in Redman's words, one thoughtfully "combining the mini-

mum of unavoidable boredom with the maximum of pleasant and active
variety." After a morning walk in Yokohama on the 7th, Shaw took a
taxicab to the Sansoms' shortly after noon. Very likely that was the day
of "a lunch party at the diplomat's house attended by members of that
restricted band of travelled and linguistically competent Japanese em-
inences who, like decimal figures and hardly more numerous, recur in
Tokyo for foreign diversion."[22] Among those attending were several
peers, including Prince Tokugawa, President of the House of Peers (the
Japanese Second Chamber), and Count Makino, Keeper of the Privy
Seal and an elder statesman. At this "hugely enjoyable affair" Shaw
"played up in his inimitable manner" to the delight of the others, who
"laughed at his outrageous replies" to their questions. To his hostess he
was certainly "the easiest of guests, as he entertained himself whilst entertaining everyone else."

Escorted by Marquis Tokugawa, Shaw paid a very brief visit to the
Upper House of the Diet that afternoon, leaving when he discovered
that his presence was distracting to the ministers, who recognized him
immediately. He returned to the Sansoms'. At 4 o'clock, accompanied
by the British consul, he appeared at the official residence of the Minister of War, General Sadao Araki. Shaw's meeting with the general was
the most publicized event, and the diplomatic climax, of his sojourn in
Japan, although the press accounts of it disagree with one another. The
Tokyo Asahi of 8 March has Shaw committing several *faux pas*: entering
the room abruptly, without a word of apology; walking on the tatami-
matted floor without removing his shoes, so that his hosts, taken aback,
hastened to offer him a chair; and adding lemon and sugar to the Japanese tea that requires no such melioration. (At home he drank no tea.)
The *Jiji Shimpo* of the same date asserts that Shaw began to take off his
shoes, but the War Minister told him to keep them on. Similarly, a few
of the statements ascribed to one of the two participants in a particular
newspaper may be found ascribed to the other in a different paper.
"Journalists' Competition Surrounding Shaw" notes that the pair had
difficulty understanding each other, and that the official interpreter had
even greater trouble trying to fathom Araki's vague language, derived
from Buddhist philosophy, than in grasping Shaw's meaning.[23]

Fortunately, an eyewitness account of the interview was submitted to
his superiors by Consul Sansom, an observer proficient in Japanese as
well as English. Told that General Araki was interested in converting
Shaw to his own political viewpoint, and knowing Shaw's tenacious ad-
herence to his own beliefs, Sansom looked forward to a lively session.

> We were introduced into a large waiting-room, whither the general, de-
> tained at the Diet, came after a short delay. The preliminary greetings
> over, some large double doors were flung open, and there poured into

the room a phalanx of press photographers, about thirty of them I should say. The protagonists posed, the air was filled with explosions and disagreeable smoke. High military officers, splendid but deprecatory, made the mildest efforts to control the camera men, who were grinning and snarling like wild beasts. It seemed as if the tumult would never end. The most daring of the photographers mauled the general and Mr. Shaw, poked cameras into their faces and altogether behaved in a disgraceful way. It was an awful scene, and I could not help thinking that it was characteristic of present-day Japan. The all-powerful militarist leader was quite unable to control this pack of ruffians.

Once free of the photographers, they moved to another room, and settled down round a table. Present, in addition to the general, Shaw, and Sansom, were an interpreter, a Colonel Homma, and "two ridiculously earnest young officers taking notes." The entry of the general's pretty daughter with refreshments interrupted the conversation. "While General Araki attempted to keep the conversation on a high philosophical plane, Mr. Shaw brushed aside his efforts and reverted to his own favorite topics—the futility of war, the blessings of communism and so on." But to everyone's surprise a rapport developed between them, and "they got on together famously. General Araki is a man of great personal charm; Mr. Shaw has a way with him, and they both like a joke. So that the symposium developed into a good-humored exchange of quips, Mr. Shaw scoring most of the points. 'Nervo and Knox, or the Two Macs,' as he put it to me later."[24]

A highlight of the exchange was their jousting on the theme of earthquakes. The general wanted to know if Shaw had a "philosophy of earthquakes." According to Sansom, this sounded odd to Shaw, who was unaware "that the Japanese, an active and empirically-minded people, are under the mistaken impression that they are a race of philosophers."

The Spartan Araki believed that earthquakes were beneficial for Japan. They bolstered the character of the people, helped them develop self-control, and precluded undue attachment to personal lives and possessions. Living with earthquakes taught the Japanese to face calamities calmly. By comparison air raids, of which they could be forewarned, were nothing to fear. He regretted that Shaw had not experienced the recent earthquakes.

Shaw asked whether Araki would favor having the War Minister in England plant dynamite in the ground to provide artificial earthquakes periodically. Laughing, the general thought that would be salutary. Shaw conceded England's moral deficiency in this regard, and the inability of the average Englishman to conceive that the solid earth could move. "'But,' he continued, . . . 'we have our earthquakes in England. When people think that their institutions, their religions, their beliefs are firm and immutable, some disagreeable fellow like me comes along and upsets their cherished convictions. Now you need that kind of earthquake in Japan!'"

The War Minister viewed with abhorrence the utter materialism of the Soviet regime. Its exclusive concern with food and trade was repulsive to a spiritual culture, such as that of the Japanese. Shaw's response was that it struck him, during their enjoyable conversation, that the general was the same type of man as Stalin—each of them a man determined to put his ideal into practice. If General Araki were to go to Moscow for a month or so, he would undoubtedly return a dedicated communist. The Japanese army, too, exemplified true communism, for every soldier—rich or poor, big or small—performed his duties on the front in the same spirit, no matter how much he was paid. Communism, he went on, had the motive power of a religion, and, anxious as the Russians were to remain at peace, they would be formidable foes for Japan if war broke out between the two nations. Araki, granting the point, insisted nevertheless that there were irreconcilable differences between the moral standards of the Russians and Japanese, and implied that they might eventually lead to war.[25] He contended that notwithstanding Japanese swings in thought and sentiment from material to spiritual, the pendulum had a secure pivot: the Imperial House. Whatever pivot the nations of the West might have, it struck him as being a fairly slack one.

Shaw shifted the discussion to the topics of slums, poison gas, bacterial warfare, and militarism. He offered advice on modern mechanized warfare and courage, drawing on his own wartime experience of air raids and his trip to the Western Front. During the air raids he felt a coward, but being also lazy, he made no effort to flee or hide. The general thought that showed true courage. Shaw brought forth his familiar proposal that octogenarians be sent to the front, followed by septuagenarians and sexagenarians, with the young kept to the rear, or at home, in order to preserve them for the future. Araki enjoyed the Shavian jesting, but was rather dismayed when advised that the immediate imperative in wartime was to shoot all the patriots and most of the politicians on one's own side.

Scheduled for half an hour, the interview lasted over an hour and a half. It was terminated by Shaw, as Sansom tells us, "in an ingenious and graceful manner":

> "Well, General," he said, "this has been a most interesting conversation. I have enjoyed it immensely and should love to prolong it. Unfortunately I have another appointment—otherwise I should like to stay talking to you until the Chinese troops get to Tokyo!" The general must have been a little disappointed, for, though he is himself a talker of great powers of endurance, he was easily beaten by Mr. Shaw, who gave him no chance

to enlarge upon Bushido and the Sacred Treasures. As soon as these subjects came up Mr. Shaw said: "Yes, but . . ." and was off on another tack. But they took to one another. Mr. Shaw told me that he thought General Araki a very good man of his type, and the general announced to reporters that he had found Mr. Shaw "a good old fellow who makes many jokes, but they are refined jokes." I think that his interviews with the Young Marshal in Peking and with General Araki in Tokyo were what interested him most in the Far East. I hope he will put both these characters in his next play.

At their parting, the general removed a drawing by Takeo Kashiki from the wall and presented it to Shaw as a gift.

Araki recorded his own impressions of his visitor in the special Shaw issue of *Kaizo*. "As I talked to Mr. Shaw, he struck me as a man of literature, critic, and an epigrammatist, rather than a satirist." Shaw unhesitatingly and unreservedly voiced his opinion "in an immediate and simple epigrammatic phrase which expressed very liberal ideas." Able to view life without prejudice (being a socialist without financial worries), he was composed and broad-minded, having confidently "established a life view that is more near to nature itself, transcending all 'isms.'"

Araki was disappointed that Shaw had missed the benefit of experiencing an earthquake during his stay. He did not think that Englishmen understood earthquakes. The general was convinced that one "does not just experience an earthquake and then forget about it."

Shaw had made metaphorical use of earthquakes in the sense he suggested to Araki—as rocking the foundations of conventional morality—as far back as in the "Author's Apology" to *Mrs Warren's Profession* and in the Preface to *Three Plays by Brieux*, as well as in *Major Barbara* and his recent *Too True to be Good*. In the Preface to *The Doctor's Dilemma* he contemplated the salubrious effect of a possible London earthquake, and in the same Preface he spoke of producing artifical earthquakes with dynamite. In addition, there is an allusion to the 1923 Tokyo earthquake in the Preface to *Saint Joan*.[26] Hence it is unclear how much his Japanese experience, including the discussion with Araki, contributed to a hyperbolic line in the second act of *On the Rocks*, the play he was then writing. There he has Hipney say, "The east is chock full of volcanoes: they think no more of an earthquake there than you would of a deputation" (*BH* 6, 656).

Shaw's penultimate day in Japan, 8 March, began with a call in the morning on the Prime Minister, Makoto Saito, with whom he conversed privately for about fifteen minutes behind closed doors. A journalist in the adjoining room, whom Sansom suspected of having listened at the keyhole, told the consul that "the two old men laughed heartily together and discussed old age and the Manchurian problem." Shaw later confided to Sansom that he failed to understand how affairs of state could be properly handled by such an "amiable old nincompoop." And in one of the two brief conversations he had with Ambassador Lindley, Shaw asked whether the prime minister was as harmless a cipher as he appeared. The ambassador assured him that Admiral Saito had been a successful and respected administrator, and though now in poor health and old beyond his years, still appeared to retain his good sense.

After his cheerful chat with Prime Minister Saito, Shaw was taken sightseeing by Katharine Sansom and Mogi. They drove around the stone wall of the Imperial Palace, then on to Ueno Park and an art museum. There, viewing an exhibit of modern Japanese water colorists, Shaw was heard to exclaim, "I now understand the trend of modern Japanese painting!" He is said to have been captivated by a variety of the exhibits: copies of Hikone screens, a painted scroll of the Tokugawa era, and especially a sculpture of a Buddha, Kudara Kwannon. From there they went to the Asakusa theater district, where he watched part of a Japanese film, showing a *chambara*, or sword fight, but had difficulty staying awake.

The sightseer continued to attract his own enthusiastic sightseers: "Fortunately he obviously enjoyed being himself a spectacle of first-class interest, for at every turn his picture was taken, and usually many times. And amusingly, when driving in the car, as we were stopped every now and then in traffic, old country-women climbing into buses, children, old men, chic girls, shop assistants—you could see each and every one with excited gaze and gaping mouth saying, 'Shaw San!' What a hero's progress!"[27]

Meanwhile, Shōō Matsui, having cleared the way for Shaw to gain easy access to Kabuki performances, learned from Kimura that though Shaw was indeed very pleased to have received the free pass, his busy schedule had so far prevented him from making use of it. Matsui then decided to pay a courtesy call on Charlotte Shaw, whom he had not seen for fourteen years, and who now lay ailing on shipboard. She greeted him gratefully, and told him that she had caught a heavy cold in Beijing after a turbulent passage at sea. Troubled by a heavy cough, she bemoaned the elements—"When on earth will Japan have fine weather?"—and her inability to see Japanese plays.

Playgoing was just what her healthy and strong-willed husband—as she had described him to Matsui—was doing late that afternoon. The event proved to be the theatrical high point of his stay in Japan. Sanehiko Yamamoto had arranged for *Kaizo* to sponsor a special performance in Shaw's honor at the Kudan Noh Theatre. The theater was packed with over 200 scholars and artists who welcomed him with virtually a standing ovation. One of the artists, Ikuma Arishima, made a sketch of Shaw and presented it to his model.[28]

Two works were presented, *Tomoe*, of the Komparu school, and *Kazumō* of the Okura school. Seated next to Shaw was Yonejirō Noguchi, who, along with Mogi and Yamamoto, helped interpret the drama for him. Noguchi doubted that Shaw would take to such a "simple and monotonous poetic drama," more to the taste of a Yeats. *Tomoe* he thought an inappropriate choice for introducing a foreigner to *Noh*. It is, however, a famous *Noh* work—a *shuramono*, or warrior-ghost play (in which the ghost of a warrior recounts his horrible death in battle). In this drama the warrior ghost is a woman named *Tomoe*, acted by a male actor, as are all roles. Its plot required little explanation, and the performance demanded absolute silence of the audience. Thus Noguchi found that he could furnish only meager explanation. Nonetheless, he sensed that Shaw was quite taken with what he saw, seeming to appreciate fully the mystical atmosphere of the drama and to grasp intuitively the rationale for this dramatic genre. Qualifying that impression somewhat is Katharine Sansom's depiction of him as "quietly asleep for a good deal of the time." To Noguchi Shaw disclosed that he had read a few of the latter's articles on *Noh* theory, which suggests that he must have had some idea in advance of the sort of theater he was going to encounter.

Shaw was quoted as saying, "I understand though I don't understand," and later adding, "Even for the Japanese it is a traditional and aristocratic art, taken up as an artistic hobby by a handful of Japanese; how could a foreigner really appreciate it without any knowledge of it, without any knowledge of the language and its tradition?"[29]

Shaw directed his attention mainly to the technical features of *Noh* drama. At Waseda University on the following day he observed, "European ghosts appear from above by machines or from a trap underneath, whereas Japanese ghosts appear along the *hashigakari* [a raised passageway extending from the auditorium entrance to the stage platform] taking more than thirty minutes to get to the main platform. This is a very interesting contrast."[30]

Additional evidence of his critical interest in *Noh* comes from his British Embassy host, who wrote an article on the subject, in Japanese, for the *Kaizo* Shaw issue, under the name Bailey Sansom. In it he reports that *Noh* was the only subject about Japan that Shaw brought up during their conversations. In commenting on the art of *Noh*, the playwright singled out three notable characteristics: "the superior quality" of its form, "the peculiarity of the chorus," and "its dimensional stage." More specifically, according to Sansom:

> He pointed out that the Noh stage can give a sense of continuity on account of the long passageway to the main stage; since the main stage is a thrust stage, it gives a dimensional effect whereas the European proscenium stage gives a flat effect because of its being a picture-frame. He said there is much to learn from various stage effects and that the acting style

was very "instructive." The Noh number he saw was *Tomoe*, which essentially has only one major character, and Shaw talked about the significance and history of the number of characters on the stage. He pointed out that Noh could improve on costume by conforming to the fashions of the period in which the play took place, thereby increasing the interest of the audience.

Sansom also noted that Shaw showed special interest in the *Noh* music. Some indication of what appealed to him is revealed in a letter he sent to his friend Edward Elgar on 30 May of the same year: "Then there is the Japanese theatre orchestra. I daresay you fancy yourself as a master of orchestration; but you should just hear what can be done in the way of producing atmosphere with one banjo string pizzicato and a bicycle bell."[31]

At the conclusion of the *Tomoe* performance Yamamoto took the stage, and in a short speech of welcome thanked their illustrious guest for accepting this invitation while declining numerous others. He regretted that Shaw's visit coincided with a disastrous earthquake in the north and so much wind and snow in Tokyo and voiced disappointment about Mrs. Shaw's inability to attend and hope for her rapid recovery. *Kaizo*, he affirmed, shared with Shaw—despite his reputation of being a satirist (the recurrent theme of writer after writer)—the aim of promoting peace.

To the delight of those assembled, Shaw rose to respond. His impromptu remarks, proudly designated in *Kaizo* as the only speech delivered during his trip through the Orient, were subsequently printed in the Shaw issue of the magazine. The performance of the *Noh* drama he pronounced so "delightful" as to make him forget the cold. It afforded him an opportunity to learn something new and interesting—the artist, no matter how old, always has something to learn. Obviously unable to understand a word of the performance, he nevertheless believed that he grasped its artistic intention and had watched it with interest throughout. Then, protesting that "humanity is hopeless!" he repudiated the pretensions of artists to pursue art for humanity's sake. Such claims should be left to the Philistines of the world outside. "We who are artists and poets in the theatre or out of it do our work because we cannot help doing it" out of the necessity to follow a sincere impulse, even if doing that were to destroy the human race. That outcome might even cause "some of us" to follow it even more enthusiastically. In their theater and among their actors he felt completely at home: "I belong to it and it belongs to me." To the outside world in which people were cutting one another's throats he did not belong. Leave humanity to that other world, he urged; "let us artists follow our sacred mission and make the best of our art regardless of consequences."

After he received and gratefully acknowledged several gift boxes, the program resumed with the second *Noh* production, *Kazumō*. According to Noguchi, Shaw betrayed signs of restlessness during that performance. When it was over, at 5 o'clock, he returned to the Sansoms'. Then, refreshed after resting there, he headed back to Yokohama with Mogi. But his long day was not yet finished. On impulse he asked to see a Japanese newspaper office and was taken to the head office of the *Tokyo Asahi*. The astonished staff welcomed him and gave him a Kabuki album and a compilation of news articles on himself. Upon completing his investigation into their operations, to see how they differed from those of Western newspapers, he returned to the ship.[32]

On his last day in Japan, Shaw was escorted to Waseda University by Professor Matahiko Ichikawa. (Many years later Professor Ichikawa founded the Shaw Society of Japan and became its president. He died a few years ago at the age of 95.) At the Waseda University Theatre Museum, a crowd of about two thousand students and faculty members shouting *"Banzai"* (Hurrah!) greeted them.

An exhibit of Shaviana had been assembled in the Museum, which housed the drama and theater collection of Professor Tsubouchi. On display were translations of Shaw plays and memorabilia of productions of them in Japan. Shaw was surprised to discover that many of his dramas had not only been translated into Japanese, but performed as well. He wryly noted that he had not received a penny from any of them. Cheerfully proceeding to a *Noh* exhibit, he donned a mask of *Hannya*, a female demon, and, imitating a *Noh* gesture he had seen the day before, set off a burst of laughter from his retinue of scholars. Encountering a drum, he beat on it, then tried out some wooden clappers. Obviously enjoying himself immensely, he was also entertaining all those clustered about him. Along the way, he stopped to inspect photographs of *Noh* drama settings. Hurried through a Japanese puppet theater display, he was guided to another building for a tea party on tatami mats, at which an actress who had once played a Shaw heroine greeted him and presented a gift for Mrs. Shaw. The University gave Shaw a *Noh* mask of an *Okina*, or old man; glowing over the gift, he put it on, and was photographed wearing it (Fig. 1). With it came wishes for a long life, which evoked from him the response that he had already lived too long. (Upon his return to London he planned to contribute the mask and the gifts from Kaizo Publishers to the Royal Academy of Dramatic Art, he told George Sansom.)

A puppeteer then performed a scene from a traditional puppet show (*Bunraku*), following which Shaw asked to see a *Hara-kiri* scene, and the artist complied. Later Shaw pointed out to the consul that in realistic stage plays actors move around too much once they have delivered their

FIG. 1. Shaw and Okina Mask.
(Photograph courtesy of Waseda
Theatre Library, Waseda University,
Tokyo, Japan.)

lines, whereas in puppet shows the puppets are kept still, imparting a
valuable lesson in acting. A passage he wrote for a book on puppets,
published the year before, begins with like counsel: "I always hold up
the wooden actors as instructive object-lessons to our flesh-and-blood
players."[33]

The museum visit lasted less than an hour, with Shaw being hastened
along whenever he tarried over anything of interest to him, for he had
an appointment to keep at the British Embassy at half-past eleven. So
absorbed was he in watching the movement of the puppet that Ichikawa
had to remind him that it was time to go. He delayed long enough for a
group photograph in the garden, before being taken to the Embassy for
his parting call on Ambassador Lindley.[34]

After lunch at the Sansoms', Shaw remained for the afternoon, com-
posing the short article for *Kaizo* that Mogi had prevailed upon him to
write. Offered a secretary and typist, he declined, suggesting that the
article would have greater value for them if he wrote it himself. *Kaizo*
reproduced in its Shaw issue the first page of the holograph pencil manuscript of his composition, inscribed beneath in ink, "Tokyo 9th March
1933 G. Bernard Shaw"—amidst several photos of Shaw: speaking at

the *Noh* performance; with Lu Xun in Shanghai; with Yamamoto, Noguchi, and Katherine Sansom; with General Araki; and with the Prime
Minister. The article, "Engels, Shaw & Lenin" recounted his sole encounter with Friedrich Engels in Hyde Park during his early Fabian
days, while, unknown to both of them, there lived in London at the time
a refugee named Vladimir Ulianov, subsequently better known as
Lenin.

When G.B.S. reboarded the luxury liner that evening he had "most
of the Empire's journalists at his heels," according to Redman. On board
he bade farewell to Mogi and Kimura, their wives, and Yamamoto. Shak-
ing their hands, Shaw told them, "I shall never forget my visit to Japan."
When Kimura said goodbye, he replied to the correspondent who had
followed him from Shanghai to Beijing and from Beppu to Tokyo, "No,
no, I shall be seeing you again in America." Before the ship weighed
anchor at eight o'clock, there was time for some last minute shopping in
shops along the dock. When the *Empress* did set sail, the newspapermen
"travelled as far with him as arrangements with the tug-master would
permit and exchanged quips with him to the end. He attended in person
the process of what he called 'chucking them overboard' and his last
words were: 'I can tell you nothing about Japan until the boat has
left.'"[35] The next day, on his way to Honolulu, he received a telegram:
"Bon voyage, no more can I follow after you. Ki Kimura."

Although Shaw's ten days in Japan had produced a flurry of publicity,
Kan Kikuchi, a Japanese playwright influenced by Shaw, dismissed
everything written about him in the press during March 1933 as "trash."
"Those who might understand Shaw," he explained, "could not speak
English, and those who speak English could not understand Shaw."[36]

G.B.S., as a global gadfly, was never one to refuse a public forum, to
hesitate to air his convictions, or to withhold his counsel and prescrip-
tions for dealing with the complex problems of the world. His prominence allowed him a latitude in speaking freely not available to everyone, and he often exploited it with wit and disarming candor. What is
less obvious is that his bold and forthright words were uttered in an
environment then inhospitable to adverse criticism. Kimura's essay on
Shaw in the Orient is dotted—literally—with deletions made to avoid
running afoul of the governmental censorship of political expression in
force at the time. Several commentators were impressed not only by
Shaw's outspokenness, but at England's forbearance in having permitted
it even in wartime. *Asahi* journalists considered trying to entice Shaw
into writing for their newspaper, but, given his unpredictability and the
prevailing political conditions, abandoned the idea as too risky. A decade earlier a more democratic era would have made possible freer be-

havior by them as well as by Shaw, "but now, one had to be careful if one did not want to be killed."[37]

In the Preface to *On the Rocks*, Shaw articulated and broadened the indictment that not even he felt free to make while still a guest on the island: "Our papers are silent about the suppression of liberty in Imperialist Japan, though in Japan it is a crime to have 'dangerous thoughts'" (*BH* 6, 608). Under the Peace Preservation Law then in effect there had been mass arrests, torture, prosecution, and severe punishment of persons suspected of harboring "dangerous thoughts," which meant espousing communism in any form. In practice it was directed against those betraying any indication of liberal leanings, including many faculty members in the high schools and colleges. A. Morgan Young, whom Shaw had met in Kobe, wrote, "It was the firm belief of the rulers of Japan that the Empire could only endure if every spark of intellectual honesty were relentlessly stamped out. This dread of truth is a phenomenon found all over the world, but seldom in such strength and abundance as in modern Japan."[38]

Shaw's performance was remarkably daring and entertainingly provocative. His session with the Japanese socialists and labor leaders takes on a somewhat different aspect, viewed from this perspective. Their desire to have him meet with them, and his agreement to do so, may well have constituted moral support sought and granted. His acquiescence in virtually all that *Kaizo*, Mogi, and Yamamoto arranged for him and his compliance with their publication requests were, in all likelihood, similarly motivated. The veneration with which most of those connected with these proceedings regarded him may also have been tinged with feelings of gratitude.

All the more provocative then does the encounter with Araki appear, with Shaw audaciously extolling communism and deriding patriotism to a military and governmental leader for whom the one was anathema and the other divinely inspired. Katharine Sansom depicted the War Minister as "that dangerous creature, a mystic fanatic," who "oozes charm," and sees both "the Sun Goddess presenting the banner of war" and "the honor and glory of Nippon as not only his but the world's beckoning star." After Shaw's departure the British ambassador shared with the Foreign Office his amusement at the furor over their visitor: "Nothing could better illustrate the love of the Japanese for a new thing and for new ideas than the reception given to Mr. Bernard Shaw during his recent visit. Fighting in Jehol, the American financial crisis and the proceedings at Geneva all took an entirely subordinate place in the press and in the minds of the statesmen and population of Japan compared to the sayings and doings of the famous playwright."

Sir Francis found Shaw "as agreeable and witty as one would have expected on general subjects." Yet there were limits to his toleration of Shavian political heterodoxy:

> Naturally Mr. Shaw could not keep off the question of Russia; and I regret to say that his attitude to this interesting subject is fundamentally dishonest, since he is obviously determined to close his mind to any facts which do not coincide with his wishes. Although no practical student of politics can take Mr. Shaw seriously in this domain, it is to be feared that the large number of ignorant people who consider him a fountain of wisdom are being grossly misled by his paradoxical absurdities.

Both the ambassador and George Sansom were struck by the good-tempered public acceptance of the "acid criticisms" Shaw leveled at various aspects of Japanese life. "In fact," Sir Francis found, "they seemed almost disappointed that he had not been more violent in this vein; and Count Makino, in a private letter to Mr. Sansom, expressed with his usual urbanity the opinion that a good dose of criticisms was salutary for his countrymen." Sansom elaborated:

> Mr. Shaw was extremely popular. The more ruthless his statements, the more the public loved him. When, instead of praising the cherry blossom and the samurai spirit, he said he didn't care twopence for Japan, and that Japanese cities were slums that ought to be blown up, and that the Japanese theatre was horrible, everybody was delighted. In fact, one prominent journalist complained to me that Mr. Shaw had been far too mild. He hadn't made enough of the offensive, paradoxical statements which are expected of him. On the other hand, a secretary in the Chinese legation told me with great pride, that Mr. Shaw had said far more awful things about China than about Japan.

Confirmation of Japanese approval of the Shavian strictures may be found scattered through reflective essays that continued to flow into periodicals in the wake of his swift transit through the land. There was counsel that Japan had something to learn from him, and wistful wishes that there had been opportunity to probe his thinking more fully. There was even a poem of homage.

Some complaints were voiced as well: that Shaw was presented to the public as a man of ideas rather than as a creative artist; that publishers made no attempt to advertise his published dramatic and other writings; that he spent most of his time with political figures, rendering him inaccessible for conversations with men of letters; and, inevitably, about his garrulity. There were detractors too, airing their dissent and disgruntlement, notably in a surprising communist-oriented polemic against his pronouncements, and an article in a business monthly wondering why so much fuss was made over a paradoxical, self-contradictory, free-spoken, harmless old man of eighty.

The most thoughtful review of his visit and its import was by H. Vere Redman. Though derogating much of "the great coming, seeing and commenting," Redman did credit Shaw with raising two important and challenging questions bearing on Japan's current political situation. First, the globe-girdling critic had questioned the psychological and material benefits to be gained from Bushido and patriotism, which might unite the nation, but would ultimately destroy it. The other question was the practical one of weighing the material cost of suppressing Chinese nationalism in Manchuria. Also valuable, thought Redman, were the only Shavian comments occasioned by his having been in Japan: on town-planning and on factory conditions. Coming from so eminent a foreign source the criticism was bound to have some impact. Indeed, "Mr. Shaw's shock tactics, which consist of saying the unpleasant truth and a half rather than the pleasant half truth, could not have been better applied than to this question of city planning." Redman considered unnecessary Shaw's playful suggestion that Japanese guns be returned from Manchuria and used on such ill-planned cities as Kobe and Osaka, because earthquakes periodically do that kind of clearance work. The real need is for "mental earthquakes" to insure that the cleared spaces, in Tokyo too, are filled in the right way. Shaw "is an earthquake of this sort; and it is to be hoped that his outspoken criticism will have some effect." "On the whole," he concluded,

> it can be said that Mr. Shaw has served Japan well. He has put some pointed questions and made some candid criticisms. Above all, he has suggested some new lines of thought, not all of them dangerous, some of them indeed perhaps extremely salutary. If one can judge by newspaper reports and the casual remarks of a fairly large circle of acquaintance, the Japanese are on the whole glad he came, sorry he saw so little, and especially thankful that he commented so much.[39]

Evidently Shaw lived up to his reputation: he came, he saw, and, even in his commenting, "conquered." Yet not with his playwriting, which never really caught on in Japan.

But what effect did Japan have upon Shaw? In the long term, any expectation that this fleeting visit would supply material for Shavian dramaturgy went essentially unfulfilled. The one noteworthy exception was the introduction of some modifications in the text of the film version of *Major Barbara*. There the Undershaft and Lazarus firm is described to the family visitors as a kind of "Totalitarian State," and Cusins claims that the Undershaft adoption plan is also a "Japanese custom." Undershaft, pronouncing it "a very sensible one," adds: "We have a Japanese temple in the village. The Shinto religion suits us exactly. I, of course, am its Mikado."[40] Shortly thereafter they all enter "the Meeting Place of All Religions," where, among others, is the Shinto temple.

When the party gathers at the temple, Undershaft explains that his Japanese experts worship there; that inside is nothing special other than a priest expecting a penny for a stick of incense to be burned at the altar. The Shinto temple, he tells them all, "is politically important to us here," as "the temple of the Totalitarian State." After Cusins eludicates that "the Shinto Totalitarian State is personified by the divine emperor, descended from the sun, who owns everything," Undershaft arrogates the same status to himself: "I own everything here. As a foundling I may be descended from the sun. At all events I am the divine emperor." This amuses Cusins, but Lomax has the last word, finding "a certain amount of tosh about this last Shinto touch" (pp. 139–40).

That is the extent of the Japanese revision. Interestingly enough, Undershaft's original third act line, "Good news from Manchuria," is altered to the more indefinite and more generally applicable "Good news from the front" (p. 147).

If at the outset he evinced little interest in the sights of Japan—fixing his eyes instead on the unsightly—Shaw came in time to see more to his liking in the environs, including the snowy scenery of Tokyo. Even more, Japan apparently caught his musical ear: the sounds of the bell at Nara, the drums in Kyoto and at Waseda University, the wooden clappers and orchestra of the theater. Even the harrassing reporters and photographers were unable to discourage him from satisfying his own journalistic curiosity about the conduct and workings of the newspaper business in Japan, which he explored at both an English and a Japanese establishment. What is more, he took the time to write a journalistic essay as a gift to the *Kaizo* management for its hospitable and helpful service to him. But it was to his role as warning prophet and moral reformer that he devoted his energies most of all. He exploited the publicity that attended his movements to communicate to an attentive nation his overriding ethical concerns: the threats to world peace, the indignities inflicted upon the victims of modern industrial society, the urban ugliness and squalor.

Shaw's eventual attitude toward Japan, it would appear, was an ambivalent one: appreciative of its charms, but disturbed by its social, political and economic policies. An indication that the negative aspects in particular lingered with him in the aftermath of his Japanese visit may be gleaned from a statement he drew up a little over a year later, but never released. Intended perhaps to be issued as an interview (self-drafted), or as a radio broadcast, it reflects concern with the same crying evils that preoccupied him when he was in Japan. Addressed in part to the Japanese, the heart of its message was that fear of Japan had spread over the entire Pacific area. The peril that the empire posed lay in its export trade and its underpaid workers. Its expansion into Manchuria and

Mongolia would cause multitudes to be exploited, and established Japan as the dire foe of every laborer.

He felt no animus towards the Japanese, from whom he had received excellent treatment. In their land he had beheld some beautiful regions, with lovely homes in natural surroundings, and the people living there well-attired and relatively content. But then there was Osaka, a hellish industrial center containing nothing but factories and slums, its sole object of beauty a superb theater. Yet the dramas presented there bore no relation to factory or slum, dealing instead with an ancient feudal experience now permanently wiped out. Japan, he concluded, could not become a promised land for the multitude because its machinery and exploited labor were too occupied with creating opulence for a handful of people. Bidding them goodbye, he suggested that there were myriad things they could do, but he had no more time.[41]

Notes

All quotations and material cited from Japanese language sources have been translated by Professor Matoba. The authors wish to acknowledge the help of Professor Masahiko Masumoto of Nagoya University, Nagoya, Japan, for alerting them to many of the Japanese sources drawn upon and for valuable critical advice. They are also indebted to John Trewin for identifying Nervo and Knox, thereby clarifying what might otherwise have been an obscure allusion, and to Stanley Weintraub for identifying the Two Macs.

1. Mount Aso, the world's largest active volcano, began erupting between 24 and 27 February and erupted again on 1 March. According to the *Osaka Asahi* (1 March 1933), the eruption occurred after an 150-year interval. "It is as though Aso is welcoming the cruiser and has beaten Shaw in the game of wit." The earthquake occurred on 3 March.

2. Shōyō Tsubouchi (1859–1935) achieved fame as the translator of Scott, Bulwer Lytton, and the complete works of Shakespeare. His "new theatre movement" introduced Ibsen and Shaw to Japan. He was far less sympathetic to Shaw than to Shakespeare, whom he ardently championed. See Mutsuko Motoyama, "Shaw in the Japanese Theatre," *Shaw Review*, 20 (1977), 51–53.

3. Kimura, the only Japanese present, shared the details with a reporter for the *Osaka Mainichi* newspaper. It and Kimura's *Jiji Shimpo* were the only Japanese papers to carry firsthand reports of the Shanghai interview. All details about Shaw's visit to Japan, unless otherwise noted, are from the following articles in the special Shaw issue of *Kaizo*, April 1933: Isoo Abe, "Political Opinions of Bernard Shaw"; Sadao Araki, "Shaw is not a Satirist"; Anon., "Noh Performance in Honor of Mr. Bernard Shaw"; Ki Kimura, "Bernard Shaw in the Orient"; Shōō Matsui, "A Visit to Mrs. Shaw in her Sickbed"; Sobei Mogi, "Meeting Bernard Shaw Again"; Yonejirō Noguchi, "Born to Be for Others"; [George] Bailey Sansom, "Shaw's Comment on Noh and Other Experiences in Tokyo"; George Bernard Shaw, "Engels, Shaw and Lenin" and "The Speech of Bernard Shaw on the Occasion

of the Performance of 'No,'" in Japanese and in English (both reprinted in *Independent Shavian*, 3 [1965]); and Sanehiko Yamamoto, "Seeing Shaw Off."

4. After Kimura's return to Japan, his dispatches from Beijing were published in two parts, "3000 Miles in Search of Shaw," *Jijo Shimpo*, 5 and 7 March 1933.

5. Yonejirō Noguchi (1875–1947), known abroad as Yone Noguchi, was a poet and professor of English and English Literature at Keio University. Kichizō Nakamura (1877–1941) was a novelist and dramatist who had studied in the United States, England, and Germany; socialist in outlook, he had been influenced by Ibsen and had studied Shaw and Maeterlinck. Shinzaburō Miyajima, who wrote perceptively on Shaw, was an art and literary critic and theorist. Hisao Homma was an English literature scholar, translator, and critic.

6. *The Japan Chronicle*, Weekly Edition, Kobe, 9 March 1933, p. 342.

7. See Blanche Patch, *Thirty Years with G.B.S.* (New York: Dodd, Mead, 1951), p. 90, and Shaw's letter to Theresa Helburn in Lawrence Langner, *G.B.S. and the Lunatic* (New York: Atheneum, 1963), pp. 126–27.

8. Si Ōsakasei, "Impressions of Shaw Landing in Japan," in *Yomiuri Shimbun*, 5 March 1933.

9. H. Vere Redman, "Shaw in and on Japan," in *Contemporary Japan: A Review of Japanese Affairs*, 2 (June 1933), 111. Notwithstanding its derisive treatment of Shaw's passage through Japan, this is a useful commentary, reflecting the perspective of an experienced observer of the Japanese scene, the Tokyo correspondent of the (London) *Daily Mail*.

10. The most detailed treatment of the press conference was that in *The Japan Chronicle*, 9 March 1933.

11. "Shaw in and on Japan," p. 112.

12. Ibid.

13. *Tokyo Asahi*, 3 March 1933, p. 11. According to this news report, Shaw's visit to the theater lasted one hour. The word that Ki Kimura received and passed on to Shōō Matsui was that Shaw was kept seated for four hours.

14. Chyōshō Yoshida, "With Mr. Shaw in Kyoto," *Osaka Asahi*, 24, 25, and 26 March 1933.

15. Katherine Sansom, *Sir George Sansom and Japan: A Memoir* (Tallahassee, Florida: Diplomatic Press, 1972). All quotations from Katharine and from George Sansom and information about Shaw's visit to Tokyo unless otherwise noted are from this book, pp. 53–68, and from the special issue of *Kaizo*.

16. Kimura indicates that he brought up the subject of Engels but credits Mogi with inducing Shaw to write the *Kaizo* article. Mogi simply says that Shaw agreed to write the piece when told that *Kaizo* was "devoted to enlightenment about socialism."

17. "Journalists' Competition Surrounding Shaw," *Jinbutsu Hyōron*, April 1933; Mukyosu Naruse, "Impressions of Bernard Shaw," *Omokage Sō* (Hokoryūkan, 1947), pp. 131–36.

18. "Shaw in and on Japan," p. 113; *Osaka Asahi*, 4 March 1933, p. 11; *Tokyo Asahi*, 4 March 1933, p. 3.

19. Shin Takatani, "On Shaw's Gloves," *PC*, No. 1, 1933, p. 5.

20. "Shaw in and on Japan," p. 121.

21. Patch, p. 116.

22. "Shaw in and on Japan," p. 114.

23. *Jinbutsu Hyōron*, p. 77. The most extensive attempts at reproducing the dialogue of the interview were those of the *Tokyo Asahi*, 8 March, and *Kaizo* in the Shaw issue. They have been drawn upon to help round out the first-hand testimony given precedence here. A translation by Masahiko Masumoto of the Araki-Shaw interview as quoted in the *Tokyo Asahi*, under the title "Bernard Shaw in Japan," was printed in the *Independent Shavian*, 15 (1977), pp. 17–19.

24. Nervo and Knox were variety artists popular on the London stage in the 1930s as a "knock about" comedy team. They were part of the comedy group known as The Crazy Gang. The Two Macs were a music-hall comedy team on the London stage in the 1880s.

25. The tone of this particular passage is milder in the press, where Shaw is portrayed as offering greater assurance that there was no need to fear Communist Russia; were that country still tsarist, the Japanese would require for their defense an army four times as large as its present one. Araki is represented as stating that Japan's defense posed no threat to other countries and that he desired only peace and happiness for the world.

26. *BH* 1, 233; *Three Plays by Brieux* (London: A.C. Fifield, 1911), p. xxxv; *BH* 3, 170, 266, 283; *BH* 6, 478, 72.

27. *Tokyo Asahi*, 9 March 1933, and K. Sansom, p. 59.

28. It was reproduced in *Kaizo*, p. 313, and *The Independent Shavian*, 3 (1965), p. 37.

29. Hiroyoshi Ohmura in *Geijutsuden*, 3 (April 1933), 1.

30. Quoted from an unidentified news report by Noguchi.

31. Reprinted in *Letters of Edward Elgar and Other Writings*, ed. Percy M. Young (London: Geoffrey Bles, 1956), p. 336. The letter also discusses Chinese music.

32. *Tokyo Asahi*, 9 March 1933, p. 11.

33. Bernard Shaw, "Note on Puppets," in Max Von Boehn, *Dolls and Puppets*, trans. Josephine Nicoll (London, Bombay, & Sydney: George C. Harrap, 1932), p. 5.

34. *Tokyo Asahi*, 10 March 1933, p. 2; "Shaw at Waseda University Theatre Museum" in *Studies in English Literature*, 13 (1933), 286–87; "Shaw in and on Japan," pp. 114–15.

35. "Shaw in and on Japan," p. 115.

36. Kan Kikuchi, "What's Going On," *Bungei Shunjū*, May 1933.

37. "Journalists' Competition Surrounding Shaw," p. 77.

38. A. Morgan Young, *Imperial Japan, 1926–1938* (London: George Allen & Unwin, 1938), p. 249.

39. "Shaw in and on Japan," pp. 115–22.

40. Bernard Shaw, *Major Barbara: A Screen Version* (Harmondsworth: Penguin Books, 1945), pp. 134–35 (in American edition, p. 127).

41. British Library, Add Ms. 50698 fols. 6–9.

Bernard F. Dukore

GBS, MGM, RKO: SHAW IN HOLLYWOOD

On 16 December 1932, Bernard Shaw and his wife Charlotte embarked on a round-the-world cruise. On Thursday, 23 March 1933, at 8:00 p.m., their ship, the *Empress of Britain*, docked at San Francisco harbor. At 10:30 the next morning they flew south to San Simeon, where they were house guests of publisher William Randolph Hearst. On Tuesday the 28th, they flew further south to Los Angeles, to visit Hollywood.[1]

The two-hundred-odd mile flight was far from smooth. The tri-motored plane encountered a sudden storm that swept in from the Pacific, lowered the ceiling, and thereby created such serious visibility problems as to render continued flight dangerous. In a perilous but necessary sudden descent that almost resulted in an accident, the pilot, Ray Crawford, flew through a hole in the fog and landed on a narrow strip of beach about two miles north of Malibu. Eventually, a UCLA sophomore named George Gray O'Connor picked up the undoubtedly shaken Shaws (both were seventy-six at the time) and drove them to Santa Monica airport, where a visiting party of civic dignitaries awaited their arrival by air. After the Shaws were deposited and exchanged cars, a cavalcade of expensive automobiles escorted them to the MGM studio in Culver City.[2]

The Shaws spent approximately two and a half hours in Hollywood. One hour or so was in the bungalow that was built on the MGM lot for Hearst's mistress, Marion Davies, who hosted a luncheon party in honor of the visiting dramatist. Davies's maid helped Charlotte, who requested a drink of Scotch, much to Davies's surprise, clean up. Shaw, as a vegetarian, found himself with nothing he could eat. At the head table with Shaw and Davies were Charlie Chaplin, Louis B. Mayer, George Hearst, and Clark Gable, who the previous year had completed the film *Polly of the Circus* with Davies. Other guests included John Barrymore, William Randolph Hearst, Una Merkel, and O. P. Heggie, who twenty years before had played Androcles in the first production of *Androcles and the Lion*, directed by Granville Barker. Shaw then visited the sets of *Dinner at Eight* and *When Ladies Meet*, and spent approximately half an hour on each. The remainder of the time consisted of photographers taking pictures of him and reporters interviewing him. The *Los Angeles Times* clocked the interviews with the press at one minute and fifty-three seconds.[3]

The encounter with the journalists elicited a series of quips. When one interviewer asked his opinion of "marvelous Southern California," Shaw asked whether Californians ever tired of superlatives.[4] Other questions revolved around the forced plane landing. "I'm not sure that you didn't arrange the whole thing for the first page of your newspapers," Shaw told one reporter.[5] To another he admitted, "I was frankly scared, when the plane swept downward to the beach in that forced landing. The pilot was the brave one. I thought he was swooping down to catch a fish."[6] And he warned a third, "Write anything you wish about it. But don't write the truth—you'll be fired."[7]

En route to the set of *Dinner at Eight*, one of that film's stars, John Barrymore, requested Shaw's autograph for his son John Jr. (later an actor under the name John Drew Barrymore). Upon learning that the child had been born the year before, Shaw refused, explaining that the boy was too young to appreciate it.[8] According to one source "Barrymore was taken aback," to another he "got sore and left," ruining his costume in the rain. Shaw did, however, sign a cowboy's hat for a makeup man Davies introduced as a "portrait artist."[9]

On the other set, a more serious disturbance occurred. Shaw met the three stars of *When Ladies Meet*: Robert Montgomery, Alice Brady, and Ann Harding. An admirer of Shaw, Harding apparently assumed that he was as familiar with her movies as she was with his plays. She smiled, extended an arm, and told him that in a few days she would again play Lady Cecily in *Captain Brassbound's Conversation*. "Where did you play it before?" asked Shaw. At the Hedgerow Theater, near Philadelphia, she replied, whereupon Shaw requested the name of that theater's manager and added, "I'm sure it must have been a piratical performance."[10] As one commentator put it, "Ann's pretty toy balloon popped. She was like a child who had been denied the proverbial stick of candy, and slapped instead."[11] But she was not speechless. "'Indeed it was not,' she said. 'We had permission in writing from your own agent.'"[12] She then left the playwright for the security of her dressing-room, whose door she closed, and according to the *Times* wept, to Edwin Schallert "wept for hours afterward," and to Davies (recalling the situation years later) "went into hysterics and said she wouldn't work any longer."[13] Hollywood's response to such treatment of one of its own was predictable. "When Ann bawled," said the *Los Angeles Times*, "a lot of people around the MGM premises looked glum. They like Miss Harding in Hollywood." [14] Schallert's more thoughtful judgment was not essentially different: "Shaw and his cortege literally swept through the movie town. Bitterness and rancor of a kind hovered in their wake, but the whole thing was dismissed finally with the appraisal that he was just showing off." [15]

In Davies's version of the story, *Androcles and the Lion* was the play Harding said she had performed and Shaw's comment was, "It must have been a pirated version." She also reported his response to the article in the *Los Angeles Times*: "Shaw was furious. He said to me, 'What kind of a country is this?'" [16]

Of those who cite the dialogue, Schallert and the unsigned reporter of the *Times* agree on the play and the response. Partly because they, unlike Davies, wrote their account at the time of the occurrence, I credit them (and since O.P. Heggie, the original Androcles, was present, Davies's memory may have confused his Shaw play with Ann Harding's). Also, Schallert states that he was within earshot of the incident and because no other newspaper that I have seen mentions it I infer that either the *Times* writer too was within earshot or that his informant was.

The same year, 1933, another studio, RKO, made and released *Morning Glory*, starring an outspoken admirer of Shaw, Katharine Hepburn,[17] in the role that would earn her her first Academy Award. In an early scene, the budding actress (Hepburn) enters the inner office of a theater producer (Adolphe Menjou), where a young playwright (Douglas Fairbanks, Jr.) is present. Trying to capture and hold the producer's attention, the actress tells him of her experience at the Little Theatre in Ordway, Vermont, where her roles included Kitty in Shaw's *You Never Can Tell*—a boner that has apparently gone undetected until now: the play contains no character of that name (possibly, the movie's author confuses it with *Mrs Warren's Profession*—the title character is named Kitty—which the actress mentions shortly after). Affectedly, the young actress remarks that she wrote to Shaw; sent him a photograph of the play; told him that when she was famous and had a theater of her own she would perform his Cleopatra until she became too old for the role, at which time she would do *Mrs Warren's Profession*; and received a reply from Shaw—which she promptly produces. Although the producer would like to get rid of the actress, the young playwright, attracted to her, asks to read it. Paraphrasing Shaw's letter, he reports that Shaw considered it cheeky of the Little Theatre to have produced any of his plays and that he was certain the one they produced was—quoting Shaw's words to Ann Harding—"a piratical performance." Returning to paraphrase, the young American playwright says that the old Irish playwright is nevertheless glad that the actress intends to see that he receives proper recognition once she has established her own repertory theater and that he hopes she will not forget him. Delighted by the letter, the young dramatist considers the rebuke to be marvelous.[18]

At MGM, Shaw's statement to Ann Harding was regarded as gratuitously rude. But such rudeness was uncharacteristic of Shaw. Even when he refused John Barrymore's request he gave a sensible reason, however much the reason may have surprised the actor. At RKO, Shaw's statement in the fictitious letter was regarded as wonderfully comic joshing that charmed the addressee, who like the young playwright admired Shaw's sense of humor. Although the response at RKO was closer to the spirit of Shaw's remark than that at MGM, both studios missed the point, which was a pun. *You Never Can Tell* was unlikely to have prompted Shaw's comment, as RKO had it do. So was *Androcles and the Lion*, as Marion Davies did. What provoked his quip about "a piratical performance" was *Captain Brassbound's Conversion*, whose title character is a pirate. In neither England nor America is *piratical* synonymous with *pirated*, and of the three plays mentioned, Shaw's pun applies only to the one that actually provoked it—a pun that Ann Harding should have recognized, since she had acted in the play.

As the reader may have noticed, a long parenthetical phrase two paragraphs earlier refers to the author of *Morning Glory*, not to that author's name. The film's credits indicate that Howard J. Green wrote the screenplay, based on the play by Zoë Akins. Which of them was responsible for the use of Shaw's line to Ann Harding?

One problem in answering this question is that the play *Morning Glory* is unpublished. The standard reference books on drama do not even mention it (for instance: Myron Matlaw's *Modern World Drama: An Encyclopedia*, John Gassner's *Masters of the Drama*, John Gassner and Edward Quinn's *Reader's Encyclopedia of World Drama*, *The McGraw-Hill Encyclopedia of World Drama*, and *The Oxford Companion to the Theatre*) and the Hepburn character, Eva Lovelace, is not listed in *Index to Characters in the Performing Arts*. Complicating the matter, *The National Cyclopedia of American Biography* cites Akins as author of the screenplay, as does Hepburn's biographer, and a film reference book says on one page that Akins wrote the screenplay, on another that Green did.[19] Further complicating it, neither the Dramatists Guild nor the Writers Guild of America, East has a record of the play.[20] The Copyright Office of the Library of Congress has not resolved the question either. Its search in the copyright card catalogues from 1898 through 1970, under the names of both author and play, has failed to disclose copyright registration.[21]

Nevertheless, both Katharine Hepburn and Pandro S. Berman, who produced the movie, assure me that Akins, a writer of movie scripts as well as plays, had indeed written *Morning Glory* as a play when Berman purchased screen rights for RKO. "Among other things that happened during this time," he says, "was the death of [Akins's] husband and it is possible that that had something to do with our adding Green to the project."[22]

As a play, *Morning Glory* was not performed until 17 October 1939,[23] when the Pasadena Playhouse produced it in what was to have been a tryout prior to a Broadway opening, which did not take place.[24] The Pasadena Public Library's archives of Pasadena Playhouse material do not include a script of *Morning Glory*. Nor do the files of Ned Esty, formerly of the Pasadena Playhouse, who reports that in those days the organization did not always keep scripts of plays it produced.[25] Ash's *Subject Collections* says that Harvard University has manuscripts of Zoë Akins, but Jeanne T. Newlin, Curator of the Harvard Theatre Collection, writes that she "cannot locate the material at Harvard" and adds, "if indeed it is at Harvard."[26] While the Huntington Library has a copy of the play *Morning Glory*, it is undated and internal evidence suggests that it might be a revision made after 1939. For this reason I will postpone consideration of this script until later.

Let us return to the question of who may have been responsible for the movie's use of Shaw's quip to Ann Harding. Since both Zoë Akins and Howard J. Green were in the Hollywood area when Shaw made his whirlwind tour on 28 March 1933, both had access to the story in the *Los Angeles Times* and perhaps had accounts from other sources. The credits of the film *Morning Glory* would suggest that the playwright Akins rather than the adapter Green was responsible for the Ann Harding line. Pandro S. Berman supports this implication: "I would say that Zoë Akins was responsible for the great majority of [the dialogue]. Howard Green was more of a screen writer and constructionist on that film and less concerned with dialogue." But Berman also points out that since the movie was written and produced half a century ago, memories of such details may be unreliable.[27]

His caveat is well justified. The available evidence suggests that Green was responsible. At the Billy Rose Collection of the Performing Arts Research Center of the New York Public Library at Lincoln Center[28] is a mimeographed copy of Green's screenplay, which is undated, though the index card in the catalogue says, "final script dated April 19, 1933"—only twenty-two days after Shaw's visit. Internal evidence indicates that the script is far from final. The opening five scenes, in the producer's offices, have neither dialogue nor action but a statement that they are to consist of atmosphere shots to be followed by the introduction of the Hepburn character. According to a parenthetical note, these five scenes, to contain a maximum of six speeches, would be worked out by Green and Lowell Sherman, the movie's director (fol. 1). A second consideration is the key scene in the producer's inner office. As on the sound track of the completed film, the young actress tells the producer of her acting experience (including the mistake of Kitty in *You Never Can Tell*) and lets the young playwright read Shaw's letter to her. In the midst of his paraphrase of the letter is a notation of something to be added in the next draft: "Line of Shaw's to Ann Harding" (fol. 22). If Akins had already written the line, this directive would have been unnecessary since Green or his typist would have copied it. It was Howard J. Green, then, who was responsible for inserting it and for reinterpreting it as comic rather than insulting.

Verifying this conclusion is the undated carbon copy of the typescript of the play *Morning Glory* at the Huntington Library.[29] The play contains the scene in question, not only with the error of Kitty in *You Never Can Tell* (fol. 26), but with an additional boner: the budding actress says (fol. 25) that she played the title role of Shaw's *Joan of Arc* (his play is called *Saint Joan*). Significantly, the scene contains neither Shaw's quip to Ann Harding nor any hint of it.

A minor difference between the scene in the play and that in the film is that the actress gained her experience in Ordway, Kansas. Probably because of Katharine Hepburn's distinctive speech, the screenwriter made the state Vermont.[30] A more important difference is that whereas the movie's actress gained experience at Ordway's Little Theatre, the play's actress gained it at Ordway's Theatre-in-the-Round (fol. 25). In 1933, even in 1939, the Ordway theater, in whatever state it was located, would likely have been called The Little Theatre, but Theatre-in-the-Round is a name that belongs to the late 1940s and the 1950s (Margo Jones, usually credited with helping to popularize the term, opened her theater in Dallas in 1947). Supporting this view is the actress's statement that Shaw wrote to her just before he died (fol. 25). Because Shaw's death occurred on 2 November 1950, I infer that the Huntington Library's copy of *Morning Glory* is a revision completed after that date. Perhaps the failure of the 1939 Pasadena Playhouse production to transfer to Broadway prompted Akins, years later, to rework the play in another effort to bring it to New York.

Nevertheless, whatever year this script was written supports the conclusion that Howard J. Green was responsible for using Shaw's remark to Ann Harding in the movie *Morning Glory*. If the Huntington's script is the 1933 original or the 1939 version (perhaps the same as 1933, perhaps revised), the reference to Shaw's death might be an error, like the mistaken title of one Shaw play and the mistaken character of another. This possibility seems unlikely since Los Angeles newspapers in the 1930s contained many items about Shaw, notably his March 1933 visit to Hollywood, and in 1939 these papers reported that Shaw won an Academy Award for the Best Screenplay of 1938, *Pygmalion*—an honor of which a screenwriter like Akins could hardly have been unaware. If this *Morning Glory* script, as I judge, was written after Shaw's death, a possible reason for omitting the line is that it was copyright by RKO, the studio that made the film. For Akins to use it in her play would be, in Ann Harding's interpretation of the word, "piratical."

Notes

1. Engagement Diary, 1933, in Shaw Material, Business Papers, Parcel 26, London School of Economics and Political Science.

2. "Shaw Arrives, Jokes, Departs/Forced Landing and Studio Visit Mark Busy Day/ Ann Harding Made to Cry; Celebrities Greeted/Filmland Boldly Twitted; Panama Next Stop," *Los Angeles Times*, 29 March 1933, Part II, p. 1; Edwin Schallert, "Mr. Shaw Shakes Up Hollywood," *Movie Classic*, 4 (June 1933), 26; Marion Davies, *The Times We Had* (New York, 1975), pp. 139, 142.

3. "Shaw Arrives," p. 1; Schallert, p. 26. For photograph of Shaw and others at the head table see *The Collected Screenplays of Bernard Shaw*, ed. Bernard F. Dukore (London and Athens, Georgia, 1980), Plate 1.

4. "Shaws at Sea After Busy Visit Here," *Los Angeles Herald-Express*, 29 March 1933, p. A–3.

5. "Shaw Thrilled by Air Trip and Studio Visit," *Los Angeles Examiner*, 29 March 1933, p. 1.

6. "Shaw Arrives," p. 1.

7. Eugene Coughlin, "Shavian Wisecracks Fizzle; But Writer Well Pleased—Haw!" *Daily News* (Los Angeles), 29 March 1933, p. 11.

8. "Shaw Arrives," pp. 1, 10; Schallert, p. 62; Davies, p. 142.

9. Respectively: Schallert, p. 62; Davies, p. 142.

10. "Shaw Arrives," p. 10; Schallert tells the same story, with the same last sentence (pp. 26, 62).

11. Schallert, p. 62.

12. "Shaw Arrives," p. 10.

13. "Shaw Arrives," p. 10; Schallert, p. 62; Davies, p. 142.

14. "Shaw Arrives," p. 1.

15. Schallert, p. 62.

16. Davies, p. 142.

17. Charles Higham, *Kate* (New York, 1975), p. 27.

18. My thanks to David Heeley, who produced and directed *Starring Katharine Hepburn* for WNET–TV (PBS), for permitting me to see the scene from *Morning Glory* in his program.

19. Higham, p. 45; *The 1934–35 Motion Picture Almanac* (New York, n.d.), pp. 37, 262.

20. Letter from Elihu Winer, Deputy Executive Director, Writers Guild of America, East, 8 July 1981.

21. Letter from Marla Y. Muse, Bibliographer, Reference and Bibliography Section, Copyright Office, Library of Congress, 16 September 1981.

22. Hepburn letter, 2 May 1981; Berman letter, 28 April 1981. See also the account in Higham, pp. 45–47. I have been unable to resolve the question of whether Akins also wrote a screen treatment or the first draft of a screenplay, as Berman thinks she did. Blanche W. Baker, Registration Administrator of the Writers Guild of America, West, writes that the Guild's records, including registration of screenplays, are confidential and may be seen only in connection with a court order (8 July 1981). But see n. 30, below.

23. For information on the opening date, I thank Ned Esty, formerly of the Pasadena Playhouse, who has a program of that production (interview, 10 June 1981), and Myron Matlaw (letter, 27 April 1981). Matlaw confirms that he did not mention the play in his *Modern World Drama*, partly because it was unpublished and was not performed in New York, and partly because Akins, a relatively unimportant dramatist, did not warrant more space than he gave her (letter, 15 July 1981).

24. James Robert Parish, *The RKO Gals* (New Rochelle, N.Y., 1974), p. 281n. Parish erroneously gives 1938 as the year the Pasadena Playhouse produced *Morning Glory*.

25. Interview, 10 June 1981.

26. Letter, 30 April 1981.

27. Letter, 28 April 1981.

28. For their help, I thank the staff of the Billy Rose Collection.

29. For their assistance, I thank James D. Akins, Mark Matousek, and the staff of the Huntington Library.

30. In addition to the play *Morning Glory*, the Huntington Library has four incomplete narrative manuscripts of the work: one holograph, the others typescripts with holograph corrections. One of the typescripts is a copy, with holograph cuts and corrections, of the holograph manuscript. Both appear to be novels (two sequences are preceded by chapter headings). The other two typed manuscripts may possibly be narrative screen treatments, which would suggest that Akins had begun working on the motion picture, as Pandro S. Berman recalls (letter, 28 April 1981), when her husband's death made him decide to assign the screen adaptation to Howard J. Green at this very early stage, before she had devoted much time to the project. Whether or not this was the case, one of the latter incomplete typescripts contains several references to Kansas as the state in which Ordway is located.

Dan H. Laurence

"THAT AWFUL COUNTRY": SHAW IN AMERICA

"And so," said Shaw in 1907 to a woman interviewing him, "you are from that awful country, that uncivilized place called the United States."[1] Although he had at the age of twenty-five momentarily contemplated the possibility of emigration to America, Shaw stubbornly avoided visiting the U.S.A. until more than half a century later—except vicariously, through the influencing pages of Charles Dickens's *Martin Chuzzlewit*. As a youth he here encountered an imposing array of American scoundrels, pettifoggers, and hypocrites: the pistol-toting Major Hannibal Chollop, self-proclaimed "worshipper of freedom," the "constant advocate of Lynch law and slavery"; the swindler Zephaniah Scadder, to whose lips "Truth" never reached; the war correspondent Jefferson Brick of the *New York Rowdy Journal*; the Hon. Elijah Pogram, windbag congressman and author of the "Pogram Defiance"; the aristocratic authoress Mrs. Hominy, "of masculine and towering intellect"; and Colonel Diver, a newspaper editor to whom the American press is "the Palladium of Rational Liberty at home, sir, and the dread of Foreign oppression abroad."

Shaw's knowledge of Americans was otherwise obtained in his formative years principally from a reading of Mark Twain, Artemus Ward, Charles Leland Godfrey, Bret Harte, and the opinions of Americans recorded in their travels by Mrs. Frances Trollope and her son Anthony. It is therefore not surprising that most of the American characters who people Shaw's works are stereotypically ingenuous, crude, and vulgar, and, in his two plays with American settings, *The Devil's Disciple* and *The Shewing-up of Blanco Posnet*, avaricious, cruel, hypocritical, and singularly lacking in charity. From the prosperous Crawfords in Shaw's second novel, *The Irrational Knot* (1880), to the Hector Malones, senior and junior, in *Man and Superman* (1903) and the American ambassador Vanhattan in *The Apple Cart* (1929), Shaw's Americans are with rare exception

painted with broad satiric strokes, seen as full of "elevated moral sentiments" (*BH* 2, 601) and "not exactly . . . the best sort of people,"[2] materialistic, ostentatious, pushy, conceited, boastful, and frenetically moving
about, "like a mouse in oxygen,"[3] incapable of being idle gracefully.

The United States was, to Shaw the socialist, a great experiment gone
wrong, a golden opportunity squandered. "America broke loose from
us at the end of the eighteenth century," he remarked in 1910; "[e]ver
since that it has been proving its utter unfitness to govern itself."[4] America, he charged, had never been successful in politics: "It was made independent largely in spite of its own teeth by a declaration of sentiments
which it did not share and principles which it barely grasped the narrow
end of. Even today," he said in 1907, "neither its ordinary security nor
its liberty is up to the monarchical standard of Central Europe."[5] Americans had long deluded themselves into believing that it was the people
who governed. But how, Shaw inquired, can you call a thing a government "which every railway king or mammoth pigsticker can bully or buy,
and every lynching mob defy?"[6] "You haven't realized yet," he told the
Americans, "that it's your money kings that rule. You think it's a government of the people, by the people, and for the people. That's how you
get your mob passion when anyone attacks the government. It's reflected
in the court room and on the bench, as well as in the street."[7]

He had no desire to experience this at firsthand, he announced, when
asked why he would not visit America. On other occasions he offered
alternative reasons for not crossing the Atlantic. "It takes," he said, "a
foreigner to understand your institutions, simply because he has a perspective on them which you have not. Why, then, go to America and lose
the perspective? To see skyscrapers? If I saw them tomorrow they'd hold
no surprise for me. I've seen them ten thousand times painted, water-
coloured, impressionised, futurised, photographed, and cinemato-
graphed from every point of view, including a bird's. The beauties of
nature? I've seen Niagara Falls, Yellowstone Park, the Grand Canyon,
Yosemite, and what not in the cinema."[8] And as he was convinced that a
veracious individual like himself would be barred from disembarking if
he admitted the truth about his political and religious convictions, and
could, further, "be arrested the moment I landed on the charge of incit-
ing the women of America to immorality by my good looks,"[9] he repeatedly declined the stream of invitations proffered to him "except on condition of receiving a safe-conduct from the President."[10]

Shaw was disturbed by the political naiveté he detected, "the childish-
ness which enables [Americans] to remain simple New England villagers
in the complicated hustle of New York and Chicago, never revising their
ideas, never enlarging their consciousness, never losing their interest in
the ideals of the Pilgrim Fathers."[11] He had never met an American, he

claimed, who had any notions of the institutions of his native land "beyond a general and most erroneous idea that they are glorious."[12] The American, Shaw told his biographer Archibald Henderson in 1907, "still has illusions about modern progress, and liberty, and God's good intentions and strong preference for the principles of the 4th [of] July. It is rather puzzling for him at first to be accepted—as all men are accepted in a thieves' kitchen—as a thief, liar, scoundrel, and hypocrite, supporting a government which would disgrace the quarter deck of a pirate ship" (CL 2, 705). The United States was, to Shaw, "a middle-class hell,"[13] the most puritanical nation on earth, whose public conscience was "a hasty, unintelligent and easily duped force."[14]

It was, as well, a country whose civilization was a century behind the times. Consider, said Shaw in 1909, the appalling poverty prevalent in America and the disgraceful misemployment of children in Carolina cotton mills, and explain how it dares call itself a free country. England had found a remedy for similar conditions in Manchester a hundred years before, but Americans prefer to ignore the lesson and remedy available to them because they are not really interested in freedom. "They want to make money and they don't care how they do it."[15] The land of the free, the home of the brave was in fact "illiberal, superstitious, crude, violent, anarchic and arbitrary,"[16] a land rife with blasphemy prosecutions, birth control persecutions, police raids of art shows, violations of free speech tenets, and a plethora of comparable indignities, a land "extremely dangerous for men who have both enlightened opinions and the courage of them."[17]

No act of American puritanism in the early years of the century escaped Shaw's baleful eye and pen. At any opportunity he would call attention to the outrages to political, economic, and social decency perpetrated by America's moral brigands: the Ku Klux Klan tarrings and featherings and the vigilante lynchings in Texas and Mississippi; the law of indissoluble marriage in South Carolina; the callous exploitation of women in New York factories and of under-age youths in Pennsylvania collieries; the "monstrous nonsense of Fundamentalism"[18] and freak legislation in Tennessee; the incarceration of the eugenics pioneer Moses Harman by postal censors and of the socialist labor leader Eugene Debs; the expulsion as "traitors" by the New York legislature of five properly elected members of the assembly because they were openly avowed members of the Socialist Party; the splenetic attacks on Mrs Warren's Profession by Anthony Comstock, secretary of the New York Society for the Suppression of Vice, who had labelled the playwright an "Irish smut dealer," and the removal of Man and Superman in 1905 from the shelves of the New York Public Library; the arrest and conviction in 1917 of a Detroit citizen for reading Shaw's novel An Unsocial Socialist in a street car! "Beneath their mask of civilization," Shaw insisted, "the American States have always remained primitive communities, and primitive communities naively persecute opinion as a matter of course." When, he inquired, "is the Bartholdi statue [of Liberty] to be pulled down?"[19]

It was not until 1933 that Shaw, at the age of seventy-seven, deigned to set foot on American soil, for the briefest of visits, as an interlude in an east to west round-the-world cruise aboard the Canadian Pacific steamship R.M.S. *Empress of Britain*, departing from Monaco on 16 December 1932. After several days in the Mediterranean and a tour of Egypt, the Shaws passed through the Suez Canal on New Year's day, and for five weeks explored the lands of the Orient. He cruised, Shaw later informed a colleague, because only on shipboard was it possible, when traveling, to get "a straight spell of work," and at the same time earn a real rest.[20] There was little work done, however, on his new play *On the Rocks*, and little opportunity for rest on the cruise. Even before they had arrived at their first "American" destination, Manila, where they lunched with the Governor of the Philippines, Theodore Roosevelt (son of the former president), on 9 February, the Shaws had been festooned with so many flowers, drenched with so much rosewater, and dotted with so much vermilion dye in the temples and homes they visited from India and Ceylon to China and Japan that, Shaw wrote to Nancy Astor, they "incessantly" cursed the day they were born and the hour of their sailing.[21]

Avoiding close-range attention was a passionate compulsion with GBS, and the ordeal of mob interviews an omnipresent terror. Even before the *Empress of Britain* called at Honolulu on 16 March, he was nervously anticipating and dreading the press furor that would inevitably await him in San Francisco. He served notice, before the docking, that he would grant neither general nor individual press interviews in Hawaii, but when a zealous and enterprising young reporter, Robert Brilliande of the *Honolulu Advertiser*, persuaded a member of the waterfront police squad guarding the Shaws to pass a note to GBS guaranteeing that Brilliande would, if granted an audience, do so "on the basis that George Bernard Shaw was a great human, a great dramatist, critic, and writer instead of the freakish picture of him one received from his latest publicity in American newspapers," Shaw consented to make an exception, provided the reporter bring no cameraman. Escorted to the top deck, Brilliande found Shaw, clad in two towels, one wrapped turban-style about his head, the other girdling his thin waist, "grunting and growling" as he exerted himself in toe-touching exercises. The ensuing interview, to Brilliande's joy, stretched out to two and a half hours.[22]

Affected by the heat the Shaws limited their exploration of the city to little more than a couple of automobile tours, though Shaw saw enough, apparently, to be able to report to Hamlin Garland that he had found the city of great interest "ethnographically" and "eugenically."[23] Receiving an invitation from Gregg M. Sinclair, President of the University of Hawaii, to attend the world première of Christopher Morley's play *Where the Blue Begins* at the university, Shaw accepted after extracting a guarantee that his presence would not be publicized, for he wished to remain as inconspicuous as possible so as not to steal the limelight from Morley, to whom he said it rightfully belonged. A student at the performance, unaware that she was violating the basic condition of Shaw's acceptance, attempted to place a lei round Shaw's neck, but was prevented by Sinclair. This elicited remarks in the press next day of "ungenerous conduct" by Shaw. He, however, apparently enjoyed the performance, being among the loudest in the audience in the cry for "Author, Author" at the finish, and encouraged presentation of the lei to Morley. Shaw had, Sinclair informed the press a few days later, been "the soul of courtesy and good humor." He neglected to mention that Shaw had dressed him down about the diction of the performers, which he referred to as "infamous."[24] A layover of several hours at Hilo on 19 March completed the Hawaiian visit.

Even before the *Empress* docked at San Francisco at eight P.M. on 23 March the ship swarmed with a regiment of reporters and cameramen that had come aboard with the immigration and health authorities.[25] Charlotte, the "pleasant, motherly-looking woman [who] appears diminutive beside her tall husband," overwhelmed by their number, clamor, and vehemence, retreated in alarm, informing her husband, "I'll wait for you in the cabin till it's all over." As the shutters clicked, the cameras ground, and the vociferous reporters snapped out questions, Shaw accepted an official welcome from Mayor Angelo J. Rossi and a delegation of municipal officers, reminding them that he had himself served as a municipal vestryman and councillor for six years. He then resigned himself to the hundreds of inane and banal questions flung at him, which he answered flippantly and with occasional asperity. Only a few times did he respond animatedly and with conviction, as when asked about the new German chancellor. "Germany is in chaos, like America, groping about like America, and willing to try Hitler like you are trying Roosevelt" (which he invariably pronounced "Roseyvelt"). He vehemently denounced the Jewish atrocities. "Why," he asked, "should the Jews be persecuted? Why should such a terrible thing go on. . . . It's horrible and unthinkable."

One subject demonstrably caused him personal torment, the imprisonment of Tom Mooney, who had been found guilty seventeen years earlier for alleged participation in a Remembrance Day parade bombing. When a letter from Mooney was delivered to him in Tokyo, through the offices of a defense committee, soliciting his intervention, Shaw apologetically cabled regrets on the grounds that the interference of a Communist foreign celebrity would carry little weight with the authorities.[26] Questioned about Mooney aboard ship, Shaw declined, "as a visitor," to express an opinion on the merits of the case, but added, his voice "tinged with fire," his frail body stiffening with indignation, "I cannot pretend that I am not shocked at having any person put into a vault for 16 or 17 years. . . . Unfortunately the Mooney case has been made an instrument of attack upon the government and the constitution and Mr. Mooney has been made a political martyr. I would like to see the case treated as simply from a humanitarian angle. I would be afraid to go to see him because it might do him more harm than good. . . . My sole concern would be to get Mr. Mooney out of that vault. . . . It would be a great relief to my feelings if the Governor would pardon him."

As the torrent of tiresome questions continued, Shaw grew perceptibly testy, finally blurting out, "You've had enough of me—and I've had enough of you. Good night." The press was, however, back in force next morning as the Shaws arrived at Mills Field to fly to San Simeon to join William Randolph Hearst and his mistress Marion Davies, having seen no more of San Francisco than the fleeting glimpse provided by the limousine ride from the dock, augmented subsequently by a view of rooftops from aloft. Boarding Hearst's black tri-motored plane, escorted by Hearst's son George, the Shaws departed, but not before GBS, apparently recuperated from the previous evening's ordeal by a good sleep, had "hurl[ed] Shavian javelins of wit" at the newsmen and camera crews.[27]

For the next four days the Shaws were entertained by Hearst at his palatial ranch, surrounded by more than forty guests, most of them women, including several of Miss Davies's chums and a bevy of "young sirens" provided by the Metro-Goldwyn-Mayer studio from its contract lists. Every afternoon at teatime Shaw held court for such fawning Hollywoodites as Constance Talmadge, Maureen O'Sullivan, Dorothy Mackail, Juliette Compton, Mary Brian, the Adolphe Menjous and the Walter Wangers. Mornings Shaw swam in the two lavish pools, preferring the out-of-doors pool to the indoor one but deprecating the heating of the water. He and Charlotte strolled in the grounds surrounding the imposing mansion. Shaw, who rose before any of the others, made dawn inspections of the considerable menagerie maintained by Hearst, commenting particularly on the eagles, zebras, and apes. He indulged Hearst's gossip columnist Louella Parsons with an interview, then entirely rewrote it. And he took time to write a lengthy letter of sympathy to Tom Mooney.

Each afternoon there was badinage and a bit of flirtation with a co-quetting hostess, who teasingly besought Shaw to cede her film rights to his plays, and long secluded talks about politics with the host, for whom he inscribed at length a copy of the American edition of his recently published book *What I Really Wrote about the War*. In the evening there were film screenings, notably of a new MGM film, *Gabriel Over the White House*, a fantasy produced by Walter Wanger in which a crook becomes president of the United States and then mysteriously reforms. Shaw, as-tutely noting the veiled allusions to the New Deal, suggested that the screenplay had been secretly written by President Roosevelt to induce the American public to grant him dictatorial powers.[28]

On 28 March the Shaws set forth for Santa Monica, where they were to be met and transported to the MGM studio at Culver City for lunch, thence to the harbor to rejoin the ship. It was raining, however, and the plane's pilot Ray Crawford, confronted with a dangerously low ceiling as the craft hugged the coast, elected to make a sudden detour, landing bumpily, barely averting disaster, on a narrow strip of sandy beach at the mouth of Puerto Canyon, two miles north of Malibu. The stranded Shaws, shaken and somewhat unnerved, accepted with alacrity an offer from a UCLA sophomore, George O'Connor, to convey them in his "ramshackle" flivver to Culver City. O'Connor, interviewed later, said he could not recall "a cockeyed thing Shaw said that was really funny," which was not at all remarkable under the circumstances.[29]

At the Metro studio Shaw was guided to the ornate bungalow built for Marion Davies, where he and Charlotte gathered at the lunch tables with Hearst (whom Shaw accused of having arranged the plane incident for newspaper headlines) and Miss Davies, studio head Louis B. Mayer, Charles Chaplin, Clark Gable, John Barrymore, O. P. Heggie (who had played Androcles in the original London production of *Androcles and the Lion* in 1913), actresses Una Merkel and Eileen Percy, writers John W. Considine, Jr., and Harry Crocker, director Robert Z. Leonard, and Mr. and Mrs. George Hearst. Lunch was followed by a tour of the studio lot and several of its sound stages, where the Shaws met a parade of stars, most of whom, to judge from the newspaper reports, were singularly lacking in sense of humor and predisposed to snub the guest of honor, possibly in retaliation for Shaw's frequent disparaging remarks in pre-vious years about cinema being, as practiced in Hollywood, an inferior art, with "conceit . . . rampant" and "good sense . . . nonexistent."[30] Few seemed amused by Shaw's sallies, with which he fumblingly sought to lighten the tense, almost frigid atmosphere, and which Marion Davies later was to derogate as "that caustic Irish wit which is very detestable."[31]

With the exception of Heggie, with whom Shaw conversed privately for a few moments, and Jean Hersholt, whom Charlotte recognized on a set, and who was led in surprise to meet the visitors, no performer they encountered that afternoon had a kind remark to make about GBS in subsequent interviews. Upon his departure for the *Empress of Britain*, where Upton Sinclair waited to greet him, Shaw, spotting the two motorcycle police escorts flanking the limousine, tossed out a comically apt parting shot: "[It's] the only time they ever called the police to get me out of town."[32]

A fortnight later, after a passage through the Panama Canal and a day's stopover at Havana, where Shaw granted an extended interview to the press, the *Empress of Britain* steamed up New York Harbor, past the Statue of Liberty, which Shaw had long before announced he had no desire to see, for "even my appetite for irony does not go as far as that,"[33] and at ten A.M. on 11 April docked at Pier 61, on West 21st Street. Again the ship was overrun with pressmen and film cameras, but Shaw, who had dined three hours earlier on porridge, grapefruit, toast, marmalade, and hot water with lemon (which reporters on both coasts mistook for tea), had retreated to his stateroom, determined not to submit to another ordeal-by-interview before giving his scheduled lecture that evening in the Metropolitan Opera House. "I don't want to [have to] lick Dempsey in the afternoon and whip Tunney in the evening," he had explained at sea several days earlier, confessing that he trembled at the prospect of "what the reporters will do to me." At first he had determined not to grant a press interview at all, preparing instead a mimeographed self-drafted interview that he arranged for the visiting Archibald Henderson to distribute to the reporters on board that morning. At breakfast, however, he relented to the extent of posting on his cabin door a drafted message: "The New York press may return to its firesides and nurse the baby until tomorrow morning, except the enterprising section which came on board at Havana, and discussed everything with me for an hour and forty minutes. Today I am in training for the Metropolitan Opera House tonight, and may be regarded as deaf and dumb for the moment. With regrets and apologies. GBS." The ship's master at arms, posted by the captain in response to Shaw's request that he be provided with protection, stood guard before the cabin door for more than two hours, keeping off the persistent pressmen, who clamored for Shaw to emerge. At last Henderson came forth from the stateroom to announce that Shaw had consented to be photographed, if they would move up to the top deck, but that he remained pledged to say nothing to reporters until after his lecture.

Striving to supplant acerbity with urbanity, Shaw appeared before the photographers and movie cameramen, relaxedly posing for them, creating "scenarios" for movie scenes that involved his greeting Henderson, and registering mock astonishment as they focused their lenses "from the tops of ventilators and deck houses, and hanging on boat davits."

One photographer, to Shaw's genuine astonishment, "crawled along an awning boom directly over the scene," clicking his shutter as GBS stared openmouthed up at him. When, however, a photographer demanded that Shaw hold a pose because color photography took longer, he impatiently grabbed the man by the shoulders and, mumbling "Damn color photography," shook him backward and forward, "looking into his face quizzically, as if he really were trying to find out how an American camera man reacted when rocked." At length, in response to an appeal for a further pose, Shaw "executed a deliberately monstrous yawn," and stalked off, grinning.[34]

By now Howard C. Lewis, director of Dodd, Mead and Company, Shaw's newly appointed American publisher (supplanting the bankrupted Brentano's), and Frank Dodd had arrived to spirit the Shaws away from the ship for a drive, suggested to Lewis by Shaw's English publisher, Otto Kyllmann. Escaping contentedly from the hundred and fifty oppressive journalists and cameramen, the Shaws rode peacefully through the incredible city, Shaw "cran[ing] his neck like any tourist to look at the Empire State Building until he almost fell out of the automobile, and . . . turn[ing] round to look over his shoulder at it so long that he rode backward through the spectacle of one of the great crossroads of the world at Fifth Avenue and Forty-Second Street." They drove through Times Square and up Broadway, Shaw remarking on the desperate men, some of them well dressed, whom he saw shamelessly begging in the streets, through Central Park and west to Riverside Drive. They lunched privately and quietly at the Claremont Restaurant overlooking the Hudson, following which they crossed the newly completed George Washington Bridge, which appealed to GBS because "you can see the water flowing under it—so different from London bridges." The Palisades he thought a scenic wonder, and he was clearly impressed, driving down the Jersey shore, by his first glimpse of the New York skyline. He preferred, however, to reserve his opinion. The return to New York was made through the white-tile-lined and brilliantly lighted Holland Tunnel, the first vehicular tunnel to be constructed under the river. Asked later what he thought of this pride and joy of New York and New Jersey, Shaw remarked that it looked very much like "a dairy lunch."

A brief stop was made at the Dodd, Mead office at 443 Fourth Avenue, after which Shaw paid an unscheduled visit to the Theatre Guild's offices and theater, on 52nd Street near Eighth Avenue. At the building he was approached by an *Evening Journal* reporter, whom GBS mistook for an attendant. Leaving Charlotte and Lewis in the automobile, Shaw allowed the reporter to escort him, via a self-service elevator, up to the Theatre Guild office, which was occupied by only one of the directors, Philip Moeller.

"I couldn't," Shaw announced, "think of coming [to New York], without coming in to pay my respects." When he expressed a desire to see the theater stage and auditorium the reporter volunteered to steer him. Moeller, mistaking the reporter for Shaw's official guide, allowed him to lead the way. GBS strode commandingly across the stage, poised himself behind the footlights, addressed a few words to the darkened house, then burst into a run of the scales in a quavering baritone. "Fine," he declared, after listening for an instant; "no echoes." Descending into the auditorium, he proceeded up an aisle and down a flight of stairs to the central lobby, where he studied a bust of himself by Troubetskoy. "It needs to be rubbed down with vaseline," he commented; "it looks a little neglected." As they departed through a lobby door to the street, the bogus attendant, whom Shaw politely thanked, confessed he was a newspaper man. "You should have told me," said Shaw; "I want to give no interviews." "You didn't ask me," said the reporter candidly, adding that he represented the Hearst press. Shaw, volunteering that he had "a genuine admiration" for Hearst, proceeded to relate to the reporter the story of the forced landing of the plane in California. Then, ducking into the waiting limousine, Shaw headed back to the *Empress of Britain* for a brief respite before the evening's ordeal.[35]

Shaw's scheduled address that evening, titled "The Future of Political Science in America," was presented under the auspices of the non-profit Academy of Political Science. For more than thirty years American entrepreneurs had dangled lucrative lecture contracts under Shaw's nose, unaware that he had never in his entire public career accepted a fee for a lecture. One New York society dowager had offered him a fee of £500 "on condition that the first words that [he] breathed with American air should be uttered in her drawing-room." Though Shaw frequently made pretense of entertaining the proposals, he had no intention of accepting them; he merely "like[d] to know [his] market-value as a matter of business and personal vanity."[36] When, however, he received on shipboard a cabled invitation from the Academy of Political Science, he set aside his resolve to make the American visit a strictly private one. It was his contention that nothing but political science could save American civilization, which in turn affected all civilization, and he looked upon the Academy as the most important institution in the United States and considered its invitation a mandate.[37] For the same reason he consented to a national radio broadcast of the lecture, so long as the talk be aired in its entirety, and on condition that the microphone be so placed as not to hamper his freedom of movement. Under the impression that the Academy would profit by the lecture, and that use of a mammoth auditorium would increase the potential profit, Shaw acquiesced in the selection of the Metropolitan Opera House, which accommodated more than 3,500 people. The Academy, however, sold its tickets at break-even prices, mostly to its own members. Consequently, many of Shaw's acquaintances were unable to gain admission.

Held back by a heavy complement of city police, frustrated ticket seekers by the hundreds formed crowds around the building as Shaw arrived at the stage door. There he was greeted by several visitors, including the omnipresent Archibald Henderson and Dr. Charles F. Pabst, advocate of vaccination with whom the anti-vaccinationist Shaw had debated in correspondence two years earlier. He posed backstage briefly for photographers, then at 8:35 was led on to the vast stage by acting chairman Jackson E. Reynolds, president of the First National Bank, and an Academy trustee, Thomas W. Lamont, senior partner of J. P. Morgan and Company. After a brief standing ovation for the guest of honor, all settled down for an uncomfortable ten minute delay for the convenience of the National Broadcasting Company's radio schedule.

Shaw appeared to be nervous and fidgety as he gazed out at the capacity audience, most of whom in the orchestra and Diamond Horseshoe circle were resplendent in evening dress, though ordinary dress predominated in the upper levels. He sat at first with arms "folded across the breast of his tightly fitting blue sack coat, then with his hands clasped in his lap, again with one hand raised to the trimmed white beard . . . now with his massive high-domed head sunk brooding on his chest so that the white beard obscured his dark four-in-hand scarf, again with his head jerked around sharply as he talked with some one [Ethel Warner, director of the Academy] sitting behind him. Continually his long, thin, pale fingers reached up and stroked his white beard or mustache." As the restless audience began to clap its hands and stamp its feet, Shaw consulted his watch, then folded his arms anew, the "picture of determination," until Reynolds rose precisely at 8:45 to introduce the speaker.

Shaw, admitting he felt "an irresistible urge to sing" in such surroundings, began to speak. Initially nervous, "he continued to clasp and unclasp his hands alternately, fold his arms across his breast occasionally and stroke his beard" as he spoke. Soon he settled down into his familiar casual platform manner. Occasionally he referred to notes (now in Cornell University's Burgunder Collection), but spoke extemporaneously, his voice clear and distinct, with only "the barest perceptible traces of an English pronunciation or an Irish brogue at times." With no strain, no apparent effort, Shaw's voice penetrated the reaches of the immense auditorium.

The address proved to be an eclectic one, loosely organized, whizzing through an overwhelming and sometimes bewildering range of topics that included American hospitality and love of publicity, "immorality" in Hollywood, Mormonism, American anarchism, U.S. relations with Soviet Russia, the World Economic Conference, dictators, war debts and their repudiation, unemployment, high finance and a policy of increased exports, and the 100% American. Much of it was shrewd dialectic in Shaw's enjoyable lighthearted style, with some surprising twists and amusingly appropriate metaphor, and though Shaw told Lowell Brentano his speech would consist of some "unpopular" but "necessary" criticisms,[38] he seemed to exercise great restraint in his remarks, trying to appear jovial rather than contentious. There was dead silence at a few places where Shaw had evidently anticipated responses, which seemed to distress him, as evidenced by ensuing remarks. He was, however, frequently interrupted by laughter and applause through most of the address, with the audience being particularly responsive when he proposed that Americans help Roosevelt by dismissing Congress and when he described America as a nation of anarchists who resent and resist being governed and who celebrate this "freedom" symbolically by setting up in New York harbor a "monstrous idol which you call Liberty. The only thing that remains to complete that monument is to put on its pedestal the inscription written by Dante on the gate of hell: 'All hope abandon ye who enter here.'"

His heaviest salvos were aimed at the American Constitution, which he had years before described as "that foolish, obsolete and obstructive document which destroys life, persecutes liberty and makes the pursuit of happiness a chase after other people's dollars,"[39] and whose existence reduced vital process to dogmatic formula. As interpreted by the United States Supreme Court and by the public at large, the Constitution, he had noted on another occasion, "is simply a charter of Anarchism in its worst form of industrial Laissez Faire, or Let It Rip."[40] Now he called again for its banishment: "get rid of it," he pleaded, "at all hazards," and make a new one, which would emancipate President Roosevelt from handicap by the old one, and which would steer America away from oppressive rule by its Trusts, dominated by John D. Rockefeller and Standard Oil, which seek to prevent Roosevelt from carrying out his programs, and from its corruptive bankers by a nationalization of the banks. Reaction to these comments varied from one section of the house to another, the attacks on capitalism meeting with stony reserve from the bankers on stage and the plutocrats in the five-dollar seats, but with vociferous enthusiasm from the one-dollar seats high in the gallery. Shaw, after a loud cheer from aloft in response to his statement that unemployment was the result of a breakdown of capitalism, conjectured that the response betokened the presence of some of the unemployed in the upper reaches of the house.

The lecture was a lengthy one—an hour and forty minutes—running until 10:25, pre-empting air performances of the previously scheduled

Willard Robison Orchestra, the soprano Alice Mock, and poet Edgar A. Guest. Shaw concluded with a tribute to Henry George, the American who had "set me on the economic trail," converting Shaw to socialism in 1883, and a call again to the Academy and its supporters to find a means to "save America," which he had earlier stressed must provide leadership that would save civilization from the ruin which previous civilizations had met in the history of the human race. Not more than half a dozen listeners exited prematurely, and the audience as it departed seemed enthusiastic, sympathetic and generally impressed. Next morning, however, there was criticism that Shaw had been garrulous, rambling, patronizing and naive. Even GBS, after glancing through a verbatim transcription of the full lecture, published in both the *New York Herald Tribune* and the *New York Times* and filling one entire page and a considerable part of the next one, lamented that "Some of it was very bad—I'm afraid I bungled a great deal of it." Nevertheless, he arranged for Dodd, Mead to publish the lecture, assigning his royalty to the Academy of Political Science. The published text was, however, considerably at variance with the verbatim text, the result, Shaw claimed, of an inaccurate and sometimes senseless transcription, which had necessitated much revision and touching up to make the lecture presentable for publication. For the English edition he altered the title to *The Political Madhouse in America and Nearer Home* and added a brief introduction.

Immediately after the lecture Shaw was escorted by Thomas Lamont to a limousine waiting outside the stage door, in which he was whisked off to Lamont's home at 107 E. 70th Street for a very brief reception. He was then driven back to the ship, which he boarded a few minutes past midnight.[41] There was little sleep, for at eight in the morning Shaw, sans Charlotte (who complained of "ptomaine" from her only meal ashore), entertained at breakfast his longtime friends Sasha Kropotkin and the actor Robert Loraine, who had created the role of Tanner in the American production of *Man and Superman* in 1906, and Lawrence Langner and his wife Armina Marshall, of the Theatre Guild. Later in the morning he received his American copyright attorney Benjamin H. Stern, the publisher William H. Wise, who had issued the Ayot St. Lawrence thirty-volume collected edition of Shaw's works in America, and Anna George de Mille, daughter of Henry George, with George's young granddaughter Agnes in tow, for whom Shaw inscribed a copy of *Progress and Poverty*. There was time only for the hastiest of conversations with his visitors, to Shaw's annoyance, for he was soon enveloped in what he called "the ballyhoo" aboard ship: the insatiable press that engulfed him whichever way he turned, the ubiquitous Chuzzlewittian representatives of the *New York Sewer*, the *New York Stabber*, the *New York Peeper*, the *New York Plunderer*, the *New York Family Spy*, and the *New York Rowdy Jour-*

nal, bombarding the trapped celebrity with mostly predictable questions, which he treated, in the opinion of one journalist, as "a form of intellectual calisthenics." Most of Shaw's replies were, however, formulaic and familiar, things he had iterated to interviewers at every ship stop across the globe. "If you ask me how I would like to contemplate an eternity of George Bernard Shaw," he told them, "I should like to know how you yourselves would like to contemplate George Bernard Shaw going on forever. You would have a shriek of despair and horror rising from humanity."

He informed the east coast journalists as he had done their west coast counterparts when they pressed him about Hitler, "The only thing I can say is that a man who may be said to base his career on an attempt to persecute the Jews is like an officer in the army who begins his career by cheating at cards"; and he injected his oft-reiterated analogy of the persecution of Catholics in America by the Ku Klux Klan. Queried about the future of civilization, he resurrected the prediction he had made in South Africa two years earlier, that "the next great civilization may come from the Negro race." Disconcerted by rude photographers who set off their "flash-lights" inches from his face; disrespectfully jostled by cameramen as they sought to catch him in awkward postures and with off-guard expressions; plagued by endless streams of asinine questions, the thoroughly exhausted writer fought to conceal his exasperation and contempt. Ultimately, having upbraided Americans for their obsessive interest in celebrities—"Americans have a passion for admiring something. Why, for instance, are you all around me here?"—and determined not to dignify with a response a question as to whether, if there were "a sort of over-dictator" of the world, Shaw would be competent to fill the job, GBS resolutely announced, "Gentlemen, the time is up," and stalked off to his cabin. Minutes later the *Empress of Britain* steamed eastward for home, and Shaw celebrated his freedom by settling into a deck-chair and returning to concentrated work on the draft of *On the Rocks*.[42]

Three years later, after a journey to New Zealand via the Panama Canal in 1934 and a west-to-east voyage round the entire African coast in 1935, the Shaws set out in 1936 on what was to be their last trip abroad, sailing from Southampton on 22 January in the Blue Star Line's S. S. *Arandora Star* on a seventy-five day cruise. The Atlantic crossing was a stormy one, which made Shaw violently ill and queasy for the first time since his crossing to Jamaica quarter of a century earlier, and he was disinclined, upon his arrival in Miami on 4 February, to undergo a chaotic press reception similar to the ones he had experienced at the hands of the American press in 1933. As the interviewers eagerly pressed round, Shaw firmly anticipated them. "I know what you are going to ask," he said. "You're going to ask me how I like Miami. . . . right? Well,

I don't like it. I haven't seen it yet." Settling determinedly in a chair, looking jaunty in tan trousers, grey pullover sweater, checkered cap, and white shoes, Shaw granted the press a controlled, low-keyed interview of approximately an hour, informing them, "You have a good President here, but your Supreme Court and Constitution hold him back. I told you Americans in New York several years ago you should abolish your Constitution. You didn't listen to me. Now you're up to your necks in trouble." Expressing vexation at the noisy salute by motorists honking auto horns along the county causeway to the ship moving down the channel, he suggested "you should greet visitors in respectable silence." Interrupting the session he accepted official greetings from Mayor A.D.H. Fossey and other city dignitaries, but declined a chamber of commerce suggestion that a tree be planted in his honor, modestly insisting that he'd be long forgotten before it was fully grown.[43]

For the two nights ashore the Shaws occupied a suite at the Hotel Deauville, of which Bernarr Macfadden, publisher of *Physical Culture* and renowned health faddist, was proprietor. In the morning, after Shaw had attempted to swim in the Atlantic surf, both Shaws visited MacFadden briefly before being conducted on a city tour in a police department limousine. Following lunch and a nap aboard ship, Shaw was escorted by the secretary of the Miami Chamber of Commerce to International Airport, where he inspected the Pan American Airways key base. Interestingly, Shaw climbed into clipper ships and questioned pilots about landings, takeoffs, blind flying, physical requirements of fliers, and all phases of aeronautics. Clambering down a ladder after inspecting the interior of one of the immense seaplanes, he suggested that his escorts not report this to Charlotte, who had stayed with the ship. Hovering in the background throughout the Miami visit, she had frequently been heard to admonish her husband not to exert himself in the heat. When one of the airline officials apprised GBS that British colonies were now only two hours' flying time from Miami, he remarked wryly, "Parliament could give several of those islands away each year and the English people would never know it."

Learning that the noted vegetarian and health apostle Dr. John Kellogg resided in Miami, Shaw scrapped the remainder of the day's scheduled sightseeing itinerary, collected Charlotte, and instructed the chauffeur to detour to Kellogg's Miami—Battle Creek Sanitarium and Health Spa, in Miami Springs, where the uninvited Shaws remained for a dinner of roast spinach, boiled cabbage, tropical fruits, and "native delicacies." Kellogg and Shaw, two abstemious octogenarians (Shaw was now in his eightieth year, with his birthday five months away), posed for the cameras, despite Shaw's insistence earlier in the day that newsmen would be barred for the remainder of the visit. His responses were brief and sharp-edged, perhaps a result of having perused the garbled reports and inaccuracies in that morning's newspapers, including the statement that one of "the better known of his many novels" was titled *The Political Madhouse in America and Nearer Home!*[44]

The Shaws returned to the *Arandora Star* on the last morning, where GBS remained secluded until the mid-afternoon departure. The ship proceeded to Havana, then southwest to the Panama Canal, which it traversed on the 11th, steaming onward to Hawaii. Shaw, affected by the heat, found that when he attempted to write he would fall asleep between each sentence. During the three-day stopover in Honolulu, from the 24th to the 27th, the Shaws visited with Charles Chaplin. On 4 March they arrived again in San Francisco, encountering the inevitable reporters and their inevitable questions, to which GBS supplied the inevitable answers, interspersed with a surprising comment that the new Golden Gate Bridge was "a beastly object" and the admission that he did not consider himself a success, for "his solutions for the world's troubles had not been accepted." The successful man, he pronounced, "is the one who has people doing what he wants them to do. . . . But they're always doing what I don't want them to do."[45]

As on the previous visit the Shaws saw virtually nothing of San Francisco, for that evening they boarded a sleeper train for a rail excursion to the Grand Canyon, which they reached early on the morning of the 6th, for a twelve-hour visit. On the south rim of the canyon they unexpectedly encountered a fellow tourist, J. B. Priestley, who had been spending the winter in Arizona and was visiting the awesome natural monument. In his autobiography Priestley recorded that Shaw had been peevish, refusing "to wonder and exclaim at the Grand Canyon, muttering something about Cheddar Gorge. The truth was, I am afraid, that he was determinedly resisting the spell of this marvel, at once awe-inspiring and beautiful, the most ego-shrinking of all earth's spectacles." Yet a *New York Times* correspondent indicated that "a strangely solemn" GBS had gazed at the canyon in wonderment and proclaimed "it reminds me of religion . . . the canyon and the truths of religion are always the same." He was attracted too by the exquisite birds that populated the area, though he admitted regretfully that "the extent of my [ornithological] knowledge is to distinguish a parrot from a canary." Asked by a park official what name he might suggest in the event a decision were made to name after him one of the scenic points in the canyon formations, Shaw promptly responded "Shawnee."[46]

A return train journey that night, to rejoin the *Arandora Star* at San Pedro, brought the Shaws to Los Angeles around noon on the 7th, with only nine hours before sailing. They decided to motor to Marion Davies's beach house, only to discover there that she had gone to Santa Barbara. Her response, "in her characteristic laconic style," when GBS tele-phoned her, was, "Well, why didn't you tell me you were coming, toots?"[47] Their chauffeur steered the Shaws to a quiet hotel dining room for lunch. Almost as soon as they were seated they were confronted, anti-climactically, by a most obnoxious reporter, who identified himself as Timothy Glutzspiegel and insisted on an interview. Shaw, glaring at him, announced resolutely that he had, at the train station, given all the interviews that he intended to give before his departure, and grew even more incensed when the unflappable young barbarian waved these off as "old stuff . . . You only repeated yourself." A series of anger-inducing questions, an uninvited partaking of some of Shaw's tomato juice, an insulting comment that Shaw "ought to keep up with current events" better than he did, and a startling burst of doubletalk culminated in the revelation that GBS had been the latest victim of a notorious Hollywood prankster, Vince Barnett. Shaw, laughing heartily, shook hands with Barnett, invited him to share the rest of the tomato juice, and departed for San Pedro.[48]

At ten that night the *Arandora Star* headed out for Mexico. Shaw never saw the United States again—except in the cinema.

Notes

I am grateful to Professors Josephine Johnson, University of Miami, Coral Gables, Florida, for research assistance on the Miami visit, and Stanley Weintraub for calling Luke Barnett's book *Between the Ribs* to my attention.

Dates and other details of Shaw's travel itinerary are derived primarily from his pocket engagements diaries, now in the British Library of Political and Economic Science.

1. "Bernard Shaw on American Women," *Cosmopolitan* (New York), 43 (September 1907), 557–61.

2. *The Irrational Knot* (London: Constable, 1931), 330.

3. Archibald Henderson, *Table-Talk of G.B.S.* (New York: Harper, 1925), 77.

4. "Roosevelt Guildhall Speech Ridiculed by Bernard Shaw," *New York American* (3 June 1910), 1.

5. "A Nation of Villagers," *Everybody's* (New York), 17 (December 1907), 861–65.

6. "Americans Cannot Govern Themselves," *New York Journal* (3 March 1901), 25.

7. "Why I Won't Go to America," *The Observer*, London (15 February 1920), 9.

8. "Why I Won't Go to America."

9. Undated letter to Charles Frohman, in "Shaw's Fatal Good Looks," *The Sun*, New York (5 December 1909), 1.

10. Letter to Frank Harris, 4 January 1918, in *The Playwright and the Pirate: Bernard*

Shaw and Frank Harris: A Correspondence, ed. Stanley Weintraub (University Park: Pennsylvania State University Press, 1982), 73.

11. "A Nation of Villagers."

12. Letter to New York Chapter of the Drama League of America, in "Shaw Gives Reasons for not Visiting Us," *New York Times* (3 January 1917), 9.

13. "What about the Middle Class? A Lay Sermon" (Part 2), *Daily Citizen*, London (19 October 1912), 4.

14. "Shaw Proud of His Play [*Mrs Warren's Profession*]," *The Sun*, New York (1 November 1905), 6.

15. "Shaw's Fatal Good Looks."

16. Letter to Frank Harris, 4 January 1918, in *The Playwright and the Pirate*, p. 74.

17. "Admirers Extol Harman as Martyr," *New York Times* (28 March 1910), 4.

18. "Where Darwin is Taboo: The Bible in America," *New Leader* (London), 12 (10 July 1925), 10–11.

19. "Savages Still, Says Shaw, of Americans," *Viereck's* (New York), 12 (March 1920), 22.

20. Postcard to W. J. Bassett-Lowke, 6 January 1936: unpublished (Humanities Research Center, University of Texas at Austin).

21. Letter to Nancy Astor, 13 January 1933: unpublished (Reading University Library).

22. Robert Brilliande, "Long-Ago Impressions of Bernard Shaw," *Independent Shavian* (New York), 12 (Winter 1973–74), 20.

23. Letter to Hamlin Garland, 2 April 1933: unpublished (Doheny Library, University of Southern California).

24. Letter from Gregg M. Sinclair to the Editor, *Honolulu Advertiser*, 23 March 1933: carbon (Sinclair Papers, University of Hawaii Library); letter to Hamlin Garland, 2 April 1933.

25. The description of the San Francisco interview is a conflation of reports: "Shaw Jovial on Arriving in San Francisco," *New York American* (24 March 1933), 3; "Shaw Hops Off for Visit to W. R. Hearst," *New York Evening Journal* (24 March 1933), 3, 8; "Happiest People Found in Cemeteries, Says Shaw, Wit Clicking with Cameras," *New York Evening Journal* (24 March 1933), 1.

26. Cable (transcription) to Tom Mooney Defence Committee, 8 March 1933: unpublished? (Mooney Papers, Bancroft Library, University of California at Berkeley).

27. "Shaw and Wife are Guests at Hearst Ranch," *New York American* (25 March 1933), 3; "Shaw Bests Army of Interviewers," *New York Times* (25 March 1933), 17.

28. Louella O. Parsons, "Witty Shaw 'Holds Court' at California Ranch," *New York American* (27 March 1933), 3; *The Speech of Mr. G. Bernard Shaw in New York*, ed. Ch. Yoshida (Osaka: privately printed, 1933), 43–62; letter (transcription) to Tom Mooney, 27 March 1933: unpublished? (Mooney Papers, Bancroft Library).

29. "Unawed Youth Gives Shaw Lift in Flivver," *St. Louis Post-Dispatch* (29 March 1933), 3B.

30. Henderson, p. 50.

31. Marion Davies, *The Times We Had*, eds. Pamela Pfau and Kenneth S. Marx (Indianapolis: Bobbs-Merrill, 1975), 138.

32. "Shavian Wit Sparkles as He Visits Studios," *New York American* (29 March 1933), 5; Edwin Schallert, "Mr. Shaw Shakes Up Hollywood," *Movie Classic* (Chicago), 4 (June 1933), 26, 62–63.

33. "Shaw's Fatal Good Looks."

34. "Shaw to Shun N.Y. Reporters," *New York Evening Journal* (7 April 1933), 19; "Shaw Here Today for 26-Hour Visit," *New York Times* (11 April 1933), 21; "Shaw Tours City, But Dodges Press," *New York Times* (12 April 1933), 15.

35. Letter from Howard C. Lewis to Otto Kyllmann, 17 April 1933: unpublished (Southern Historical Collection, University of North Carolina at Chapel Hill); Ernest S.

Greene, "Shaw in New York": unpublished typescript, 2 pp., 12 December 1959 (Henry W. and Albert A. Berg Collection, New York Public Library); "Shaw Tours City, But Dodges Press"; "Goes Aboard Ship to Rest for Speech," *New York Evening Journal* (11 April 1933), 1, 6.

36. Undated letter to Anthony Hope Hawkins, in Sir Charles Mallet, *Anthony Hope and His Books* (London: Hutchinson, 1935), 171.

37. Letter (transcription) to Ethel Warner, 14 March 1933: unpublished (Columbia University Library).

38. Letter to Lowell Brentano, 14 March 1933: unpublished (University of Oregon Library).

39. "Americans Cannot Govern Themselves."

40. "A Nation of Villagers."

41. "Shaw Tells Nation It Must Lead to Save Civilization from Ruin" (accompanied by full verbatim text of lecture), *New York Times* (12 April 1933), 1, 14–15; *The Future of Political Science in America* (New York: Dodd, Mead, 1933); "All Americans Are—You're Right, It's Shaw Finally Facing Press Battery—and a Bit Testy," with by-line of Joseph Mitchell, *New York World-Telegram* (12 April 1933), 1, 2; letter to Theresa Helburn, 13–14 March 1933: unpublished (Beinecke Library, Yale University); letter to Elbridge L. Adams, 5 May 1933: unpublished (Humanities Research Center); "Shaw, Sailing, Fears He Bungled Speech," *New York Times* (13 April 1933), 19.

42. Lawrence Langner, "A Morning with G.B.S.," *The Stage* (New York), 10 (June 1933), 16; "Shaw, Sailing, Fears He Bungled Speech."

43. "George Bernard Shaw Arrives Here on Cruise from England," *Miami Herald* (5 February 1936), 1, 4.

44. "Shaw, Visiting Miami, Advises Us To Chuck Constitution Into Ocean," *New York Times* (5 February 1936), 21; "Shaw Talks of New Play as He Eats Spinach and Cabbage," *Miami Herald* (6 February 1936), 9B; "'Not for $50,000,000,' Says Shaw at Miami," *New York Times* (6 February 1936), 8; "Arandora Star Sails from Port of Miami," *Miami Herald* (7 February 1936), 13.

45. "People Love Him Shaw Tells Press," *New York Times* (5 March 1936), 24.

46. J. B. Priestley, *Margin Released* (New York: Harper and Row, 1962), 166; "Shaw Sees Grand Canyon," *New York Times* (7 March 1936), 11.

47. Louella O. Parsons, "Marion Davies and G.B.S. Go on Spoofing Jaunt," *New York American* (11 March 1936), 8.

48. Luke Barnett (as told to George E. Kelly), *Between the Ribs* (Philadelphia: Dorrance, 1945), 219–21; "Shaw is Badgered by an Interviewer," *New York Times* (8 March 1936), 36.

Murray S. Martin

"IF I SHOWED MY TRUE FEELINGS": SHAW IN NEW ZEALAND

Shaw's visit to New Zealand, although a minor event in his busy life, took place at a time when he was belligerently anti-democratic and provided him with a ready platform for expounding his views. He had just finished writing (22 October 1933) the Preface to *On the Rocks*, although it had not yet been published. After his return, he replied to a questionnaire from Andrew E. Malone concerning the play; when read in the context of that response, most of his New Zealand remarks, collected in *What I Said in New Zealand*,[1] seem part of a continuum. During the voyage he worked upon two other plays, *The Simpleton of the Unexpected Isles: a Vision of Judgment* and *The Millionairess*. The question of any interaction between the experiences of the voyage and the plays themselves can probably never be satisfactorily resolved and is perhaps relatively unimportant. The major interest is to trace the parallels between what he said and what he wrote. There is also the interest of having a relatively well documented episode in the life of Shaw the public man. To this can be added a variety of small but revealing details, such as a list of the books he donated to the ship's library and the dietary instructions issued by Charlotte.

Although the voyage was simply one of several undertaken at the insistence of his wife, the visit of so important a man of letters to a country which felt so keenly its remoteness from Europe could not be a private event. One of the minor controversies of the visit turns on New Zealand's ambivalent relationship with England. Shaw was, however, good at the role of tourist and found much scenery to admire in New Zealand. There was also a personal link, since in his early Fabian Society days Shaw had met some of New Zealand's influential early politicians and was interested to see what had happened to this far-flung social democracy. We sometimes forget how much occurs during a single life span, and it is a salutary reminder of our foreshortened perspective to realize that Shaw in 1934 could greet Peter Fraser, who was to be prime minister from 1941 to 1949, and Walter Nash (prime minister, 1957–1960) and recall having met W. Pember Reeves and Richard Seddon, premier from 1893 to 1906. A very striking example of this span occurred later in the visit when Shaw attended the film of *The Guardsman*, starring Lynne Fontanne, whose death was reported only in 1983 while this article was being written, and he could comment on her as an actress in his plays.

For Shaw, no doubt, the incidents of his tour were simply that, events soon to be displaced by many more, similar events. Yet what he said during that month epitomizes much of what is difficult to accept in the later Shaw. It is hard to separate Shaw the clown from Shaw the iconoclast. It is equally hard to know when he is speaking from the heart and when he is performing. The reported record of his interviews and addresses sparkles with the expected wit, but sometimes reporters and audiences were not sure what to accept as genuine. The few editorials were very disapproving of his attitudes on democracy.

The tour taken by the Shaws would still, despite the changes of fifty years, be a fairly standard itinerary. The Government Tourist Bureau might suggest the same things to a present-day visitor (except for the spectacular South Island scenery not then so readily accessible)—the sights of Auckland, the Waitomo Caves, Rotorua and the thermal region, the Chateau Tongariro, the Wanganui River, Wellington and Christchurch. The newspaper reports of the itinerary are frequently misleading, for the Shaws did make a major change by substituting a visit to Christchurch for an intended visit to Nelson. The Shaws, who had personal friends in New Zealand, also made time to meet political groups and undertook a few personal side-trips with their friends. Otherwise they were in the hands of the Bureau, which apparently performed very satisfactorily. At least they were thanked in a generous letter. (An itinerary is included as Appendix A.)

In the pretour publicity it was suggested erroneously that a major purpose of the visit was to study the Maori.[2] To this end Shaw was given several books by the High Commissioner, but some of these were, in fact, donated to the ship's library. Except in Rotorua, where he spent some time with Guide Rangi, Shaw had minimal contact with Maoris during his tour. He was more interested in airing his views on government and frequently sidestepped enquiries concerning race relations.

The New Zealand visited by the Shaws was beginning to emerge from the depths of the depression, and New Zealanders were consequently very interested in the economic and political upheavals affecting their overseas markets. Shaw appeared to be unaware of how traumatic an experience the Great Depression had been; even before setting foot in New Zealand he had remarked, "Apparently you have not experienced completely the smash we have had." Shaw was presumably speaking off the cuff, but he seems to have remained unaware of how deeply the worldwide economic collapse had affected New Zealand. After all, his own contacts were with those who were influential, affluent, and employed. He did comment that public works, on which the government had relied, were a poor solution, but the economic nationalism he preached was no better. Moreover, his fascination with Fascism and Communism forestalled his sympathy with and understanding of other political solutions. New Zealand was, in fact, preparing for a political revolution of far-reaching consequences that should have appealed to Shaw the Fabian. Peter Fraser, who met him at the ship, would become in 1935 the minister for health and education in the first Labour government, carrying on the first steps towards state socialism taken by Seddon in the 1890s. But facts never did seem to stand in Shaw's way when an *idée fixe* intervened or a witty riposte was possible.

During the tour his public utterances concentrated almost entirely on the disease of parliamentary democracy, but he showed great interest in seeing such practical things as the Wellington town milk supply and the Karitane children's home, and on speculating about the possibilities of thermal power—an apparent split between his public and private interests. With his disillusion at the turn which events had taken in the 1930s, his misanthropism had emerged strongly. While this is most clearly seen in his public utterances, it also shows in the plays and prefaces written at that time. What he said in New Zealand continues what he had written in the Preface to *On the Rocks*, completed only six months earlier, and reappears in the Malone interview published in the following August. Equally, however, it reflects a very strong current in contemporary European politics, a frustration at the seeming incompetence of all politicians and a willingness to surrender the future to any strong man who seemed to be able to overcome the effects of the depression.

Given this background it would be naive to expect addresses on literature and the arts, but it is surprising to find that in his first interview, on board RMS *Rangitane*, he concentrated on the evils of parliament and capitalism almost to the exclusion of any other topic. As the editor of the *Evening Post* remarked in an editorial on the press conference: "Once a fervent democrat, he has now a profound contempt for democracy and elective Parliament and a vaguer but apparently equally genuine admiration for dictators. So obsessed is he with his new faith and his new scepticism that he started talking about it before he landed."[3] It is instructive to place Shaw's remarks in his own context. In the Preface to

FIG. 1. "Our Adviser-General," *Free Lance*, 11 April 1934 (courtesy The Alexander Turnbull Library, Wellington, New Zealand). Text: "GBS (with a parting smile): Thank you. Enjoyed myself so much! Sorry I can't stop to answer all your questions but accept from me this little keepsake. [Mr. G. B. Shaw will leave for England by the Rangitane on Friday.—News item.]"

On the Rocks he refers to the illusions held about personal liberty as "threatened by the dictatorships which are springing up all over the world as our pseudodemocratic parliamentary institutions reduce themselves more and more disastrously to absurdity" (*BH* 6, 605). A reporter at the press conference on board RMS *Rangitane* wrote that Shaw felt "European dictators had merely to say: 'No democracy,' and the response by most of the people was 'hear, hear.' Yet he was sorry to see the newspapers talking of liberty and democracy, and that they were still going strong."[4]

Unfortunately, Shaw's terms are frequently imprecise. *Democracy, dictatorship, Communism,* and *Socialism* recur again and again, yet their meanings shift to accommodate to the context in which they are being used. Some of this was undoubtedly due to Shaw's desire to shock his hearers and some to the English tendency to capitalize words, but much is due to his fifty-year-old memories of Pember Reeves[5] and Fabianism now muddled with more recent memories of Russia.

> If communism were discontinued in Auckland and Wellington from today, in a week they would be heaps of ruins, with starving people looting them, no roads, no lights, no water supply, no power, no police, no morals, no religion, only individual bandits. New Zealand's eminence among the Dominions is due solely to her Communism.[6]

At a later interview a reporter who questioned this use of labels was dismissed with, "If you don't recognize your institutions as socialist or communist it simply shows that you don't know what communism and socialism are, or else that you don't know the meaning of two very common English words."[7] Yet earlier he had said of Fascism that "any movement which increases State control of the existing dictatorship of private capital is part of the general movement towards Communism. But Fascism does not go the whole way. . . . When I began political life the Capitalists would not hear of State interference in business. But the Socialists cured them of that folly so effectually that nowadays they will not build a Cunarder unless the Government takes a hand in it."[8] And of communism he claimed that "after seventeen years of Bolshevik rule the Soviets are still hard at work on the foundation of Socialism. There is no difference between Socialism with a policy of gradualness and Communism. Lenin's aim was precisely that of the Fabian Society."[9] Such quotations could be multiplied.

In hindsight, one must question Shaw's grasp of contemporary history, but he is in many ways representative of his times. In the same way, he appears to misunderstand the flux in economic thinking and frequently urges New Zealand towards economic nationalism, and—although he was there as a tourist himself—he is scathing in his retorts to those who wished to promote tourism as an industry. One of the strangest of his aberrations, however, is his apparent concept of the monarchy. A recent conference in Ottawa had promoted the idea of a commonwealth of nations and England had passed the Statute of Westminster in 1931, which permitted the individual countries of the Commonwealth to define themselves as nations. New Zealand, not unexpectedly, was slow to do so and adopted the statute only in 1949. Many questions were directed to Shaw, seeking to determine British attitudes to the colonies; though he generally sidestepped them, he nevertheless disposed very quickly of any sentimental notion of special attachment: "They [the average Briton] have none really. The Dominions can indulge in all sorts of imaginative illusions about the British islands and even call them Home in their sentimental moments; but that side of life does not exist in England."[10] Despite the wordy rebuttal in an editorial[11] and the protests of another visitor, the Earl of Wemyss,[12] Shaw was in this more prescient than his hearers, as New Zealanders were to learn to their cost in the later upheavals following Britain's decision to join the Common Market. Curiously, however, he associated nationhood with a direct relationship with the king, even though the latter was now merely a figurehead. The colonies, he insisted, "have now got the right to go direct to the King himself without the intervention of Parliament,"[13] and he expanded greatly on this concept in a later interview in Blenheim:

> You have direct access to the King past Mr. MacDonald and Mr. Baldwin, and can have it out with him personally. That is all very nice for you, and the more you get on top of us the more you wave the flag of Empire. But it is pretty poor fun for us, and we are becoming the bottom dog. In the end, something like America, we shall break off and insist on not being trampled on by those colonies.[14]

To some extent this represents the thinking behind such plays as *The Apple Cart*. Even more they show how much Shaw was concentrating on strong personalities as leaders—a very different Superman from that intimated in earlier writings—and how this fascination was overwhelming all other considerations.

To be fair, he did have a connection, tenuous but real, with New Zealand. Invited by the Hon. W. Downie Stewart to speak kindly of New Zealand, he "plunged into memories of the late Hon. W. Pember Reeves, and claimed that through his Socialist activities he was one of the promoters of the social legislation carried out in New Zealand in the nineties."[15] This historical anecdote was repeated, in modified form, on at least three occasions and tended to exaggerate Shaw's own role; however, with a finer sensibility, he admitted that "the proper way to consider me is as a back number, with Fabian Socialism all played out."[16]

In most other ways, Shaw (perhaps more correctly the Shaws) was an exemplary tourist, interested in the sights but also eager to see nontourist attractions. Though he frequently refused the opportunity to react as a tourist to what he had seen and confessed to some vagueness as to where he had actually been, he did praise the Waitomo Caves and expressed surprise that so many New Zealanders had never seen them.[17] He was also impressed by the Lakes of Rotorua. Here he also showed that he kept in touch with modern technology when he predicted the utilization of thermal power, which is today a reality.[18]

He showed also that his aesthetic senses were as active as ever when he commented on the ugliness of "the cut and burnt and dead trees left standing" in the haste to make over the wilderness. Nevertheless, his chief interest was in people, and he enjoyed a day at a local sports and axeman's carnival—not surprising for Shaw, who chopped wood at his country home for recreation. A more carefree Shaw emerges at times, as in the description of his swim at Mount Maunganui: "The menacing surf that was running on Sunday seemed to challenge Mr. Shaw, and somewhat impulsively and with characteristic flouting of the conventions, he borrowed a lady's most modern bathing suit and plunged into the breakers."[19]

It was not possible, of course, that the voyage or his travels in New Zealand should occupy him entirely. He is frequently shown as occupied in writing letters or otherwise busy on personal matters. Asked on his arrival "whether he was completing another play," he replied, "Of course I am. I am always writing plays. I am a playwright."

"Did you write on ship?" Mr. Shaw was asked. "Yes," he replied. "Had I not been writing I would have gone over the side."[20] This was not an altogether honest reply, since the comments of a ship's officer make it quite clear that he was also physically active.

> Mr. Shaw read a tremendous amount during the voyage. He read all the way through his meals, and, it seemed, during the greater part of each day. His best exercises came after his morning swim in the ship's baths. This was without fail at about 7 o'clock, and after it he made good entertainment for the others by going through a system of exercises on his back. He and Mrs. Shaw were very much liked by the other passengers.[21]

A less attractive anecdote illustrates his more opinionated self. On March 13 he heard publisher John Lane, of the Bodley Head, making less than complimentary remarks about Shaw over the wireless and took matters into his own hands.

> "I can't turn this thing off," said a voice from near the floor of the drawing room.
> Mr. George Bernard Shaw was on his hands and knees near the loudspeaker, working at screws at the base of the wall where the radio was connected.
> Then the words of the broadcast ceased abruptly. Mr. Shaw had managed to "turn it off."[22]

Although Shaw did not say at that time what he was working on, near the end of the return voyage (12 May 1934) he wrote to Leonora Ervine, "I have written two plays on the double voyage. . . . My bolt is shot as far

as any definite target is concerned and now, as my playwright faculty
still goes on with the impetus of 30 years' vital activity I shoot in the air
more and more extravagantly without any premeditation whatever." On
16 May 1934 he sent to Blanche Patch shorthand drafts of the last portion of *The Simpleton*, a second play, *The Millionairess*, and a draft of *The
Six of Calais*. Given that both voyages were via the Panama Canal and
still constitute the longest passenger sea-voyage in the world without
regular ports-of-call, he had very few possible shore diversions during
more than two months at sea, sufficient time for much reading and writing. It would be difficult, if not impossible—and probably fruitless—to
determine now when he wrote what during those voyages, and to a certain extent it does not matter. Whenever the various scenes of *The Simpleton* were actually written, the ideas expressed in them were certainly
in his head during his New Zealand visit. Whether there was a reverse
effect is more problematic. We have his own word for it (letters to translator Floryan Sobienowski written in 1935) that the third scene of the
prologue is taken from the caves of Elephanta, near Bombay, seen during earlier travels; yet it is not unlikely that the sights seen on this journey should make their way into the play, concerned as it is with another
exotic part of the Commonwealth.

Shaw claimed that his reason for visiting New Zealand was that he was
interested in seeing how its social experimentation was succeeding. The
same interest is evident in *The Simpleton*, as is also a feeling that what will
not change should cease to be. If these ideas were not already on paper,
they were certainly already in Shaw's head. How otherwise explain the
following extraordinary combination of ideas, spoken before Shaw had
even set foot in New Zealand!

> New Zealand is an interesting place in many ways. I want to know what
> the future of New Zealand is going to be. Apparently you have not ex-
> perienced the complete crash we have had. Nowadays everything is
> changing, and New Zealand in many respects is the last place that is likely
> to change. Probably all the people of New Zealand should be extermi-
> nated to make room for an advanced people. You are an advanced
> people: you are ahead of the world apparently in your vital statistics. You
> are multiplying quickly in spite of your birth control.[23]

The two themes of building and destroying, birth and death, are here
set together in stark simplicity as they are in *The Simpleton*, and recur in
several variations during Shaw's visit, together with a wide range of remarks that may loosely be termed *eugenic*.

In his thinking, social amelioration is closely linked with violence and
religion. As he wrote, "The world's troubles can be cured only by long
and laboured social reconstruction by thinkers and workers religiously

devoted to the general welfare and ruthlessly intolerant of idleness and waste."[24] As an example of such reconstruction he frequently cited the Russian treatment of the peasants who as a class "could not be exterminated, so the authorities came to the decision to take the children from their parents and place them on collective farms," where they had a better time of it away from the "thrashings" and "whippings" they had received at home. Immediately, however, he balanced that freedom by saying "what the world needed and was getting under dictators was rigid discipline."[25]

The combination of experimentation, discipline and force is characteristic. Indeed at times Shaw even seems to be gloating over the possibilities of human brutality. While in his brighter moments he rejected the possibility of war, he seemed to find violence inborn. "Men are always ready to kill one another on the slightest provocation, and so long as there are that sort of people perhaps it is just as well that they should kill one another."[26] This may be directly compared to the patriotic prattle of the children in *The Simpleton* about killing and death (*BH* 6, 818–19), but is presented, under philosophic guise, in Prola's summation: "We shall plan commonwealths when our empires have brought us to the brink of destruction; but our plans will still lead us to the Unexpected Isles. We shall make wars because only under the strain of war are we capable of changing the world; but the changes our wars will make will never be the changes we intended them to make" (*BH* 6, 839–40).

It is not impossible that the ideas of Empire and Commonwealth and the problem of war—there is an interesting account of an interchange about New Zealand's participation in England's wars in one interview[27] and there are many other references to war—crystallized in the course of this visit.

Seeing the unsatisfactory state of the world as having a close linkage to the Victorian past so often praised for its progress, he was quick to decry that virtuous time. "The Victorian age was an especially abominable period—perhaps the worst in human history. I should certainly not have chosen it if I had had both the choice and the necessary information. The world is not yet fit for decent people to live in: those who think it is are living in a fool's paradise. We must hasten to change it for the better."[28] To him such change had religious force not in an institutional but in a personal sense. "There will have to be new political ideas, new religious ideas, because you will want a great deal more religion than you have had in the past. A great deal of what you call religion is not religion at all. Indeed some of it may be called anti-religion. In any case you want more religion and complete reconstruction of many of your ideas, social ideas and prejudices, and political ideas."[29]

New Zealand, by accident or by political obtuseness, presented him with an ideal occasion for supporting free speech, in this case with religious overtones. *Androcles and the Lion* had been broadcast, but with the epilogue censored. Shaw laughed about it because the epilogue was not really a part of the play; however, he was more serious in his condemnation of a ban on Krishnamurti. "A far less excusable case is the refusal to allow Krishnamurti to broadcast. He is a religious teacher of greatest distinction, who is listened to with profit and assent by members of all Churches and sects, and the prohibition is an ignorant mistake."[30]

He followed this up with comments on education. "No person should presumably meddle in the affairs of Empire without a competent general knowledge of the Moslem and Hindu religions or Buddhism, Shinto, Communism, Fascism, capitalism, party Parliamentary government, municipal government and all the forces which are really alive in the world to-day. Universities where these things are not taught and discussed are not universities at all; they are booby traps, and should be turned into mental hospitals."[31]

Then, as on other occasions, he referred to his own concept of a life force: "I don't, you see, believe in the faith in which I was brought up— that we are created by a god who is an elderly gentleman who went out of business several thousand years ago. I believe that the life force is going on working all the time and that it will never stop."[32]

The linkage of a life force with motherhood and therefore with childbearing and eugenic experimentation is central to *The Simpleton*, and it is not surprising that the same issues surface in his interviews. Although Shaw explicitly rejected the idea that he had come to New Zealand to study the Maori and declined to suggest any impression of the Maori race on the reasonable grounds of ignorance, he did show considerable interest in the characteristics of the New Zealand population, warning New Zealanders against reliance on inferior immigrants from England. "This raises the nice question of the most suitable stock to invite. . . . If an experiment were made with, say, Italians or Chinese, the immigrants should be allowed to marry one another. The breeds should be crossed or mixed."[33] The metaphor may perhaps be forgiven in an agricultural country, but it is not a flattering one. Asked about relations with the Maoris, he agreed that widespread intermarriage was not perhaps likely but opened the question of what would happen to the European settlers. "Well it is going to be extraordinarily interesting to see what the people of European descent will do with themselves. The climate here is different and they are so isolated. Yes, it will be extraordinarily interesting."[34]

The parallel with the situation in the Unexpected Isles is clear, and is confirmed by his choice of words on the same occasion. "New Zealand is a more interesting place because you have here a lot of people—who have come in from the outside to a very curious island; of course, one can only look on you as children and ask oneself: 'In God's name, what is going to happen to them?'"[35]

A further interesting parallel presents itself as a possibility: the resemblances between Sir Charles Farwaters, Governor of the Unexpected Isles, and Viscount Bledisloe, Governor General of New Zealand. The latter appeared to Shaw as a prime example of the benefits of belonging to the Empire and he went out of his way to praise him. Characteristically, Shaw indirectly takes some of the credit for this fortunate appointment. "Nine times out of ten a Governor-General is merely a territorial aristocrat but is not a very enlightened and stimulating sort of man. By a great piece of luck, Lord Passfield, a fellow Fabian of mine, when the Labour Government took office in England, was at the Colonial Office and saw that what New Zealand wanted was a Governor General [an aristocrat] who was a man of scientific interests and an agricultural chemist. And so you have your agricultural chemist and a Governor-General who is very much interested in New Zealand."[36] There is some hint of this in Sir Charles's remark to his wife after the Judgment. "You might take a turn in the garden, dear; gardening is the only unquestionably useful job" (*BH* 6, 836). By coincidence, on the day of Shaw's departure Viscount Bledisloe was laying the foundation stone for the new Dominion Museum, an interesting practical demonstration of Sir Charles Farwaters' claim that the Unexpected Isles must go on being governed even in the Day of Judgment (*BH*, 6, 836).

An even more suggestive parallel shows up in the description of the setting which precedes Act 1. "The lawn of a stately house on the north coast of a tropical island in the Pacific commands a fine view of the ocean and of a break-water enclosing a harbor" (*BH* 6, 783). Although Shaw himself did not visit Waitangi and there are no records of his conversations with Lord Bledisloe, the latter had made it one of his prime projects to purchase and restore the Treaty House at Waitangi (the house of the British Resident, James Busby, where the Treaty of Waitangi was signed) and to present it to the New Zealand people. It is not, therefore, improbable that he should talk about this project with Shaw. The house itself and its location match. It is a stately home in Georgian colonial style, set among wide lawns and gardens, looking across the Bay of Islands to the Pacific, and it is in the north of New Zealand. There is little reason, otherwise, why the north coast or the Pacific should be specified, particularly in view of Shaw's reference elsewhere to an Indian derivation.

Although that is speculative and is unlikely either to be confirmed or denied, there are several other geographic references which clearly derive from his voyage and sojourn in New Zealand. They follow on the proclamation of the Day of Judgment: "Someday Heaven will get tired of lazy people; and the Pitcairn Islanders will see their day of Judgment at last" (*BH* 6, 820). Pitcairn Islanders at that time frequently made contact with passing liners to transfer mail and supplies, and the *Rangitane* with the Shaws on board would have done so. There is little reason otherwise for Pitcairn Island to show up here. It is also of interest that the Pitcairn Islanders are Seventh Day Adventists with their strong belief in the Second Coming and the accompanying Day of Judgment.[37]

Finally there is the comic business of mistaking the Angel for an albatross. The albatross is one of the most fascinating of pelagic birds and common in the Pacific, though usually further south than the Shaws would have sailed. It is, however, a prime symbol in Coleridge's *Rime of the Ancient Mariner*, where the shooting of an albatross precipitates judgment on the sailors, and Coleridge's poem derived directly from accounts of Cook's voyages in the Pacific. In the play the link is specific and is in turn referred back to the Pitcairn Islanders. The Angel announces the Judgment Day and Hyering says, "Do you mean that the Pitcairn Islanders were right after all?" (*BH* 6, 821).

One final parallel relates to the ways of distinguishing between the useful and the useless. At his civic reception in Christchurch (then and for a long time Christchurch was unique in that the Labour Party was strong in municipal affairs), Shaw offered a definition of true ladies and gentlemen: "One [conception] that was largely prevalent in the Old Country, was that a gentleman was only an idle and useless person who lived entirely by the labour of others. . . . The true lady and gentleman was the man who said he was not going to be in anybody's debt. . . . If you want to be a true gentleman you must produce more than you have consumed. You must make it a point of honour that just as you at the beginning of life find yourself in debt to the community, when you die you will leave the community in debt to you."[38] This definition appears in the preface to *The Simpleton* (*BH* 6, 757–58) and is the basis of the judgment passed by the Angel (*BH* 6, 833–35).

These direct associations are small enough, but both the play and Shaw's interviews contain expositions of the same ideas. The themes of violent social change, the uselessness of the existing order and of those who preside over it, the need for social experimentation, including eugenic experimentation, and the role of the life force are clear, as is the obsessive nature of Shaw's contemporary concentration on violent politics.

The people of New Zealand took it all with a grain of salt and went about their business, conducting their own political revolution in 1935. Shaw met and disparaged the Labour leaders, Peter Fraser and Walter Nash among them, but they persisted in their goal of working within the system. As we would say now, a good deal of hype surrounded Shaw's visit. Clearer minds recognized what had happened: a serious mind had challenged "solemn personages" to stir up their thought processes.[39]

One interesting follow-up was a series of lectures delivered by Professor G. W. Von Zedlitz to the Wellington WEA (Workers' Educational Association) in July 1934. In these four lectures Professor Von Zedlitz attempted to summarize Shaw's life and demonstrate his importance as writer and thinker. He commented on Shaw's self-education and his relative independence, but stressed his reaction to "the sham and pretences practised by the shabby gentility with whom he came in contact—and the entire lack of vitality in the Irish Protestant Church" as a basic formative influence. He shrewdly assessed Shaw's role within the Fabian Society as apologist and peacemaker. Shaw's experience in journalism and public speaking brought extraordinary skill to his dialogue. "His sentences were so built that they ran easily from the tongue of a public speaker, and allowed his players to get their points over the footlights with ease." In this comment Professor Von Zedlitz accurately recognized the polemical nature of many of Shaw's plays. In his summation, he eulogized Shaw as "unquestionably the most important and distinguished citizen in the British Empire to-day" but was compelled to admit some degree of shallowness. "Shaw has always been exceedingly well acquainted with the trend of events in Europe . . . but he knew things as a journalist knows them [rather] than as a man engaged in scientific research." He also characterized Shaw as "a slave to his sense of the ridiculous. He has always preferred to amuse rather than to be impressive." Finally in relation to his clear emphasis on violent change: "He has made a distinction between any reorganization of society which could be reached with little alteration and inconvenience, and a reformation that could only be accompanied by a chaotic upheaval." This balanced view of Shaw underplays the vehemence of the later Shaw, but probably recognizes accurately the feelings held by educated New Zealanders.[40]

In 1957 *Freedom* published a retrospective on the visit, which includes a wry comment on public expectations: "Certain well-meaning citizens had advocated his being disbarred from entry into our earthly paradise, as being anti-social and a menace, and the admiration of those who looked upon him worshipfully as the superman of letters was tinged with timidity lest the lion in whose playfully-ferocious growlings they delighted, might suddenly flash out his formidable jaws."[41] In the event, nothing turned out quite so badly and the country had a field day with its important visitor.

Departure by ship from New Zealand in those days was a festive event and was on this occasion additionally so, since the ship carried the naval complement of the *Laburnum* who were being paid off and the *Rangitane* flew a 200-foot pennant. For some unexplained reason the traditional bouquets of flowers were late and had to be passed through portholes after the ship had cast off. Although this last incident is perhaps a fitting one with which to conclude a visit to a rather rough-edged society full of friendliness and fumbling, the most appropriate epigraphs come from the Shaws themselves. Their letter to the Tourist Department reads:

> Dear Mr. Marshall—we cannot leave New Zealand without acknowledging our obligation to your Tourist Department in the conduct of our tour. Everything has been done for us in the friendliest and completest fashion. We have had no trouble at all, and we quite agree that we never had such a tour in our lives. Traveling without worries did not seem possible, but you have achieved it for us. Many, many thanks.

Shaw himself said on the ship, "If I showed my true feelings I would cry; its the best country I've been in."[42]

Notes

This article could not have been written without the assistance of J. Ross Somerville who, from the distance of Wellington, N.Z., has searched out relevant materials and supplied photocopies, suggestions, and advice.

All materials not otherwise cited are from contemporary newspaper accounts of the visit.

1. *What I Said in N.Z.: The Newspaper Utterances of Mr. George Bernard Shaw in New Zealand. March 15 to April 15th, 1934* (Wellington, N.Z.: reprinted by The Commercial Printing and Publishing Company of N.Z., [20 April] 1934). This 32-page publication contains the major part of what was reported about Shaw in the newspapers, though its coverage of editorial comment is selective.

Shaw's address to the Fabians in Wellington was also published as *Address by Mr. G. Bernard Shaw to the Wellington Fabians and Members of the N.Z. Labour Party* (Wellington, N.Z.: Blundell Bros. Ltd., 1934).

2. *The Dominion* on 9 Feb. 1934 reports that "Mr. G. B. Shaw is to spend a month on a motor tour through New Zealand studying Maori life and ways. Sir James Parr [the High Commissioner for New Zealand] presented him with two of James Cowan's Maori ethnological books, and also a novel with a Maori background."

3. *Evening Post*, 24 March 1934.

4. *Evening Post*, 16 March 1934.

5. Biographical information on prominent New Zealand figures mentioned in this article can be found in *The Encyclopedia of New Zealand*.

6. A letter from Shaw quoted in *The Auckland Star*, 2 April 1934. The date is cited as 2 March 1934 in *What I Said*, and unfortunately such errors are frequent.

7. *Christchurch Press*, 9 April 1934.

8. The agreement had recently been announced whereby the British Government

would subsidize the building of the *Queen Mary* in order to provide work in the Scottish shipyards.

9. *Evening Post*, 4 April 1934.

10. *Auckland Star*, 15 March 1934.

11. *Evening Post*, 31 March 1934.

12. *Dominion*, 22 March 1934.

13. *Dominion*, 4 April 1934.

14. *Dominion*, 6 April 1934.

15. *New Zealand Herald*, 16 March 1934.

16. *Dominion*, 4 April 1934.

17. *Auckland Star*, 22 March 1934.

18. *New Zealand Herald*, 4 April 1934.

19. *Bay of Plenty Times*, 29 March 1934; contributed to the *Journal of the Tauranga Historical Society* (no. 43, 1971), by Alistair Matheson.

20. *Auckland Star*, 15 March 1934.

21. *Dominion*, 11 April 1934.

22. *Dominion*, 14 April 1934.

23. *Dominion*, 16 March 1934.

24. *Dominion*, 27 March 1934.

25. *Auckland Star*, 16 March 1934.

26. *Dominion*, 4 April 1934.

27. *Dominion*, 6 April 1934.

28. *Sun*, 9 April 1934.

29. *Dominion*, 4 March 1934.

30. *New Zealand Herald*, 28 March 1934.

31. *Auckland Star*, 2 April 1934 (cited in *What I Said* as 2 March 1934).

32. *Christchurch Press*, 9 April 1934.

33. *Evening Post*, 4 April 1934.

34. *Christchurch Press*, 9 April 1934. It is interesting that Shaw shows no particular awareness of a parliamentary enquiry into native affairs, a Royal Commission on Western Samoa, and a very intricate trial resulting from a revolt on that island, although all these matters were reported in the newspapers alongside references to his tour.

35. Ibid.

36. *Dominion*, 4 March 1934.

37. There is a more disputable Pitcairn connection. Iddy, the clergyman, was captured by pirates and released. The Pitcairn islanders combine in their history a strange mixture of near-piracy (mutiny) and devout religion.

38. *Christchurch Press*, 10 April 1934.

39. Editorial in the *North Canterbury Gazette*, 10 April 1934.

40. Professor Von Zedlitz's lectures are reported in *The Dominion* for 12 July, 19 July, 26 July, and 3 August 1934 from which these quotations are taken. The professor himself has the unique distinction of having been, as a German, deprived of his professorial chair by Act of Parliament during the First World War, despite the fact that he was totally out of sympathy with the German cause.

41. *Freedom*, 15 May 1957.

42. Even on this occasion there is a striking parallel between his journey and his play. In *The Simpleton* the Emigration Officer hurls the Young Woman over the edge of the cliff (*BH* 6, 781–82). In response to an interruption of his discussion with a woman reporter the following interchange occurred:
OFFICIAL. "That is, I do not want to break in on your talk with your friend."
SHAW."Oh! It is all right. I had just lured her to the ship's side and was thinking of throwing her overboard; so you came in time to save her life." [*Dominion*, 16 April 1934]
The reporter in question was Ness Mackay.

Appendix A
Itinerary of George Bernard Shaw in New Zealand

Feb. 8 Leave U.K. in R.M.S. *Rangitane*, via Panama.

Mar. 15 Arrive Auckland. Press interview. Garden party at Government House. Dinner with the Governor of the Reserve Bank of New Zealand and guests.

16 Lunch with Lord Bledisloe.

17 Meet Labour officials. Evening guest of Fabian Club.

18 Private.

19 Private.

20 Drive from Auckland to Waitomo.

21 Visit Waitomo Caves. Drive to Rotorua via Arapuni.

22 Guest of Mr. A. Warbride. Private visits.

23 Private.

24 Tour of Rotorua Lakes.

25 Visit to Tauranga. Guest of Dr. J.D.C. Duncan. Swim at Mount Maunganui.

26 Private.

27 Private.

28 Evening. Attended private Maori concert given by Guide Rangi at Whakarewarewa.

29 Drive from Rotorua to Wairakei. Visit Thermal area.

30 Drive from Wairakei to Chateau Tongariro.

31 Visit Sports and Axemen's Carnival, Owhango.

April 1 Chateau Tongariro. Evening. Speech and public question period.

2 Chateau Tongariro.

3 Drive via Wanganui (lunch and interview at Wanganui) to Palmerston North. Public press interview.

4 Drive to Wellington. Sail to Picton on the *Tamahine*. Stay at Picton.

5 Drive via Blenheim (interview) to Kaikoura. Stay at Kaikoura.

6 Kaikoura.

7 Arrive Christchurch. Stay at United Service Hotel. Press interview. Evening attend showing of "The Guardsman" with Alfred Lunt and Lynne Fontanne.

8 Christchurch. Guest of Sir Joseph Kinsey.

9 Civic reception by the Mayor, D.G. Sullivan (Labour M.P.). Brief tour of city. Evening ferry to Wellington.

10 Wellington, Cabinet reception. Tour of Hutt Valley.

11 Visit to Karitane Hospital and its founder, Sir Truby King.
12 Visit Alexander Turnbull Library and Wellington Public Library and Museum. National Broadcast (2YA), 10:00 P.M.
13 Address to Wellington Fabians and members of the Labour Party.
14 Leave New Zealand, 11:00 A.M., on R.M.S. *Rangitane*.
May 15 Arrive London.

The itinerary was changed several times and many newspaper reports of where the Shaws were carried misleading dates.

Appendix B
Shaw's Reading Matter

On arrival at Auckland, Shaw donated to the ship's library 23 books he had read during the voyage out. Since one seldom has the chance to discover the reading matter of a major writer during a specific period of time, they are listed below.

Berners, Gerald Hugh Tyrwhitt-Wilson, Baron. *First Childhood*. London: Constable, 1934.

Bridie, James. *Marriage Is No Joke: A Melodrama*. London: Constable, 1934.

Buick, Thomas Lindsay. *The Treaty of Waitangi, or how New Zealand became a British Colony*. New Plymouth: Avery, 1933.

Condliffe, John Bell. *New Zealand in the Making: a survey of economic and social development*. London: G. Allen, 1930.

Cowan, James. *Travel in New Zealand, the Island Dominion, its Life and Scenery, Pleasure Routes and Sport*. Auckland: Whitcombe and Tombs, 1926.

Chapple, James Henry George. *Divine Need of a Rebel: Addresses from texts from the wider Bible of literature*. London: C.W. Daniel, 1924.*

———. *A Rebel's Vision Splendid*. London: C.W. Daniel, 1925.

Gwynn, Dennis Rolleston. *DeValera*. London: Jarrolds, 1933.

Harrop, Angus John. *Amazing Career of Edward Gibbon Wakefield: With extracts from "A Letter to Sydney."* London: G. Allen, 1928.

Henry, James Maxwell. *A New Fundamentalism*. London: Macmillan, 1934.

Hitler, Adolf. *My Struggle*. London: Hurst and Blackett, 1933.

*Interestingly enough, these lectures were "delivered in the Unitarian service held in the Masonic Hall, Christchurch, New Zealand."

Kenworthy, Joseph Montague (later Baron Strabolgi). *Sailors, Statesmen and Others: an autobiography*. London: Rich and Cowan, 1933.

Lloyd-George, David. *War Memoirs*. London: Nicholson and Watson, 1933–36. (vols. 1 and 2 only)

Lockhart, Robert Hamilton Bruce. *Memoirs of a British Agent: being an account of the author's life in many lands and of his official visit to Moscow in 1918*. London: Putnam, 1932.

Macdonel, Archibald Gordon. *Napoleon and His Marshals*. London: Macmillan, 1934.

Maurois, André. *King Edward and His Times*. London: Cassell, 1933.

Millin, Sarah Gertrude. *Rhodes*. London: Chatto and Windus, 1933.

Pearson, Hesketh. *The Smith of Smiths: Being the Life, wit and humour of Sydney Smith*. London: Hamilton, 1934.

Rattray, Robert Fleming. *Bernard Shaw: a chronicle and introduction*. London: Duckworth, 1934.

Rees, Rosemary Frances. *New Zealand Holiday*. London: Chapman and Hall, 1933.

Young, Francis Brett. *My Brother Jonathan*, London: Heinemann, 1928.

———. *Portrait of Clare*. London: Heinemann, 1927.

Appendix C
George Bernard Shaw's Diet

During the tour Dr. H.I.J. Thacker asked for a reply-paid telegram of 12 words concerning his diet. Shaw replied: "Dr. Thacker, Christchurch. Vegetarian 50 years. Teetotal always. Milk, butter, eggs. Shaw."

For the guidance of hotels, Mrs. Shaw issued a set of instructions:

Mr. George Bernard Shaw does not eat meat, game, fowl or fish, or take tea or coffee. Instead he will want one of the undermentioned dishes at lunch and dinner. He will eat green vegetables, puddings, pastry, etc., cheese and dessert like other people. He likes oranges and salads and nuts—especially other nuts.

For Breakfast
Oatmeal porridge or other cereals and always grapefruit. For drink: "Instant Postum."

Other Meals
One of the following dishes at lunch and dinner:
Haricot Beans, dry, white: Butter Beans. May be plain boiled or with a sauce, or curried or formed into cutlets.
Lentils. As above.

Macaroni. Au gratin, or with tomato, cheese, or other sauce, or curried.

Spaghetti. As above.

Welsh Rarebit

Yorkshire Pudding

Rice. Savoury, or Milanese (No ham), or curried with haricots or eggs or nuts, raisins, etc.

Pease Pudding

Eggs (not too often). Curried, cutlets, mayonnaise, Espagnoli, en cocotte à la crème, omelette, etc.

Gnocchi

Sweet Corn

Curried Chestnuts

Minced Walnuts

Soups. Any thick vegetable soup, such as lentil, Haricot, Pea (St. Germain), Barley (crème d'orge), Rice (crème de riz), Artichoke (Palestine), Celery, Onion, Tomato.

Review

The Life as a Bibliography

Dan H. Laurence. *Bernard Shaw: A Bibliography.* Volumes One and Two. 1,058 pp. Oxford: Clarendon Press. £80. New York: Oxford University Press, $152.00.

Dan H. Laurence's bibliography, the result of some thirty years' research, tells us so much about Shaw's work that it is indispensable for the serious student. This is not a book merely for Shaw collectors, or for dealers in Shaw's first editions, though they will be immensely grateful for it; it is a work which adds greatly to our store of knowledge of the dissemination of Shaw's writings and tells us not only of little-known pieces but also of material hitherto unrecorded.

Mr. Laurence follows his own modification of the Soho formula, which has become the norm for the best descriptive bibliographies of modern writers. Thus Section A is for books and ephemeral publications written wholly by Shaw, Section B for his contributions to books, and Section C for contributions to periodicals and newspapers. There are ten other sections besides, but it is instructive to use the first three as a yardstick to measure the gargantuan task which Dan Laurence set himself. This bibliography extends to 1,058 closely set pages. Comparison with two of the next longest bibliographies of contemporary figures, those of Winston S. Churchill and Edmund Blunden—each, like Shaw, living a long life; each, like Shaw, prolific with the products of his pen; and one, like Shaw, including political polemics in his output—yields these figures: For Section A: Churchill 142 items, Blunden 177, Shaw 311; Section B: Churchill 66 items, Blunden 293, Shaw 444; Section C: Churchill 528 items, Blunden 3,370, Shaw 3,975.

Mr. Laurence deals faithfully with the task of giving full bibliographical descriptions of the items he lists, providing transcriptions of title pages, page sizes, signatures, imprints, details of binding, publication dates, print runs, prices, and, in the case of the scarcer items, locations. Where binding variants, issues, or states exist, they are duly recorded and an attempt is made to establish the relative priorities. What makes the bibliography so useful—and such a delight to work with—is the extent and nature of the compiler's notes and commentary. Mr. Laurence clearly recognized what he had achieved (note the title of his recent Engelhard lecture at the Center for the Book, Library of Congress, *Bernard Shaw; a portrait of the author as a bibliography*): it is a rich portrait of the author that he has given us, a mine of information presented in an enjoyably readable form. Here is a bibliographer who, when the cold and clinical task of giving collations is done, writes with style and élan.

The bibliography is amply larded with quotations from Shaw, mostly from apposite letters. The texts of the printed postcards that Shaw used as a form of reply (or at least as the basis of a reply) to troublesome correspondents are here published in full. Quotations from Shaw used as promotional blurbs on the dust-wrappers of other peoples' books are fully listed—and moreover quoted *in extenso*—in Section E. In Section C, Contributions to Periodicals, Laurence follows the titles of contributions with a brief explanatory synopsis of the subjects dealt with. This is a practice I heartily commend to other bibliographers called on to deal with such a prolific output of journalism.

Almost in passing, as it were, Laurence clears up many a problem that has troubled collectors and dealers for decades. Let me give one example: the multifarious forms in which the 44-page *Press Cuttings: a Topical Sketch* (1909) presented itself. We saw it in blue-flecked pink paper wrappers and blue-flecked grey paper wrappers. We saw it priced at one shilling. After the price on some copies the word "Net" was rubber-stamped. Other copies had the word "Net" added from metal type, but not always in the same position. Still more had the price information printed correctly and *at one time*: "Price One Shilling net." Yet others had the imprint as "Constable and Company," replacing the earlier "Archibald Constable & Co." Lastly there were copies with four pages of advertisements, causing a revision in the signature pattern. Confusion reigned. Now the exact sequence and exact status of each variant has been made clear beyond peradventure. Similar cases abound.

Mr. Laurence benefits of course from his many years at the very epicentre of Shaw scholarship. He has been in a position to consult "Shaw's shorthand diaries and account books, literary manuscripts and corrected typescripts, 'opus' card file, draft income tax returns, and scrapbooks, as well as correspondence; publishers' royalty statements and house records; printers' invoices and day books; binders' ledgers; minute books of Fabian Society members' meetings, executive committee meetings, and sub-committee meetings; minutes of Dramatists' Club meetings; and marked files of newspapers and journals." All this grist has been ground to good purpose in Mr. Laurence's mill. He is able to attribute to Shaw much anonymous and pseudonymous material (James Timewell's *The Police and the Public* is one such example). Scarcely less important is his ability to deal with the misattribution to Shaw of *Lady Wilt Thou Love Me*, the eighteen manuscript love poems allegedly addressed by Shaw to Ellen Terry, sold at auction in 1958 (when the auctioneers stated that Shaw had attempted "to disguise his normal hand"), and published in the United Kingdom in 1980 and in the United States a year later. In 1958 I knew no one, apart, presumably, from the purchaser at the auction, who was taken in by the "disguised hand"; Dan Laurence now proves categorically in four pages of convincing and well-argued prose that the attribution was entirely devoid of solid foundation.

In another passage he again demonstrates that, regardless of which is mightier, the pen can cut through a reputation as swiftly as the sword, laying bare shoddy work and ill-deserved fame. I speak of his devastating critique of F.E. Loewenstein's *The Rehearsal Copies of Bernard Shaw's Plays*. Laurence does this in the introduction to his Section AA, "Rough Proofs/Rehearsal Copies." He points out that less than half the entries in Loewenstein's work can accurately be described as "rehearsal copies" in the first place. In a few blistering paragraphs Loewenstein is accused of arrogance, failure to examine many of the copies he described, and "inane rationalization" when he attempted to make newly discovered variants fit his preconceptions. His work is dismissed as "chaotic in form, technically unsound, and appallingly dense." Happily, Mr. Laurence then goes on to make an exemplary task of the codification and description of the wrappered proofs which had defeated poor Loewenstein.

A word must be said about the illustrations, which have been unusually well-chosen. Most reproduce the wrappers of pamphlets or the rectos of leaflets so rare that few of us can ever hope to see the originals outside one of the major Shaw collections in research libraries. But at least we now know what we are looking for! Examples are the *Bill . . . to Increase the Powers of Local Authorities* (A5), which Shaw introduced in the debating society, the Charing Cross Parliament, in 1887; *A Word to Women Electors about the Borough Councils* (A53), an unsigned leaflet put out during the Metropolitan Borough Elections of 1903; and *The Speech of Mr. G. Bernard Shaw in New York* (A212b), the unauthorized Japanese edition of *The Future of Political Science in America*, 1933. But the best and most tantalizing of the facsimiles is that of the sole surviving proof page, containing the last three stanzas, of the "Sir Knight" verses, 1883–84 (B1).

These verses were published by W. Mack and were written to fit engraved blocks which Mack already owned. The verses are otherwise known to us only from the shorthand manuscript. Dan Laurence and the anonymous owner of the fragmentary proof hope that this illustration will help the search for the elusive book of which the verses were to form a part.

Have I no quibbles? Well, yes, a few. One concerns Laurence's slightly cavalier attitude to dust-wrappers. He tells us that "most of [Shaw's] principal books have been issued in dust-wrappers since at least 1902," but he makes no attempt to record them all. If he had to restrict himself then he has certainly chosen the important ones: "those instances where Shaw either provided text, aided in the design, or commissioned and passed judgement on the finished dust-wrapper." Laurence adds that "designers are identified when their names have some special significance." The justification for this approach appears to be that "dust-wrappers have never figured notably in the collecting of Shaw's works." Never say "never," Mr. Laurence: any politician will tell you that. The presence or absence of dust-wrappers has now assumed an importance in the buying and selling of twentieth-century books infinitely greater than at any previous time in my thirty or more years' experience of the market. Some among us may decide that this "dust-wrapper syndrome" has gone too far, but we cannot deny its existence, nor that there is some logic in seeking to own and preserve a book as it first appeared, *with the jacket*, if one was present originally. It follows that it is the best practice in a descriptive bibliography to describe dust-wrappers too—and to name all designers, where they are known, not just those that a subjective contemporary judgement rates "significant."

I quarrel just a little with Mr. Laurence's descriptions of color (usually the color of binding cloths, but occasionally the color of the stock on which texts, e.g. the celebrated printed postcards on common topics of correspondence, were printed). Since he rightly implies that "differentiation of shade" is seldom of importance in determining variant states or issues in Shaw, I am not on the strongest ground, but I would respectfully point out that unless the known variants are described quite precisely, we have no way of recognizing what might be an *unknown* variant.

In dealing specifically with the colors of the "stereotyped postcards" I have referred to above, Mr. Laurence says that he has tried to use "simple nomenclature." I wish he had bowed to the growing fashion and identified colors by reference to an identifiable constant, preferably, *faute de mieux*, to the Inter-Society Color Council/National Bureau of Standards Centroid Color Chart. That might have helped me with my own copies of Laurence D.1(a) and (b), the two texts of the printed postcard on Capital Punishment. The bibliography describes them as "pale green," which my copies undoubtedly are; the trouble is, one of them is a paler green than the other.

I am less than perfectly happy with one element of the organization of the bibliography, *viz.* the treatment of foreign language editions of Shaw's writings. Laurence lists them only if they constitute the first appearance of a text, if they are "known to contain significant new material . . . supplied by Shaw to the Translator," or if they are specially written contributions to foreign periodicals. I would have liked, in an ideal world, to see at least the first translation of each work into each language listed, albeit briefly, in order to gain a picture of the spread of Shaw's influence in the non-English-speaking world. As it is, his entries for foreign translations of books and ephemeral publications wholly by Shaw are listed chronologically in Section A. There is an argument for adapting even the excellent and now widely accepted Soho formula to the needs of the pattern of the author whose works are under review, but I would have preferred to see all translations listed in a separate section in the more usual Soho manner.

It would be unfair to complain about the price. To be sure £80 seems a great deal of money to English eyes, however it might or might not look in the United States at the present rate of exchange, but then one gets what might be termed "a great deal of book" in return. Admirably and, it would seem, durably produced, with 26 illustrations and a wide-ranging, comprehensive index covering 112 double-column pages, meticulously proofed (and where necessary proofed again until it *was* right), it must have been an expensive book to make. The question which every serious reader of Shaw must ask himself is not "Can I afford to own it?" but "How can I afford not to own it?"

Anthony Rota

John R. Pfeiffer*

A CONTINUING CHECKLIST OF SHAVIANA

I. Works by Shaw

Shaw, Bernard. "Capital Punishment," in *Prose Models*, ed. Gerald Levin. Sixth edition. San Diego: Harcourt, Brace, Jovanovich, 1983. Found in "Arguments and Persuasion," under the subheading "controversy." Not seen.

———. Excerpt from "The Revolutionist's Handbook," in *The Norton Reader*, ed. Caesar R. Blake, et al. Sixth edition. New York: W. W. Norton, 1983. Not seen.

———. Excerpted in "Bernard Shaw and Music Hall" by David F. Cheshire. *Theatre Quarterly*, X, no. 37 (1980), 19–22. The piece is over half in quotations from GBS's comments on the music halls of the 1890s, taken from his articles in *The World* between 1889 and 1894. See also Cheshire in "Periodicals," below.

———. "Images, Farewells." *Time* (December 26, 1983), p. 49. On Rebecca West who died at 90 in 1983 GBS is quoted: "Rebecca can handle a pen as brilliantly as ever I could and much more savagely."

———. Postcard to Robert Graves in Robert Graves' *In Broken Images. Selected Letters of Robert Graves, 1914–1946*. Edited, with commentary, by Paul O'Prey. London, Melbourne, etc.: Hutchinson, 1982; p. 362. GBS answered a request for information on T. E. Lawrence that he thought came from Robert Graves: "A great mistake. You might as well try to write a funny book about Mark Twain. T.E. has got all out of himself that is to be got. His name will rouse expectations which you will necessarily disappoint. Cape will curse his folly for proposing such a thing, and never give you another commission. Write a book (if you must) about the dullest person you know; clerical if possible. Give yourself a chance." But Shaw had mistaken Robert for his brother Charles Graves, the gossip columnist. See also Graves, and Seymour-Smith under "Books and Pamphlets," below.

———. *Pygmalion*, in *Literature, The Human Experience*, ed. Richard Abcarian and Marvin Klotz. Revised shorter edition. New York: St. Martin's Press, 1984; pp. 573–652. The Dodd/Mead text, added as a new inclusion in this edition. Includes "Questions" and

*Thanks for special assistance in the preparation of this checklist to Andrea M. Dawe, Scott K. Hamilton and Jean L. Rowe. Professor Pfeiffer, SHAW Bibliographer, welcomes information about new or forthcoming Shaviana: books, articles, pamphlets, monographs, dissertations, reprints, etc. His address is Department of English, Central Michigan University, Mount Pleasant, Michigan 48859.

"Writing Topics." Instructor's manual provides "Bernard Shaw, Pygmalion" commentary, pp. 74–76.

———. Quoted in "Short Views," in *The Little Brown Reader*, ed. Marcia Stubbs and Sylvan Barnet. Third edition. Boston and Toronto: Little, Brown and Company, 1983; p. 86. The single GBS item is, "The great secret of vegetarianism is never to eat vegetables." "George Bernard Shaw" is on the cover between "Shakespeare" and "Mary Shelley" (Percy B. not included), just above the book title. A very little bit of Shaw is made to go a long way here.

———. Quoted in *The Traveller's Dictionary of Quotation*, ed. Peter Yapp. London, Boston, Melbourne and Henley: Routledge and Kegan Paul, 1983. Shaw is tapped for quotes on Dublin, England, France, Greece, Ireland, Letchworth, London, Oxford, Paris, Russia, Scotland, Switzerland, U.S., and other subjects, drawing mostly from the plays—about twenty-five citations in all. The entries for Shakespeare and Shelley are about one-third longer.

———. Quoted in *Victorian Actors and Actresses in Review: A Dictionary of Contemporary Views of Representative British and American Actors and Actresses, 1837–1901*, ed. and comp. Donald Mullin. Westport, Connecticut and London: Greenwood Press, 1983. Thirty-eight excavations of Shaw's opinions are indexed, on Janet Achurch to Mrs. John Wood. Sources are Shaw's *Dramatic Opinions and Essays* (New York, 1901), vol. I; and *Our Theatres in the Nineties* (London, 1932).

———. Quoted in Winston Fletcher's *Meetings, Meetings: How to Manipulate Them and Make Them More Fun*. Morrow, 1983. From *Publishers Weekly* review. Not seen.

———. Statements attributed by Clarissa Lorenz in *Lorelei Two, My Life with Conrad Aiken*. Athens: The University of Georgia Press, 1983; p. 193. Samples: "'Whenever I'm told something has been especially prepared for me, I notice everybody helps himself first,' Shaw complained. He reached for a cucumber sandwich, frowning at Laura's [Knight, the painter and friend of GBS who had set up a tea party for the Aikens and the Shaws] cigarette, ash dropping on her yellow frock as she poured tea. What was to be the climax of my long pursuit began and ended with a nonstop monologue brooking no interruptions.

"'I seem to be losing my memory—can't remember a person five minutes after meeting him. One of these days I'll see Charlotte in the street and ask who she is. I'm certainly becoming more solitary, but as I grow older I find I have no great need of people.' . . . 'And the critics dissatisfied with *Fanny's First Play* were those I had omitted to caricature in the epilogue. It's quite true,' Shaw continued, 'you can caricature a man on the stage so precisely that his identity is unmistakable, and he will feel flattered. But if you're writing an autobiography, in England at any rate, you can be malicious only to a certain extent, calling somebody a pig or swine or old goat. But if you say his check's no good, or that he keeps two domestic establishments, you're hauled into court. No, an autobiography is a dull book unless you're malicious, and unless you disclose yourself subtly it's like a bad photograph.'" See also Lorenz, Clarissa, under "Books and Pamphlets," below.

II. Books and Pamphlets

Abelove, Henry, et al. *Visions of History. Interviews with . . . Sheila Rowbotham*. New York: Pantheon Books, 1983. Diana Copelman's interview of Rowbotham as British socialist, feminist historian and playwright produced the following acknowledgment of GBS influence: "I was searching, I suppose, for a new kind of sexual morality. When I was in school I read Shaw's prefaces and had very iconoclastic views about how you shouldn't be a virgin. But I found it was a bit difficult in practice because (a) I didn't know anything at all about contraception, I mean nothing at all, until I met those socialists when I was nineteen, and then (b) people's attitudes weren't quite so rational as mine were from reading Shaw."

Allen, John. "Shaw, Barker and Galsworthy," in *A History of the Theatre in Europe*. Totowa, New Jersey: Barnes and Noble; London: Heinemann, 1983; pp. 260–62. About one paragraph each on dramatists "who carried the tradition of social realism into the mainstream of the British theatre."

Atkinson, Brooks. *Sean O'Casey: From Times Past*. Totowa, New Jersey: Barnes and Noble, 1982. About ten references to the relationship of O'Casey and GBS.

Balashov, Peter Stepanovich. *The Artistic World of Bernard Shaw*. Moscow: Publishing House of "Artistic Literature," 1982. Title here is a translation of the Russian language title. The contents are as follows: Introduction, I) "The Paradoxical Fiction Writer," II) Aesthetic Positions, III) The Comedy of Contrasts, IV) From "Comedy with Philosophy" to "Fantasy in the Russian Style on English Themes," V) The October Revolution and the Public Writings of Shaw, VI) Two Worlds of Artistic Division, VII) In Other Genres: Shaw and Film; Shaw the Novelist; Epistolary Legacy. In Place of a Conclusion. All the references or sources appear to be at least twenty years old. A photo of GBS, signed, adjoins the title page.

Bannister, Ivy. *The Shavian Woman: A Study of Women in the Life and Works of George Bernard Shaw*. Dublin: University Press of Ireland, promised for publication in Spring/Summer 1984. From the advertisement: "Covers all the plays. . . ." "Traces the developing characterization of the 'new women,' the tempestuous 'siren,' and finally the 'superwoman'—the sorceress who embodied Shaw's final dramatic, religious, and social aspirations." (As of March 1985 still not released.)

Barzun, Jacques. *A Stroll with William James*. New York: Harper and Row, 1983. Barzun, who honors GBS, mentions *Misalliance, Methuselah,* and *Major Barbara* among a number of references. He compares James to Shaw more than once. "The real handicap one notes in James as writer of philosophy is his irrepressible humor. He shares with Swift, Lamb, Samuel Butler, Shaw, Chesterton and Mark Twain the disadvantage of having used yet one more rhetorical means which, though legitimate in itself and generally pleasing, somehow distracts all but the fittest readers . . ." from the serious content.

Calonne, David Stephen. *William Saroyan. My Real Work is Being*. Chapel Hill and London: University of North Carolina Press, 1983. A few references review Saroyan's great respect for and debt to GBS. Shaw was "probably the greatest influence of them all when an influence is most effective—when the man being influenced is nowhere near being solid in his own right . . ."; Shaw was "health, wisdom, and comedy." "If it matters which of the writing men I have felt close to, and by whom my writing has been influenced, that man has not been Ernest Hemingway, as Mr. Edmund Wilson seems to feel, but George Bernard Shaw."

Donnelly, Honoria Murphy. *Sara and Gerald, Villa America and After*. New York: Times Books, 1982. The author is the daughter of the subject couple of this book, best known for their friendship with Fitzgerald and Hemingway. The author called Mrs. Patrick Campbell "Aunt Stella," though they weren't related. She knew her like an aunt as well, though Campbell was the only one of her parents' friends she didn't call by first name. Also included is a brief account of the conditions imposed by GBS for the posthumous publication of his letters to Campbell—the money to be used for the secondary education of her great grandchildren.

Edwards, Owen Dudley. *The Quest for Sherlock Holmes, A Biographical Study of Arthur Conan Doyle*. Totowa, New Jersey: Barnes and Noble, 1983. Excerpts: "Shaw was a neighbour of his in South Norwood before he removed to Hindhead; the kindly Conan Doyle was repelled by the streak of cruelty in Shaw, but the two men were much closer in thought than is generally realised, especially in their analyses of social gradations achieved in the Sherlock Holmes stories, and imitated in Shaw's *Pygmalion.*" Edwards says Doyle's *The Tragedy of the Korosho* "reads as though Conan Doyle had anticipated Bernard Shaw in contrasting the romantic English with the practical Irish. . . . In general, the evidence suggests that Conan Doyle tended to use his Irishness as Bernard Shaw used his, to strengthen his objective analysis of the English and occasionally to satirise them." There is a fair debt to GBS in the Professor George E. Challenger character of Doyle's science fiction stories.

Eisenstein, Sergei M. *Immoral Memories. An Autobiography.* Translated by Herbert Marshall. Boston: Houghton Mifflin, 1983. Includes the following reference to GBS, among others: "The third impression was gleaned from George Bernard Shaw's *Chocolate Soldier* during my tender, romantic, and heroically inclined years. By its pitiless irony, the play cooled my ardent and youthful craving for pathos. Afterward for my whole life I shouldered the heroic-pathetic yoke of screen 'canvases' in the heroic style.

"My visit to Shaw in London in 1929 culminated in his sending me a radio telegram, which, reaching me in mid-Atlantic on my way to the United States, invited me to make a film of the *Chocolate Soldier*, 'on condition that the text is kept full and in completely undistorted form.' This proposition was a great honor, coming from a man who had previously refused, for any amount of money, to give anyone the rights to make a film version of his works. Just as with Maxim Gorky, another great writer, whose propositions to film his work were *turned down* by me."

Fink, Augusta. *I—Mary: A Biography of Mary Austin.* Tucson: The University of Arizona Press, 1983. Austin knew Beatrice Webb and GBS. Shaw captivated her and he was glad to have her to tea—without formal invitation. She used this to deflate Sinclair Lewis when he visited her, just as the sales of his novel *Main Street* were reaching 300,000. "For once, Lewis, who had met his master, kept relatively quiet, but Mary was cast into the limelight when Shaw referred to her lecture on rhythm and urged her to expand and publish the material. Naturally, Mr. Brace [Sinclair Lewis's publisher] asked to see the book as soon as it was finished. Mary gloated over her triumph."

Finneran, Richard J., ed. *Recent Research on Anglo-Irish Writers.* New York: The Modern Language Association of America, 1983. Lots of references to GBS; see also Weintraub, Stanley, "Bernard Shaw," below, for description of the Shaw chapter in Finneran's volume.

Fitch, Noel Riley. *Sylvia Beach and the Lost Generation: A History of Literary Paris in the Twenties and the Thirties.* New York and London: W. W. Norton and Co., 1983. Shaw, along with James, Hardy, and Masters, was favorite reading for Beach in college, but she felt GBS a coward for his refusal to subscribe to Joyce's *Ulysses.* Fitch gives an exposition of the by-play surrounding the disagreement of the two, including the text of a letter to Shaw from Beach long afterwards that chides him again.

Fitz-Simon, Christopher. *The Irish Theatre.* London: Thames and Hudson, Ltd., 1983. Provides a chapter "The Unspeakable Irishman, George Bernard Shaw." In addition a number of illustrations reproduce Augustus John's portrait of GBS, Dermod O'Brian's painting of a scene from *Devil's Disciple*, and a photo of a scene from *John Bull* revived in 1980 by Patrick Mason—all in color. There are also photos of the 1978 Mason revival of *You Never Can Tell*, the cast on stage of the original Abbey Theatre production of *Blanco Posnet* (1909), the televised 1968 production by Christopher Fitz-Simon of *O'Flaherty V.C.*, a scene from the 1951 Dan O'Connell revival of *Man and Superman*, and Siobhān McKenna as St. Joan in her Irish translation of the GBS play at Taibhdhearc, Galway in 1952.

Forster, E. M. *Selected Letters of E. M. Forster.* Vol. 1. Ed. Mary Lago and P. N. Furbank. Cambridge: Harvard University Press, 1983. Includes a number of references to

GBS, such as the following: November 5, 1899. "I have been reading Bernard Shaw's plays. Wonderfully clever & amusing, but they make me feel bad inside." Also remarks in February and March 1920 on his writing of *The Government of Egypt*: "I have written a memorandum on Egypt for the Labour Party. This entailed a pleasant tête-à-tête with Woolf and Shaw." "The pamphlet has Bernard Shaw's corrections, which may interest you. He was very complimentary about it."

Ganz, Arthur. *George Bernard Shaw*. London and Basingstoke: Macmillan; New York: Grove, 1983. Contents include 1) The Life, 2) The Life of the Intellect: Political Economy and Religion, 3) The Life of the Theatre: Shakespeare, Wagner, Ibsen and the Theatre of the Age, 4) Plays of the Nineties: Unpleasant, Pleasant, Puritans, 5) Plays of Maturity: The Initial Group, Disquisitory Plays on Family and Religion, The Later Group, 6) Last Plays: *The Apple Cart* and After. Part of Macmillan/Grove Modern Dramatists series.

Gibbs, A. M. *The Art and Mind of Shaw. Essays in Criticism*. London: Macmillan; New York: St. Martin's Press, 1983. 224 pp. See Emrys Jones's review in "Periodicals," below. Gibbs sees Shaw's reputation as resting primarily on *Man and Superman, John Bull's Other Island, Major Barbara* and *Heartbreak House*, omitting *Saint Joan* because he claims it has been written about too much relative to the other major plays. He also considers *You Never Can Tell* as a substantial comedy unduly neglected by critics.

Goldberg, Marshall. *Nerve*. New York: Coward, McCann & Geoghegan, 1981; New York: Berkley, 1983 (paper). Adam, the superman hero, to the woman with whom he is falling in love, says, "To love—'a triumph of hope over experience.'" The woman replies, "That's George Bernard Shaw's line. And he was referring to marriage, not love" (p. 133, paper).

Graves, Robert. *In Broken Images. Selected Letters of Robert Graves, 1914–1946*. Edited, with commentary, by Paul O'Prey. London, Melbourne, etc.: Hutchinson, 1982. Several references to GBS including, "All these Councils of Nicaea and Quinquagent Gospels in the new early-Christian era: Arnie functioning well as James the brother of the Lord, and G. B. Shaw as St Joseph the pseudo-father and Pope, Lady Astor as the Magdalen . . ." (3 July 1935?). To Liddell Hart: "Irishness. A vein of seriousness, which easily becomes treachery. G. B. Shaw has it. Joyce is the extreme example . . ." (21 December 1935). Basil Liddell Hart later wrote to Graves and included the following curious allusion. "I should love a chance of seeing your notes on G.B.S. and Fuller . . ." (14 July 1941). See also Postcard to Robert Graves under "Works by Shaw," above, and Seymour-Smith, Martin, below.

Grawe, Paul H. *Comedy in Space, Time, and the Imagination*. Chicago: Nelson-Hall, 1983. Listed as "not seen" in last year's checklist. A number of references to Shaw plus a chapter, "Romantic Comedy in Perspective: Shaw." Excerpts: "Perhaps no playwright has spent more philosophical attention on the role of romance in humanity's destined survival than has George Bernard Shaw. His play *Pygmalion* and its later musical adaptation, *My Fair Lady*, present a fascinating problem in comedic structure and use of a virtual future. . . . Probably no less romantically sentimental writer was ever so completely fascinated by romance and the battle of the sexes as George Bernard Shaw." "*Pygmalion* and *My Fair Lady* are central both to romantic comedy in particular and comedy in general in working so assiduously toward a 'virtual future' beyond the final curtain." The future may be vague but we can be sure of Eliza having Higgins and "of having what to Shaw was more important in any case, his children, designed by the life force to embody their complementary powers. Marry Freddie? Ha!"

Grote, David. *The End of Comedy*. Hamden: Archon Books, 1983. Includes a discussion of the situation comedy and the comic tradition and finds GBS a major contributor.

Hawkins, Desmond. *Concerning Agnes: Thomas Hardy's 'Good Little Pupil.'* Atlantic Highlands, New Jersey: Humanities Press, 1982. Not seen. The subject is Lady Agnes Grove, sometimes in the company of GBS, who chose to take offense at a remark he made in a lecture she heard. An account of her reaction is presented here.

Hayman, Ronald. *Brecht, A Biography.* New York: Oxford University Press, 1983. Twelve references including ones to *Major Barbara* and *Saint Joan.* GBS is an occasional touchstone.

Herzinger, Kim A. *D. H. Lawrence in His Time: 1908–1915.* Lewisburg, London and Toronto: Bucknell University Press; Associated University Press, 1982. A few references confirm that GBS was a big part of Lawrence's time, as well as an influence upon him.

Higgins, D. S. *Rider Haggard: A Biography.* New York: Stein and Day, 1983. In March 1906 in London Haggard attended a lecture by GBS at a meeting of the Fabian Society. No other references, although Shaw knew him.

Houseman, John. *Final Dress.* New York: Simon and Schuster, 1983. An autobiographical account that gives several paragraphs each to Houseman's role in the late 1950s television production of *Misalliance,* and the early 1970s production of *Don Juan in Hell* which he directed.

James, Henry. *Letters. IV. 1895–1916.* Ed. Leon Edel. Cambridge: Harvard University Press, 1984. Only two letters to G.B.S. appear, both from early 1909, when James was chafing over the rejection by the Stage Society of his dramatization of the ghost story "Owen Wingrave," then called *The Saloon* and later retitled *The High Bid.* Shaw disapproved of the pessimistic ending; James characteristically insisted on his right to a "luxurious perversity."

Johnson, Paul. *Modern Times: The World from the Twenties to the Eighties.* New York: Harper and Row, 1983. Several references to GBS to represent the political left.

Kosok, Heinz. "Shaw," in "A Bibliographical Checklist," *German Studies in Anglo-Irish Literature, 1972–1982.* Dublin: The Goethe Institute/The National Library, 1983; pp. 30–32. Twenty-one entries, many never listed in this checklist, mostly in German-language publications.

Kuhn, Reinhard. *Corruption in Paradise. The Child in Western Literature.* Hanover and London: University Press of New England, 1982. Uses quotations from Shaw about confusion with and the abuse of children to begin and end this study.

Lahr, John. *Coward the Playwright.* London: Methuen, 1982. Shaw's early influence on Coward is established. "He had to absorb influences before he could discard them." Coward was the only one to top GBS in earnings between 1929 and 1932, according to the *Sunday Daily Express.* Coward was first; Shaw second; A. A. Milne was third. Coward's annual income was 50,000 pounds. Shaw's is not specified.

Laurence, Dan H. *Bernard Shaw: A Bibliography.* Two volumes. Oxford and New York: Clarendon Press, 1983; 1,058 pp. Reviewed in this volume.

————. *A Portrait of the Author as a Bibliography.* Washington: Library of Congress, 1983; 20 pp. The Engelhard Lecture on the Book, at the Library of Congress on November 3, 1982. A personal account of the contribution that bibliography makes to scholarship. Laurence on bibliographers: "Their most significant contribution, however, has been one that biographers and autobiographers have seldom been capable of accomplishing, in those instances when they have made the attempt: the graphic recreation of the subjects' lives in the context of their struggles and frustrations and yearnings reflected through commercial intercourse, as when Hardy, after optimistically anteing up £75 toward the cost of production of his first novel *Desperate Remedies* (1871), discovers from the final royalty accounting that he has recovered only £59.12.7 of it. . . ."

LeVot, André. *F. Scott Fitzgerald: A Biography.* Garden City, New York: Doubleday, 1983. Three GBS references, one of which notes again that the subtitles of *This Side of Paradise* are mostly borrowed from Shaw's Prefaces.

Lindberg-Seyersted, Brita, ed. *Pound/Ford: The Story of a Literary Friendship.* New York: New

Directions, 1982. Reprints a Ford invention about GBS: "Now, to the right of me lived a most beautiful lady. She was so beautiful that Mr. Bernard Shaw broke up the City Socialist Club by drinking champagne out of her shoe."

Lloyd-Jones, Hugh. *Blood for the Ghosts, Classical Influences in the Nineteenth and Twentieth Centuries*. Baltimore: Johns Hopkins University Press, 1982. A chapter on Gilbert Murray notes, "Murray's distortion of the style of Greek tragedy went together with a distortion of the meaning. His master, the great Wilamowitz, had given the world an Ibsenian Euripides; Murray's Euripides was Shavian."

Lorenz, Clarissa M. *Lorelei Two—My Life with Conrad Aiken*. Athens: The University of Georgia Press, 1983. This account by Aiken's second wife presents a number of remarkable references to GBS. Paul has a dream which Aiken is asked to interpret: "'I was walking up a steep hill to G. B. Shaw's house and saw several hideous old women, all naked, one with her derrière marked off in squares like a preliminary sketch. Only Shaw's pretty secretary was clothed. Now what do you make of that, Dr. Freud?'

'Too complicated and abridged as you tell it,' Conrad said stiffly. 'But I'll hazard a guess. The climb to Shaw's house might symbolize intellectual inferiority, the nude and unattractive old women suggest suppressed sensuality, while the fully clothed secretary could be the unattainable object of desire.'" Lorenz also recalls her relationship with Laura Knight, who had painted a portrait of Shaw—whom Lorenz refers to as "my idol" at least twice in this volume. "Laura's studio was stacked with canvasses, in one corner a shaggy-browed pixie with a quizzical mouth and prominent red-veined nose—G. B. Shaw, my idol. Laura sighed. 'The trouble I've had with that portrait! He's so changeable and difficult, one minute a tired old man of seventy-six, the next an absolute devil.' He sang operatic airs and told fanciful tales. For instance, and she quoted him: 'My nurse used to hold the back of my petticoats so they wouldn't act as sails and carry me away.' This apropos of his big ears. 'And have you noticed the projection at the base of my skull? Catherine of Russia had the same. I'm told it means excessive sexual development.'" There are others. See also Statements attributed by Clarissa Lorenz under "Works by Shaw" above.

Macfarlane, Gwyn. *Alexander Fleming: The Man and the Myth*. Cambridge: Harvard University Press, 1984. This account of Fleming, who gave the world penicillin, gives space to Dr. Almroth Wright, a radical eccentric who presided over St. Mary's Hospital where Fleming began his work. GBS would visit Wright at the hospital for a good argument. When he wrote *Doctor's Dilemma*, the character Sir Colenso Ridgeon emerged as a somewhat exaggerated picture of Wright.

Malpede, Karen. *Women In Theatre: Compassion and Hope*. New York: Drama Book Publishers, 1983. Shaw's empathy with feminism is generally acknowledged here. A paragraph from a letter of February 1956 by Lorraine Hansberry (Nemiroff at the time), author of *Raisin in the Sun*, is representative: "I suspect that, among others, one reason there have probably been more Bertha Albergs than Marie Curies is because there have been, as of yet, too many Strindbergs (in one degree or another) and too few Ibsens and Shaws.—Which is hardly a 'feminist' statement."

Matthews, James. *Voices: A Life of Frank O'Connor*. New York: Antenium, 1983. O'Connor was an associate of George Russell and Yeats who fought censorship to preserve Abbey Theatre ideals. He helped GBS when the novella *The Black Girl* met with disfavor by the Catholic hierarchy in Dublin.

O'Donovan, John. *George Bernard Shaw*. Dublin: Gill and Macmillan, 1983. Not seen. In a series called "Gill's Irish Lives," brief biographies of leading persons in Irish history, literature, social and political life.

Partnow, Elaine. *The Quotable Woman, 1800–1981*. New York: Facts on File, 1982. Only one on GBS, by Mrs. Patrick Campbell: "To be made to hold his tongue is the greatest insult you can offer him—though he might be ready with a poker to make you hold yours."

Pfeiffer, John R. "*Androcles and the Lion*, A Fable Play," in *A Survey of Modern Fantasy Literature*, ed. Frank N. Magill. La Cañada, California: Salem Press, 1983; vol. 1, pp. 42–44. The discourse and matter of the Androcles fable is used by GBS to demythologize the ideas of heroism attributed to the early Christian experience.

Pratt, E. J. *E. J. Pratt on His Life and Poetry*. Edited by Susan Gingell. Toronto, Buffalo, London: University of Toronto Press, 1983. A single reference: "May I spend a minute or two upon an attempt to understand the spirit behind heroic action. . . . (I have just been reading with a class the great sixth scene of Shaw's *St Joan* [sic] and its overwhelming pathos lies in the contrast between the decision of the maid when she tears up the recantation paper and the consequences which she knows she must face—the contrast of the maid with her youth, simplicity, honesty and naturalness, her love of life and flowers and birds and sunshine—the contrast of these things with that judicial assembly representing the world's most terrible, most uncompromising authority, interested only in one juridical point—the disobedience of making a personal independent judgement.)"

Rogers, Will. *The Writings of Will Rogers*. Vol. 6. Stillwater: Oklahoma State University Press, 1983. Lady Astor "arranged my meeting with George Bernard Shaw. She thinks a lot of Shaw, but Shaw keeps her worried to death, the same as he does all England. You know, England wonders what he is going to pull on them every minute."

Rosen, Ruth. *The Lost Sisterhood*. Baltimore and London: The Johns Hopkins University Press, 1982. Shaw's well-known views on the subject of prostitution, especially as put in *Mrs Warren*, are referenced.

Rosenberg, Helane S., and Christine Prendergast. *Theatre for Young People: A Sense of Occasion*. New York, Chicago, etc.: Holt, Rinehart and Winston, 1983. Five GBS references. "The truly great playwrights—Shakespeare, Moliere, Chekhov, Shaw—. . . ." Included is a photo of Chris Kauffmann as General Mitchner in *Press Cuttings*. Also two quotes from *Art of Rehearsal*.

Rossel, Sven H. *A History of Scandinavian Literature: 1870–1980*. Minneapolis: University of Minnesota Press, 1982. "It is unthinkable that Bernard Shaw's *Saint Joan* and Eugene O'Neill's *Mourning Becomes Electra*, with their modern psychological approach and dialogue, could have been written without the examples of Strindberg's history plays"—*To Damascus* and *A Dream Play*.

Salmon, Eric. *Granville Barker, A Secret Life*. London: Heinemann Educational Books, 1983. Many pages of this book, which combines biography and criticism, deal with Shaw, including an argument that Barker could have been GBS's illegitimate son. See also Michael Holroyd's "Between Secrecy and Sex" under "Periodicals," below, in which Holroyd makes a special point of demolishing Salmon's argument.

Schmiechen, James A. *Sweated Industries and Sweated Labor, The London Clothing Trades 1860–1914*. Urbana and Chicago: University of Illinois Press, 1984. The sweated worker turns up everywhere, including allusions in GBS's plays. *Mrs Warren* suggests that prostitution is better than sweated labor.

Seymour-Smith, Martin. *Robert Graves: His Life and Work*. New York: Holt, Rinehart, and Winston, 1982. George Mallory, the Everest mountaineer, introduced Graves to the works of Shaw. Trying to write a play related to war with detailed knowledge of modern theater, he chose GBS as his model. He had one piece of correspondence with GBS requesting information on T. E. Lawrence. GBS apparently refused (but see also Postcard to Robert Graves under "Works by Shaw," above, and Graves, above).

Soloway, Richard Allen. *Birth Control and the Population Question in England, 1877–1930*.

London and Chapel Hill: University of North Carolina Press, 1982. A number of references to Shaw, including his acquaintance with Marie Stopes.

Spoto, Donald. *The Dark Side of Genius, The Life of Alfred Hitchcock.* Boston and Toronto: Little, Brown and Company, 1983. Hitchcock made much of having known GBS. He owned a complete set of Shaw's work. Shaw came to dinner at Hitchcock's, and autographed thirty-one volumes.

Stansky, Peter. *William Morris.* New York: Oxford University Press, 1983. Several references to Shaw, including a claim that he was once on the verge of marrying May Morris, William's daughter who later became her father's amanuensis and literary executor.

Straumanis, Alfred. "Latvian-American Theatre" in *Ethnic Theatre in the United States.* Edited by Maxine Schwartz Seller. Westport, Connecticut, and London: Greenwood Press, 1983. GBS, the "superman" among social critics, was neglected completely in the old Latvian theater repertoire, but the new Latvian theater's most praised production was *Pygmalion,* produced by Valfrids Streips in Boston, opening 2 May 1959.

Thornton, R. K. R. *The Decadent Dilemma.* London: Edward Arnold, 1983. "Bernard Shaw, for example, would not normally be classed as a Decadent (although his review first appeared in the American Anarchist paper *Liberty* on 27 July 1895, under the heading 'A Degenerate's View of Nordau' [Max Nordau, author of *Entartung* (*Degeneration*), 1893]), but his defence, or rather his attack on Nordau's methods and conclusions, is convincing. Yet even his *The Sanity of Art* does not dismiss finally one of Nordau's major themes, that of the insanity of genius." Substantial extracts of *Sanity* follow.

Torvey, E. Fuller. *The Roots of Treason: Ezra Pound and the Secret of St. Elizabeths.* New York, Toronto, etc.: McGraw-Hill, 1984. A handful of GBS references including the following: "Someone diagnosed Shaw years ago by saying he had a tight foreskin. The whole of puritan idiocy is produced by badly built foreskins." Attributed to Pound.

Tredell, Nicholas. *The Novels of Colin Wilson.* London and Totowa: Vision Press, Ltd., and Barnes and Noble, 1982. Lots of references to GBS, as is predictable since Wilson has always represented himself as inspired by Shaw.

Updike, John. *Hugging the Shore, Essays and Criticism.* New York: Alfred A. Knopf, 1983. Updike respects Shaw, but can also say, "Céline has the gift (like no one in modern English so much as Bernard Shaw) of irresponsible exaggeration."

Van Amerongen, Martin. *Wagner: A Case History.* Translated by Stewart Spencer and Dominic Cakebread. New York: George Braziller, 1984; London: Dent, 1983. "The *Ring*, Shaw believed, is a radical socialist parable on the curse of gold. . . . After having been ignored for almost three-quarters of a century, the justness of Shaw's interpretation has finally been confirmed by the publication of Cosima's Diaries: 'The other day R. said that it gave him pleasure to have offered in the *Ring* a complete picture of the curse of greed, together with the ruin which it entails.'"

Weintraub, Stanley. "Lawrence of Arabia: The Portraits from Imagination," in *The T. E. Lawrence Puzzle,* ed. Stephen E. Tabachnick. Athens: University of Georgia Press, 1984; pp. 269–92. The essay on creative transmutations of Lawrence by Graves, Auden, Forster, D. H. Lawrence, Anthony West, Alan Bennett, and Anthony Burgess among others, also includes Shaw's *Too True to Be Good,* where T.E.'s personality is split into the characters Private Meek and Aubrey Bagot.

———. "Bernard Shaw," in *Recent Research on Anglo-Irish Writers,* ed. Richard J. Finneran. New York: The Modern Language Association of America, 1983; pp. 66–84. Opens with a notice of the calendar of copyrights remaining on Shaw's works, and continues with sections on Bibliographies, Editions, Biographies and Autobiographies, General Critical Evaluations, The Novels and Early Musical, Dramatic, and Literary Journalism, Criticism of Individual Plays, Criticism in Languages Other than English, and Influence and Reputation. See also Finneran, Richard J., above.

————. "Uneasy Friendship: Shaw and Yeats," in *Yeats, An Annual of Critical and Textual Studies*, ed. Richard J. Finneran. Vol. 1. Ithaca and London: Cornell University Press, 1983; pp. 125–53. "To Shaw, Yeats had style: . . . To Yeats, Shaw had been not only his century's only equivalent of Swift and Burke, but also the creator of the inimitable Father Keegan, who possessed more of the real Ireland than Yeats had succeeded in portraying in Cathleen ni Houlihan herself. Theirs was an uneasy friendship, but rewarding, and true."

Wilson, Edmund. *The Forties.* New York: Farrar, Straus and Giroux, 1983. Two mentions of GBS as a touchstone.

III. Periodicals

Berst, Charles A. Review of Arnold Silver's *Bernard Shaw: The Darker Side. Modern Language Quarterly*, 40, no. 2 (June 1982), 190–93.

Bradford, Sarah. "Sale of Autograph Letters and MSS." *TLS* (March 11, 1983), p. 252. Article is principally about the sale by Mrs. Patrick Campbell's grandson of her letters to GBS.

————. "Sales of Books and MSS." *TLS* (August 5, 1983), p. 843. "Quaritch paid a high price, £594, for a letter dictated and signed by Shaw to the editor of *The Standard* criticizing a review of *The Doctor's Dilemma* with the perennial cry of the celebrity: 'it shows the extent to which I am the victim of preconceptions as to my character and attitude towards life for which there is no warrant in my authentic utterances.'"

"Briefly: Shaw Photo Treasures in Minsk." *Detroit Free Press* (February 21, 1984), Section D, p. 8. "Found: More than 70 photos of George Bernard Shaw, in an old building in Minsk." Tass said the collection was a mystery, noting Shaw visited the Soviet Union in 1931.

Brown, Barbara B. "Bernard Shaw's 'Unreasonable Man.'" *Modern Drama*, 26, no. 1 (March 1983), 76–84. "Shaw's Unreasonable Man is in no sense a Superman, but instead a 'conglomeration of contradictory traits.'" "Joan, Caesar, Undershaft, and others are indeed extraordinary individuals, but because Shaw includes human weaknesses and errors in their personalities, he implies that certain of their superior, admirable qualities are not beyond the reach of ordinary men and women."

Burgess, Anthony. "The Apocalypse and After." *TLS* (March 18, 1983), p. 256. W. Warren Wagar's *Terminal Visions*, the book Burgess is reviewing, does not mention Shaw's *Methuselah*; so Burgess does: "Shaw's *Back to Methuselah* (again unmentioned here) sees life itself as the great mutable élan: the human world may end, but as servants of the life force, we should regard this consummation with indifference."

Carpenter, Charles A. "Shaw," in "Modern Drama Studies: An Annual Bibliography." *Modern Drama*, 26, no. 2 (June 1983), 172–73. About thirty-five entries, some of which have not appeared in this checklist, by a former bibliographer of *The Shaw Review*. Carpenter's lists on GBS are indispensable.

Caesar, Sid. "How to Make Television Funnier." *TV Guide*, 31 (November 5, 1983), pp. 8–12. Caesar saw the SCTV troupe "do a satire of 'My Fair Lady' that was absolutely hilarious. With all the ball gowns and introductions to London high society, the Eliza Doolittle character learns absolutely *nothing* from speech expert Professor Higgins. Despite his frenetic attempts to convert her from a slum flower girl to a lady, she remains a raucous klutz who *still* speaks something unintelligible that sounds like Bulgarian."

Cheshire, David F. "Bernard Shaw and Music Hall." *Theatre Quarterly*, 9, no. 37 (1980), 19–22. See "Bernard Shaw and Music Hall" in "Works by Shaw," above.

Corliss, Richard. "Distant Thunder," a review of the Broadway, Rex Harrison production of *Heartbreak House. Time* (December 26, 1983), p. 80.

Czarnecki, Mark. Review of Shaw Festival productions of *Candida*, *O'Flaherty*, *V. C.*, and *Simpleton of the Unexpected Isles. Maclean's* (July 18, 1983), p. 54.

Dukore, Bernard F. "The Time of *Major Barbara." Theatre Survey*, 23, no. 1 (May 1982), 110–11. Considers the evidence and speculates upon why Shaw set the time of the play in January 1906.

Freund, James C. "Shaw spins in Grave as Pygmalion Learns Law." *Legal Times* (Washington, D.C.), February/March, 1984, 8, 10–11. A skit in dramatic form tracing the development, under the tutelage of Professor Huggins and Major Dickering, of a personable clerk in a flower shop named Lisa, into a legal-jargon-spouting pseudo-lawyer.

"George Bernard Shaw," in "1982–1983 Annual Review." *Journal of Modern Literature*, 10, no. 3/4 (November 1983), 567–69. Seventeen entries, plus cross-references to ten other entries, with some annotations.

Grene, Nicholas. "Benevolence and Beneath," a review of Stanley Weintraub's, ed., *The Playwright and the Pirate: Bernard Shaw and Frank Harris, a Correspondence*, and Weintraub's *The Unexpected Shaw: Biographical Approaches to G.B.S. and His Work. TLS* (April 8, 1983), p. 359.

Harris, Sydney J. "Why Many Tennis Stars Don't Make Good Teachers." *Tennis* (September 1983), p. 22. Opens this 500 word essay with Shaw's "He who can, does; he who cannot, teaches." It ends announcing the "flagrant falsity of Shaw's maxim."

Henry, William A., III. "Great Expectations in Canada." *Time* (October 24, 1983), p. 100. In part a review of the Grand Theater Company's London, Ontario, production of *Doctor's Dilemma.*

Hobson, Harold. "Hobson's Choice." *Drama*, no. 148 (Summer 1983), pp. 36–37. Review note on the Haymarket production of *Man and Superman.*

Holroyd, Michael. "Between Secrecy and Sex." *TLS* (May 13, 1983), p. 485. Holroyd finds much to disagree with in this review of Eric Salmon's *Granville Barker: A Secret Life*, especially in the GBS/Barker connection. See also Salmon, Eric, in "Books and Pamphlets," above.

———. "Shaw and Biography." *TLS* (April 22, 1983), pp. 413–14. Adapted from the Giff Edmonds Memorial Lecture delivered at the Royal Society of Literature and the Keith Morden Memorial Lecture at Portland State University, Oregon. Holroyd describes some of the pattern of GBS's idea of biography and autobiography. Excerpts: For what Shaw "is really beginning to say is that biography should support the work, if necessary at the expense of the life; that it should (as with the gospel of St John) fulfil the career of the artist which takes over from the life of the man. Later still, he refers to 'the dramatic faculty that enables me to see the stage effect I am producing, and to exploit it histrionically for the inner purpose that drives me on without any real complicity in its artificiality.' And yet, since you may not separate style from content in art, there is a complicity. Artificial histrionics had become part of his reality." "The man who, in the nineteenth century, had called for a new type of truth-telling in biography had grown into a twentieth-century subject for biographies wryly reminding his readers that 'when you read a biography remember that the truth is never fit for publication.'"

Hubert, Judd. "Upstaging *The Devil's Disciple." Theatre Journal*, 35, no. 1 (March 1983), 51–57. The play "relies on the psychological verisimilitude and ethical sophistication typical of Shavian comedy while making skillful and sometimes devious use of intertexts, which frequently provide a basis for the theatrical practice of upstaging. Melodrama tends to function within the play as just another intertext." "In systematically thwarting the audiences's expectations by switching from [one dramatic code to another], Shaw goes way beyond the mimetic boundaries of dramatic art and makes his comedy–melodrama–tragi-comedy or what you will, to an unusual extent, self-referential." The confrontations of Richard and Judith Anderson in different moods function as upstagings of one another: "each principal manages to cramp the style of the other."

Imlah, Mick. "Temporary Forfeits," a review of the Theatre Royal, Haymarket production of *Heartbreak House*. *TLS* (March 25, 1983), p. 297.

Jones, Emrys. "Classics and Fakes," a review of A. M. Gibbs' *The Art and Mind of Shaw*. *TLS* (March 30, 1984), p. 325. See also Gibbs, A. M., in "Books and Pamphlets," above.

Kauffmann, Stanley. "Stanley Kauffmann on Films." *The New Republic* (November 21, 1983), pp. 32–34. *Educating Rita* has been compared with *Pygmalion*. It resembles it "only in that the seemingly forecast romance between student and teacher does not happen. In Willy Russell's script, from a London theatre hit, the teacher, *unlike* Henry Higgins, tries to persuade the student to remain as she is, to convince her that she is in reality better off than he is."

Keates, Jonathan. "With the Pen-pushers." *TLS* (March 23, 1984), p. 294. From this review of Jerome K. Jerome's *My Life and Times*: "The company which includes Swinburne, Barrie and Marx's son-in-law Edward Aveling, sets off to finish the evening in the rooms of a blind poet called Philip Bourke Marston in the Euston Road, pausing on the way to consider the question of whether or not to ask Bernard Shaw, living in Fitzroy Square, to join them. But nobody can recall the number of the house and 'the chances were a hundred to one that, even if we ever got there, Shaw wouldn't come down, but would throw his boot at the first man who opened the door.'"

Kelly, John. Review of May Hyde's, ed., *Bernard Shaw and Alfred Douglas: A Correspondence*. *British Book News* (April 1983), p. 254.

Kummings, Donald D. "G. B. Shaw on Whitman (IX: 122)." *American Notes and Queries*, 20, nos. 9–10 (May/June 1982), 151–52. Collects and names the sources of GBS's few remarks on Walt Whitman, whom he regarded as a classic. Kummings' first name is incorrectly given as "David" in *AN&Q*.

Mendelson, Edward. "A Family Frivolity." *TLS* (November 11, 1983), p. 1248. From this review of the New York University Theatre production of Virginia Woolf's *Freshwater*: "The casting of Nathalie Sarraute . . . in the invented part of James the Butler has a lucky aptness, as the lines given to her character from the abandoned 1923 version echo the visionary speeches of Captain Shotover in *Heartbreak House*—which Virginia Woolf had seen late in 1921. *Freshwater* as a whole, in the New York production, seems something of a burlesque on Shaw's play. Joyce Mansour plays Mrs Cameron in the mood of Hesione Hushabye; Florence Delay's Ellen Terry has the hymeneal resolution of Ellie Dunn; the baffled idealism of Mazzini Dunn reappears in Guy Dumur's George Frederick Watts. And the arrival—loud and astonishing—of Jean-Paul Aron as Queen Victoria, in make-up that could stop a clock, takes the place of the bombs."

Newlin, Jeanne T. "L'amitié amoureuse." *Harvard Magazine* (March-April 1984), 56H. A discussion of the disposition of the surviving letters of the Shaw/Mrs. Campbell correspondence. Campbell's 239 letters to GBS were acquired in 1983 for the Harvard Theatre Collection by Frederick R. Koch, Harvard 1955. See also Peters, Margot, below.

Ontario, Yours to Discover. Toronto: Ministry of Tourism and Recreation, May 13, 1983. An advertising supplement to approximately fifty newspapers that refers to the Shaw Festival at Niagara-on-the-Lake five times on four different pages.

"People." *Time* (March 28, 1983), p. 63. A photograph of Diana Rigg and Rex Harrison in the London production (Haymarket) of *Heartbreak House*, accompanied by a one-paragraph comment.

"People." *Time* (October 5, 1983), p. 159. GBS is the entry for 1946 in this anniversary number of *Time*. A photo of Shaw is on page 31.

Peters, Margot. "Shaw vs. Stella: The Battle of 'The Apple Cart.'" *Harvard Magazine* (March-April 1984), 56A–H. "Suppressed passages from their correspondence— some appearing in letters recently given to the Harvard Theatre Collection—as well as the shorthand draft and unpublished rehearsal copies of *The Apple Cart*, reveal the sources of a heated dispute over one of Shaw's most brilliant and successful plays." The article forms the content of "Discovery," bound into *Harvard Magazine*. See also Donnelly, Honoria Murphy, under "Books and Pamphlets," above; and Newlin, Jeanne T., above.

Peterson, Bettlou. "If Actors Could Play Their Dream Roles." *Detroit Free Press* (Sunday, 1 June 1984), Section C, p. 1. Ed Flanders of "St. Elsewhere": "I'd like to do Shaw. I can't tell you which play, there are so many good ones, I'd do any of them. I read (King) Lear a lot but I'm a long way away from that. I haven't seen Olivier's Lear but it can be pretty intimidating to follow that fellow."

Potter, Rosanne G. "The Rhetoric of a Shavian Exposition: Act I of *Major Barbara*." *Modern Drama*, 26, no. 1 (March 1983), 62–74. "I shall approach the rhetoric in *Major Barbara* through Aristotle by way of James Kinneavy's theory of discourse, and divide the sorts of proofs that characters put forth on their own behalf into ethical, emotional, and logical." The investigation of rhetoric leads her to divide the act into three scenes. "In each of the three corresponding sections of this article, I shall examine the dominant character, the message that is being transmitted (both the intended message of the character to his or her audience and, where applicable, the ironic message of the author to the implied audience), the stylistic traits that mark the character's speech, and the rhetorical appeals made by the character. The first scene is dominated by Lady Britomart, whereas the shorter second and third scenes are dominated by Undershaft."

Rabey, David Ian. Review of Stanley Weintraub's, ed., *The Playwright and the Pirate*. *Hermathena*, 134 (Summer 1983), 97–98.

"Shaw, George Bernard," in "Bibliography." *Irish University Review* (1983), 247–48. Over forty entries, some from as early as the 1960s, a number never included in this checklist.

Taylor, John Russell. "Plays in Performance—London," includes reviews of the Haymarket productions of *Heartbreak House* and *Man and Superman*. *Drama*, no. 148 (Summer 1983), 40.

Tobias, Richard C. "Shaw" in "Victorian Bibliography for 1982/Section VI." *Victorian Studies*, 26, no. 4 (Summer 1983), 552–53. Includes fourteen entries and a couple of cross-referenced items, retrospective to 1979.

Watt, Stephen M. "Boucicault and Whitbread: The Dublin Stage at the End of the Nineteenth Century." *Eire-Ireland*, 18, no. 3 (Fall 1983), 23–53. Introduces the essay with a Shaw/British–Yeats, Synge, O'Casey/Irish contrast, noting that each contrived a popular theatrical tradition. Moreover, "Shaw and O'Casey, in particular, wrote history plays that were repudiations of a reaction against the popular history plays and romanticized, comic melodrama of their youth. They rebelled, for example, against both the form and content of popular history plays. Shaw's appropriation of the medieval 'chronicle-play' form and O'Casey's earthy, sardonic realism amount to deliberate rejections of the form of the popular Irish history play, analogues of the anti-Romantic views of history *Saint Joan* and *The Plough and the Stars*, in their different ways, presented. Nevertheless, traces of the popular Irish tradition are evident in these plays, however transformed or reversed."

Wearing, J. P. Review of Arnold Silver's *Bernard Shaw: The Darker Side*. *Victorian Studies*, 26, no. 3 (Spring 1983), 364–65.

Weinreb, Ruth Plaut. "In Defense of Don Juan: Deceit and Hypocrisy in Tirso De Molina, Molière, Mozart, and G. B. Shaw." *Romanic Review*, 74, no. 4 (November 1983), 425–

40. "Specifically, the elements of deceit and hypocrisy will be examined here in relation to Don Juan and the other characters in each work. They will be studied according to the three forms they consistently assume: 1) in the deeds designed to deceive;
2) in the masks and disguises worn to deceive; 3) in the vocabulary used by the victims
of deceit and hypocrisy or by the deceivers and hypocrites themselves." "Within each
work, Don Juan proves himself a man of honor. Tirso's hero never reveals Ana's
secret, Molière's Don Juan remains true to his word and principles, and Mozart's, the
least sympathetic, nevertheless keeps his promise to the Statue. Shaw's John Tanner,
by sharing the role with Ann, and leaving hypocrisy and deceit, along with seduction,
to the woman, carries the legend to its limits."

Whitman, Robert F. Review of Charles Berst's, ed., *Shaw and Religion* (*SHAW: The Annual
of Bernard Shaw Studies*, vol. 1). *Modern Drama*, 26, no. 1 (March 1983), 116–20.

Wisenthal, J. L. "Having the Last Word: Plot and Counterplot in Bernard Shaw." *ELH*, 50,
no. 1 (Spring 1983), 175–96. The beginning of one of Shaw's "plays takes place exactly where an unwritten one ended, in the sense that he disposes of the unwritten
play and then proceeds with his own. What then of the unwritten play that follows
the ending of Shaw's play?" "In *Pygmalion*, the play in a way becomes the prologue to
a short story about what Eliza will do once she becomes a woman. *Candida* leaves its
sequel unwritten. . . .

"These endings that are beginnings are very much part of Shaw's general outlook.
In his Hegelian view of history, process never stops; every dialectical resolution is
merely a resting place or jumping-off point. There is no finality in life or history;
every ending is a new beginning; there is always something to add."

Zelenak, Michael. "Philandering with Shaw: GBS 'Made in America.'" *Theater*, 14, no. 3
(Summer/Fall 1983), 72–77. An interview by Zelenak of director and cast members
for the Yale Repertory Theater production of *The Philanderer* in November and December, 1982. David Hammond, the director: "Not one person, not one critic, complained of the play as being 'talky.' I think we found the essential life of the play with
the result that Shaw's ideas came through with vitality and immediacy for a present-
day American audience."

GBS, no. 9 (September 1981). Newsletter of the Bernard Shaw Society of Japan. Includes
"To Our Japanese Friends" by T. F. Evans, "*Mrs Warren's Profession* and *Yvette*" by
Asako Ueno, "Shaw's Views on Christianity Seen through His Plays and Prefaces" by
Masako Obata, "London 1980" by Masafumi Ogiso, and "Shaw Festival at Niagara-
on-the-Lake" by Ryoichi Nakagawa.

GBS, no. 10 (December 1982). Newsletter of the Bernard Shaw Society of Japan. Includes
"Memorial Tribute to Professor Ichikawa, Honorary President," "Shaw and His Fel-
low Townsmen Yeats and Joyce" by Stanley Weintraub, "Shaw's View of War—on
Heartbreak House and *Back to Methuselah*" by Toshihiro Iida, "Shaw's Mystification in
Saint Joan" by Yoshikazu Shimizu, "Bernard Shaw—Fiction and Reality" by Tatsuo
Yamamoto, and "Various Texts of *Pygmalion*" by Totaro Shimamura.

The Independent Shavian, 21, nos. 1 and 2 (1983). Journal of the Bernard Shaw Society.
Includes "What the Films May Do to the Drama" by Bernard Shaw, "Shavian Screen
Notes" by Douglas Laurie, "The Girlish Shaw," "Rape of the Socks," "It Takes One to
Know One," "Man of Letters as Reformer: Thornton Wilder on George Bernard
Shaw" by Sidney Feshbach, "Shaw and Wilder: A Rejoinder" by Jacques Barzun, "A
Shaw-Wilder Postscript" by Dan H. Laurence, "H. G. Wells Was a Man Without Mal-
ice" by Bernard Shaw, "Shaw Cornered," "Book Review [of Arnold Silver's *Bernard
Shaw: The Darker Side*]" by Richard Nickson, "Signed 'G.B.S.,'" "Society Activities,"
"News About Our Members," and "Our Cover."

The Independent Shavian, 21, no. 3 (1983). Journal of the Bernard Shaw Society. Includes
"The Law of Changes is the Law of God But the Church Does Not Change" by

Bernard Shaw, "Scientists: The Mystical Quackeries of Dangerough Nuisances" by Bernard Shaw, "Bibliographical Portraitist," "Worthy and Valuable—Not Unexpected" by Jacques Barzun, "G.B.S. on Palestine," "Shavian Notes from Springtime London" by Richard Nickson, "George Bernard Shaw as Photographer" by Robert Lassam, "No Place for Best Sellers," "Autograph Letter," "Enter George Bernard Shaw" by Harcourt Williams, "Shaw Cornered," "The Shavian Sound of Music," "Professional Shame!" and "Our Cover."

IV. Dissertations

Amalric, Jean-Claude. "George Bernard Shaw: du réformateur victorien au prophète édouardien" [George Bernard Shaw: from the Victorian Reformer to the Edwardian Prophet]. Université de Paris, 1976. *DAI*, 44 (March 1983), 137-C. Examines trends in the criticism of Shaw's work and the developments and changes that occurred in the criticism at different periods. Looks at why the attitudes of the critics have changed over three periods: 1893–1930, 1930–1950, and since 1950.

Elliott, Robert Frederick. "Shadows of the Shaughraun: Reflections on the Use of the Stage Irishman Tradition in Plays by Boucicault, Shaw, Synge and O'Casey." Cornell, 1983. *DAI*, 44 (December 1983), 1627-A. "Each, in his own way, created variations of the stereotype and played heavily upon audience expectations about Stage Irishmen to discredit spectators' theatrical and moral/social ideals. Shaw parodies and inverts the Stage Irishman tradition in the masterfully constructed *John Bull's Other Island*, which attacks the illusions of both English and Irish audiences."

Herzog, Callie Jeanne. "Nora's Sisters: Female Characters in the Plays of Ibsen, Strindberg, Shaw and O'Neill." University of Illinois, 1982. *DAI*, 43 (March 1983), 2988-A. In the plays by Ibsen, Strindberg and Shaw the stock female character types are used to challenge the "conventional cliches, stereotypes and myths about women." O'Neill's plays "reaffirm conventional attitudes towards women." Each playwright has favorite types: "Shaw's favorite type is his 'man in petticoats,'" young, unmarried, and a "new" woman. In each playwright woman is always the "other."

Thaler, Estelle Manette. "Major Strategies in Twentieth-Century Drama: Apocalyptic Vision, Allegory and Open Form." St. John's University, 1983. *DAI*, 44 (July 1983), 163-A. "The metaphor of the Apocalypse appears in various theatrically powerful forms. Chekhov's *The Cherry Orchard* and Shaw's *Heartbreak House* present the end of an ineffectual social structure." Selected plays of Chekhov, Shaw, Pinter, Shepard, Witkiewicz, and Beckett "represent a sort of Cubist collage, reducing meaning to its barest monochrome shapes, the ultimate poetic simplicity beautifully conveying the profoundest truth."

Watt, Stephen Myers. "The Making of the Modern History Play." University of Illinois, 1982. *DAI*, 43 (March 1983), 2991-A. Almost every major modern dramatist, Shaw included, has written a history play. The thesis examines the best-known historical and popular dramatists of the later nineteenth century—Tom Taylor, W. C. Wills, Augustus Harris, and Lord Tennyson in London and Dion Boucicault and J. W. Whitbread in Dublin—to discover the conventions and ideological implications of the late nineteenth century. Then the thesis demonstrates how Shaw and O'Casey "appropriate, manipulate, and finally undermine the codes of the historical drama of their predecessors."

Williams, Katherine Gamewell. "Heroic Archetypes in the Comedies of Aristophanes and Later Playwrights." Florida State, 1983. *DAI*, 44 (December 1983), 1785-5-A. Works by GBS among many other playwrights illustrate both heroic and non-heroic comedy archetypes.

V. Recordings

"Shaw and His Contemporaries," in "The Theater of Social Problems," History of the Drama, Unit 7. Price: $59.95; from Films for the Humanities. P.O. Box 2053, Princeton, New Jersey 08540. Phone: 800–257–5126. Covers Shaw and Wagner, Ibsen, Marx, Chekhov, and Brecht, noting *Man and Superman, Heartbreak House, Saint Joan, Pygmalion* and *Major Barbara*. Package includes two fifteen-minute sound filmstrips.

"Shaw, Bernard" and "Shaw, George Bernard." *The Magazine Index*. Belmont, California: Information Access Company. Microfilm reel: 1978 to March 1984; microfiche: 1977–78. Present reel lists about ninety entries under both headings, including many not noted in this checklist. Example: Elizabeth Lambert. "Historic Homes: George Bernard Shaw," *Architectural Digest*, 39 (May 1982), 180–87.

"Shaw, Bernard" and "Shaw, George Bernard." *The National Newspaper Index*. Los Altos, California: Information Access Company. Microfilm reel: 1980 to March 1984; microfiche: 1979. About thirty items, mostly on recent productions of the plays in the U.S.

Contributors

Elsie Adams, Professor of English at San Diego State University, is author of *Bernard Shaw and the Aesthetes* and a member of the *SHAW* Editorial Board.

Sidney P. Albert, Professor Emeritus of Philosophy at California State University, Los Angeles, and a member of the editorial board of *SHAW*, has visited and lectured in Japan. His many articles on Shaw are especially crucial for the study of *Major Barbara*.

Jean-Claude Amalric is Professor of English at the University of Montpellier, France, an editor of *Cahiers victoriens & édouardiens*, and author of *George Bernard Shaw: du réformateur victorien au prophète édouardien*.

Charles A. Berst is Professor of English at the University of California, Los Angeles, and author of *Bernard Shaw and the Art of Drama*. He was guest editor of *SHAW 1, Shaw and Religion*.

Bernard F. Dukore is Professor of Drama and Theatre at the University of Hawaii. His recent books include *The Collected Screenplays of Bernard Shaw, Harold Pinter*, and *The Theatre of Peter Barnes*.

T. F. Evans, editor of *The Shavian*, has recently retired as Deputy Director of Extra-Mural Studies at the University of London. He is the editor of *Shaw: The Critical Heritage*.

Piers Gray, Senior Lecturer in English at Hong Kong University, is author of *T. S. Eliot's Intellectual and Poetic Development, 1909–1922*. He is currently working on a book about Modernist Poetry and the Modern.

Nicholas Grene is Fellow and Director of Studies in the Department of Modern English at Trinity College, Dublin. His most recent book is *Bernard Shaw: A Critical View*.

Leon Hugo is Professor of English at the University of South Africa and author of *Bernard Shaw: Playwright and Preacher*.

Damir Kalogjera is Professor of English at the University of Zagreb, Yugoslavia, and at the time of writing also Visiting Professor at the University of Nottingham.

342

Dan H. Laurence, Literary and Dramatic Advisor to the Shaw Estate, is author of *Shaw: A Bibliography* and is now completing his edition of Shaw's *Collected Letters*.

Ishrat Lindblad is Docent, at the Department of English, University of Stockholm, Stockholm. Her writings on G.B.S. have appeared in the *Shaw Review*.

Murray S. Martin, University Librarian at Tufts University, Medford, Massachusetts, is a native of New Zealand.

Junko Matoba is Professor of English at the University of the Sacred Heart, Tokyo, Japan.

John Pfeiffer, *SHAW* Bibliographer, is Professor of English at Central Michigan University and a contributor, as well, to standard bibliographies of science fiction.

Valli Rao teaches English at Flinders University, Adelaide, Australia. Her writings on G.B.S. have appeared before in *SHAW*.

Anthony Rota, director of the distinguished London rare book firm, Bertram Rota Ltd., lectured at the Library of Congress in April 1984 on "Points at Issue: A Bookseller Looks at Bibliography."

Rodelle Weintraub, guest editor for this issue, is editor of *Fabian Feminist: Bernard Shaw and Woman* and the *Captain Brassbound's Conversion* volume in the Garland *Early Texts: Play Manuscripts in Facsimile*.

Stanley Weintraub, general editor of *SHAW*, has written and edited a number of books on G.B.S., including *The Unexpected Shaw: Biographical Approaches to G.B.S. and His Work*.

John J. Weisert is Professor Emeritus of German at the University of Louisville and author of "Shaw in Central Europe before 1914."

DATE DUE

GAYLORD			PRINTED IN U.S.A.